ANGUS - CULTURAL SERVICES

3 8046 09860 437 3

CW00690669

BRADFORD
PALS

The Soldiers

Down some cold field in a world unspoken
the young men are walking together, slim and tall,
and though they laugh to one another, silence is not broken;
there is no sound however clear they call.

They are speaking together of what they loved in vain here,
but the air is too thin to carry the things they say.
They were young and golden, but they came on pain here,
and their youth is age now, their gold is grey.

Yet their hearts are not changed, and they cry to one another,
'What have they done with the lives we laid aside?
Are they young with our youth, gold with our gold, my brother?
Do they smile in the face of death, because we died?'

Down some cold field in a world uncharted
the young seek each other with questioning eyes.
They question each other, the young, the golden hearted,
of the world that they were robbed of in their quiet paradise.

HUMBERT WOLFE, REQUIEM: THE SOLDIERS (1916)[1]

1. Umberto (Humbert) Wolfe (1886-1940), poet and old boy of Bradford Grammar School. Wolfe was the son of a Bradford wool merchant of German/Jewish origins, and was a senior career civil servant establishing amongst other things the Beveridge Labour Exchange scheme. The Soldier (1916) was part of Wolfe's *Requiem*, first published in 1927.

LABOR · OMNIA · VINCIT

BRADFORD
PALS

A Comprehensive History of the 16th, 18th & 20th
(Service) Battalions of the Prince of Wales Own
West Yorkshire Regiment 1914-1918

DAVID RAW

Pen & Sword
MILITARY

First published in Great Britain in 2005 by

PEN & SWORD MILITARY
an imprint of
Pen & Sword Books Limited
47 Church Street
Barnsley
South Yorkshire
S70 2AS

Copyright © David Raw, 2005

ISBN: 0 85052 350 8

The right of David Raw to be identified as Author
of this Work has been asserted by him in accordance
with the Copyright, Designs and Patents Act 1988.

A CIP catalogue record for this book
is available from the British Library

All rights reserved. No part of this book may
be reproduced or transmitted in any form or
by any means, electronic or mechanical
including photocopying, recording or by any
information storage and retrieval system,
without permission from the Publisher in writing.

Typeset in 10pt Palatino by Pen & Sword Books Limited

Printed and bound in England by
CPI UK

For a complete list of Pen & Sword titles please contact:
PEN & SWORD BOOKS LIMITED
47 Church Street, Barnsley, South Yorkshire, S70 2AS, England
email: enquiries@pen-and-sword.co.uk • website: www.pen-and-sword.co.uk

Contents

Second Pals at Bowling Park May 1915.

Introduction and Acknowledgements

THERE WERE TWO EARLY STRANDS to my awareness of the Bradford Pals. A former Pal was the sole booming bass in the Church choir of which I was a member. This formidable gentleman had a strong West Yorkshire accent, but he nodded towards respectable gentility by lengthening his vowels. To our lasting shame, we young choirboys nudged and winked at a solemn moment in The Creed when the bass voice boomed that Our Lord had 'Ascended into Heaven'. Later, at Bradford Grammar School, I became aware of so many names and photographs of the Pals generation in the disturbing yet impressive gloom of the School War Memorial chamber. As we of a more fortunate generation passed through to a science lesson, a hushed respectful silence was enforced by Masters with their own memories of both World Wars.

Many years later I was fortunate enough to meet some of the surviving Pals, John McGrath, George Grunwell and Sam Wainwright and to hear their stories. Another Pal, Walter Hare, became a close friend and a remarkably accurate fount of knowledge. He was also a travelling companion to the battlefields many times well into his nineties. My one regret is that I failed to complete this work in Walter's lifetime, although he read drafts of the events in which he was involved. I dedicate the book to Walter and to his fellow Pals with admiration for their bravery and fortitude. They were ordinary men who, for the most part, did extraordinary things.

My research has taken many years and it has been extremely difficult to decide what to leave out given the publisher's limit of three hundred and twenty pages. I have much more material than it has been possible to include here, but there are hopes that the publishers will produce a follow up volume with complete medal rolls of both battalions, full casualty lists, and muster rolls of the battalions at break up. In addition there are literally hundreds of photographs which it has not been possible to include.

I would like to thank everyone who has helped by providing material for the book. I am especially grateful to Steve Kerry, formerly of the Bradford Industrial Museum for sharing his own research with me and for allowing me access to the Museum's oral history and photographic collection. I owe Steve a great deal and his work has made a massive contribution to the book. His colleague Ian Ward has also been more than helpful and taken much trouble on my behalf. The Editor of the *Telegraph and Argus* has kindly given permission for me to reproduce photographs from their archives. I acknowledge her help and that of her former colleague Bill Berry for the introductions they made. There are many others to thank. Martin Middlebrook, author of the classic *First Day of the Somme* allowed me to use interview material he collected from the Pals in the 1960's. Malcolm Brown provided introductions and tape recordings of interviews with the Pals. Laurie Milner of the Imperial War Museum and author of the companion volume, *Leeds Pals*, cheerfully discussed ideas and shared information. The late Dr. Alf Peacock was generous with his research and always knew somebody who knew where something was. Julian Sykes and Julian Putkowski, co-authors of *Shot at Dawn*, provided a range of information and technical information, and in Julian P.'s case welcome hospitality and lively conversation during visits to the Public Record Office.

Staff at the Public Record Office, The Imperial War Museum and the Regimental Museum in York took much trouble on my behalf which I would like to acknowledge .

I owe a huge debt of gratitude to the many family members of Pals who entrusted me with much information and material including diaries, letters and photographs. They number almost into three figures and I have acknowledged individual help during the course of notes at the end of each chapter. I hope they enjoy the book and feel that it pays a fitting tribute to their late relatives.

At Pen & Sword, Roni and Sylvia were always kind and patient and always had a technical answer to problems. To First World War buffs, Roni Wilkinson has become a bigger Barnsley institution than Dickie Bird could ever be and I wish him every happiness in his forthcoming retirement. Thanks also to Rupert Harding for his gentle velvet glove diplomacy in getting me to commit pen to paper and to meet deadlines.

Inevitably there will be mistakes or omissions for which I apologise and take full responsibility. It has been a profoundly moving experience to work on the story of the Bradford Pals and I hope my book is worthy of them.

DAVID RAW *April, 2005*

Chapter One

WORSTEDOPOLIS

*If we look around at our mills, our warehouses and our public buildings it
needs no great effort to imagine that Bradford is built of Wool.*
THE BRADFORD OBSERVER, 31 December, 1900.

IN THE SUMMER of 1914, Bradford was a bustling self-confident city
with a growing population approaching 300,000[1]. In just over one
hundred and fifty years, the city had undergone a rapid and dramatic
transformation. In 1750 it was a small market town with a population of
only 5,000 and a miniscule textile industry based on the domestic system.
Within a hundred years it had grown twenty fold to become a major
manufacturing centre with a population of 103,771 in the 1851 Census
return. Growth continued throughout the second half of the nineteenth
century at a pace exceeded only by Middlesbrough in the United Kingdom.

The pace of change brought wealth for the few and employment for the
many. There were also problems of poor housing, health, education and
sanitation. In 1845, the German writer George Weerth remarked of
Bradford, 'every other factory town in England is a paradise compared to

Tyrrel Street, Bradford. Bradford Town Hall can be seen in the distance.

this hole'. Yet despite this there was an undeniable vitality and in the latter half of the nineteenth century determined local efforts were made to improve conditions.

By 1914 the vast majority of the population had a feeling of pride in their city even though many felt there were still enormous social problems to overcome. There were some early signs of the future long-term decline of the textile industry, but this was only apparent to those who looked closely into the matter. For the vast majority, long term confidence in the possibility of social, economic and political progress still remained.

The census of 1911 reveals the dominance of wool. No less than 70,243 persons were directly employed in textile manufacture, with thousands more employed in the engineering, transport and commercial service industries that were dependent on the industry.

Bradford came to regard itself with justification as the world centre of the wool manufacturing industry, particularly in the field of fine worsted stuff. Worsted 'stuff', be it noted, not cloth. Worsted was a distinctive fine smooth cloth with a world-wide reputation for excellent quality. In simple terms, in worsted the yarn was made from wool where the short fibres are removed by combing. The long fibres were then laid parallel to produce a smooth even yarn quite different to the intermingled fibre used in the Heavy Woollen district of Dewsbury and carpet manufacture in Halifax.[2]

To quote J. B. Priestley, an eighteen year old contemporary of the Pals in 1914,

> Bradford was very fortunately placed for its own staple trade of worsted and woollen manufacture. It was near some large coalfields, and what was even more important, it had an excellent supply of soft water free from lime, good for both washing wool and dyeing it. All the processes of worsted manufacture – combing, spinning, weaving, dyeing and finishing – are carried on in Bradford. It also deals in alpaca, mohair and silk. Indeed there is nothing that can be spun and woven that does not come from Bradford.[4]

Worsted, was first introduced in the early 1700s after the Turkey cloth (fabric used to cover chairs and furniture) trade collapsed following a change in fashion to cane bottomed chairs. However, the building of the Bradford Canal in 1777, driven through by the Quaker worsted entrepreneur John Hustler, gave the biggest impetus to the expansion of the Bradford trade. The new canal, linking Bradford to the Leeds-Liverpool Canal, provided a cheap and easy alternative to the expensive and often appalling turnpike road system.

By its very nature, the worsted industry was more capital dependent than the woollen industry, and it was the availability of capital which made it possible to move on to the next stage. As the local historian David James has pointed out, a worsted man of business was often a man of means who had to organise and finance a complex entrepreneurial chain process involving a large number of domestic outworkers. By 1750, half of Bradford's workforce was employed by such worsted entrepreneurs, the most prominent being the Quaker John Hustler. Hustler's dissenting connections gave him a networking connection to many of the great business dynasties of the north, and led to the establishment of a commercial infrastructure of banks and other financial organizations.[5]

The combination of cheap transport, available capital and entrepreneurial skill gave Bradford the essential pre-conditions necessary to take full advantage of mechanisation with the coming of the Industrial Revolution. When the first steam engine was set to work in a Bradford Mill in 1800 the transition from domestic to industrial production began. By 1820 there were twenty steam powered mills, by 1841 over seventy, and by 1873 more than 200 as the familiar Bradford skyline of tall smoking chimneys was established.

The drive and determination to establish this industrial powerhouse came from a remarkable group of individual entrepreneurs who made their wealth and left their mark on Bradford in more than just the economic sense. But the rapid growth and change in the first half of the nineteenth century was often achieved at a heavy and terrible social price. The great geographical bowl of a town suffered terrible smoke pollution, the streets were filthy with animal waste, human waste and mud. The waterways were polluted with factory wastes and dyes. There was unrest and disturbance and resistance to the change as a whole way of life in the domestic system was overturned and replaced by the factory system. Opposition and violence flared up.

The Luddite movement spread throughout the West Riding in the 1820's when mills were attacked, frames broken and some mill owners

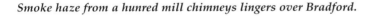

Smoke haze from a hunred mill chimneys lingers over Bradford.

attacked or murdered. The military were called in. Seventeen Luddites were hanged at York and many others were transported for life. Dispossessed hand workers broke a power loom in Shipley in 1822, and after the Riot Act was read shots were exchanged resulting in two deaths and a number of non-fatal casualties. In 1825 the Great Bradford Strike convulsed the town and lasted six months when the weavers and combers joined forces to demand an increase in wages. They were eventually forced back at reduced rates and the pace of mechanization increased.

In the 1840's there were more social convulsions as the radical Chartist movement gained support in Bradford. Plugs were pulled from factory boilers to stop the mill engines. In Bradford in 1840 there were plans to use violent force. This was only thwarted when forty armed men and their leader Robert Peddie were arrested and imprisoned.

Work there was a plenty in the mills, but there were also terrible living and sanitary conditions for the less fortunate. The pressure of rapid growth exacerbated these problems. In the 1840s average life expectancy was a mere 18.69 years. The mass of the workers lived in cheap jerry-built housing without water or sanitation. The average income was less than £1 per week and children worked from 6.00 am to 7.30 pm.

Whilst much of the new population came from rural Yorkshire (including the author's family), the city also attracted workers from other parts of the country as well as Scotland and Wales. In the hungry forties, ten thousand Irish immigrants settled in the city in search of a better future, but what they often found was a miserable squalor – and in some cases hostility from what had been a largely nonconformist protestant population.

Back o't mill houses.

After an outbreak of cholera in West Yorkshire in 1849, the *Morning Chronicle* newspaper sent its political correspondent Angus Reach (successor to Charles Dickens) to investigate living conditions in the industrial West Riding. He described his visit to Bradford.

Mr. Smith of Deanston, in a sanitary report made about 1837, describes Bradford as being the dirtiest town in England. Mills abound in great plenty, and their number is daily increasing, while the town itself extends in like proportion. Bradford is essentially a new town. Half a century ago it was a mere cluster of huts: now the district of which it is the heart contains upwards of 132,000 inhabitants. Fortunes have been made in Bradford with a rapidity almost unequalled even in the manufacturing districts.

The houses of the work people are very inferior. They are one and all constructed back to back, or rather built double, with a partition running down the ridge of the roof. This is the case even in rows and streets at present building. "The plan," said my informant, "is adopted because of its cheapness, and because it saves ground rent". [7]

But there were positive forces crying for change and reform. Their voice was the recently formed *Bradford Observer* newspaper whose Editor William Byles campaigned for a Mayor and elected Town Council to tackle the problems. In 1847 they got their way and the Council was set up by a Charter of Incorporation. In the second half of the nineteenth century Bradford was dominated and shaped by a remarkable collection of successful entrepreneurs, not all with local roots, who had made their fortunes out of the textile industry. They lived in the town and lived with its problems – the delights of Morecambe, Harrogate and the Yorkshire dales were for a future generation. They were mostly non-conformist by religion and Liberal by politics. The Council became a focus of power for this extremely wealthy but politically radical business elite.

The Council re-shaped the infrastructure of the town practising what amounts to a form of 'municipal socialism' which seems positively revolutionary compared with today's culture of privatisation and out-sourcing. Municipal socialism it certainly was, even though the make up of the Council was largely Liberal. The powerful group who ran the Council were the textile barons, men such as Sir Titus Salt, Briggs Priestley, John Venimore Godwin, Daniel Illingworth and Robert Milligan. The central group of power brokers all attended the Congregational Independent Chapel on Horton Lane and were dubbed the 'Nine Muses'. Today they would probably be described as the Bradford Mafia, but they were men of ideas and initiative used to getting things done and getting their own way. They set to in the task of 'Improvement' with energy and drive. Nothing was too good for Bradford and if it was good, then Bradford must have it.

Clean water and a sewerage system were obvious priorities after the cholera outbreak of 1849 when over 400 died. Street lighting and street improvements were also tackled. A fire service was established, essential greasy wool in mills was a constant fire hazard. After the Chartist riots, law and order was imposed with a Chief Constable and a police force. The Council opened cemeteries, established libraries, organised markets, built schools and were the first to develop secondary education, generated gas and electricity (a national first), cleared slums and built houses. They provided museums and took over three parks to provide a healthy lung of recreation for workers who never imagined a cheap flight to Majorca. The three parks were Lister Park, (named after Samuel Cunliffe Lister the biggest of all the textile barons who sold his former mansion and grounds in Manningham to the Council), Peel Park at Undercliffe (negotiated by Titus Salt and named after the champion of free trade Sir Robert Peel), and Bowling Park at the southern end of the town. The boating lake in Lister Park was built to provide work for the unemployed. In 1914 and 1915 Lister Park and Bowling Park became regular places for drilling for the embryonic Pals Battalions. The parks were also where many met their first sweethearts on a Sunday promenade above the band stand.

The coming of the railway provided a further boost. Robert Milligan, the town's first Mayor and later Liberal M.P., campaigned to get Bradford onto the emerging railway network. What later became the Midland Railway opened Market Street Station in 1846 (later named Forster Square to honour the town's M.P., W.E. Forster, sponsor of national universal elementary education in 1870). What became Exchange station connected with the Lancashire & Yorkshire Railway in 1850. Milligan built his massive Italianate warehouse (now home of the *Telegraph & Argus*) next to the new station, and campaigned for the two lines to join – without success.

The Council led the way with great public buildings which still stand today, also designed in the Italianate style by the local architects Lockwood and Mawson. There was a magnificent Town Hall for administration and politics, there was the St. George's Hall for entertainment and edification, and the Wool Exchange for business. The town became a city in 1897, but the name 'town hall' was to linger on for many years. The City Hall is still the focal point of the city today, as familiar to us as it was to the volunteer Pals of 1914 and 1915.

But the biggest building in the town, again in the Italianate style, was Lister's Manningham Mills. A third of a mile long with a 250 foot high chimney, it still dominates the city skyline today. Built in 1873, it was the largest textile mill in the world employing up to 11,000 workers. Lister's invention, the 'nip comb', a machine for combing the fine botany wool being shipped from Australia was crucial to the success of the worsted industry. Samuel Cunliffe-Lister (1815-1906), was a dominant force in the town, and unlike most of his contemporaries a Conservative. He made his fortune by selling a machine costing £ 200 for £ 1,200. He also produced high quality velvet. Known as the 'King of Velvet' and 'King of the Patents', he became Viscount Masham in 1892.

Cunliffe-Lister built the biggest mill but, Sir Titus Salt built the most impressive comprehensive development in 1853. Near his new mill in Shipley, which had 1,200 looms, he built a model village (Saltaire) for his

3,500 workers with good quality housing, churches and a school. The architects, Lockwood and Mawson, went on to design Bradford Town Hall, the Wool Exchange, and St. George's Hall. As befitted a paternalistic Liberal Non-conformist tee-totaller, there was to be no alcohol and no public house, although there was a library and a workmen's institute. The Italianate Renaissance design indicates Salt's attitude that God's will was fulfilled by Mankind's material aspirations to reform and improve. Salt made his fortune by spinning the hair of the alpaca llama from Peru and weaving it with wool to produce fine lustrous 'mixed fabrics'.

The manufacturers and the Council were not the only catalysts for change. There was a third element adding spice and difference to the cocktail mixture of Bradford. The textile industry was an international trade with contacts throughout the world and its development attracted immigrants from Germany and Central Europe who became the merchant princes of Bradford. The pioneer of these immigrant merchants was Sir Jacob Behrens who came to Yorkshire from Hamburg in 1832. He was followed by others and their monument today is the area of elegant warehouses and offices known as 'Little Germany' situated between the Cathedral and Leeds Road. Many, but not all were Jewish.

In 1914 there was a Lutheran Church as well as a Reform Synagogue in Bradford. Also in 1914 one of the Bradford Pals' officers returned from Danzig in order to volunteer. The foreign sounding names in 'Little Germany' soon became familiar to Bradfordians. Hertz, Lowenthal, Reichenheim, Schlesinger, Schonfeld, Schuster, and Schwabe. Edelstein, Moser & Co, Herels, Simonson & Co, B. Reif Ltd., Kesslers & Co. In 1902, twenty-one out of thirty-six yarn merchants and thirty-one out of sixty-three piece merchants were of German origin.[8]

> *Their great forte was not a technical one. They knew very little about the manufacturing side of the industry, but they allied their powers as salesmen to the prowess of their Yorkshire colleagues as craftsmen and between them Bradford captured the markets of the world.*
>
> THE YORKSHIRE OBSERVER, 6 December 1934.[9]

Bradford was heavily dependent upon the German chemical industry for the supply of aniline dyes, with over 80% coming from Germany before the war. In Manningham, just off Toller Lane, there was and still is Heidelberg Road, Bonn Road, and Mannheim Road, indeed one of Pals casualties Ernest Dearden lived in Heidelberg Road.[10]

The Central European immigrants were an educated and cultured lot and their impact on the cultural life of the city far outweighed their numbers. Their views were progressive, liberal and humanitarian. They established a Literary Club named after the German poet Freidrich von Schiller, the Schiller-Verein, and established classical concerts in the town. They took a full part in the life of Bradford. Charles Semon, born in Danzig in 1814 was elected Mayor of Bradford in 1874. Jacob Moser born in Schleswig Holstein in 1839 was Lord Mayor in 1910.

In health, Bradford had much cause to be grateful to German

immigrants. Dr. Bronner, a refugee from the riots of 1848, founded the Bradford Eye and Ear hospital. Anthrax, 'the wool-sorters' disease', had an incidence of one new case every week, a third of which were fatal. Dr John Henry Bell, a founder with Bronner of the Royal Eye and Ear Hospital in 1879, he confirmed the identification of woolsorters' disease with anthrax. Dr Fritz Eurich set up a practice in 1896 with Bell, and in 1905 was appointed as bacteriologist to the Anthrax Investigation Board. His work led to the institution of various measures against anthrax, including the building of the Wool Disinfecting Station at Liverpool.

The German connection included the parents of the Delius, the artist William Rothenstein, and the poet Humbert Wolfe. They were generous employers and benefactors to the town endowing hospitals and schools. Bradford Grammar School, was transformed to achieve national status as a centre of excellence, by the efforts of Sir Jacob Behrens. In 1914, the Grammar School was to provide many of the officers and men of the Bradford Pals, and the Pals first commanding officer, Colonel Muller, was himself of German descent.

This then was the City that the Bradford Pals knew. It would change in the years up to 1914. The textile industry moved from boom to slump and back to recovery again. Compared to the cotton industry in Lancashire, the West Yorkshire textile industry had been relatively under unionised, but a great six months strike at Lister's Mill in 1891, when Cunliffe-Lister successfully cut wages by up to 30%, transformed industrial relations in the city. It led directly to the election of the first Labour Councillor, Fred Jowett in 1892, and to the foundation of a new national Independent Labour Party at a conference in Bradford in 1893.

Jowett failed to be elected to Parliament by a mere forty-one votes in 1900, but in 1906 after persuading the City Council to introduce free school meals he became Bradford's first Labour M.P. His campaign was supported by the educationalist Margaret McMillan and Jonathan Priestley (Head of Green Lane School and father of J.B. Priestley). Brockway described the childhood of some of the Pals of 1914:

> In the winter of 1903-1904, following the Boer War, there was a severe depression in Bradford, and destitution was widespread. The schoolteachers in the poorer districts were in despair as they faced children pinched and emaciated through want of food. They asked the Education Committee to receive a deputation, and one after another told of the sorrowful condition of those in their charge. Moved by these stories, it was agreed on the initiative of Jowett to appoint a Poor Children's special sub-committee with power to investigate and act. This investigation revealed 2,574 cases of underfed children in the schools. Of these 329 were stated to attend school without breakfasts. The Poor Children's sub-committee impressed by the evidence of hunger, decided to provide school meals. This was the first decision by any local authority in Britain to assume public responsibility for feeding school children.[11]

The balance of political power slowly and inexorably changed. In 1914 the

Bales of wool. 70,000 worked in the Bradford textile industry on the eve of war.

Liberals still formed the national government of the day but the City Council was virtually split three ways between the three parties. The old order was gradually changing. There were signs of stagnation in the textile industry as the younger generation of mill owners and merchants moved out to more rural climes, and markets and fashions changed. Samuel Cunliffe-Lister's transformation from inventor and entrepreneur into the aristocratic Lord Masham with a huge estate in the Yorkshire dales was of a more than symbolic significance.

Nevertheless, the new cinemas, the theatres and the music halls flourished. The first trolley bus in the country ran in Bradford in 1911. Professional sport began. Cricket, rugby and football all flourished as vast crowds came to be entertained away from their workaday lives in a pre-television era. Bradford City won the F.A. Cup in 1911 and in 1914 both professional soccer teams, City and Park Avenue were in the First Division.

Whilst there was gradual change and old memories faded, Bradford may have been a provincial city but it still had world horizons. In the hazy summer days of 1914, Bradford still had problems and difficulties, but it was also a city with a right to feel much self-confidence and pride.

Main entrance to Lister Park, often known as Manningham Park. The Pals trained here regularly until the move to Skipton in January 1915. Their HQ at the skating rink was just half a mile down Manningham Lane.

NOTES

1. The population was recorded as 288,458 in the 1911 Census, compared with 279,767 in 1901.

2. Worsted owes its name to the village of Worstead in Norfolk where Flemish Weavers settled in the middle ages and first introduced the method. See *Bradford* by David James, Ryburn Publishing 1990, for an excellent overview of the development of the textile industry in Bradford.

3. J.B.Priestley, *English Journey*, 1934. Priestley was working as an 18 year old clerk in a wool office in Bradford in September, 1914. Surprisingly he walked to Halifax to join the Duke of Wellington's Regiment rather than join the Bradford Pals, but the author has been unable to find any reason for this. J.B. was commissioned and wounded before returning to Bradford after the War.

4. James, *opus cit.*

5. p. 67. *Bradford, A Centenary City*, by Tom Montgomery, published by Bradford Metropolitan District Council, 1997.

6. Directory of Yorkshire Textile Districts, Angus Bethune Reach, 1849.

7. J.S. Roberts, *Little Germany*, City of Bradford Metropolitan Council, Bradford 1977. See also A.R. Rollin, 'The Jewish Contribution to the British Textile Industry', paper read to the Jewish Historical Society of England, 12th April 1948. See also an article by Harry Leach, a former director of the Bradford Dyers Association in JSDC, Volume 115, July, 1999 and available on line.

8. *Yorkshire Observer*, 6th December 1934. Special supplement to mark the centenary of the firm Sir Jacob Behrens and Sons Ltd.

9. Fenner Brockway, *Socialism over Sixty Years : The Life of Jowett of Bradford 1864-1944*, London, 1946.

Chapter 2

WAR

This will be the greatest war that this world has ever seen.
I hope Great Britain will not be drawn into this crime against civilisation.
Fred Jowett, MP for Bradford East, 2 August, 1914.

AT 11.00PM (MIDNIGHT IN BERLIN) on Tuesday 4th August 1914
Great Britain declared war on Germany. It was the day after Bank
Holiday Monday. A British ultimatum demanding the withdrawal of
the invading German troops from neutral Belgium had been ignored. Great
Britain was bound by treaty to guarantee Belgian neutrality, and as the
Foreign Secretary Sir Edward Grey had explained to a hushed House of
Commons, this guarantee was at the heart of Great Britain's action.

The chain of events following the assassination of Archduke Franz
Ferdinand of Austria has been well chronicled elsewhere.[1] Austria, on very
slim evidence, held Serbia responsible for the murder. The Austrians decided
to use the event as an excuse to settle old scores and to assert their crumbling
authority in the Balkans. The Serbians asked for Russian support whilst
Austria in turn got backing from Germany. The German government saw an
opportunity to re-vitalize their Austrian allies through an invasion of Serbia
whilst at the same time challenging what they saw as the encircling threat of
the Franco-Russian alliance. The Germans believed the time was ripe for a
quick victory given what they thought was inherent weakness in that alliance.
The dominoes were about to fall.

Germany encouraged Austria to invade Serbia whilst declaring war on
Russia citing Russian mobilization as a *causus belli*. German strategic planning
calculated on a quick strike and victory in the West to protect themselves from
Russia's ally France. The key to such a victory was an advance through
neutral Belgium avoiding the French defensive system. The Kaiser dismissed
British guarantees of Belgian neutrality as a meaningless 'scrap of paper'. He
believed the British were far too preoccupied with Ireland to have the will to
get involved in a continental war, and that in any event British military might
was centred on sea power whilst Britain's 'contemptible little army' would
have no impact in a continental land war. An inter-connecting system of
alliances, and German miscalculation of the consequences of their aggression,
led to a World War with British involvement.

Although there had been tension in Europe since 1911, and the tactless
blustering Kaiser had given rise to a mixture of alarm and amusement in
Great Britain for a number of years, the events of the last days of July 1914
moved at a remarkable pace. A game of political poker was played with
reckless abandon by the German Government. It was to result in over four

years of misery and tragedy for millions of ordinary people throughout the world.

The astonishing speed of events, and the pre-occupation with Irish affairs, can be gauged by the fact that when the British Cabinet discussed the Austrian ultimatum to Serbia 24 July it was their first foreign affairs discussion of the month.[2] The Cabinet's initial reaction was that Britain would not be involved. But within eleven days we were at war.

*   *   *

The speed of events was reflected in Bradford. The socialist *Bradford Pioneer* newspaper regularly carried items of interest to its Clarion Cycling Club readers. On 31 July they acknowledged receipt of an excellently written itinerary of a tour of Belgium and Germany,

from which I hope to have quotations in the near future... With unconscious irony, the editor went on, *it is as well to remember that a chronicle of what may seem to be trifling adventures and experiences is infinitely more interesting to the reader than an elaborate description of the places visited.*[3]

Kaiser Wilhelm.

But for most Bradford folk foreign holidays were a pipe dream. The rack railway in Shipley Glen was a treat, or there was the trek up the hill from Bingley through Eldwick to have ham and eggs at Dick Hudson's pub on the moor. Stepping through the snicket onto the moors gave a special feeling of freedom, for it was no longer possible to see the dominating presence of the 249 feet high chimney at Lister's Manningham Mills.

A Bank Holiday excursion to Scarborough from Exchange Station via the Great Northern and North Eastern Railways, or to Morecambe on the Midland line from Forster Square, were treats to be saved up for all year round in countless holiday clubs. On Bank Holiday Saturday, when Germany declared war on Russia, more than 60,000 visitors were staying in Scarborough, whilst in Morecambe,

The weather was fine and people spent a most enjoyable time amidst the round of entertainments provided. Everybody was talking of the War, and the vendors of newspapers did a roaring trade all day. Considerable interest was taken in the departure of a number of naval reservists from Heysham.[4]

Cricket was a Yorkshire religion and the traditional Bank Holiday Roses match against the old enemy Lancashire was in full swing at Old Trafford despite the usual Manchester showers. Roses matches could draw 26,000 crowds into Bradford's Park Avenue ground with a further 50,000 reported locked out.[5] A cricketer awarded the white rose cap acquired an almost immortal status in the land of mills, mines and stone built terraces.

But the looming impact of war affected the Roses match. The two captains, both 'gentlemen' with military connections, were called away during the course of the match. A.H. Hornby the Lancashire skipper was summoned to the War Office on the first day. On the second day, the Yorkshire captain, Sir Archibald White was summoned to report to the Royal Notts Artillery. Sir Archibald (an amateur with a career batting average of 14) was hardly missed. Two tough old pro's, George Hirst and Wilfred Rhodes, effectively ran the team anyway and went on to lead the Tykes to eleven wins out of twelve by the end of the season. But war was to leave its mark. Three of Yorkshire's winning team in the Roses match joined the Leeds Pals in September. All were casualties on 1 July, 1916 at Serre on the Somme : Kilner and Dolphin were wounded, whilst Booth was killed.[6]

Back in Bradford, a *Telegraph* photographer caught an anxious group of men studying a newspaper. The score at Old Trafford was the last thing on their minds. Through the mercantile connections of the wool trade, Bradford had a sizeable German population. Under the caption, 'A personal interest in the War news', a group of German subjects was seen standing outside the German Consul's office in Leeds Road. The *Telegraph* also reported that in Bradford's German Church the congregation was in tears.

There were some warning voices amidst the growing tension. On Sunday 2 August the vicar of Bradford, the Reverend Theodore Woods, led prayers for peace in the Parish Church. One of the curates at the service was the vicar's brother-in-law the Reverend John G.Thornton: in little over a month he would become Chaplain to the Bradford Pals and go on to witness events which he was loath to discuss in future years.[7]

Also on that first Sunday in August, at a public meeting in Manningham Tide Field, Fred Jowett, Labour M.P. for Bradford West, pleaded for non-involvement in a remarkably prophetic statement.

This will be the greatest war the world has ever seen, and I hope Great Britain will not be drawn into such a crime against civilization... Why should we be contemplating, at the present moment, a declaration of war to assist France? ...The time has come when it should not be in the power of any man or clique of men to say that men should slay each other. It is the people who ought to determine. Don't make any mistake, it is the people who will have to suffer. It is all very well for those who make their money producing armaments – that filthy gang which makes profits by creating jealousies and bad blood between nations. The high prices which will immediately follow will not cause any hardship to the capitalists. The working classes have to pay now, and I wonder how long it is going to continue.[8]

Jowett's anguished prophecy was in vain. The 1911 Census revealed that over 70,000 Bradfordians were directly employed in the textile industry, but there were only forty-eight Army personnel living in the City. The balance was to shift with dramatic speed.[9]

Elsewhere in Manningham, all was hustle and bustle at Belle Vue Barracks, the home of Bradford's 'Saturday night' Territorial soldiers. Known as the 6th Battalion of the West Yorkshire Regiment, they had just come back from their Summer camp on the coast at Redcar.

In August 1914, the West Yorkshire Regiment consisted of four full time regular battalions (the 1st, 2nd, 3rd and 4th) of about 1,000 men each. The regulars were backed up for home defence purposes by four part-time Territorial battalions (the 5th at York, the 6th at Bradford, with the 7th and 8th at Leeds).

The Territorial Force had been re-organised out of the old Volunteer Companies by the Liberal Government under Richard Haldane's Army Reforms of 1908. The Territorial soldiers were civilians who carried out military training in their spare time and were under no obligation to serve overseas. Whilst training was carried out with seriousness and thoroughness, for many the prospect of a free 'holiday' (usually on the Yorkshire coast in Bradford's case) in the annual camp, together with comradeship away from the monotony of work, were great attractions. Many of the 6th's officers had enjoyed membership of the Bradford Grammar School O.T.C. and decided to carry on with the Territorials. A former commander of the 6th, and another old boy of Bradford Grammar School, Colonel G.H. Muller, was destined to play a vital role in the training of the Bradford Pals despite his German family background, whilst a private, John Stanley, went on to a commission, became adjutant of the First Pals, and went on to win a D.S.O. in 1917.[10]

Throughout the country Territorial battalions received orders from the War Office to mobilize. At Belle Vue barracks the orders arrived during the morning of Tuesday, 4 August only hours before the outbreak of war. The following morning, the men received a long green envelope franked 'Mobilization – Urgent' containing Army Form E635. By 9.00 a.m. the vast majority had reported to the barracks, and by 6.00 p.m. a telegram was sent to Regimental Headquarters in York reporting that 575 out of the full strength of 581 were now present at Belle Vue – an amazing response and an indication of the air of excitement in the city following the declaration of war.[11]

*   *   *

On Wednesday, 5 August, the first full day of the war, Lord Kitchener of Khartoum was appointed Secretary of State for War by the Prime Minister, H. H. Asquith. The post of Secretary of State for War had been vacant since March following the Curragh incident in Ireland when the possibility of an Army Mutiny meant that Asquith had taken over responsibility for the duties himself.[12]

Although Asquith had some doubts about 'K', they were not as pronounced as his wife Margot, who characteristically described 'K' as, 'if not a great soldier, at least a great poster'. The hero of Khartoum and the South African War was a man of enormous prestige and his appointment was warmly welcomed by the public at large.

The psychological effect of his appointment, the tonic to public confidence,
were instantaneous and over-whelming[13]

How the news of the outbreak of war was presented to the people of Bradford.

Unlike many of his contemporaries, Kitchener was convinced that the war would not 'be over by Christmas'. He had the vision to realise it would be a long drawn out affair of at least three years duration and that the size of the Army must be increased dramatically. The pre-war regular Army was essentially a colonial police force, and even with back up by the 250,000 Territorials it would be insufficient for a European campaign, indeed, no British Army had seen action in Europe since the battle of Waterloo ninety nine years before. Kitchener's first act was to launch a massive recruiting drive and he sought parliamentary approval to increase the Army by 500,000 men, with an immediate increase in the regular army of 100,000.[14]

On Friday morning, like everywhere else in the country, the citizens of Bradford woke up to find a dramatic recruiting advertisement, 'Your King and Your Country Need You', in their morning newspapers. Under the royal crest, *The Bradford Daily Telegraph* carried, 'A Call to Arms' to men between the ages of 19 and 30 to enlist for a period of three years or until the war was concluded. Lord Kitchener it stated, 'is confident that this appeal will be at once responded to by all those who have the safety of the Empire at heart'.[15]

There was an immediate response. The next few days saw a flurry of activity, with hundreds of men applying to join the 6th West Yorks at Belle Vue Barracks. About twenty per cent were turned away because they failed to meet the medical standards (a telling point about health and poverty in the City), but many others were turned away because the Battalion very quickly became fully recruited. By Saturday, 9 August, the 6th had been brought up to full war strength of 979 men and twenty-nine officers. They were the first Territorial unit in the country to be able to report 'Ready to move', and they had all accepted 'foreign service' as well as their expected role of coastal defence.[16]

This was a remarkable achievement given the problems of equipment. Sufficient khaki uniforms, 'still creased', were brought out of the Quarter-Master's Stores. By the second day of mobilization, the Purchasing Officer had obtained fifty-seven horses in the City and a fledgling transport unit had been set up in Lister Park.

The constant comings and goings at Belle Vue drew huge crowds to the barrack gates as relatives and the curious gathered to pick up the latest gossip and information. Rumours flew that the Battalion was off to France, or would it be Egypt? Within a week of mobilization they were indeed off – but only to Selby.

At 7.30 am on Tuesday, 11 August the 6th West Yorks marched down Manningham Lane to the Midland Railway Station at Forster Square. The

Territorials of 6th West Yorks arrive at Forster Square Station 11 August, 1914.

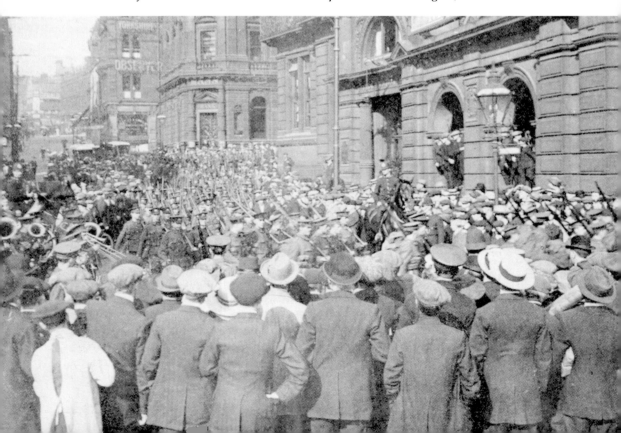

Yorkshire Observer reported their departure

> *When it was at last disgorged from the barracks the column reached almost from Belle Vue to Penny Bank – a resolute body, heavily accoutred, embracing men of all ages. There were youths scarce out of school and grizzled men who must have signed on afresh after the expiration of their time.*[17]

On 12 August the 2nd West Riding Battery, a Territorial Unit of the Royal Field Artillery, left the city at 5.00 am. They had spent the previous week based at Valley Parade, the Bradford City football ground just over the road from Belle Vue barracks, and had exercised their horses in Lister Park. Not everyone went by train from Forster Square, and the good citizens of Dudley Hill and Tong must have rubbed their eyes to see a tram towing an obsolete fifteen pounder artillery piece, up the hill to Tong Street and Wakefield Road to the city boundary at Drighlington to spare the horses.

It was a quiet departure for both Territorial units, and unlike the Pals Battalions, there was no huge crowd to see them off. The 6th West Yorks finally arrived in France in April, 1915, and many never saw Bradford again. Many in the Territorials came to resent the publicity given to the as yet unformed Pals Battalions, and sadly it became a cause of bitter comment in later years.

Two days after the Territorials' departure, the *Bradford Daily Telegraph* reported the arrival of the 125,000 strong regular Army British Expeditionary Force in Boulogne under the command of Sir John French. The B.E.F. were rushed to Mons just across the Belgian-French border to prepare for the German onslaught.

> *The declaration of war with the best customer of the wool and textile trades of this country was a blow which staggered every section of the industry, and for the time being no-one knew what to do.*[18]

The Government prolonged the Bank holiday to prevent a run on the banks, and this proved effective in stopping an immediate panic reaction. Nevertheless, the impact of war on the textile industry was enormous. Later, looking back at the end of December in the 'Review of Bradford Trade in 1914' the *Weekly Telegraph* recorded that demand came to an absolute standstill, and a large volume of business cancelled made the outlook very black.

On 13 August, a special meeting of woolmen was held in the Bradford Exchange to consider the situation. Two of the City's senior figures, Alfred Illingworth and Sir Algernon Firth had been appointed to a special advisory committee by the Board of Trade and reported back on the Government's intentions to support the textile industry. Illingworth was well connected, his brother Percy being the Liberal MP for Shipley and Government Chief Whip.

Although there was immediate uncertainty and wool prices continued to fall throughout August and September, those with foresight realised that a mass Army would need mass uniforms and that war would bring plenty of trade to Bradford despite the loss of the German market.

In such a feverish atmosphere, and with a large German community in Bradford, it was not long before all sorts of rumours and spy stories began to circulate in the city.

Bradford Territorials loading up at Forster Square Station.

On Saturday, 8 August all none naturalised Germans in Bradford were arrested, although many in the community had already departed for Germany never to return.[19] Those arrested were interned on the Isle of Man for the rest of the War.

On 15 August spy fever was boosted by a report in the *Yorkshire Observer* that a Rolls Royce of German registration, driven by a German chauffeur and belonging to a German gentleman had been garaged with Mr Eric S. Myers of Manningham Lane. Myers ran an enterprising car business and his logo dominated the main stand at Valley Parade football ground. After a week, in which the car went out early and came back late, the party left for Germany leaving the car behind. The police had been contacted and,

> a large number of German and English maps were found in their car, together with detailed accounts of journeys made, a ruler, a whistle and camera stand, some unused films and a quantity of rope. There were also a number of German newspapers with paragraphs marked in blue pencil relating to Irish Riots, insurrection in India, commercial war in England etc.[20]

But editorial comment in the *Observer* was in a more liberal vein,

> It is a matter for much congratulation that so far there have not been in this country any popular demonstrations. Their position (Bradford's German community) is indeed terribly distressing and it would be a brutal and disgraceful thing to add to the misery which the war must inevitably cause them by any demonstrations.[21]

Such high-minded sentiments did not last long in the editorial columns of the *Yorkshire Observer* or in the streets of Bradford and Keighley. Dr. Eurich, the German born doctor who had done so much to combat the horrors of anthrax amongst wool sorters in the Bradford textile industry, found old friends crossing the street to avoid the embarrassment of being seen talking to him.

On 20 August, the *Bradford Daily Telegraph* reported,

> *The Bradford registration of aliens is now complete and shows a larger proportion of Germans and Austrians within our city than many people might imagine. Many of these occupy important positions in our commercial life and may be regarded as friendly. They will have no use of a telephone or motor car and all their correspondence is subject to careful scrutiny. They are not allowed to leave town without a police permit.*

But from reports in the same edition, it is clear that prominent Bradfordians of German descent were taking care to be seen to have a positive attitude to the war. Mrs Annie Hoffmann had set up the 'Ladies of Bradford Soldiers' Dependents Relief Committee', and there were generous public donations from Colonel and Mrs. Muller, Mrs. Hoffmann and Messrs Mahler, Sichel & Company.[23] They had good reason to advertise their loyalty. On 22 August the *Yorkshire Observer* reported the fall of Brussels. The tone had changed.

> *Germany has sown so many seeds of hatred and she is now reaping the whirlwind of retribution. Her militarism is a cancerous growth if you like, which must be rooted out.*[24]

On the following day, the British and German Armies clashed for the first time at Mons. In the House of Commons, the Prime Minister indicated that 'casualties were heavy'.[25] News soon followed of the British Army's fighting retreat towards Paris from Mons. The initial mood changed from a mixture of

German citizens under arrest. They were interned on the Isle of Man for the duration of the War.

Phototpie J. Bouveret, Le Man

almost euphoric excitement to bitterness, anger and anxiety. It was a mood which led to some nasty incidents involving the local German community.

In Keighley police reinforcements were called in from Bradford, Shipley, Bingley and Cleckheaton as a largely Irish mob stoned the High Street house and shop of a German pork butcher, Carl Andrassy, whilst the family were inside. The Chief Constable of Bradford attended with the Mayor of Keighley, but matters only cooled down when the local Catholic priest, Father Russell intervened and persuaded the rioters to calm down. The following night the shops of a Mr Schulz in Low Street were looted and the mob returned to Andrassy's home where they broke in and burnt the furniture. The mob moved on to South Street where Stein's shop was smashed up and Church Street where Hoffman's shop was looted. At 1.00 am the *Riot Act* was read and the police dispersed the mob after a baton charge.[27]

In Bradford there were similar scenes. John McGrath who was to become the last living survivor of the 2nd Bradford Pals recalled,

> There were like a public outcry against all the Germans. Anybody that had a pork butchers shop with a German name, their windows were going in regular, and there was a lot of pork butchers in Bradford at that period. Where I lived in Manchester Road there were the Stieges, the Susslers – two Susslers – and the Lamonts, and they all set about them, it were all propaganda. It was just...well, it was an outcry against the Germans.[27]

Fred Jowett, the Labour MP, felt it politic to shift his ground. Speaking outside Bradford Moor Barracks where recruiting was going on, he denied charges that he had been trying to discourage the flow of recruits.

> It is not true. All I said is that adequate pay and compensation should be provided for those who feel it their duty to go to the front and fight the Nation's battle.[28]

*   *   *

Three days after the British Army's initial clash with the Germans at Mons, General Smith-Dorrien's II Corps made a stand at Le Cateau south of the Franco-Belgian border. On 26 August, in a brilliant rear-guard action, the British inflicted severe punishment on the pursuing Germans before resuming the long retreat south to the Marne and the defence of Paris.

Amongst the casualties at Le Cateau was the Adjutant of the 2nd Kings Own Yorkshire Light Infantry. Captain Charles Ackroyd from Manningham became the first Bradford casualty of the war.[29] By strange coincidence one of Ackroyd's successors as Adjutant of 2nd KOYLI, was Captain Herbert Carter, who was to become Commanding Officer of the 2nd Bradford Pals.

The regular Army fought on magnificently throughout 1914 even though it was heavily outnumbered. Casualties mounted as the Germans steam-rollered on into France before finally losing their momentum as men tired and supply lines struggled to cope. In the late Autumn the fighting was to turn into the stalemate of trench warfare after a series of flanking movements by both sides in a race for the channel ports ended in failure. Kitcheners vision

Herr Andrassy's pork butchers shop smashed in the Keighley riots.

of a long war and the need for a mass army would prove to be correct.

Efforts to recruit a mass army for this lengthy war were essential, but the resources of the War Office were simply insufficient to cope with the flood of recruits. The concept of men from a similar background or community joining up together had first been suggested by the Director-General of Recruiting, Sir Henry Rawlinson in mid-August.[30] By a twist of fate, Rawlinson was to be in command when so many of those recruits perished on the opening day of the Battle of the Somme on 1 July, 1916.

On 28 August, Kitchener appealed for a second 100,000 men for the 'New Army'. On the same evening, at an emotional recruiting meeting in Liverpool, Lord Derby coined the term 'Pals Battalion' for the first time.

> *I am not going to make you a speech of heroics... You have given me your answer... We have got to see this through to the bitter end and dictate our terms of peace in Berlin if it takes every man and every penny in the country. This should be a Battalion of Pals, a battalion in which friends from the same office will fight shoulder to shoulder for the honour of Britain and the credit of Liverpool...*[31]

'Pals' was an inspired turn of phrase. It appealed to the imagination, the deepest feelings of identity and comradeship. Picked up by the national press, it echoed round the industrial towns and cities of the north. Ninety years later, the echo lingers on.

Local initiative and organisation stepped in to fill the recruiting gap. Anything Liverpool could do, so could the rest. Manchester, Leeds, Sheffield, Barnsley, Hull and even little Accrington would not be outdone. And there was no northern city with a greater sense of its own worth and civic pride than Bradford. Its enterprising 'can do' worthies were determined to play their full part.

NOTES

1. See the works of A.J.P. Taylor and also the collections of official documents, telegrams etc., published by the British Government and used to establish German responsibility for the War at the Versailles conference in 1919.

2. 'Asquith', Roy Jenkins, pub. Collins, 1964, gives this surprising information, but also reveals the British Government's pre-occupation with Ireland and domestic matters. The Kaiser calculated on this pre-occupation in his view that the British would not intervene.

3. *The Bradford Pioneer*, 31 July, 1914.

4. *Clayton Times & Express*, 7 August, 1914.

5. *Yorkshire Observer*, 8 August, 1914.

6. *The History of Yorkshire County Cricket Club*, J.M. Kilburn, 1932.

7. In 1914 the Parish Church had yet to achieve Cathedral status. The Reverend Theodore Woods went on to become Bishop of Peterborough and later of Winchester. John Gordon Thornton was 29 years old and an M.A. of Trinity College, Cambridge. Mr. Thornton's son, Mr. J.H. Thornton, informs me that 'I am quite sure (my father) absolutely hated the war and went through it as a matter of duty. (Letter to author, 27.1.91)

8. Fred Jowett M.P., *Bradford Daily Telegraph*, 4 August, 1914.

9. 1911 Census enumerators returns available in Bradford City Library.

10. *A History of the 6th Battalion West Yorkshire Regiment*, Captain E.V. Tempest D.S.O., M.C., pub. Percy Lund Humphries & Go, London, 1921.

11. Ibid. p. 4.

12. In March 1914 the Government and military establishment were rocked when senior British officers (including Hubert Gough, the future commander of the Fifth Army) threatened to resign if they were required to take action against Ulster Unionists in the event of Irish Home Rule. The matter was patched up but left mutual suspicions between the military and the Liberal Government.

13. The quotation is from Asquith's daughter, Lady Violet Bonham Carter in her biography, *Winston Churchill as I knew him*; Eyre, Spottiswood & Collins, London, 1965. p 316 p. See also *Asquith*, op.cit p 343, for the Prime Minster's view and Margot Asquith's comment, p 343.

14. For a detailed account see *Kitchener's Army*, by Peter Simkins, Manchester University Press, 1988.

15. *Bradford Daily Telegraph*, 7 August, 1914.

16. Tempest, opus cit. p.5.

17. *Yorkshire Observer*, 15 August, 1914.

18. *Bradford Weekly Telegraph*, Review of Bradford Trade in 1914, 1 January, 1915.

19. *Bradford Daily Telegraph*, 8 August, 1914.

20. *Yorkshire Observer*, 15 August, 1914.

21. ibid.

22. *Clayton Times and Express*, 21 August, 1914.

23. *Bradford Daily Telegraph*, 19 August, 1914.

24. *Yorkshire Observer*, 22 August, 1914

25. *Yorkshire Observer*, 29 August, 1914.

26. *Yorkshire Observer*, 5 September, 1914.

27. John McGrath, tape recording in Bradford Museum archive kindly supplied by Mr. Steve Kerry.

28. *Yorkshire Observer*, 26 September, 1914.

29. Obituary of Captain Ackroyd in the *Bradford Daily Telegraph*, 3 September, 1914.

30. See Peter Simkins, *Kitchener's Army, The Raising of the New Armies*, 1914-16, Manchester University Press, 1988. pp 83/84.

31. Lord Derby speaking at a recruiting meeting in St. Anne's Street Drill Hall, 28 August, 1914. See Graham Maddocks, *Liverpool Pals*, Pen & Sword, in this series.

Chapter Three

A BRADFORD PALS
BATTALION

The ideal to be aimed at is a congenial companionship and a community of interest and association. THE YORKSHIRE OBSERVER, 5th September, 1914.

I thought it would be the end of the world if I didn't pass.

16/1205 PRIVATE GEORGE MORGAN

ON THURSDAY 3 SEPTEMBER, The Lord Mayor of Bradford, Alderman John Arnold, called a meeting 'of influential and prominent persons' in the Victoria Hotel to form a 'Bradford Citizens Army League, According to the Lord Mayor, the League would,

Push men into the recruiting office and form a commercial battalion in Bradford as had happened in Liverpool, Manchester and Birmingham.[1]

To loud applause, he concluded,

This war has been thrust upon us, and what we have to do is look to our homes and defend the dignity of the Nation. I trust that Bradford will rise to the occasion.[2]

In scenes of great enthusiasm, the meeting unanimously agreed with the Lord Mayor that an application be made to Lord Kitchener at the War Office to form what they hoped would be called the 10th (City of Bradford) Battalion of the Prince of Wales Own West Yorkshire Regiment.[3]

The West Yorkshire Regiment already had eight battalions (four regular and four territorial). The meeting was aware that War Office sanction had been sought for a Leeds Battalion and assumed the Leeds recruits would become the 9th West Yorks. In fact, by the time the Battalions were numbered, the Leeds Pals became the 15th West Yorks, the first Bradford Pals became the 16th West Yorks, and the 2nd Bradford Pals which began to recruit at the end of January 1915 became the 18th West Yorks.

Thus established, the newly formed Bradford Citizens' Army League went on to elect an Executive Committee to administer its affairs. The *Bradford Weekly Telegraph* described the members of the Executive as 'the great businessmen of the city', – the *Telegraph* reporter no doubt being mindful that his own Chairman, Sir James Hill, was on the Committee. It was undoubtedly a powerful group commanding national as well as local influence and political power. They were immensely wealthy, used to getting things done and used to getting what they wanted.[4]

The new Chairman, John Holdsworth Robinson J.P. (1855-1927) from Greenhill Hall, Bingley, was Chairman of the Bradford Chamber of

Commerce and the Yorkshire Provincial Unionist (Conservative) Association. He was knighted after the war and made a Chevalier of the Legion of Honour, but this must have been small compensation for the loss of his son, Second Lieutenant John Holdsworth Robinson junior who died with the Pals on the first day of the Battle of the Somme.

The Chairman of the Finance Committee, Sir William Priestley J.P., M.P., was Chairman of Priestley's Ltd., dress manufacturers of Pudsey. Sir William, a former Mayor of Bradford, was Liberal M.P. for Bradford East. His father had been M.P. for Pudsey, whilst his wife's father had been M.P. for Skipton. Sir William immediately donated £1,000 to the funds of the League, an immense sum in 1914. Another powerful committee figure was Sir James Hill (1849-1936). In addition to his textile interests, he controlled the local press as Chairman of the *Yorkshire Observer*, the *Bradford Daily & Weekly Telegraph* and the *Keighley News*. He also found time to be Chairman of the local directors of Barclays Bank and was Liberal M.P. for Bradford Central from 1916 to 1918.

Sir Arthur Godwin J.P. (1852-1921) was another prominent Liberal with textile interests and a knighthood. The son of a Mayor, he became the City's first Lord Mayor in 1907, and was also a Senior Grand Deacon in the Freemasons. Sidney Illingworth, was related to the Lister and the Holden textile dynasties, and was a director of the National Provincial Bank. His brother Percy was the Liberal M.P. for Shipley, and at the centre of national power as Chief Whip in the Liberal Government.

The Committee was a roll call of powerful textile and commercial interests: Colonel Armitage, G. Douglas, J.J. Oddy, J.H. Walker, Councillor E.J. Smith, Charles Ogden (brother of the M.P. for Pudsey), S. S. Midgley, and Councillor John Bland who later joined the Second Pals as an officer. Captain Burton, the Recruiting Officer for Bradford made up the numbers.

A notable absentee was Fred Jowett, the Labour M.P. for Bradford West and a future Cabinet Minister in the first Labour Government. The *Bradford Daily Telegraph* reported his refusal to have anything to do with the recruiting campaign. However, a prominent Labour Councillor and future Mayor of the City, J.H. Palin, gave his enthusiastic support to the recruiting campaign, particularly when the second Battalion was formed.[5]

On 4 September, the *Clayton Times* indicated the special character of the new battalion.

> It is being suggested that Shipley should unite with Bradford, Keighley and Bingley in forming a Battalion of friends.[6]

On the same day, it was reported that Evelyn Lintott the former Bradford City captain and England football international had joined the Leeds Pals. Lintott, a teacher at Dudley Hill School, had become impatient with recruitment delays in Bradford.[7]

The new Executive Committee of the Citizens Army League was in virtually continuous session. Before waiting to receive official sanction from the War Office, an advertisement was placed in the press announcing that registration of recruits would commence in the lecture hall of the Mechanics Institute on the following Tuesday morning, 8 September. Town Hall clerks were instructed to make preparations for the register.

On 5 September, having failed to receive a reply to the Lord Mayor's initial application, another telegram was fired off to the War Office stating that the Bradford Battalion would,

> be raised, clothed and equipped for the West Yorkshire Regiment at the cost of the citizens of Bradford by subscription.[8]

Angry words were expressed when a dampening reply was received later in the day asking the League to send fuller details by letter. No doubt after a word from his Chairman, Sir James Hill, the editor of the *Yorkshire Observer* thundered under the heading RECRUITING DELAYED:

> This state of affairs cannot be regarded as satisfactory. It exists throughout the North of England in varying degrees. It is to be hoped for the nation's good that the remedy will be very different from the expedients now being adopted by the War Office to cope with the situation.[9]

To be fair, the War Office was overwhelmed with the demands being made on it, and it was only reasonable to be certain that any new Battalion was a viable proposition before granting sanction.

The *Observer* went on to explain, with a hint of snobbery, that the scheme for the new battalion,

> seems to have taken firm root in the minds of the young commercial and professional men of the city, who appear only too anxious to get started. This, of course, cannot yet be done, as the official sanction of the War Office to form the battalion has not yet been received, though it is expected at any moment. Thus, the registration is not enlistment proper but a means of raising the battalion first of all "on paper" after which it can be converted into actual existence in a very short time.[10]

The Executive of the League, however, were able to move quickly to appoint a commanding officer for their new battalion. They were aware of the irony that the new C.O. was of German descent, but there is no doubt he was the right man for the job.

Fifty-eight year old Lieutenant Colonel George Herbert Muller was the Yorkshire yarn agent for Courtaulds and was well connected in the business and social circles of the city. He had attended Bradford Grammar School and became President of the Old Boys Association in 1904. He was a prominent member of the congregation at Bradford Parish Church (not yet a Cathedral) and commanded the Bradford Church Lads Brigade. Most relevant, as a retired Colonel of the 6th West Yorks Territorials, he knew how to run a battalion and had a network of contacts of former officers and N.C.O.'s to call on both in the Territorials and through Bradford Grammar School. As a young man he had joined the old 2nd Volunteer Battalion of the West Yorks (Bradford Rifles) as a private. He went on to succeed his father as C.O., and in 1908 was appointed Colonel of the newly formed Territorial battalion after the Haldane reforms.

The Colonel on his white horse became a familiar figure in the City and in the local press. The fact that the press abbreviated the Volunteer Decoration (long service) medal after his name to V.D. provoked the odd smirk amongst his new charges, but there is no doubt he was well respected. When he eventually relinquished command of the First Bradford Pals at Skipton, he moved on to take charge of the formation of the Second Pals Battalion until the move to Ripon in May, 1915.

* * *

On Monday night 7 September hundreds of young Bradfordians got out their best Sunday suits ready for an early start the next morning to register at the Mechanics Institute. They wanted to make a good impression and be regarded as 'the right sort of men' having read another somewhat pompous comment in the *Yorkshire Observer*.

> *The advantage of the system described is that it restricts admission to the battalion to the right sort of men. An exact definition of suitability for this purpose can hardly be obtained, but the ideal to be aimed at is a congenial companionship and a community of interest and association, and the question of suitability in this respect will be in the discretion of the employers who distribute the tickets or the responsible league representatives who will supervise the registration and form their own judgement upon each of the men who come forward.*[11]

On Tuesday morning there were scenes of great excitement and patriotic fervour as the Mechanics Institute in Bridge Street was besieged by young men anxious to register. It is ironic that when the Institute was first founded in 1832 one of its four specialist subjects was the German language.

The Mechanics Institute was at the heart of the city just across the large

The Mechanics Institute, Bradford. In the lecture room in September 1914 men signed up for the 16th Battalion, West Yorkshire Regiment.

No 17 Platoon at Cartright Hall, Manningham Park. Major Haworth with walking stick.

open space outside the main entrance to the Town Hall. The Lord Mayor and the Executive Committee of the Citizens' Army League were cheered as they made their way through the crowds from the Town Hall to the Institute in time for the opening of the doors.

The band of the 6th West Yorks Territorials had been specially recalled from Selby to set the tone with military music, whilst a Sergeant Major resplendent with waxed moustache and in full regimentals supervised the queue.

Inside the lecture hall three tables had been set out, each manned by two Town Hall clerks, to enable the eager recruits to be dealt with three at a time. Behind the clerks, the Lord Mayor, Alderman Arnold, and the worthies of the League stood in shiny top hatted corporate splendour in front of an enormous fire blazing away in the fireplace. With thumbs in waistcoats, they fingered watch chains and beamed approval as the young men filed in.

The first to register, and given the number 1, was twenty-four year old Bradford solicitor, P.M. Crowther. He was rewarded with a handshake from the Lord Mayor and congratulated on his spirit. Number 2 to be registered was, Walter Turner, an estate agent, Boer War veteran and former member of the Territorials. He became the new battalion's first regimental sergeant major. Each man was given a number. Later, when the Battalion became the 16th West Yorks, the prefix 16 was added to every number, whilst in the later 2nd Pals, the prefix 18 was used. Each recruit was asked his age, full name and address and whether he was in good health. He then signed the registration book and was given a registration card with his number and name. There was as yet no medical examination or attestation because formal

War Office sanction was still awaited for the new battalion.

Scrubbed faces; polished boots, pressed suits, birthday tie-pin, grand-dad's watch, macassared hair and bright eyes under best caps. Adventure, a patriotic glow, doing one's bit, approval from the most powerful figures in the city, no more boredom at the ledger desk or noise, sweat and drudgery in the mills, the chance to be a hero, to thrash the Hun, admiring glances from young women – or possibly to get away from a nagging wife or the creditors. Who knows what mixture of motives and emotions these young men felt as they joshed and chatted in the queue as the band played on that late summer morning.

"Are we down-hearted? Nooooo...". "We don't want to lose you, but we think you ought to go"... "It'll all be over by Christmas. If they don't get a move on we're going to miss our chance to be in it".

Would they have been so eager if they had known their fate?

If we take the first one hundred recruits as a random sample, thirty-nine were killed and nineteen were so severely wounded that they were discharged as unfit for service before the end of the War. The ratio of killed to wounded was one to three, so of the remaining forty-two who served throughout the war most would suffer at least one wound. Eight were decorated for gallantry (one D.C.M., two M.C.s and five M.M.s) whilst seventeen were later commissioned from the ranks.[12]

On 10 September, as registration continued, the *Yorkshire Observer* reported that the Lord Mayor had called a meeting of 'prominent employers' in the Town Hall. He was happy to announce that,

> *he had received a telegram from Lord Kitchener thanking him on behalf of the Army Council for the offer of the citizens to, clothe and equip a Bradford Service battalion of the West Yorkshire Regiment, and stating that the proposal is sanctioned subject to conditions which are to follow by post.*[13]

The purposes of the meeting was to encourage employers to make a financial contribution to League funds to equip the battalion, at least £7,500 was needed, and to persuade them to offer recruiting incentives to their employees. £6,000 was raised immediately and the *Observer* reported,

> *The employers of Bradford are, generally speaking, making most generous offers to such of their men as are enlisting. The Bradford Manufacturers' Association, consisting of some eighty to ninety firms, are offering re-instatement in the present position after the war, half wages for all married men*

BRADFORD SERVICE BATTALION.
WEST YORKSHIRE REGIMENT.

Enrolment No. *168*

Name *Mr Herbert Taylor*

You have been duly registered as a Candidate for enlistment in the Bradford Service Battalion of the West Yorkshire Regiment.

You will in due course receive instructions when and where to present yourself for medical examination and attestation. In order to facilitate enlistment it is necessary you should have ready the following particulars when you attend for attestation :—

1. Your correct age (year and month).
2. The name of the Town or place where you were born.
3. Are you, or have you been an apprentice? if so, where? to whom? for what period? and when did, or will the period of your apprenticeship expire?

If you are married :—

4. The Christian and Surname of woman to whom married.
5. Place and date of marriage.
6. Name of officiating Minister or Registrar.
7. And names of two witnesses.

If you have any children :—

8. Their Christian name or names.
9. Date and place of Birth.
10. Name and place of Baptism and name of Officiating Minister.

Special Recruiting Office,
BRADFORD MECHANICS' INSTITUTE

The recruiting boom, Valley Parade Barracks.

while serving in the Army ; and special arrangements for single men having relatives dependent upon them according to circumstances. It will therefore be seen that the wife of a man earning from any of the firms mentioned 30 shillings (£1.50) per week and having two children would receive the following amounts per week :

From the employer, half wages	*15s. 0d*
From the Government, separation allowance (wife)	*7s. 7d*
From the Government, two children at 1s 2d each	*2s. 4d*
Allotments out of husband's Army Pay to wife	*3s. 6d*
Ditto for two children	*1s. 2d*
Total	*£1. 9s. 7d*

Moreover the household bills would be lessened by the cost of the husband's keep. There are a great many employers apart from the manufacturers who are offering substantial benefits to those in their employ who are enlisting.[14]

One wonders whether the manufacturers would have been quite so generous if they known how long the war would last. It is not known how widespread or sustained this beneficence was, although Fred Rawnsley certainly benefited from it.

I was in the cloth export section with a firm called Sharp, Sonnenthal & Company. I was only nineteen, and just a bit of a superior clerk at the time but I wasn't anything special. When I came back I'd my job to come back to and I will say this about the firm, they were very good. Of course I volunteered, and they paid us half wages all through the war to those of us who had joined up voluntary, not those who were called up. At that time I was getting a pound a week, so my mother collected ten shillings all through the war for me. This was a lot of money when I came out, and it seemed very nice to have a hundred pounds to come back to.

16/853 PRIVATE FRED RAWNSLEY[15]

But it may be that the employers' generosity was inspired by more than patriotism. The Mayor, a canny politician, had a splendid carrot to dangle at the meeting,

> *Local industry has received further big support by an enquiry from the War Office authorities for 15,000 pieces of blue serge cloth, to be delivered at the rate of 500 pieces a day. The Lord Mayor, Alderman John Arnold, was asked to place the orders and he immediately had enquiries made of merchants and manufacturers as to what quantity of suitable material they had.... The Chamber of Commerce was also acquainted by the Lord Mayor of the order and the members communicated with, indicating that the Government were prepared to buy, through the Lord Mayor, a large quantity of serges.[16]*

Tactfully, the *Yorkshire Observer* failed to report this happy co-incidence in its round up of recruiting news. It was left to the *Clayton Times* and *Express* to carry the story as a separate item of business news.

Profit and patriotism were comfortable companions. By the end of 1914 demand from the War Office ensured that wool prices and profits shot through the roof. The price of Forties to Sixties Tops, used in the manufacture of Army uniforms, rose from one shilling and eight pence (8 pence) to two shillings and three pence (11 pence) per pound, a rise of 36% in three months. By the end of 1916 the price was three shillings and seven pence (17 pence), a rise of over 200 % from August, 1914.[17]

One hopes more than just Fred Rawnsley's employer kept the promise of jobs and half pay to the 42% of recruits who returned relatively whole. Their war profits meant they could afford to do so.

*   *   *

By the end of the first week, over four hundred applicants had registered – with no less than 106 different occupations. The League 'felt confident to announce' in the press that consideration was being given to the forming of eight companies of 150 men. In line with their earlier comments about restricting selection to 'the right sort of men', the statement indicated that the different companies would be graded in a hierarchy of particular groups of occupations echoed their earlier comments of restricting selection to 'the right sort of men':

A Company	*Professional men and Bradford Trade Employers*
B Company	*Cashiers, foreign correspondents, higher grade office workers.*
C Company	*Clerks*
D Company	*Warehousemen*
E Company	*Master Tradesmen*
F Company	*Tradesmen's assistants*
G Company	*'Pals', meaning friends who wish to stand together despite differences of civilian occupation.*
H Company	*Miscellaneous.[18]*

This quaint segregated structure was quietly abandoned. H Company never became the company required to do all the potato peeling, and the Company of Clerks never sent a memo to the Germans thanking them for theirs of the 30th ultimo but respectfully requiring an early surrender by return of post. What we are left with is a strong hint of class consciousness by the Bradford Citizens Army League Executive. As we will see this may have been reflected in the selection policy, but G Company, 'the Pals', became the generality for the whole battalion.

*   *   *

Having registered with such enthusiasm, the first four hundred recruits must have felt a sense of anti-climax when they had to return home and go back to work as normal But on Monday the 14 September, their pulses must have quickened when they received their first Battalion orders by special postal delivery. They were ordered to parade at 7.30 p.m. sharp on Tuesday 15 September for Preliminary Drill at the Artillery Drill Hall, Valley Parade, Manningham Lane near to the Bradford City football ground. They were also instructed to parade at 6.30 p.m. sharp on Wednesday 16 September in order to march to the Eastbrook Hall for a Recruiting Campaign Meeting.

On Tuesday evening, 'without a single late-comer', the keen young men gathered as the Bradford Pals for the first time. They were introduced to their new commanding officer by the Lord Mayor. No doubt the odd eyebrow was raised at the C.O.'s name, for although he was born in Bradford Colonel Muller's parents were born in Germany. Perhaps the more reflective remembered that the Kaiser was a grandson of Queen Victoria and first cousin of King George V. The Royal family later changed its name from Saxe-Coburg-Gotha to Windsor. Private Eric Weintz of the Second Bradford Pals served under the alias of White, even though he lived in Britannia Street, Shipley.

Whatever their initial feelings, the Pals came to respect Colonel Muller and there were genuine expressions of regret when he left them to take command of the Second Pals five months later.

After a brief pep talk, Colonel Muller introduced his second in command, Major William Mitchell. The Major, who was well into his sixties, was a cashier with a firm of solicitors Watson, Son & Smith. He was an old colleague of Colonel Muller having served in the Bradford Volunteers for 37 years. He joined as a private in 1877 but was commissioned in 1896 when he became the Volunteers' quartermaster.[19]

Colonel Muller and Major Mitchell had been busy in preparation for the meeting. They used their Territorial and Volunteer contacts to recruit a number of retired N.C.O.s. Most were Boer War veterans with suitably waxed military moustaches. Old campaign medals clanked on uniforms which seemed to have become more tight-fitting over the intervening years. Under Acting Regimental Sergeant Major Walter Turner, orders were barked out asking for anyone with previous military experience to step forward. Those that did, quickly found themselves marked out to be additional N.C.O.s.

The rest of the evening was spent getting the men into lines and learning the rudiments of drill. And with the parade down Manningham Lane to come the following evening – how to march. Even though they had no uniforms or rifles, they began to feel like proper soldiers. The Belle Vue Hotel and public houses in Manningharn Lane did a roaring trade as the excited young men swapped experiences after the evening's activities were over.

On Wednesday evening 16 September came their first public showing in a great parade to a recruiting meeting in the Eastbrook Hall. Led by the band of the 6th West Yorks Territorials, and followed by companies of Boy Scouts and Colonel Muller's old charges in the Boys' Brigade, they marched down Manningham Lane and North Parade.

It must have been an exhilarating experience for these impressionable young men. All were in their Sunday best, trying to keep in step for the first time despite the showers and equine contributions on the slippery stone sets.

Despite the rain, 40,000 Bradfordians lined the streets to cheer them on their way. The Pals made a detour to the Town Hall where the Lord Mayor and his guests took the salute before heading past St. George's Hall, along Hall Ings to Forster Square, and then on to Eastbrook Hall. The *Telegraph* described the scene in highly enthusiastic terms.

BRADFORD SERVICE BATTALION,

WEST YORKSHIRE REGIMENT.

RECRUITING OFFICES,
MECHANICS' INSTITUTE, BRADFORD.
September 14th, 1914.

BATTALION ORDERS.

All registered men will parade for Preliminary Drill at the

ARTILLERY DRILL HALL, Valley Parade,
Manningham Lane, Bradford,

at 7-30 p.m. sharp, on Tuesday, Sept. 15th, 1914.

All ranks will parade at the same place on **Wednesday, Sept. 16th,** at 6-30 p.m. sharp, to march to EASTBROOK HALL for the **Recruiting Campaign Meeting.**

The Area at EASTBROOK HALL will be reserved for the Men of the Battalion and the Members of the **Bradford Citizens' Army League.**

All the chief Speakers at the St. George's Hall Meeting will address the Eastbrook Hall Meeting also.

☞ This notification will serve for admission to the DRILL HALL (*both evenings*) and the EASTBROOK HALL, and must be shewn at the doors.

BY ORDER.

NEW BATTALION'S GALLANT PARADE

The Bradford Pals Battalion withstood the elemental adversity.... They are a fine body of men, and the crowds of onlookers were impressed to such remarks as, "Bravo, boys", "Them's the sort of lads", and other commendations.

Their ranks were as solid as their steps were in order. Their first parade was a distinct success. The Battalion showed what the men of Bradford were ready to do. The men were already stamped with order and discipline and they were ready to sustain the honour and glory of the British Empire in times to come.[20]

Times to come? There would be no cheering crowds at Serre, Rossignol Wood or Gavrelle. There would be rain and mud... and there would be shrapnel, bullets, grenades and gas.

And when they ask us how dangerous it was...
Oh, we'll never tell them,
No, we'll never tell them...
We spent our pay in some cafe,

And fought wild women night and day,
T'was the cushiest job we ever had

*   *   *

Outside Eastbrook Hall, the Pals lined up for inspection by former Admiral of the Fleet, Lord Charles Beresford. When they moved to their reserved places in the well of the hall they were cheered to the echo.

Eastbrook Hall, rebuilt and extended only a few years before, was a vast Methodist Hall with over 2,000 seats. The meeting was a packed emotional affair with hundreds turned away. It was a double header with a similar event in St. George's Hall and the main speakers moving between the two halls. Newspaper reports indicate the passion and depth of feeling of the time.

THRILLING SCENES AT ST. GEORGE'S HALL

Never before in its sixty years' history has St. George's hall presented such a scene as it did last night. It was a scene which touched the emotions, and the memory of it makes a vivid chapter in the history of Bradford.

The vast audience simply breathed patriotic fervour, which was heightened to an indescribable intensity as the national songs followed one on another. Again and again the audience rose and cheered, and even the pressmen for once in a way threw custom aside and forgot their traditional impassivity.[21]

The main speakers were Admiral Lord Charles Beresford (Conservative M.P. for Portsmouth), Stanley Buckmaster M.P. (Solicitor General and a member of the Liberal Cabinet), G.H. Roberts the Labour M.P. for Norwich (a future Junior Minister), and the Vicar of Bradford, the Reverend Theodore Woods.

Lord Charles had stepped in at short notice to replace Lord Haldane (the Lord Chancellor and former Secretary of State for War) who was kept in London by Government business.[22] For the purpose of the meeting, Beresford was probably more attuned to what was expected than the cool intellectual Haldane. He was a fiery jingo on the far right of the Tory Party – with no inhibitions about laying into Germany and all things German. Beresford was also in hot water with his relative by marriage, Winston Churchill, (then First Lord of the Admiralty) for crude remarks about the First Sea Lord, Prince Louis of Battenberg.[23] According to Beresford:

Prince Louis was an exceedingly able officer, but nothing could alter the fact that he is a German and, as such, should not be occupying his present position.

Churchill had fired back,

The interests of the country do not permit the spreading of such wicked allegations by an officer of your rank, even though retired.[24]

One wonders whether Lord Charles was introduced to Colonel Muller.

After everyone had been whipped up into a frenzy with all the old patriotic songs, Beresford's speech was par for the course:

The Germans do not understand honour... they have broken every law, human and divine, and they have to be taught a swift violent lesson... the so-called German culture is a culture Europe can well do without...We have got to settle this issue in Berlin and nowhere else.[25]

Buckmaster was more cerebral, outlining the legal obligations of the Belgian

Treaty, whilst Roberts said their mission was to save humanity. The Vicar, before closing the meeting with prayers and the National Anthem, said,

> *War is horrible to every true Christian – but there are worse things than war. One is to break your plighted word. England never went into war with a cleaner sheet or a brighter conscience.*[26]

George Morgan was one of the young recruits in the hall. He remembered his feelings at the time.

> *We had been brought up to believe that Britain was the best country in the world and we wanted to defend her. The history taught us at school showed that we were better than other people (didn't we always win the last war?) and now all the news was that Germany was the aggressor and we wanted to show the Germans what we could do.*
>
> 16/1205 PRIVATE GEORGE MORGAN[27]

On 19 September, it was announced that the Battalion register was fully subscribed with over 1,200 potential recruits. Formal written sanction had been received from Lord Kitchener, but the War Office made it clear that the Bradford Citizens' Army League would have to be responsible for the running costs, uniforms and equipment for an indefinite period. Attestation and medicals began the following week. Some very disappointed recruits were turned away because they failed the medical or dental examination. In a speech in December, Sir William Priestley M.P. confirmed that over 1,700 men had presented themselves, but only 1,000 were accepted. Others were turned away because they were discovered to be under the required age of nineteen, -although a large number of under-age youngsters did manage to get through the net. We get an indication of the atmosphere and the close knit nature of the Pals from some of their stories. George Morgan was only sixteen:

> *When they started the Pals battalion I wanted to get in very much. My brother-in-law had joined and four cousins had already joined so of course I wanted to join. Only I was only 16. I thought I wouldn't be big enough 'cos I wasn't what you might call big, well made or owt. Just a skinny bit of a lad.*
>
> *And 'course I went and joined the queue to join the Bradford Pals and they were very particular who they took because such a lot wanted to join. They were very choosy about it all... they passed you from one doctor to another, one doctor would do one thing and another another and the last one was chest measurement. I thought it would be the end of the world if I didn't pass. People were being failed for all sorts of reasons, if they hadn't got sufficient teeth, for example: they were glad enough to get them later! When I came to have my chest measured I took a deep breath and puffed out my chest as far as I could and the doctor said 'You've just scraped through'. It was marvellous being accepted. When I went back home home and told my mother she said I was a fool and she'd give me a good hiding: but I told her, "I'm a man now, you can't hit a man".*
>
> 16/1205 PRIVATE GEORGE MORGAN[28]

Stanley Wright, who became batman to the Battalion Chaplain, the Reverend John Thornton, was also under age, having just passed his eighteenth birthday.

I was 18...a year under age. I joined with my brother who was about eight years older – and as far as I was concerned he was the very best... to his dying day he was a 'buddy' brother. He joined and I wanted to go with him and for that reason my parents allowed it. PRIVATE STANLEY WRIGHT, 16th West Yorks[29]

Eighteen year old Rhodes Akam was a timber merchant who had played on the wing for Bradford Grammar School. He was later commissioned in the 2nd Bradford Pals and was last seen charging towards the German line at Serre. Private Norman Waddilove (16/313), a school friend of Akam, grandly described himself as 'a gentleman'. A more accurate description would have been seventeen year old son of a textile millionaire. Like Akam, young Waddilove was killed on 1 July, 1916. There were plenty of other youngsters. John Bower (16/263) was another seventeen year old killed at Serre. Probably the youngest was Bill Brayshay (16/1391), a strapping fifteen year old farm worker from Bradley near Keighley. He was only sixteen when he died of pneumonia in hospital at Fovant a year later in October, 1915.

Tony Miller tried to join the First Pals, but he found the standards at his medical examination more demanding than for George Morgan.

In the first instance when you go before the Doctor you're stripped naked, as mother nature, like when you're first born. No clothes on at all. You go before the Doctor, he does various measurements on you, he puts a tape on you and they take all the measurements on you. And then he says, 'Cough' and if the cough isn't right you're discharged. It's a matter of, well, old soldiers know

1st Pals in their best suits at Cartwright Hall, September 1914.

what I mean. Anyhow, my chest was a little bit too narrow, you might say, and they sent me to a chap called Crawshaw, he was manager at Salmon and Glucksteins, and he used to be a member of the All Saints Gymnastic Club. And he gave me exercise for several weeks thus expanding my chest to the required measurement. And after that I went through a second examination and Doctor Lodge, on Manningham Lane just past the old Grammar School, passed me for the Army. By that time the First Pals had filled up and they put me in the Second Pals, the 18th West Yorks. 18/856 PRIVATE TONY MILLER[30]

*   *   *

Who, then, were the young men who rushed so eagerly to volunteer for the new Bradford Battalion? We are fortunate in being able to analyse a full list of the names and occupations of the twenty-five officers and 1,064 other ranks published in the *Bradford Weekly Telegraph* in November, 1914,[31] to which has been coupled an analysis of their ages from the Commonwealth War Graves Commission records. They were generally of a higher social class, taller and in better health, more articulate and better educated than the general population of the City of Bradford. They were also very young with a large proportion younger than the official age of nineteen for foreign service.

Bradford was an industrial manufacturing city with the majority of the population involved in manual work. Yet despite this, the other ranks of the Pals Battalion were overwhelmingly white collar rather than blue collar. An analysis of occupations in the City in the 1911 Census reveals that commercial or business clerks accounted for less than four per cent of the employed male population. Yet nearly one in five members of the new Battalion were clerks (202 or 19%) compared with only 16 general labourers (1.5%).

It is not surprising that so many clerks joined the Pals, often joining together as groups of friends. In 1914 computers were not even a pipe dream and typewriters were often regarded as a new fangled American toy. The commercial life of the city was maintained by an army of male clerks. They had to be intelligent, articulate and sometimes to have a foreign language. Yet the work was often claustrophobic, boring and repetitive. They often worked in groups in a large office, and when the boss's back was turned, in normal times there would be a great deal of talk about football, cricket and amorous exploits (real or imaginary). Now the talk was of war and adventures in foreign lands. The summer holiday was over and the long drag until the next one seemed endless. All that was needed was one strong voice to empty an entire office. One does not have to be a 1914 version of Billy Liar to see the excitement and appeal to the imagination of the recruiting campaign.

After the clerks, the next largest groups were 113 warehousemen (11%), 55 dyer's labourers (5%), and 30 (3%) travellers and salesmen. Only 11% of the total came from totally unskilled manual occupations. If the occupations of the other ranks are consolidated into social class groups the following pattern emerges:

	Number	Percentage
Professional (Solicitors/Accountants)	11	1.0 %
Managers, teachers, high grade technical engineers, and chemists etc.	89	8.3 %
Clerks and Commercial Travellers	232	21.8 %
Self employed trades	58	5.4 %
Skilled employees (electricians, mechanics and skilled craftsmen etc.)	156	14.6 %
Retail (shop assistants)	56	5.4 %
Semi-skilled (tram drivers, wool trade skills etc)	275	25.8 %
Unskilled (dyers labourers etc)	118	11.0 %
Miscellaneous (actors, boxers, musicians, and no given occupation)	69	6.7 %
TOTAL	1,064	100.0 %

The analysis confirms reports in the *Yorkshire Observer* that admission to the Battalion was to be selective and restricted:

> *The league representatives will supervise the registration and form their own judgement upon each of the men who come forward. The advantage is that it restricts admission to the right sort of men.*[32]

A further example of the white collar flavour is the fact that no less than 61 (6 %) of the recruits had attended the prestigious Alma Mater of the prosperous Bradford middle classes, Bradford Grammar School.[33] The figure of 6% is six times bigger than a proportionate number would be for the city as a whole. In August, 1914, Bradford Grammar School ranked second only to Rugby (but ahead of Eton, Winchester, Oundle, Marlborough and Charterhouse) in the Oxford and Cambridge Schools Examination Board results.[34] It is fair to assume that the general quality of other ranks in the Pals was much higher than a typical pre-war recruit to the Regular Army. Their more prosperous social background may also account for the fact that they were taller than the average for the period. This became evident when contracts were issued for their uniforms. The battalion has been specially measured, and an interesting feature is that on a 5ft 6in standard only about 120 would be under that height, the average height of the battalion being 5ft 8½ in.[35] The other predominant factor was that they were extremely young. An analysis of the casualty lists reveals that well over 50% of all casualties two years later in 1916 were aged twenty-two or younger with the largest single year group number being aged nineteen. This is true of both battalions but was even more pronounced in the Second Pals. A fair number of fifteen and sixteen year olds must have been let through the net. The impression of a lively group of articulate intelligent men was confirmed for the author by reading many surviving diaries and letters. George Grunwell (16/1042) recalled that at Skipton orders were always posted on a notice-board rather than announced because it was assumed that everyone was literate.[36]

No less than 240 different occupations were represented with an astonishing variety of different skills and talents, and there were also some unusual characters. Will Blakeborough and Jack Manley were professional boxers. Blakeborough was regarded as one of the best three featherweights in the country and 'Stoker' Manley was the Yorkshire area middleweight champion. The 'stoker' nickname came from Jack Manley's day job – he was a stoker for the massive steam engine at Lister's mill.

On a more cerebral level in the other ranks, a twenty-two year old Cambridge graduate, Edward Victor Appleton, was destined to be the future Sir Edward Appleton, winner of the Nobel Prize for his work on Radio and Space Research at the Cavendish Laboratory. In 1914 he was described as a University Coach. He was the son of a warehouseman born in a small back to back terraced house in the Barkerend Road district of Bradford behind the Parish Church. He was educated at Hanson School, which had a strong scientific reputation, and went on to graduate with a Double First in Physics and Natural Sciences at Cambridge University. His abilities were soon noticed in the Pals, and he left to join the Royal Engineers as an officer towards the end of 1914. He was to specialize in Radio Communications including developing eavesdropping methods to penetrate German wire communications.[37]

Edward Victor Appleton, Nobel Prize winner.

Three professional musicians (John Cooper, Franklin Morrell and James Sheldon) formed the core of the Battalion band alongside a number of semi-professional musicians. As bandsmen they would learn first aid and be stretcher-bearers. Tim Wharton, a lively humorous character, was an accomplished sportsman and musician and joined the band as a bugler/drummer. He was so unhappy with the quality of the regimental issue drum that he went out and bought his own drum[38]. The drum came home to Bradford and his family still have it. Alas, Tim didn't come home. He was killed shortly before the end of the war despite valiant efforts by Franklin Morrell to save his life. There was also talent for future concert parties. Ernest Swain was professional singer. Albert Sands (father of the well known actor in television 'Z' Cars series, Leslie Sands) was a semi-professional entertainer and comedian although his occupation is described as brush maker in the *Telegraph*.

One of the Parish Church curates, the Reverend John Thornton became the Battalion Chaplain. He did not lack for spiritual support. John William Worsnop, a solicitor's clerk later commissioned in the Second Pals Battalion, was considering taking holy orders. Frank Fairfax was a non-conformist minister and John Wallbank was a lay evangelist. No doubt Colonel Muller could also reflect upon the special talents of George Brown, described as a lunatic attendant, if training schemes went awry.

*　　　*　　　*

The twenty-five officers were a mixture of older men with Regular Army or Volunteer and Territorial experience (known rather unkindly as 'dug outs'), and younger men often with family or business connections with members of the Executive Committee of the League. Nearly all were Bradford men. Most of the older officers dropped out to help with the formation of a second Pals Battalion in the Spring of 1915 when the First Pals moved to Skipton. Only fourteen of the 1914 original officers were still with the Battalion when it arrived in France in March 1916. The oldest officer, Captain James Grimshaw Crossley of Saltaire, had served in the Egyptian and Sudan campaigns with the 12th Lancers in the 1880's. His spell training the Pals was a final flourish for he died in May, 1916 of liver cancer. Captain Arthur Howarth, Chairman of a woolcombing firm and brother of a future Lord Mayor, had seen action with the Royal Fusiliers and Royal Marines in East, West and South Africa and was 'several times wounded'. He arranged for his son Arthur Junior to become a 2nd Lieutenant in the Pals. The younger Howarth survived, but was captured in a trench raid by German troops in 1916 after transferring to the Second Pals. Three of the older officers did get to France. Captain Frank Holmes joined the Volunteers in the 1890's – the *Telegraph* stating he was 'stationed at Halifax Barracks as an officer during the South African War', but there is no record of a Boer attack on West Yorkshire. The Quartermaster, Lieutenant Frederick Reynolds, joined the regular Army in 1892 and was with the Mountain Artillery in India and Aden. Captain (later Major) Sydney Moore was 37, and an Inland Revenue official. He fought in the Boer War with the Civil Service Rifles and later served in the colonial Uganda Protectorate Service. Moore soon got a reputation as a stiff unbending officer. When the Pals moved to Skipton each hut was given an unofficial name (for example Buckingham Palace), but one hut rejoiced in the name of 'Sycamore'. For a short period after the Battalion arrived in France, Major Moore became the acting C.O.of the Battalion but returned home after losing a leg early in June, 1916.

Captain George S. Blagbrough, at 31, was the youngest of the senior officers. After Bradford Grammar School and University he became a schoolmaster at Bridlington Grammar School where he was in charge of the Officer Training Corps. Technically his commission remained with the East Yorkshire Regiment. He was killed by a shell splinter at Hebuterne just before Christmas, 1916. Lieutenant Albert W. Robinson was thirty-four and yet another former Bradford Grammar School old boy. He was Senior Science and Mathematics master at University School, Hastings, and in charge of the school O.T.C. He was an excellent athlete representing Yorkshire at Rugby Union and played cricket for Bradford. He later transferred to the Second Pals where he was promoted to Major and became second in command of the Battalion. A bout of pleurisy saved him from the Somme offensive and he survived the war to became a farmer in Suffolk.

Second Lieutenant John Holdsworth Robinson was the twenty-two year old son of his namesake Alderman father, the Chairman of the Citizens' Army League. Young John had been educated at Woodhouse Grove School, a school with strong Methodist connections. Second Lieutenant Donald Smith from Batley, was educated at Mill Hill – the Nonconformists' Eton. He was a staunch Methodist and teetotaller and achieved a certain notoriety amongst the Pals for his reluctance to distribute the rum ration in the trenches. Nevertheless he was well respected as a Yorkshire County Rugby player.

Drill in Manningham Park, officer is Lieutenant Sutcliffe.

Donald Smith's father, E.J. Smith, like John Robinson's father, was a prominent Liberal member of the City Council and Chairman of the Health Committee. Both officers were killed on 1 July 1916.

Two of the Lieutenants, Robert Sutcliffe and Owen Morgan, were solicitors in the city and both were old boys of Bradford Grammar School. Robert Sutcliffe, a bespectacled thirty-four year old, was runner up in the Yorkshire Amateur Golf Championship in 1907. He had responded to a newspaper advertisement to join the Public Schools Battalion (16th Middlesex) as a private in August, 1914, but within weeks he was back in Bradford with a commission in the Pals. He died of wounds 5 July, 1916. Owen Morgan was wounded soon after the Pals arrived in France, but later recovered and transferred to the Second Pals.

Robert Pringle was a tall twenty-one year old Scot educated at Fettes College in Edinburgh where he was in the O.T.C. He joined the Pals shortly after graduating from Merton College, Oxford and joining a textile firm in Bradford. He was destined to be another casualty on 1 July.

The two tall Hoffmann brothers, James (twenty) and Frank (eighteen), from Prospect House in Oak Lane, were descendants of a well established German merchant family in Bradford. They were educated at Giggleswick School and were thoroughly anglicized. James was badly shell shocked in 1916. He was an accountant, whilst Frank was 'learning the business' in a spinning mill. Lieutenant Frank Gray was yet another old Bradford Grammar School boy. He originally joined the Cameron Highlanders as a Private, but a commission was arranged for him in the Pals by his relative the Acting Adjutant Captain Gray.

The Hoffmann's weren't the only members of the Pals of German descent.

Norman Halstead Schneider, who joined as a private, was educated at Fulneck College and Bradford Grammar School and was working in Hamburg when the war broke out. His father was a principal in Schneider Gerharts & Co in Bradford. John Schultess later commissioned in the Duke of Wellington's Regiment was another of German descent, as were Privates Ernest Rasche and Oscar Hasse. Private Sam Wainwright had a middle name of Fritz although he did not advertise the fact.

The Reverend John Gordon Thornton, served as the Pals' Chaplain until May 1917, and was Mentioned in Despatches. John Thornton was twenty-nine and a native of Nottingham. He had graduated at Trinity College, Cambridge, and after a spell as a curate in Durham, was now a curate at Bradford Parish Church.[39]

Given the high standard of recruits, it is not surprising that a number of other ranks received commissions during the course of the next few months. From the medal rolls we know that 17% of the first hundred recruits were commissioned – but this has to be an underestimate. There are gaps in the rolls because others were commissioned before qualifying for a medal. For example, the Chief Constable of the West Riding's two sons, Tom and Harold Quest joined the Pals as other ranks, but were later commissioned into the Second Barnsley Pals. Harold Quest was awarded an M.C. before being killed in 1916.

The Bradford Citizens' Army League successfully raised its Battalion in a little over three weeks. They now had to pay, feed, clothe and house it for an indefinite period. The task of the Colonel and his officers was to turn a thousand civilians into fit, disciplined and effective soldiers.

*   *   *

It was one thing to get a thousand men to sign a register but quite another to find a place for them to train. The League's problem was solved when Messrs. H.W. Moorhouse & Co. offered the use of the Rollerina skating rink on Manningham Lane near the Bradford City football ground and Belle Vue Barracks. The rink became the Battalion's Headquarters until their departure to Raikes Camp, Skipton in January, 1915.[40] The rink was a huge domed building made out of corrugated iron bolted onto girders not unlike an aircraft hangar. It was unlikely to win any architectural prizes and was built in a hurry a few years before to cash-in on a roller-skating craze. Moorhouses were delighted to let it out. Crazes come and go and the building had been closed for some time. The author was to ballroom dance there and to learn a great deal about life there in his teenage years.

The rink was ideal for drill with a good hard surface and plenty of space. It had the advantage of being on the main road with a good tram service and was within easy distance of the city centre. It was convenient for Lister Park (usually known as Manningham Park) which was used for outdoor activities. An enormous poster bearing the legend, HEADQUARTERS OF THE BRADFORD BATTALION soon covered the gable end overlooking Manningham Lane. An administrative centre continued at the Mechanics Institute for a few weeks until office space and an Officers' Mess was created at the rink.

There was a thorough review of which other rank recruits were suitable to be an N.C.O. (although a number of men refused the rank because they were worried about rifts with their friends if they were in a position of authority). By the end of October, the Battalion had a regimental sergeant major, three company sergeant majors, four quarter master sergeants, twenty-seven sergeants, eight lance sergeants, thirty-five corporals and thirty-nine lance corporals. As with the officers, a number of the N.C.O.'s were veterans and as time went on they were replaced by younger men. In addition, a number of the younger men went off to be commissioned elsewhere and there was a constant change and state of flux in the early days.

Compared to their former work routine, many of the men must have thought they were living the life of Riley. If they lived more than two miles from the rink they were given a free tram pass and instructed to report at the rink at 9.00 a.m. each morning – long after many of them would have normally started work. There was a fifteen minute break for refreshments in the morning and afternoon but, best of all, they had a two hour lunch break when they could walk round the city in groups as if they owned the place. Cheery evenings could be spent in the pubs and clubs and at night they could sleep in their own beds. Afterwards many of them reflected that this was the best time of their lives.Compared with the Leeds Pals who were sent off to camp in the wilds of Colsterdale near Masham as early as September, the Bradford men knew they were having a 'cushy time'.[41] They were determined to enjoy it.

The men still wore their civilian clothes, and it was mid-November before they began to obtain uniforms. The League felt it was important for morale, and to stimulate recruitment, for the Pals to be recognised in the streets. Armbands were issued, but the men were particularly pleased with the enamel lapel badges they were given bearing the City coat of arms and Battalion name. The badges were made by the city jewellers, Fattorini's, and paid for by Sir William Priestley M.P. The Pals could now bask in admiring glances as they strolled round the city centre at lunchtime. The badge was no handicap as an icebreaker when it came to making conversation with the opposite sex.

The early weeks of training consisted of learning how to drill and march in the rink arena. In order to get fit there were also 'show the flag' route marches round the city led by Colonel Muller on his white horse. The marching gradually improved and the number of men with two left feet began to dwindle. An aid to the marching was the band. The bandsmen were the first to receive a uniform and instruments were provided from subscriptions to the League. The bandsmen were trained in first aid because they would double as the battalion's stretcher bearers. One of their first tasks was to learn to play the West Yorkshire Regimental march, 'Ah, Ca Ira', a catchy French tune adopted by the Regiment after the battle of Famars during the Napoleonic Wars. Whether the more conservative officers were aware of the revolutionary sentiments of the words which mention stringing up aristocrats from lamp-posts and abolishing priests one can only surmise.

On 3 October the men received their first pay. Then, with the newly formed but well rehearsed band, they marched off to Shipley for what was the first of a regular series of recruiting rallies around the district. By now the term 'Pals' was used by the local press, and which young man could fail to be pleased with their description in the *Yorkshire Observer* as, 'literally the pick of Bradford's manhood....this fine body of men should make a strong appeal to the young manhood of Shipley'.[42]

There were physical jerks in Lister Park when, as a concession to athleticism, they took off their caps, jackets and ties. There were cross-country runs into Heaton Woods with a race to a finish round the curving footpath of the boating lake. Shirts and shorts were borrowed from City and Park Avenue for soccer matches, and from Bradford R.F.C. for games of rugby union. There were posed photographs with Belgian refugees and with bewhiskered veterans of the Indian Mutiny and Crimean War.

Early drill was often a case of imagination over reality. A few obsolete long Lee Metford rifles were obtained from the Territorial Barracks at Belle Vue, but they had to be shared out. More often broom handles were used to practice drill movements. The O.T.C. experience of Captain Blagbrough and Lieutenant A.W. Robinson was particularly useful when learning how to present and slope arms. The only grumble was wear and tear to Sunday suits and best boots. However, the League was busy inviting tenders for clothing, equipment and uniforms. On 10 October it was announced that contracts had been placed: shirts and drawers would be supplied by the Bradford Manufacturing Company ; Davisons Stores provided socks; braces from Sports and Pastimes; jerseys, hairbrushes and hold-alls from Lingards, and

Physical jerks in Manningham Park. Caps and coats piled up to the front and back.

toothbrushes and kitbags by Brown Muff and Company. A Mr. Dobson of Charles Street even provided every recruit with a comb. Two pairs of boots were also provided.[43]

There was also a limit on how much could be achieved in a few hours daily training in Bradford with the men living at home. Plans had to be made to build a camp to house the Battalion. After a false start with a site in Harrogate, the League obtained a site above the town of Skipton on the Grassington road. Work began to prepare the site in mid-November.

> It would have been difficult to find a more suitable site in the Craven District. It is well elevated, and there is an excellent water supply. The camp will consist of wooden huts, each hut being a barrack room 60ft. by 20ft., and good accommodation for horses etc. Water and gas will be laid on, and the necessary drainage is to receive the most careful consideration. The work of construction will commence at once, and it is expected that 1,200 men will be in residence in about four or five weeks.[44]

On 6 November, the *Bradford Weekly Telegraph* published a complete roll call of the 25 officers and 1,064 other ranks of the new Battalion under the heading:

> "BRADFORD'S OWN" The City's Patriotism "Pals in Hard Training"
> When the history of our time comes to be written, the local historians will have abundant information as to how the citizens of Bradford rallied to serve their country.

The *Telegraph's* assiduity has been a useful research tool, and it would be churlish to suggest that at least 1,000 families rushed out to buy extra copies of the newspaper that weekend. All the local press carried lavish accounts and photographs of the doings of the Pals. Concerts and dances were put on for their benefit. A handsome brass case containing chocolates and cigarettes was presented to each man by Francis Laidler the owner of the Alhambra Theatre. Each case contained a slip with the optimistic slogan 'Good luck to the Bradford Boys. A Souvenir of the Great European War 1914-1915'.

But the fulsome media coverage began to cause a backlash, particular from relatives of men in the Regulars and the Territorials who were failing to get the same attention. There were muttered comments about 'chocolate soldiers' and 'when are you going to go'. As the novelty of the training wore off, the men began to feel restive and wished to get on with things before the war was over.

By November the war had virtually ceased to be a war of movement. After a series of attempts to outflank each other in a desperate race for the Channel ports, the two sets of armies had entrenched. As winter set in, in a line stretching for over four hundred miles from the Channel to the Swiss border, men huddled together in muddy ditches and faced each other across barbed wire and No Man's Land. Back in Bradford, the first uniforms began to arrive. The officers already had khaki uniforms, but the men were provided with two uniforms of the finest navy blue serge and a shiny peaked cap. Sir William Priestley M.P provided silver buttons, again with the city coat of arms. West Yorkshire Regiment cap badges with the horse of Hanover (another germanic touch) also filtered in. There is no doubt the new uniforms looked extremely smart: They were also of very good quality, as would be expected in the city

16/61 Drummer Tim Wharton in Manningham Park. He bought his own drum.

which regarded itself as the leading textile city in the world. The powerful textile barons on the Bradford Citizens Army League had pre-empted any quality problem by stating in the contract that no payment would be made until the Committee itself was satisfied with the items supplied.[45]

The serious work of arranging contracts for the clothing of the Bradford Service Battalion... has now been completed, and stipulations have been made for quick delivery. Tenders have been accepted as follows: Greatcoats, Messrs. Wright Burrows, Burrows & Co., Huddersfield; jackets and trousers, divided between Mr. David Murie (Bradford), Mr. R. Mettrick (Guiseley), Miller, Rayner & Haysom Limited (London), and Messrs. George Brown & Son (Bradford); puttees, Messrs. Fox & Todd (Bradford); regulation Army caps, Brown Muff & Co.,Limited (Bradford). The whole of the serge for the jackets and trousers is Bradford made, and the luster lining and the other linings are from Bradford houses. The puttees are made in Bradford. The buttons – a great source of difficulty – have been specially made to Government pattern by a Bradford firm.[46]

When the Pals came into contact with the Accrington Pals at Ripon the following summer, they were amused to hear stories of blue dye running from the Lancashire men's uniforms because a cost cutting cheap tender had been accepted.[47] Yorkshire's innate superiority over the red rose county was proved to the Pals' satisfaction.

On 3 December, the Bradford Citizens Army League Executive, under the Chairmanship of the Lord Mayor, held a meeting in the Mechanics Institute and formally agreed to form a Second Pals Battalion when the First Pals left for Skipton. They resolved:

That the Lord Mayor be requested to apply to the War Office on the behalf of the citizens of Bradford for leave to raise a second battalion of infantry on the terms and conditions that applied to the raising of the Bradford Battalion of the West Yorkshire Regiment.[48]

Sir William Priestley M.P. reported that the League had sufficient funds to do this and that £ 10,000 had been subscribed in a fortnight after the launch of the First Pals. After the usual round of patriotic speeches from other local worthies, including the wish to form a third Battalion if possible, the Second Bradford Pals, the future 18th West Yorks, were born.

There was indeed a third Battalion, the 20th West Yorks. The 20th were formed in August, 1915 but never saw foreign service as a unit and were based at Clipstone. They were formed out of surplus numbers from the depot companies of the 16th and 18th West Yorks and to provided a reserve when the First and Second Pals went abroad. The 20th did this, but also provided troops for other the West Yorkshire Regiment battalions.

Christmas came and went with a handsome Christmas card from the Lord Mayor and a splendid dinner paid for by the League. There were stories of fraternization with the enemy in the trenches, but northern France and Belgium still seemed a very long way from Bradford. It was the last Christmas many of the young men would spend in their home city. Many of them realized this might be the case, and in their hearts they were determined to enjoy it. No doubt there were family worries and tears behind the outward jollity of the Christmas celebrations.

On the last day of 1914, the trade section of the *Yorkshire Observer* carried the headlines, HUGE ORDERS FOR ARMY CLOTH. One wonders whether four years later the writer of the article felt any ambivalence if he ever checked his old files. The *Observer* went on to report 'There has been no more

Drum and bugle band of the 15th (Bradford) Battalion. Colonel Muller on the white horse.

Major A.W. Robinson holds the football.

wonderful and eventful year than that which is just drawing to a close in the whole history of the woollen industry'.[49]

And so, 1915 arrived to a chorus of mechanical tunes echoing over the city from the magnificent Town Hall clock. A few days later came the news the Pals had been waiting for. At last on 15 January, the time came for the Battalion to leave Bradford.

NOTES

1. *Yorkshire Observer*, 5 September, 1914.
2. *Ibid.*
3. The actual 10th West Yorks was formed in York with mostly Leeds and Harrogate recruits, although surplus members of the First Bradford Pals were transferred to the 10th in the Summer of 1915. Sadly, the 10th West Yorks suffered the highest single battalion casualty figures on the first day of the Battle of the Somme when they attacked Fricourt (710 officers and men, including some transferred from the First Bradford Pals).
4. *Bradford Weekly Telegraph*, 6 November, 1914.
5. *Bradford Daily Telegraph*, 3 September, 1914.
6. *Clayton Times and Express*, 4 September, 1914.
7. *Bradford Daily Telegraph*, 4 September, 1914
8. *Yorkshire Observer*, 12 September, 1914.
9. *Ibid.*
10. *Ibid.*
11. *Ibid.*
12. Analysis based on Medal Roll for British Medal and Victory Medal, the West Yorkshire Regiment, WO 329 899/900, Public Record Office, Kew.
13. *Clayton Times & Express*, 11 September, 1914
14. *Yorkshire Observer*, 12 September, 1914.
15. Fred Rawnsley, transcript interview kindly supplied by Steve Kerry
16. *Clayton Times & Express*, 11 September, 1914
17. Statistics taken from *Bradford Daily Telegraph* review of trade, 2 January, 1917.
18. *Yorkshire Observer*, 12 September, 1914
19. *Bradford Weekly Telegraph*, 6 November, 1914, carries biographical details.
20. *Bradford Daily Telegraph*, 17 September, 1914.
21. *Ibid.*

22. Lord Haldane was the Lord Chancellor and a close colleague of the Liberal Prime Minister Asquith. He was an extremely competent Secretary of State for War between 1905 and 1912. He is now given credit for creating the Territorial Army and for excellent contingency planning in the event of war. He spoke fluent German and was a leading authority on the philosopher Goethe. Many years before the war he had said that Germany was his spiritual home. This phrase was picked up and used to drive him from office (by, amongst others, Lord Charles Beresford) in a vicious press campaign when the Conservatives joined the coalition Government.

23. Prince Louis of Battenberg (1854-1921), a cousin of King George V and father of Lord Mountbatten, was born in Germany but naturalised as a British subject in 1868. Beresford made his remarks in August, 1914. Lord Louis resigned as First Sea Lord in October, 1914 after a scurrilous press campaign impugning his loyalty. There was an added poignancy because on the previous day his nephew Prince Maurice was killed in the defence of Ypres.

24. *Winston S. Churchill, 1914-16, The Challenge of War*, (p.148), Martin Gilbert, Heinemann, 1971.

25. *Bradford Daily Telegraph*, 17th September, 1914

26. *Ibid.*

27. George Morgan, tape recording kindly loaned to author by Malcolm Brown.

28. *Ibid.*

29. Stanley Wright, tape recording kindly loaned to the author by Stephen Kerry, Bradford Oral History Archive.

30. Tony Miller, tape recording kindly loaned to the author by Stephen Kerry, Bradford Oral History Archive.

31. *Bradford Weekly Telegraph*, 6 November, 1914.

32. *Yorkshire Observer*, 12 September, 1914.

33. Information culled from *The Bradfordian*, school magazine of Bradford Grammar School. No less than seventeen of the officers in the two Pals Battalions attended Bradford Grammar School.

34. *Yorkshire Observer*, 12 September, 1914.

35. *The Yorkshire Observer*, 23 October, 1914.

36. George Grunwell, conversation with author, 10 May, 1989

37. I am grateful to Professor Peter Excell of Bradford University for supplying information and photographs of Sir Edward Appleton. Professor Excell has an archive of Appleton's work and an excellent web site where details of Appleton's career can be perused.

38. Information kindly supplied by the Wharton family.

39. Information kindly supplied by Mr. J.H. Thornton, the Rev. J.G. Thornton's son.

40. The author remembers seeing the smoking remains of the by then derelict building on his way to school after it burned down in the 1950's.

41. See, *The Leeds Pals*, Laurie Milner, in this series.

42. *Yorkshire Observer*, 10 October, 1914

43. *Bradford Daily Telegraph*, 10 October, 1914.

44. *Bradford Weekly Telegraph*, 6 November, 1914.

45. Tender advertisement in the *Bradford Daily Telegraph*, 8th October, 1914.

46. *Yorkshire Observer*, 23rd October, 1914

47. See, *Accrington Pals*, William Turner, in this series for details of the Lancashire men's predicament.

48. *Bradford Weekly Telegraph*, 4 December, 1914.

49. *Yorkshire Observer*, 31 December, 1914.

The Lord Mayor & Lady Mayoress (Ald Geo.H. Robinson, J.P. and Mrs Robinson) and the Citizens of Bradford send Christmas Greetings To Albert House May the thought of your Father's Service to his King and Country, and this little token of loving regard for you, make you as happy as you can be.

Signed "Bradford Daily Telegraph"

Xmas 1914. SANTA CLAUS.

BRADFORD BATTALION (P.W.O.) WEST YORKSHIRE REGIMENT.

First Complete Roll Call.—A Credit to the City.

"BRADFORD'S OWN."

The City's Patriotism.

"PALS" IN HARD TRAINING.

Winter Quarters Selected.

THE BATTALION'S OFFICERS

COL. G. H. MULLER, V.D.

MAJOR W. MITCHELL.

CAPTAIN F. N. A. GRAY.

CAPTAIN JAMES G. CROSSLEY.

CAPT. FRANK HOLMES.

CAPTAIN G. S. BLAGBROUGH.

CAPTAIN S. MOORE.

CAPTAIN A. HOWARTH.

LIEUTENANT D. L. CRANTREE.

LIEUT. T. LINTON RHODES.

LIEUT. A. W. ROBINSON.

LIEUT. AND QUARTERMASTER GEO. FREDK. REYNOLDS.

LIEUTENANT O. MORGAN.

2nd LIEUT. ROBERT SUTCLIFFE.

SECOND LIEUT. R. W. N. PRINGLE.

SECOND LIEUTENANT A. HOWARTH.

SECOND LIEUT. J. M. N. HOFFMANN.

SECOND LIEUT. S. L. F. HOFFMANN.

SECOND LIEUT. F. R. B. JOWITT.

SECOND LIEUT. C. M. CROMBEAW.

SECOND LIEUT. F. B. WEBSTER.

SECOND-LIEUT. R. RYAN.

SECOND LIEUT. J. H. ROBINSON.

SECOND LIEUT. N. CRANTREE.

SECOND LIEUT. D. SMITH.

NON-COMMISSIONED OFFICERS.

RANK AND FILE.

COLONEL G. H. MULLER, V.D.

MAJOR W. MITCHELL.

OFFICERS OF THE BRADFORD BATTALION.

A group of the senior officers of the Bradford Battalion, West Yorkshire Regiment. Standing in front are: Captain J. G. Crossley, Major W. Mitchell, Colonel G. H. Muller, Captain Gray (adjutant), and Captain F. Holmes. In the rear: Captain Moore, Captain A. Howarth, and Captain G. S. Blagborough.

The junior officers. Front row (left to right): Second-Lieutenant A. Howarth, Second-Lieutenant H. Russell, Lieutenant A. W. Robinson, Lieutenant D. L. Crabtree, Second-Lieutenant A. Clough. Second-Lieutenant F. R. B. Jowitt, Second-Lieutenant F. R. Webster, and Second-Lieutenant F. Hoffmann. Behind: Lieutenant R. W. H. Pringle, Second-Lieutenant J. Hoffmann, Second-Lieutenant B. Ryan, Second-Lieutenant H. R. Watling, Lieutenant G. F. Reynold, Lieutenant N. Crabtree, Second-Lieutenant J. H. Robinson, Second-Lieutenant C. H. Grimshaw, Second-Lieutenant Morant, Second-Lieutenant D. C. Smith, Second-Lieutenant B. Sutcliffe, and Lieutenant Owen Morgan.

Chapter Four

SKIPTON AND A
SECOND BATTALION

*I went back to work and I told the boss, I'm in the Army, and he said,
'Thank God we've got a Navy.*

ERNEST WILSON, Second Bradford Pals

THE HEADY EXCITEMENT of the late summer days in September
seemed far away when New Year dawned in 1915. Notions of facing up
to the Germans in a matter of weeks were long gone as was the notion
of the war being over by Christmas. The war of movement had come to an
end in November with the two sides dug into a series of trenches 400 miles
long stretching from the North Sea at Nieuport in Belgium down to the Swiss
frontier. As Kitchener had foreseen when issuing his call for recruits to the
'New Army', it was going to be a long war.

The feeling of frustration in the ranks of the Pals was not helped by
comments expressed in some parts of the city that 'the fancy blue uniforms'
had had more than their fair share of publicity whilst enjoying all the
comforts of home. The Bradford Territorials of the 6th West Yorks had spent
Christmas digging trenches on the Yorkshire coast where it was wet, windy
and uncomfortable – and too far for any Bradford newspaper photographer
to bother visiting even if the censor permitted.

On 16 December, a German naval bombardment of the east coast at
Scarborough and Hartlepool did nothing to lessen mutterings about
'chocolate soldiers in blue uniforms' having a 'cushy number', but it gave
added impetus to recruitment in Bradford with a huge banner, 'Remember

*March 1915, Drill at Skipton. Two men at the back are in khaki, but the rest are still in dark
blue.*

Hartlepool', surmounting the Recruiting Office. A fifth company of the Pals, E Company, was quickly recruited taking the numbers up to over 1,300. Troops from the 18th Durham Light Infantry (Durham Pals) suffered casualties in the raid and became the first troops of Kitchener's New Armies to come under enemy fire. The Durhams were to join the Bradford and Leeds Pals in 93 Brigade at Ripon in the Summer of 1915.

There had been numerous delays at Skipton in the arrival of construction materials and equipment for the Pals' camp. The *Telegraph* tried to put a positive gloss on everything and blamed the bad winter weather for the delays. There may have been some truth in it, but it is hardly surprising that there should be muddle and mistakes in a country newly at war. It came as a relief when the Pals received orders on 1 January to begin preparations to move to their newly completed camp on the northern edge of Skipton. A, B, C and D Companies, fully equipped and wearing their blue uniforms, were to march to Skipton on 15 January, 1915. E company were to remain in Bradford as a depot company under Captain Howarth until 5 February when they would have received their uniforms and equipment and their huts at Skipton would be completed. At short notice, the Citizens Army League Committee made rapid plans to give the Pals a spectacular Farewell Entertainment and Civic Send Off. The Entertainment was a huge affair held on two nights, 5 and 6 January, in the Central Baths next to the Alhambra Theatre in Morley Street. Sixty years later, outside the baths in Morley Street was still the departure point for the surviving Pals when they joined their coach for pilgrimages to France. The city War Memorial would also be built on the corner of Morley Street opposite the theatre.

> *In addition to the members of the Executive and the Battalion and their ladies, invitations have been sent to a number of civilians who have rendered voluntary service in the important work of raising this fine body of men. Altogether over 3,000 people are expected to be present at the Central Baths tomorrow and Wednesday evenings, about half of this number each evening.*[2]

The evenings lived up to expectations. There was dancing, food and drink. Francis Laidler, owner of the Alhambra Theatre and Princes Theatre, arranged for Music Hall artistes to provide entertainment. Mona Vivian and Bessie Butt, topping the bill in the Aladdin pantomime at the Princes Theatre, 'Contributed items of a patriotic flavour and the audience was often heard giving full voice to well known choruses'.[3]

'Wee Mona' Vivian was only nineteen and described in the press as 'an alluring coquette'. Her Principal Boy legs and fine singing voice led on to a very successful theatrical and recording career, and she appeared at the Royal Command Performance in 1921. She also did well for herself by marrying J. Hilton Crowther, a millionaire mill owner from Milnsbridge. Crowther aroused hostile passions in his native Huddersfield in 1919 by trying to move Huddersfield Town football club 'lock, stock and barrel' to merge with the newly formed Leeds United. 'Yes, we'll win the fight', sang the choir of the Bradford Battalion. It was a night for enjoyment and the spirit of it was upon them all.[4]

The next few days consisted of a mixture of hectic family farewells and the continuing round of P.E. drill and marches round the city in all weathers to build up fitness. Fitness was going to be needed, because it was decided that the move to Skipton would be done by marching rather than rail. The need to put on a display and stimulate recruiting may have lain behind this decision.

At 11.00 am on the morning of Thursday, 14 January, A, B, C, and D Companies in their uniforms, and E Company in their best civilian clothes, lined up in a heaving Town Hall Square for a Civic Farewell Parade in front of the Lord Mayor and City Worthies. In addition to the Pals, units of the Territorial Reserve, the Bradford Artillery, and the Army Service Corps based in Bradford also took part , and according to the *Telegraph*, over 4,000 troops were on parade with Colonel Muller on his white horse in overall command. In his farewell speech, the Lord Mayor expressed the hope that,

> *You will remember the words of Lord Kitchener, "Cherish honour in your hearts; strive to be honourable; strive to be sober, and strive to do your duty".*
> *England expects of you and we know that you will loyally do your duty.*[5]

The Artillery band played as the Pals marched out of the Square watched by thousands of relatives, sweethearts, friends and well wishers. The ceremonial over, they went home for last goodbyes, and prepared for morning. Before dawn on Friday, 15 January, the 16th West Yorks assembled in the skating rink for the last time. Shortly before nine o'clock, a huge roar of welcome came from a crowded Manningham Lane as they marched out in fours in companies led by their officers with Colonel Muller at their head. The Pals own band was limited to bugles and drums, and in view of the distance of the march it was decided that they should be led as far as Bingley by the Band of

Second Pals recruiting in Town Hall Square.

the Bradford Artillery. A few men at the front carried the old fashioned Lee Metford rifles, but most had yet to receive them. Their kits, accompanied by the Officers' orderlies, were sent on to Skipton by train. A lunch of two substantial ham sandwiches and a piece of cake were stowed in the men's pockets. The *Telegraph* reported that the Battalion strength was now 1,316 (three hundred more than would be eventually required). The band struck up the West Yorkshire's Regiment's March, 'Ca Ira'. The music, a French Revolutionary song, has a certain poignancy. The words roughly translate as, 'We'll make it, we're going to win, it's going to be fine.' It was a lively optimistic tune and the men struck up a good pace as they passed a Guard of Honour who presented arms outside Belle Vue Barracks. Sadly for many of the Pals marching away from home up Manningham Lane the optimism of the music failed to match the reality of their experience. The Pals marched north to a mixture of tears and cheers as thousands of well wishers lined the streets. Within the hour the men had passed through Saltaire and reached Bingley where the streets were just as crowded, and they gave a special salute to the Belgian refugees given a temporary home in the Old Post Office.

Unfortunately the weather became much worse, rain falling heavily, but the spirits of the men were in no way damped. They joined lustily in various choruses, Widow Twankey's 'S'nice, S'mince, s'pie' evidently being a favourite, while 'Oh, Oh ! Who's your lady friend' and the inevitable 'Tipperary' were included in their vocal programme.[6]

The Pals' drum and bugle band took over from the Artillery Band in Bingley, and despite a huge downpour, large crowds cheered the Pals through Keighley. At Eastburn House there was a welcome stop for lunch and hot tea was provided. The full band of the 6th West Yorks Reserve Territorials played the thoroughly soaked Pals into Skipton at 3.30 pm.

The main streets were thronged with people, all anxious to give their visitors a splendid reception and thus make up as far as possible for the discomforts which they had suffered during the march.[7]

After covering over twenty miles in a little under seven hours, much of it in cold driving January rain, the Pals marched wearily up the hill to what was to be their home for the next four months. It marked their transition from part-time soldiering at home to the more demanding rigours of a full time military life. One of the Pals, Joe Linford (a former Bradford City footballer who had become a reporter on the *Bradford Telegraph* and sent regular reports of camp life to his old paper) described his feelings on arrival in Skipton.

It rains and it rains, and it rains like, well – I mustn't give away a military password. Trudging through wind and rain is symbolic of the kind of thing this time of war demands of men. A joyous nonchalance seized us when we entered Skipton. We were wet. We were further from home. But we were to get to business and we were well satisfied. 16/665 PRIVATE JOE LINFORD, M.M.[8]

Raikes Camp had been paid for by the Citizens' Army League. As befitted an organization of hardnosed Bradford businessmen, the League had driven a hard bargain to obtain the site and the tactics used aroused suspicion. Secret negotiations to obtain the site by two un-named 'gentlemen from Bradford'

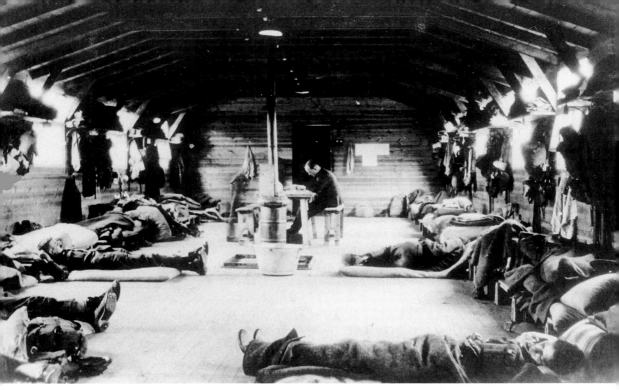

Inside a hut at Skipton. Catching up on sleep after a night march.

were undertaken with the local Council Clerk and Council Surveyor without the knowledge of Skipton Urban District Council. There were hints of unorthodox dealings and threats to obtain the site by compulsory purchase when the deal was questioned later at a meeting of Skipton Council. After a fulsome apology by the Council Clerk for not referring the matter to the Council, coupled with the usual appeal to patriotism, the matter was glossed over.[9]

The new camp was on an exposed site on top of a hill overlooking the town to the north of Skipton, next to what is now Salisbury Street. The camp consisted of thirty-six huts for the men with additional huts for the officers, baths, a canteen and a cookhouse as well as stables for nine officers' horses. There was also an institute which could hold up to 500 for concerts and recreation. The men quickly personalized the huts with names such as 'North Pole', 'Buckingham Palace', and more dubiously 'Sycamore' from men in Captain Moore's Company.[10] As full time soldiers, the men now had to adjust to a new routine with Reveille at 6.00 am and lights out at 10.00 pm. They also began the hard work of preparing roads around the camp and dealing with the mud and slush of a Yorkshire Dales winter. Corporal Herbert Taylor's diary (see Appendix A at the end of this chapter) gives a fascinating and detailed record of their daily routine.

The new routine involved drill, digging trenches, route marches, fieldwork and maintaining and improving the infrastructure of the camp. Specialist groups such as signallers and cooks learned their trade, sometimes being sent off to Aldershot to receive specialist tuition. Sundays saw a march into Skipton for Church Parade, and there was the occasional leave pass to return to Bradford by train. Equally, at weekends family visitors came to Skipton for an afternoon visit to their men. There were occasional lectures from visiting soldiers with war experience. At first small parties of the men went to York for shooting practice, but more rifles eventually arrived, although of the obsolete Lee Metford variety, and the men began to practice on their own shooting range. The route marches were demanding and took place at night as well as in the day. The overall intention was to toughen and harden the men. The officers, too, were learning their trade, and their learning curve was not without its humour. George Grunwell recalled how the bespectacled Lieutenant Robert Sutcliffe found soldiering rather different from being a solicitor,

> *He once got confused and said 'right' when he meant 'left'. Our platoon would have ended up in the canal if we had obeyed him. He was a nice chap, but he wasn't much of a soldier. None of the officers were at that time if I've got to be honest.*
> 16/1042 PRIVATE GEORGE GRUNWELL[11]

The route marches in filthy weather earlier in January exacted a price. 16/886, Private Gerald Gray, a shop assistant from Otley Road, developed pneumonia and died at home on 18 January, the Pals' first loss. He was buried in Undercliffe Cemetery with full military honours including a gun carriage and a Union Jack draped coffin on 22 January. The procession was led by the Artillery Band, the whole of E Company, and a firing party travelled from Skipton.

The death of Private Gray stimulated a series of rumours and concerns about the health of the Battalion. The march to Skipton through the downpour may have been good theatre for recruiting, but it did nothing for the men's health. The concerns pale into insignificance compared with the future realities of the trenches, but the rumours were not helped by an admission that the men's uniforms were still soaking wet two days after their arrival and that sanitation was of a very primitive kind with trenches having to be dug around the huts. The glamour of the early recruiting days was by now long gone.

> *Everything is surrounded in fog today... The ground which surrounds some of the huts is still in a terrible condition and only the ample use of planks saves one from a mud bath, or at any rate, sinking in the slimy earth up to the knees.*[12]

On 29 January, referring to concerns about health, under the heading 'SCARE' RUMOURS OFFICIALLY DENIED, the *Telegraph* reported,

> *Our representative was again assured that the rumours were incorrect, and that there had not been a single death in camp since the men came to Skipton. It is true that a large number of cases are at present under treatment, mainly for colds and influenza, and that two men had to be removed to hospital, but in all cases we are assured, the men are doing very well.*[13]

The accuracy of the official denial was somewhat undermined by a report further down the same page referring to ten cases in hospital. Certainly, the local Doctor in Skipton, Dr Fisher, was trying to deal with over 1,000 more patients than he had just a fortnight before.

With the arrival of E Company after the completion of their huts on 5

February, there were now over 1,300 men on site. There was no grand Civic send-off for E Company, but on 3 February they were entertained with their wives and sweethearts at the Central Baths. Speeches were made by the Mayor and Colonel Muller, and the professional entertainment was led by the top ranking music hall artiste, Florrie Forde, famous for her hit songs, 'Goodbye-ee', 'Pack Up Your Troubles', and 'It's A Long Way To Tipperary'. The nature of the Pals was demonstrated by the fact that no less than twelve members of the Victoria Rangers Rugby League team had joined E Company together, and Florrie Forde presented them with a rugby ball. Two days later, E Company, led by Captain Howarth, covered the same route march to Skipton as the first four companies. Herbert Taylor recorded in his diary, 'Arrived Skipton 3.30. Well. Place dirty but were welcome.'[14]

The medical situation was retrieved on 1 February when the Pals were joined by their own Medical Officer, Lieutenant Charles Roche. 'Paddy' Roche was the twenty-five year old son of a Land Agent in Queenstown, County Cork, and had only recently qualified at Dublin in 1914. He stayed with the Bradford Pals until 1918, giving devoted and courageous service to the men in his care. He was twice decorated for gallantry, Military Cross and Bar, for rescuing the wounded in No Man's Land. He married a Bradford girl, Ivy Millner, but sadly had a short life. In the trenches in the winter of 1917 he contracted what was thought to be pneumonia. He soldiered on to the end of the war, but in fact he had contracted tuberculosis. He died at Peterculter Sanatorium near Aberdeen in March 1921 at the age of only 31.[15]

At Skipton, one of the new M.O.'s first tasks was to carry out a series of

One of the many hut photographs taken at Skipton. The high morale and good spirit is evident in the pose.

innoculations against typhoid and small pox. The colonel and the officers led the way. There was a subdued air, some fevered nights and sore arms for a period – although the special leave home by train for the weekend was a welcome treat.

*   *   *

The departure of E Company from Bradford on 5 February, co-incided with a meeting of the Citizens Army League who made arrangements for recruitment for the Second Pals. The Army Council had signified agreement to raising the second battalion on 29 January, and registration began in the Labour Exchange on the following Monday. The second battalion,

> Will be known as the 17th Service Battalion of the West Yorkshire Regiment (2nd Bradford)... The new battalion is to be attached to the same Brigade as the first one...namely the 114th Brigade, 38th Division of Fourth Army... The raising of the new Bradford Battalion will not involve further camp building. The men are to be billeted in some way.[16]

In fact the Second Pals became the 18th West Yorks. The actual 17th West Yorks was a bantam battalion from Leeds. By April, 1915 the Fourth Army had been broken up and 38th Division was re-numbered as 31st Division with the intertwined red and white roses of Lancashire and Yorkshire as its badge. The Pals were attached to 93rd Brigade in June, 1915 where they remained for the rest of their existence.

The League announced that the medical demands in the Second Pals were to be relaxed, with a reduced minimum chest size of thirty-three inches being permitted and recruitment began in early February. Arrangements to recruit the new battalion in Cleckheaton, Keighley and Skipton and gave priority to providing a band to help with recruitment. The first recruits were soon signed up but sent home to await orders until arrangements could be made to officer and equip the battalion. It was also agreed that the Second Pals would wear khaki uniforms rather than blue.

The Citizens League agreed that Colonel Muller should move back to Bradford from Skipton to take command of the Second Battalion and that Lieutenant Albert W. Robinson would go with him as second in command and be promoted to Major. Company Sergeant Major Hammond, a museum curator, was commissioned to Lieutenant to be the Quartermaster – probably an appropriate appointment when the first few ancient rifles were acquired.

Several of the older officers in the First Pals including Major Crossley and Major Haworth moved with Colonel Muller and Major Robinson to train the new battalion. Their places were taken by what became known as the Norfolk connection. Captain Thomas Herbert Russell (Tom) and his cousin Captain Henry Russell (Harry) were Conservative Party Organisers in Bradford although they were originally from Thetford in Norfolk. Both had experience in the Norfolk Territorials and Tom was a member of the England Rifle Team at Bisley. They were friends of Colonel Muller and their commission reference came from Sir Arthur Godwin J.P. (Bradford's first Lord Mayor in 1907, and Senior Grand Deacon in the Freemasons).[17]

Tom Russell's organising skills soon led to his appointment as Adjutant of the First Pals, and he clearly had clout with Colonel Muller and the Citizens' Army League. Tom's networking and influence led to his third brother and his cousin joining the First Pals as officers. Brother Frank, a Company Sergeant Major in the R.A.S.C. (but with a farm in Suffolk) became the Transport Officer. Brother William was appointed as a 2nd Lieutenant from the ranks of the 19th Royal Fusiliers (Public Schools) Battalion. Three other members of the Norfolk Territorials connection were recruited as officers, Ralph Stead, Frank Symonds and Cecil Ransome.[18] Colonel C. W. Warden took over command of the First Pals from Colonel Muller on 22 February. He belonged to the breed of retired Army Officers often unkindly described as 'dug outs' who answered the War Office's call to train Kitchener's New Armies. Fifty-nine year old Lt. Colonel Charles Wallace Warden J.P., D.L., came from a long military line. He had a splendid walrus moustache and was Protestant High Sheriff and Deputy Lieutenant of Catholic County Kerry in Ireland. He had joined the 57th Regiment (later, the Middlesex Regiment) forty years before in 1874 and seen action in the Zulu War of 1879. He eventually rose to be Colonel of the Middlesex before retiring on pension in 1895. He was wealthy enough to buy the splendid estate of Derryquin Castle in County Kerry. He then served in the Boer War with the Imperial Yeomanry.

Colonel Warden's purchase of Derryquin reveals the interconnections of the pre-war officer class. The castle was sold because of the bankruptcy of the brother-in-law of Warden's future Divisional Commander, General Robert Wanless-O'Gowan. Whether the transaction was an embarrassment that had anything to do with O'Gowan's refusal to let Warden accompany the Battalion abroad in 1915, it is impossible to say. Instead, he commanded various training battalions of the West Yorks at home until the end of the war.

Colonel Warden was clearly a survivor. When Derryquin was burned down by the I.R.A. during 'the troubles' in 1922, the Colonel wisely moved to Devon where he lived on to the grand old age of 99.[19]

*   *   *

At Skipton, a boxing tournament against the West Riding Regiment on 4 February offered light relief from the back breaking work of trench digging, road building and route marches. Boxing was much more active and widespread in the early part of the twentieth century than it is now with over a thousand venues staging professional contests. The Pals had two very successful professional boxers in their ranks, as well as a number of skilled amateurs, and no doubt a few bets were placed on the results. Top of the bill in a ten round fight against another professional, Private Dan Demaine, was twenty-two year old Private Will Blakeborough (16/369). Blakeborough was a small man but he was an extremely skilful star performer. He had had thirty-two professional fights, was North of England Featherweight Champion at 8st 6lb, and currently ranked third in Great Britain. Private Jack 'Stoker' Manley (16/913) was also a professional and the tough durable

Lightweight Champion of Yorkshire.[20] There seems to have been universal affection for Will Blakeborough. Former footballer turned reporter Joe Linford described him.

I shall not forget the night when the gloves were brought into our hut and Bill kindly undertook to box in turn any of us... I had four rounds with him and had no fear. Bill was a perfect gentleman. He 'biffed' me occasionally to spur me, but he was exceedingly gentle. When he had left half a dozen of us panting and realising our inefficiency, he thanked us and smiling remarked that it had helped to keep him in training. There is no mock modesty about Bill. He knows he is a clever boxer and will frankly tell you his success depends upon his cleverness rather than upon brute force... There are many things I like about Bill Blakeborough. I have never seen him do a rotten or unkind or mean thing. I like Bill's shy way of revealing his love for his home. I have never seen him lose his temper. I will sum him up with the remark he is a man and a gentleman, a cheery wit and a good comrade, a credit to society and to our battalion.   16/665 PRIVATE JOE LINFORD, M.M.[21]

Bill Blakeborough won his fight, and Joe described it,

Bill knew he had a good man to face in Demaine, but he kept calm and won full confidence by the third round. He knows how to use his feet; it was a real treat to watch his nimble feints and tricky footwork. And when he hit home I was glad I wasn't his opponent. Long before the tenth round it was evident Bill's experience and superior art would mean victory. When the referee announced 'Blakeborough the winner on points' his behaviour was characteristic. He did a sort of war dance, flinging up his arms and inspiring us to cheers, following up this by – O grievous irregularity ! – and frantic shaking of hands with our officers. Well, Bill was victorious and I was happy.

16/665 PRIVATE JOE LINFORD, M.M.[22]

Sadly, it was Bill Blakeborough's last proper fight. He took part in a short exhibition bout in Bradford to aid recruitment on 20 March, but died of pneumonia at Skipton camp on 13 May shortly before the move to Ripon. Huge crowds lined the streets to see his funeral which had full military honours from the Pals at Bethel Chapel, Shelf.

Will Blakeborough's military funeral.

Will Blakeborough.

*   *   *

At Skipton, a number of the First Pals obtained commissions in other battalions or who transferred to more technical units for specialist work. Edward Appleton, the future Nobel prizewinner had already gone. A number joined the engineers or the Royal Flying Corps. Nineteen year old Horace Cannon, a motor engineer, joined the Royal Flying Corps, as did a number of other Pals with engineering qualifications. Flight Sergeant Cannon was later awarded the George Cross rescuing the pilot from a blazing aircraft.[23] James Midgley (16/259), a research chemist, was transferred to the Royal Engineers. In October 1915 he was awarded the Distinguished Conduct Medal for bringing in the wounded under heavy fire. He died of his wounds a month later and the Pals sent an escort party back to Bradford for his funeral.[24]

The Pals officers at Skipton began French and German lessons with Harold Colley, a twenty-two year old foreign language master at Skipton Grammar School. Colley, a Bradfordian educated at Hanson School, had experienced an interesting eighteen months after graduating from Liverpool University in 1913. He was appointed English Lektor at the University of Posen in Prussia but war broke out during his first summer vacation at home in Bradford. He was dismissed by the German government but his possessions were returned in a civilised way via Berlin. He obtained the teaching post at Skipton and was soon encouraged to apply for a commission with the Second Pals. He went on to become the Intelligence Officer with the Second Pals, but was yet another of the missing on the first day of the Somme.[25]

No less than nine other ranks from the First Pals were granted commissions as officers in the Second Pals. Rhodes Akam was in the timber

First Pals at Skipton.

trade, Allan Booth an architect, Morris Clough a clothier's manager, David Hellewell a yarn merchant, Francis Nowell in the wool trade, Lionel Watson an assistant engineer, Frank Watson an engineer's draughtsman, John L. Wood and John W. Worsnop a solicitor's clerk. They were mostly old boys of Bradford Grammar School, boys which no doubt appealed to their C.O., Colonel Muller and his Second in Command, Major Albert W. Robinson, themselves both old Bradfordians. All the new officers were in white collar middle class jobs without any particular military background other than the school O.T.C. – John Worsnop was even thinking of taking Holy Orders.

A number were also recruited from the other ranks of the Leeds Pals. Sydney Newlands was just nineteen and joined the Leeds Pals straight from Silcoates School. His father was the Congregational Minister at Providence Place Chapel in Cleckheaton (now the largest and most spectacular Indian Restaurant in the country). Charles Hyde was the son of the vicar of Cleckheaton, a bank clerk, and yet another Bradford Grammar School boy. The brothers Charles and Reginald Laxton were from Dewsbury where their father was in the heavy woollen trade and President of the Conservative Association. Harry Dalley was in the wool trade in Leeds.[26]

First Pals at Skipton.

Colonel Muller also arranged a commission for another local worthy. Councillor John Bland, a prominent Conservative member of the City Council and prospective Parliamentary Candidate for Spen Valley, was a large man of forty-five. He had played an active part in Citizen's Army League and was a prominent freemason. He was a partner in Moore and Bland, a prosperous Colonial top-making wool firm. Although he got to Egypt and France with the Second Pals, he was diagnosed with diabetes in May, 1916 and had to return to Bradford. He became the Mayor in 1917, but died during his year of office at the early age of forty-seven. [27]

The Second Pals recruited steadily in Bradford, Keighley and Cleckheaton.

Harold Scott in Coldstream Guard days.

The first 500 khaki uniforms arrived at the end of February even though the men were still living at home. Colonel Muller and Major Robinson became familiar figures riding at the head of their men. An illuminated tramcar was used in Bradford to stimulate recruitment. The Citizen's League also arranged for a cinema film to be made by the Gaumont Company of the Pals at Skipton which could be shown to aid recruiting. Sadly the film disappeared somewhere in the Yorkshire Television archive in the 1970s.

No less than twenty policemen from the City Force joined the Second Pals together. They were led by their formidable Drill Sergeant, Harold Scott, late of the Coldstream Guards. Harold Scott soon became Regimental Sergeant Major of the 18th West Yorks, and arranged for his brother Alf to transfer from the First Pals to be Quartermaster Sergeant. Together they ran the battalion with impressive authority and precision. R.S.M. Harold Scott made a deep impression on one eighteen year old recruit.

Ooh, he were a smart feller. Oooh, he were as straight as a die. He frightened me to death. Oh, he had a word of command. Oh, you could hear him from hear to Wigan. He didn't half put us through it. He did that.

18/1150 PRIVATE ALBERT JOWETT[28]

Ernest Wilson was keen to join, but he had already been turned down by the First Pals for being too young when his mother turned up at the Recruiting Office to fetch him out and reclaim him. He tried again with the Second Pals.

I was still an apprentice woolsorter so they sent me with some samples down to Bradford to different firms. As I'm coming back I call in the recruiting office. I was only a lad, like. Anyway I go on the scale and I weigh 108 lbs and the doctor says, Oh, this fellow will swell out, so they passed me and I got a shilling. I went across to the Theatre De Luxe and had a right good time. I went back to work and told the boss, I'm in the Army, and he said, Thank God we've got a Navy.

PRIVATE ERNEST WILSON, 18WY[29]

For seventeen year old Ernest Brook it was more a matter of brass. His attitude makes an interesting comparison with the enthusiastic patriotism of the newspapers.

I was t'only lad working in a saw mill and I were doing all t'work. I went to t'boss, I says, 'Can't you give me some more money?' He says, 'You'll get your rise when your birthday comes'. I never said a word to anybody. I went straight down and enlisted, joined t'Army, they'd a pound a week there. They'd formed Pals Battalion then, this was Second Battalion. It were a gimmick were Pals. How can I explain? They wouldn't get 'em to join now like they did in them days. Britons never shall be slaves? We were all slaves in't olden days, workin' in't mills.

18/761 PRIVATE ERNEST BROOK [30]

The *Telegraph* took countless photographs of posed hut groups at Skipton, and of marching men in Bradford. No doubt relatives rushed out to buy copies of the paper. The paper even organised a competition for a suitable 'Song for the Pals'. There was a round of kit inspections, football matches, rugby matches, hockey matches, cross country races, recruiting marches and concerts. The Divisional General, General Molesworth, inspected Skipton Camp and expressed his satisfaction as did Brigadier Charlesworth. The last week of March also saw a transition from blue to Khaki at Skipton.

At Keighley, after a half-time drill by the Second Pals, the Mayor, W. A. Brigg, and members of the mill owning Clough family posed awkwardly for a recruiting photograph with the Keighley team at Lawkholme Lane after the Rugby League Cup Tie with St. Helens. There was a similar event when Bradford Northern played York at Birch Lane – preceded by a match between the First and Second Pals which the Second won by six points to three.

Spy fever was still around. There was a scare about a 'clergyman and his daughter' sketching Skipton Camp and then disappearing when challenged by a sentry. Oddly enough a sketch appeared in the *Bradford Telegraph* the following week. On 1 April a few heads were scratched as to the authenticity of an official warning posted on the camp notice boards:

Reports from various quarters point to the conclusion that individuals are using officers' uniform as a disguise in which to question soldiers and to visit guarded points. Soldiers are questioned as to numbers, corps, progress made in training, probable movements etc. Non-commissioned officers and men are warned of this danger. In the event of

R.S.M. Harold Scott and his little brother Q.M.S. Alf Scott.

any non-commissioned officer or private being questioned in this way by a strange officer he should take steps to ensure the questioner being brought before the nearest officer of his own unit. [31]

Authentic it certainly was, although all a spy had to do was to be an assiduous reader of the *Bradford Telegraph* and *Yorkshire Observer* who detailed almost every potato peeled at Skipton. Yet as Winter turned to Spring there was still no news of a move abroad.

The Citizens' Army League continued to hold recruiting meetings in Bradford with a number of Second Pals officers and men on the platform as well as the Lord Mayor and Sir William Priestley M.P. On 2 April at St. George's Hall the principal speaker was the East London Labour M.P. Will Crooks. Unlike the Bradford MP Fred Jowett, Crooks was a whole hearted supporter of the War and his expenses were paid by the War Office. In a sideswipe at his fellow MP, Crooks demonstrated the division in the Labour party.

> *There were a few people – who were not yet certified – who thought we ought not to be at war and thought we could live as well under the Kaiser as George V ("Shame")*[32]

Councillor J. H. Palin, Labour Chairman of the Tramways Committee and a railway trades union official, joined in the chorus.

> *He was not concerned about the few people who would impeach the Labour Party. They were only a few and unfortunately being the newest party contained the most number of cranks. It was only a family trouble and we have to put up with it.*[33]

One wonders whether relations had been restored in 1924 when the 'crank'

Pals recruiting at Keighley Rugby League ground. Mayor of Keighley, left centre, Sir John Clough on his right.

Jowett was a member of the Labour Cabinet and Palin (having been Lord Mayor of Bradford) was the back bench Labour MP for Newcastle upon Tyne West.

By early April, numbers in the Second Pals had grown to 750 men and twenty-five officers. At an inspection in Lister Park, General Molesworth, 'accompanied by a large staff', 'expressed satisfaction' yet again, and 'congratulated Colonel Muller on the clean looking new battalion'.[34] Perhaps the General thought washing was an unusual practice in Bradford.

By now Army plans were afoot to move both the Bradford Battalions to a new camp at Ripon. The First Pals were to stay at Skipton until Ripon Camp was ready, but it was decided that it was essential to get the Second Pals living and working together as a military unit in a temporary tented camp before the Ripon move and a search for a tented site began. The need for a camp became even more necessary when the owners of the Manningham HQ said they wanted their skating rink back.

On Sunday, 19 April, the Second Pals were caught up in an embarrassing spy scare which illuminates the feverish attitude of the time. William Whitenmair, a naturalized German pork butcher, lived in Thurnscoe Road near the Pals' HQ in Manningham Lane. Pals officers were told of mysterious flashlight signals seen during the night and armed guards were sent to surround the unfortunate Mr Whitenmair's house as he prepared for a Sunday morning stroll. He was arrested and marched up Manningham Lane to the Police Station in front of a large crowd waiting to watch the Battalion depart for Church Parade. There were red faces all round when the case against Mr Whitenmair, who 'had the appearance of a prosperous tradesman', was laughed out of court. The *Telegraph* commented,

> It is to be regretted that the name of a well-known Bradford gentleman has been connected with the affair, and we need hardly add that there was not the slightest truth in the rumour.

The reporter put the best face he could on the Pals' embarrassment.

> The effect of this little military display has shown itself in the recruiting boom that has since taken place. The Second Battalion is receiving its fair share of new applications and at the present rate of progress the full strength should be reached in a short time.[35]

"NOW LADS, PLAY THE GAME!"

Join the Keighley Team!!

2nd Bradford   Pals' Battalion

GOAL:
LORD KITCHENER

FULL BACKS:
GENERAL FRENCH   ADMIRAL JELLICOE

CENTRE HALF:
LORD FISHER

WANTED AT ONCE
1000 DASHING FORWARDS
To complete the 2nd Battalion.

Apply for all Particulars :
RECRUITING OFFICE, DRILL HALL, KEIGHLEY.

"Pals'" Recruiting Song.

Tune—" Marching Through Georgia."

Come on, boys, and join the "Flag," our
   country needs us all,
Can you hear the bugle sound and not obey
   the call ?
Join us, then, and we can feel whatever may
   befall
England is doing its duty.

CHORUS.
Come on, come on, the Pals are calling you,
Come on, come on, be loyal, brave and true ;
All have sacrifices made, this is what you
   can do.
Follow the call of the bugle.

Belgium, France, and Russia, all are sending
   of their best,
Canada, Australia, have followed like the rest,
Surely you will not hold back, we put you
   to the test.
Follow the call of the bugle.—CHORUS.

Mothers, wives, and sweethearts, all have
   worked for soldiers too,
They have done their duty, and it's plainly
   up to you
Now to follow bravely and your little share
   to do.
Follow the call of the bugle.—CHORUS.

The Second Pals camp at Bowling Park.

There was better recruitment publicity later in the week when it was announced that two of Bradford City's international footballers, outside right Dickie Bond and centre forward Harold Walden had joined the Pals. There had always been an affinity between the football club and the West Yorkshire Regiment at Belle Vue Barracks on the opposite side of Manningham Lane. City's claret and amber strip was based on the colours of the regiment. Twenty-eight year old Harold Walden had distinguished himself by winning a Gold Medal in the 1912 Stockholm Olympics as part of the Great Britain football team, scoring an amazing six goals in the 7-0 demolition of Hungary. He also had previous Army experience as a sergeant in the Cheshire Regiment. According to the *Telegraph*,

Band of the 18th West Yorks by the boating lake in Manningham Park.

He has the highest certificates as a gymnastic instructor, and held the position of a first class instructor of drill and musketry; in fact, he was regarded as one of the best qualified and smartest instructors in the army.[36]

Walden was soon commissioned and acted for a time as Adjutant to the Second Pals, although he was transferred to the 20th Reserve Battalion in August, 1915. After the war he left City and signed for Arsenal in 1920. He then had an unusual career change, becoming a professional comedian in Leeds. Dickie Bond also had army experience as a private in the Artillery, although he was bought out of the Army when he was signed by Preston North End. He won several England caps but missed the 1911 Cup Final victory because of a ban for swearing at the Arsenal crowd. He was promoted to sergeant in the Pals and was in charge of a Lewis Gun team on the Somme. He was with the Pals until he was captured and became a prisoner of war at the end of July, 1916. On 21 April, the Second Pals held a recruiting parade at the First Division local derby match between Bradford City and Bradford Park Avenue. Walden and Bond both put on their army great coats over their football kit to address the crowd at half-time. The attendance of 21,000 was lower than usual, partly because the match was on a Wednesday afternoon, and also because many supporters had already joined the Army. The result was a comprehensive win for Park Avenue by 3-0, and Avenue moved to ninth place immediately above City in the final First Division table.

Dickie Bond.

St George's Day, 23 April, saw a major parade by the Second Pals in Peel Park with an inspection by the Lord Mayor. The Second Pals continued to use route marches as an aid to recruitment through the district as far as the Spen Valley to Birkenshaw, Cleckheaton and Heckmondwike.

The Scottish music hall singer and comedian Harry Lauder had formed a Scottish pipe band at his own expense to be part of a national recruiting campaign by the War Office. They arrived in Bradford on 26 April and performed through the City, leading route marches by the Second Pals. Their most spectacular effort was a march from Keighley down the Worth Valley and up to Foster's Black Dyke Mill at Queensbury. [37]

Harold Walden.

This concerted effort resulted in a rush of new recruits. In the two weeks up to 26 April no fewer than 576 men registered although not all passed the medical. The *Telegraph* report for the first time used the term 'world war':

The wastage is considerable, but the rush of men shows that great numbers of Bradford lads are willing and every young man who fails to pass the tests has at any rate the consolation of receiving a certificate which for the rest of his lifetime will stand as proof that it is not his fault that he did not serve in the great world war.[38]

A further trigger for a late rush of recruits may have been the sinking of the passenger liner *Lusitania* on 7 May by a U boat off the southern coast of Ireland with the loss of 1,198 passengers, including a number of Americans. What was not disclosed is the fact that the vessel was almost certainly carrying secret munitions. The *Bradford Telegraph* gave huge prominence to the sinking including a photograph of a Mr and Mrs Eddie Riley from Great

Horton and their two young children who survived the tragedy. The paper also described numerous anti-German riots in various parts of the country with attacks on individuals and property, including looting of German shops.

By the end of April, the Second Pals had reached full strength. In addition to the older officers who had transferred from the First Pals, a number of new officers had been appointed.

Although a move to Ripon was imminent a tented camp known as Bowling Park Colony was erected with over a hundred tents and large marquees in Bowling Park on the southern end of the city. The camp was on flat land beyond the ornamental gardens next to the old Bradford Northern Rugby League ground at Birch Lane. The intention was to enable the battalion to live together and train together for the first time as a complete unit. The men took part in a formal parade and march from Manningham Lane to the new camp led by the Lauder Pipe Band on 30 April, and they enjoyed a sports day on the natural amphitheatre in the park next to the camp. Their route to Bowling Park took them past the Town Hall where the Lord Mayor took the salute. Unfortunately, a huge thunder storm on the first night destroyed the camp and the soaked men were sent home again until new tents and equipment could be obtained two weeks later.

The two Bradford battalions came together in full strength for the first time on 8 May at a huge recruiting rally with over twelve thousand troops from 38th Division in Huddersfield. The First Pals travelled by train from Skipton and donned their old blue uniforms again for the last time for special effect.

War Office anxiety about poor recruitment in Huddersfield and the need for the rally underlines certain undercurrents which received little prominence in the press at the time. Both Halifax and Huddersfield failed to form their own Pals Battalions and in his excellent book, *Comrades in*

Second Pals at Bowling Park. After ablutions. Note cookers in background.

Conscience: The story of an English community's opposition to the Great War, Cyril Pearce describes how the War Office appointed a certain John Hunter Watts, as a paid recruiting agent and established him in a room at the George Hotel. Watts had been a prominent member and organiser of the Social Democratic Federation wing of the Labour Party since the 1880's, but like Will Crooks MP, he came out in support of the War. Watts claimed, 'The War Office informed him that the most serious opposition to recruiting came from this district.'[39] The Second Pals finally moved into Bowling Camp on 13 May. The *Telegraph* reporter dutifully and enthusiastically praised all the arrangements. His readers were edified to learn that,

> *The sanitary arrangements are as near perfection as possible thanks to the personal supervision of Councillor Ezra Hoyle and Superintendent Call of the Street Cleansing Department. Nothing has been overlooked apparently and when the weather improves the men will be able to take their morning dip in a pretty little spot which has been prepared by diverting a stream from its natural course.*[40]

The reporter no doubt returned home to a cosy fireside. The men were probably grateful for the efforts of Ezra, but their main memory was of huddling together for body warmth in tents of twelve and suffering sleepless nights with only three army blankets. Cheerful smiles were put on for the cameras, but the men were delighted to receive orders to march to Ripon Camp to join the First Pals on 20th May.

The march to Ripon. Men of the First Pals freshen up at a horse trough after a night in a barn at Hampswaite.

A two day march to Ripon ensued for both battalions with the First Pals spending the night in school rooms, barns and the village at Hampsthwaite, whilst the Second Pals did the same at Pannel near Harrogate. All the First Pals managed the march, but a number of the Second Pals who had had less time to toughen up under march conditions dropped out and completed the journey by train.

After the Pals departure, Raikes Camp at Skipton was used by other units, the first being the 17th West Yorks (Leeds Bantams). The camp was eventually used as a Prisoner of War Camp for captured German troops, holding 500 officers and 130 men, and was operational until October, 1919 when it was dismantled. Today much of the land has been developed for private housing, although large animal bones still sometimes get dug up in the gardens of local residents where the Cookhouse once stood.

Appendix

Daily routine at Raikes Camp, Skipton from the diary of 16/458 Corporal Herbert Taylor, 'E' Company, 16th West Yorks.

February 1915
5. Arrived Skipton 3.30. Well. Place dirty but were welcome.
6. Great job shifting in rain. Afternoon and evening in town shopping.
7. Sunday.
8. Physical and fieldwork morning. Fieldwork and route march. Transferred to 17 Platoon.
9. Trenching round huts in morning. After, easy, then 4.30 picket until 6.30 Wednesday.
10. Off till afternoon, trenching round huts and walk in town till 9.30.
11. Company drill in morning then large fieldwork operations in afternoon.
12. Battalion drill before dinner then hut trenching.
13. Battalion drill under Brigadier. Wife's visit home 8.30.
14. Sunday. Church Parade, out evening.
15. Squad drill till dinner and bayonet drill after. Not out.
16. Field operations before and after noon.
17. Route march and lecture. Company drill.
18. Platoon drill in morning. Route march to Gargrave. Corporals, meeting.
19. Company drill before and after noon. Fire Picket. Outpost work on moors.
20. Kit inspection. Wife's surprise visit. Home 10.
21. Sunday. Church parade. Splendid walk afternoon and evening. Home 10.
22. Company drill before noon. Guard at 5.00. Colonel Warden took command of Battalion.
23. Guard till 5.00. Not out
24. Company drill before noon. Retiring movement with D Company between Gargrave and Carleton. Home 9.00.
25. Company drill. Operations with D Company against A Company between Bolton Abbey and Eastly Sanatorium. The B.O.C.
26. B.O.C. till 5.00.
27. Kit inspection and visit home.
28. Sunday. Home till 9.20 train.

March 1915
1. Morning work on road. Inoculation at 2.00.
2. Feeling bad. In bed mostly.
3. Rather better, home till Thursday.
4. Back to camp by 10.30 train.
5. Attack practice near Embsay. Lecture by Major Moore, then flying piquet at 5.
6 . Reveille at 6.30. Easy morning.
7. Sunday Church Parade and foot inspection. Splendid walk in evening.
8. Miniature firing before noon. Physical drill and bayonet fighting.
9. Attacking Embsay quarries before noon, then defending, then route march. Corporals' concert in evening.
10. Operations in fields near Embsay before noon, then easy till 7.30 pm. Night march on Draughton road for relief of C Coy in trenches. Back at 10.45.
11. Lecture on aiming before noon. Miniature practice at Embsay after.
12. Battalion drill near Broughton before noon. Second inoculation after.
13. Easy morning. Feeling better.
14. Sunday. Home by 10.20 train.
15. Bradford on leave.
16. Barracks by 6.55 train. Easy morning in fields towards Embsay. Afternoon in fields between camp and Craven Heifer.
17. Extended order from 'none gone by' to hilltop. Afternoon in fields near camp for visual training.
18. Blizzard, lectures all day.
19. March to Gargrave and back before noon. Company drill near camp.
20. Easy morning, no visitors.
21. Sunday. Church Parade.
22. Company drill near camp before noon. Issue of khaki after.
23. Easy field drill before noon. Afternoon extended across moor. Corporals' concert.
24. Company drill before and after noon.
25. Vaccination. Easy all day.
26. Route march through Gargarve and Broughton Park. Imaginary billeting at Embsay.
27. Easy morning. Wife's visit.
28. Sunday. Church Parade. Walk after tea.
29. Extended order drill towards Broughton. Medical inspection, feeling bad.
30. Visual training past Craven Heifer. Easy afternoon.
31. Visual Training as before. Medical Officer's inspection, confined to barracks.

April 1915
1. Morning nil after same.
2. Church Parade. Feeling better, but c.b.
3. Easy morning, wet after, evening rec. orders for transfer to C Company.
4. Sunday. Church Parade. Transferred to C Company.
5. Morning getting settled in new quarters. Holiday for day. Visited castle in afternoon, walk to Gargrave in evening, back 9.30.
6. Road repairing round huts before noon. After nil.
7. Road repairing all day. Pic (....)
8. Wet morning, kit inspection, easy.
9. Full day on Flasby Fell all day, trench digging, hard day but enjoyable.
10. Easy morning, home for weekend on pass.

11. Sunday. At home until 9.20 train.

12. Trenching on Flasby Fell all day.

13. Battalion Inspection by G.O.C. Lawson before noon. Holiday after, fine. Trip to Keighley, back by 9.30.

14. Trenching all day.

15. Vaccination for company, easy morning, gardening afternoon.

16. Trenching all day.

17. Hut cleaning and gardening before noon.

18. Sunday. Church Parade. Visit of motor party.

19. Khaki parade before noon, route march nearly to Cracoe.

20. Lecture by NCO's to sections before noon. Route march again with visual training on Embsay Hill.

21. Trenching on Flashy Fell all day.

22. Trenching all day.

23. Squad and company drill before noon. Visual Training behind Craven Heifer.

24. Easy morning.

25. Sunday. Church Parade. Sisters visit.

26. 5.30 Reveille. Short route march past Craven Heifer and bugle calls instruction. Afternoon route march towards Eastby and Draughton. A and D fright.

27. Company drill before noon, afternoon visit to Skipton Castle.

28. Company drill near Craven Heifer forenoon, afternoon extended on Flashy moor, outbreak of big fire, back to camp at 7.00.

29. Physical and company drill on barrack square, before noon, after message practice in fields, Draughton road.

30. Physical drill and lecture by Captain Chatterton on personal experiences in War. Afternoon visual training near Craven Heifer.

May 1915

1. Easy morning, home on pass by 12.20.

2. Sunday, home.

3. Miniature practice, first class, and marksman. Issue of rifles.

4. Battalion parade by CO. before noon. After shooting at Embsay first class. Concert in Y.M.C.A. hut. Baby born, Annie.

5. Shooting at Embsay all day. Flying piquet 7 till 5.30.

6. Battalion parade before noon, firing practice after. Flying piquet 7-5.30.

7. Firing practice before noon, easy after.

8. Battalion parade to Huddersfield, recruiting campaign, back 9.30.

9. Sunday. Church Parade. Visit by motorists party. Flashy Fell.

10. Outpost practice in fields to left of Craven Heifer, back at 2.30. Short lecture by Captain Blagborough 3.45 to 5.00.

11. Outpost practice again 2.00. Physical drill 3.45 to tea time. Y.M.C.A. Concert.

12. Inspector-General inspection of Outpost work before noon, company drill after, though we did not see him. Brigadier General Gainsford CB CMG

13. Great route march by Grassington, 26 miles, Burnsall, Appletreewick, Barden, Eastby etc. Back at 6.30.

14. Company and physical drill before noon. Khaki parade and kit inspection after. News of going to Ripon. Corporals' mess meeting.

15. Easy morning except for moving clothing to stores. Home by 12.20 train.

16. Sunday. Home on pass. Registered Annie.

17. Filling trenches in all day on Flashy Fell. Departure of Advance party to Ripon.

18. Easy morning after receiving dr(afts?). Route march afternoon Embsay, Eastby etc.

19. Physical drill, packing of kits etc., afternoon off.
20. Departure for Ripon 10.00. Long march, billeted at Hampsthwaite. Late dinner.
21. Left Hampsthwaite 9.30. Hot and long march to Ripon, arrived 3.00.

NOTES

1. *Bradford Daily Telegraph*, 16 January 1915.
2. *Bradford Daily Telegraph*, 4 January 1915.
3. *ibid.*
4. *ibid.*
5. *ibid.*
6. *ibid*, 22 January 1915.
7. *ibid.*
8. *ibid.*
9. *ibid*, 4 January.
10. The full list of names for the huts at Skipton was :
Buckingham Palace, Carleton View, Carry On Cottage, Chumley Hall, Craig Villa, Cross Lea, Devil's Hall, Dew Drop Inn, Downing Street, Eaten Hall, French Villa, Full Inside, Harmony Hall, Haworth Cottage, House O'the Hill, Hun Cottage, Hungry-an-Villans, Intelligence Department, The Jungle, KBO, Liberty Hall, Little Grey Home in the West, Mudlarks, No Worry Hut, North Pole, Nulli Secundus, On Parle Francais, One Step Nearer, Paradise Hall, Ponn Thune Villa, Pro Patria, Russell Villa, Sailor's Rest, South Parade, South Pole, Stone Ridge, Sycamore, The Terrible 33, Venes par Ici, Vicarage, 2nd West Villa, We Can Whack 'Em, White City, Windsor Castle.
11. George Grunwell, taped conversation with author, 10 May 1989.
12. *Bradford Weekly Telegraph,* 29 January 1915.
13. *ibid.*
14. Herbert Taylor, diary kindly supplied by Mr C J Taylor.
15. Letter to author from General Medical Council, 19 March 1991.
16. *Bradford Weekly Telegraph,* 5 February 1915.
17. Officers' Records, PRO WO/339.
18. *ibid.*
19. Information on Colonel Warden from Officers' Records WO/339, and on connection with O'Gowan and Derryquin 'Who was Who' and Derryquin Hotel website.
20. I am grateful to boxing historian Harold Alderman for supplying details of Will Blakeborough's career.
21. *ibid,* 12 February 1915.
22. *ibid.*
23. Horace James Cannon, G.C., 1895-1975. The original award was the Albert Medal, later transformed into the George Cross. The award was equivalent to the Victoria Cross and would have been such if the event had taken place in France. Citation: On 21 January, while flying in England, a pilot when attempting to land lost control of his machine, which crashed to the ground from a height of about 150 feet. Flight Sergeant Cannon and another Flight Sergeant went to the rescue of the pilot at great personal risk, as one petrol tank blew up and another was on fire; moreover, the machine was equipped with a belt of live cartridges, which they dragged out of the flames. They managed to extricate the pilot, but he died shortly afterwards from his injuries and burns.
24. Citation: *London Gazette,* 29 November 1915.
25. WO 339 PRO Officers Records.
26. *The Bradfordian Magazine.* Journal of Bradford Grammar School, termly issues between 1914 and 1918.
27. *Bradford Daily Telegraph,* 23 March 1915.
28. Tape of 18/1150 Albert Jowett by Steve Kerry, Bradford Industrial Museum.
29. Ernest Wilson, tape by Steve Kerry.
30. Tape of 18/761 Ernest Brook, Kerry *ibid.*
31. *Bradford Daily Telegraph,* 2 April 1915.
32. *ibid.*
33. *ibid.*
34. *Bradford Daily Telegraph,* 23 April 1915.
35. *ibid.*
36. *ibid.*
37. Harry Lauder's son, Captain John Lauder of the Argyll and Sutherland Highlanders, was killed at Ovillers on the Somme in December, 1916. His father was moved to write his most famous song, 'Keep Right On To The End Of The Road'. Sadly there is now a strong tradition in Scotland that the unpopular Captain was shot in the back by his own men.
38. *Bradford Daily Telegraph,* 30 April 1915.
39. Cyril Pearce, p. 120, in *Comrades in Conscience,* pub Francis Boutle, 2001.
40. *Bradford Weekly Telegraph,* 14 May 1915.

Chapter Five

RIPON

THE PALS ARRIVED dirty, sweaty and exhausted at their new camp on 21 May, watched by curious locals who applauded as they marched past headed by their respective bands. The Pals were delighted with what they found. They were the first occupants of what was to become a massive military area and at first they had it to themselves.

Although Ripon styled itself a city because of its ancient Cathedral, it was in reality a sleepy market town with a population of 7,000 in 1914. It was certainly attractive and a marked contrast to the experience of the urban dwellers from smoky industrial Bradford.

Ripon lay on the banks of the River Ure as the gateway to Wensleydale and on the edge of the Vale of York not far from the Great North Road. It had a rail link to Harrogate and Leeds to the south, and to Northallerton and the East Coast main line to the north. Its racecourse was fashionable and long established and it was surrounded by the great estates of Newby Hall, Norton Conyers, and Studley Royal (with Fountains Abbey).

Attempts had been made to stimulate the local economy by setting up a spa to rival Harrogate immediately before the War. In 1900, the radical Marquis of Ripon of Studley Royal had sold land for a spa pump room and pleasure gardens. There was a Bradford connection, for Ripon was W. E. Forster's deputy when the 1870 *Education Act* was passed, and he unveiled Forster's statue in Bradford in 1890. The *art nouveau* Spa Baths were built in 1905 and the Spa Hotel opened in 1909. Unfortunately the fashion for spa

MARKET PLACE, RIPON

treatments had passed Ripon by, and the local council was on the look out for a new project to stimulate trade. On 12 August 1914, eight days after the outbreak of war, it was announced that Lord Kitchener had ordered the construction of 2,000 huts to accommodate 40,000 troops on land to the south of neighbouring Richmond – it was to become Catterick Camp. The shopkeepers, hoteliers and publicans on Ripon City Council spotted an opportunity to combine patriotism with more than a bit of enlightened self-interest.

Negotiations for a camp at Ripon opened in September, and in December Kitchener approved proposals for a camp likely to become permanent, housing two divisions amounting to over 30,000 troops, at a total expenditure of £350,000 and with a completion date of April 1915.[1]

The camp would dwarf the town. It covered nearly 1,000 acres spreading in an arc from Red Bank to the south of the town clockwise to Clotherhole to the north-west. Two rifle ranges were built, one towards How Hill and the other across the River Laver to Ellington Banks. The camp required the construction of ten miles of main roads, sixteen miles of secondary roads and twelve miles of footpaths. It also had its own eight mile long standard gauge railway connecting up with the main line. Two large reservoirs were built supplying up to 700,000 gallons a day, and forty-eight miles of sewers and drains were built. This new state of the art camp was to be lit and powered by electricity from its own generating station.

The camp was not universally popular with the locals. At a council meeting in January 1915, a fiery nonconformist councillor named Kearsley,

Second Pals take a break on the march to Ripon.

Marching through Ripon.

> *voiced strong feeling against the desecration of the Sabbath, pointing out that whilst the mayor and Corporation were worshipping in the Cathedral the streets resounded with passing engines and wagons.*[2]

Letters also appeared in the local press complaining of drunken behaviour by the labourers building the camp who, it was claimed, were wandering the streets in an intoxicated state at mid-day. The response was to put public houses out of bounds until 6.00 pm. The Temperance Hall was put at the disposal of the Y.M.C.A. to provide 'rest and refreshment' for the men in the evening – with what success we do not know.

The Bishop of Ripon attempted to calm local feeling by announcing that the War Office would provide eight chaplains for the camp. There would also be two recreation and refreshment huts, a music and cinema hall, and a soldiers' institute. As is often the way with the church, the Bishop then appealed for money, £15,000, to pay for the projects. The Sheffield Cutler's Company provided £5,000 when they heard that the 12th Yorks & Lancs (Sheffield Pals) were to be sent to Ripon as part of 31st Division, and Lady Radcliffe of Rudding Park provided funds for a hut to be used for the celebration of Mass.[3]

The two Bradford Battalions were joined by the 18th (Service) Battalion of the Durham Light Infantry (the Durham Pals) as the first occupants of the camp. Advance parties arrived on 17 May to make preparations, and the rest of the men arrived on the afternoon of Friday, 21 May. They were to stay for four months. The Leeds Pals (15th West Yorks) were nearby at Colsterdale beyond Masham but soon arrived to join the Bradfords and Durhams to form

93rd Brigade of 31st Division at Ripon.

The 31st Division of Kitchener's Fourth New Army consisted of thirteen battalions in all from Lancashire and Yorkshire and their badge was the intertwined red and white roses of the two counties. The Division was sub-divided into three Brigades (92nd, 93rd and 94th) each with four battalions, whilst the 13th Battalion acted as Pioneers. Later, specialist units to do with the artillery and medical services were added.

The time was spent on route marches, trench digging, drill, P.E., use of the bayonet and shooting. Movements were also practised at company, battalion and brigade levels during the day and in the night. How far these practices were relevant to a war that was spent in the trenches is a moot point.

Again we get a daily record of the battalion's activity through the diary of Sergeant Herbert Taylor (16/458) in Appendix B. Herbert Taylor was thirty-seven and older than many of the other recruits. He had been a tram driver for Bradford Corporation and was regarded as a leader amongst his colleagues at work. He was an active union member and his papers reveal him to be an intelligent careful man. On one occasion he organised a petition for the re-instatement of a dismissed colleague on compassionate grounds. Sergeant Taylor was a capable stonemason and joiner, but he was also musically talented capable of playing a number of instruments, especially the violin and bassoon. Not surprisingly he became a member of the Pals band and was promoted to sergeant.[4]

The Pals finally received a rifle each on 17 June, and on 24 June they had a

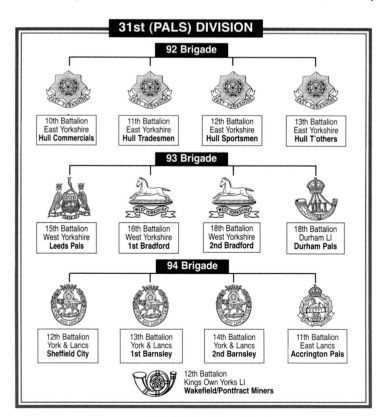

formal parade and were inspected by Sir Archibald Murray, Deputy Chief of the Imperial General Staff. They were to meet Murray again several months later when he was appointed GOC in Egypt.[5]

It was not all sweetness and light. On 30 June, Sergeant Herbert Taylor made one of the few sharply critical personal remarks in his diary 'Returned wet through, never forget Pringle the bully.'[6] C Company was returning from rifle drill after an afternoon on the range in a heavy thunderstorm. Whatever was said and done by the tall ex-Fettes public schoolboy Captain Robert Pringle, it certainly caused offence. Specialist training also took place with the signallers learning their craft and co-operating with the shooting practice.

> *I joined the signallers because I thought I'd get out of drilling and guard duty, and I did. Instead of doing a lot of guard duty we were learning the signals. We had a field telephone, like a little black square box, and we used to have dinon accumulators. We used to have rolls of wire to hug around and we used to have morse code flags – a big flag about six foot odd length handle, and we used to have a smaller flag to signal morse code. The more proficient you became the sooner you got your tanner a day extra. I got six pence a day extra for being a signaller and we used to wear crossed flags on our sleeves.*
>
> 18/856 PRIVATE TONY MILLER[7]

Tony Miller discovered that though he had less guard duty and drilling to do, he still had to be trained for bayonet combat.

> *Oh deary me, we used to have sacks hung between posts and we used to charge these sacks and jab 'em with a bayonet, and it used to terrify me to death did that sort of work, bare bayonets. I thought if I were to miss these and these particular sacks in the charge and stab somebody it'd be awkward.*
>
> 18/856 PRIVATE TONY MILLER[8]

First Pals Signaller Section at Ripon.

The War Office took over formal responsibility for the Pals from the Bradford Citizens' Army League on 16 July 1915 and there was a farewell visit by Bradford worthies the next day. Sergeant Herbert Taylor joined the Pals with a group of tram driver colleagues, and his diary reveals a visit from the City Tramways Manager and Councillor J. H. Palin (Labour Chairman of the Tramways Committee, future Lord Mayor of Bradford, and MP for Newcastle West 1924-31).[9] A series of changes followed the takeover by the War Office. There was a weeding process when the number of active companies in each battalion was effectively reduced from five to four – the fifth company becoming a depot company to which the less fit men were transferred.

On 20 July, Colonel Muller bade farewell to the two Pals Battalions he had helped to nurture. He was replaced as C.O. of the 18th West Yorks by forty year old Major E. C. H. Kennard, a regular officer in the Duke of Wellington's West Riding Regiment although he was originally from Norfolk. The Second Pals' new Colonel had begun his career as a 2nd Lieutenant in the Grenadier Guards in 1896, but gone on to serve in the Boer War where he was wounded with the Imperial Yeomanry. E. C. H. Kennard and his new second in command Major W. G. Johnson stayed with the Second Pals until the following April, but both were replaced when the Battalion arrived in France.[10]

On 4 August there was a last grand parade in Bradford to mark the first anniversary of the Declaration of War. The First Pals were taken by train to Bradford and assembled at Valley Parade football ground where they were given a beef sandwich and a drink. There was then a march down Manningham Lane led by the band to the Town Hall Square for a thirty minute ceremony.

The gathering was so great that it filled completely the space before the Town

Transport Section at Ripon. An unsuspecting young soldier about to be 'dripped' from a wet sponge.

Route march near Ripon. Note the young Pal carrying the rifle of his older comrade.

Hall and stretched in tentacles along the converging thoroughfares. It was a sober decorous crowd, and seemed rather too impressed to cheer, though emotional enough to join heartily in the singing of the appointed hymns.

The Pals were received with cheers... but the crowd was so great that it was impossible to draw the men up in any impressive formation. Very soon, indeed the troops were almost inundated by the press of civilians.[11]

It was the last time the First Pals marched together in Bradford as a complete unit. It was also the last parade for the First Pals amiable and elderly Second in Command Major Crossley. He transferred to join Colonel Muller to form what was to become the 20th West Yorks, but died shortly afterwards of liver cancer. Captain Harold Walden the Bradford City centre forward and Olympic gold medal winner went with Colonel Muller to act as adjutant. Two of Walden's City team mates, Oscar (Fox 20/184) and Irvine Boocock (20/245) also joined the 20th Battalion at this time. Boocock, from Cleckheaton, was selected to represent the football league and was regarded as one of the best uncapped left-backs in the country. Fox was Dickie Bond's inside forward partner, and both he and Boocock made nearly 200 First Division appearances. The professional boxer Fred Blakeborough became a Lance Corporal and fitness instructor in the 20th West Yorks. The brother of Will, he was a contender for the British Lightweight title, became Lightweight Champion of all the command home forces. Joe Delaney (20/200) was also a useful professional boxer (his brother Jerry was a world championship contender) – but after service with the Leeds Pals in 1918 he deserted shortly after the armistice only to receive a twelve month prison sentence for his pains.

The two depot companies of the 16th and 18th West Yorks were amalgamated and moved to Colsterdale Camp which had been vacated by the Leeds Pals. New recruits were allocated a '20' prefix to their regimental number. The unit did supply reinforcements to the two Pals battalions and to other units. They were eventually re-designated as the 51st RTR batalion and moved to Whitley Bay, still under the command of Colonel Muller. A number of wounded officers from both the 16th and 18th West Yorks were to spend time at Whitley Bay after the Somme when they were on light duties as part of their recuperation. A number of the men transferred to the 20th Battalion were transferred back again in the last few weeks before the Pals left Fovant, and also in the Spring of 1916 in France before the Battle of the Somme.

Major Crossley's replacement as Second in Command of the First Pals was thirty-three year old Captain Humfrey Heyes Kennedy. Kennedy was a regular soldier with experience of the Western Front who had recovered from a wound received whilst serving with the Seaforth Highlanders in Flanders. Kennedy was promoted to major and played an important part in the history of the First Pals.

Major Kennedy had joined the Seaforth Highlanders in 1900 and served as a young 2nd Lieutenant in the Boer War, winning the Queen's Medal with five clasps. He was promoted to full Lieutenant in 1908, and in 1912 was employed with the West African Frontier Force. He returned to Europe at the outbreak of war and took part in the defence of Ypres where he was wounded. He was promoted to Captain in November, 1914.[12]

Humfrey Kennedy was a tall, genteel Scot although his home was in Dorking because of his army career. He was respected and well liked by the rank and file in the Bradford Pals. According to Walter Hare he was, 'a decent man, approachable, you could talk to him'.[13]

On 23 August, Major-General Robert Wanless-O'Gowan took over the command of 31st Division from General Molesworth. The fifty year old general was a very different character to his genial predecessor. He was a bleak no-nonsense man with staring eyes and came from the Anglo-Irish protestant conveyor belt which supplied so many Generals to the British Army. More significantly, he had recent active service experience in command of the 13th Brigade when Hill 60 was captured in Flanders. His task was to prepare the Pals for war. Future events proved him to be a harsh disciplinarian.[14]

One advantage of Ripon was that it was still possible to make home visits or to receive visits, and it was still possible for the Bradford newspapers to send photographers to chronicle the doings of the Pals. The fact was though that the doings of the Pals were becoming repetitive and boring to the men. It became more and more difficult to deflect the question 'When are you lot going to France' when they visited Bradford.

Eventually a move came as a consequence of events elsewhere. Throughout the summer, plans were afoot to break the stalemate on the Western Front with a major offensive. The place selected by the commander of the British Expeditionary Force, Sir John French, was Loos in the coal mining area to the north of Lens. After the losses in the Regular and Territorial battalions, more men were needed and three of the Kitchener's New Army Divisions, the 21st, 24th and 26th were despatched to France early in

18th West Yorks Bugle band at Ripon.

September.

It was decided that 31st Division should move further south to be nearer the action if called upon, and they were to take over the accommodation vacated by 26th Division at Fovant. On the 16 September the Lord Mayor of Bradford, Alderman George H. Robinson, sent what the *Yorkshire Observer* described as 'a stirring letter' to Colonel Warden and Colonel Kennard to wish the Pals well.

> *The citizens of Bradford will watch with the deepest interest all the doings of the battalions abroad, and with the certainty that, from the time of their departure until the moment of their return we shall hear of nothing in the story of the battalions which will fail to arouse feelings of pride in, and deep satisfaction with, the brave men who will represent Bradford in the war.*[15]

It was impossible for the mayor to anticipate the feelings of sorrow and grief that would also be aroused.

On 22 September the Pals left Ripon for Fovant Camp near Salisbury. On 25 September, the Battle of Loos commenced. It proved to be a massive failure with huge losses and no advantage gained. It also led to the replacement of Sir John French as Commander-in-Chief by Sir Douglas Haig.

Appendix

Daily record of activity at Ripon Camp of the 16th West Yorks

From the diary of 16/458 Corporal Herbert Taylor, 'E' Company, 16th West Yorks.

May 1915

21. Left Hampsthwaite at 9.30 am. Hot and long march to Ripon, arr. 3.00 pm.
22. Fatigue party, easy morning and afternoon walk.
23. Sunday. Church parade at Cathedral. Walk by river in afternoon. Walk and adventure beyond Cathedral.
24. Short company drill. Half day off, visited Fountains Abbey, back by 8.30.

25. Battalion parade and alarm before noon. 3 mile route march to Hollin Ridge and reading of Army Act.

26. Extended order drill above camp before noon. Company drill on parade ground after. Fire alarm 6.30 at ropeworks, paraded 10.00 to 12 midnight.

27. Extended order drill before noon after short route march round camp, good rest.

28. Off 8.15, Battalion and Brigade route march past left of Fountains Abbey and through Markington (Normald Green). Back by 12.30. Easy after.

29. Easy and wet day.

30. Sunday. Camp service on parade ground. Fire alarm for hut on fire, 15 minute parade.

31. 7.30 Guard until 7.30 Tuesday.

June 1915

1. Guard to 7.30 am. Sergeants Mess fatigue 1 hour, easy remainder of day.

2. Easy morning, Canteen Corporal 12.00 to 9.00. Staff parade.

3. No duties. All day off for King's birthday. Walk by river in afternoon, bowls before, walk round town evening.

4. Easy morning and afternoon bowling. Set off 10.15 pm via Tanfield and Masham, arrived at 2.30 bivouac.

5. Battalion left at 10.00 for operations, self left behind for cooking. Battalion returned at 3.00, and left for Ripon at 6.15. Ripon at 10.00.

6. Sunday. No church parade. Visit of several friends.

7. Extended order drill before noon, route march and rest in wood. Walk by river in evening.

8. Battalion march round camp and lecture by Captain Chatterton. Afternoon company drill on parade ground. Bowls.

9. Battalion march to Studley Park. Battalion drill. Afternoon bathing parade, walk in town.

10. Company and pick and shovel drill before noon. Route march after by Sharow, Copt Hewick, Hewick Bridge and past race course.

11. Pick and shovel drill before noon. Easy after. Walk in town.

12. Battalion Parade to Studley Park, home on pass 1.05 special from Ripon 2.35.

13. Sunday. Back to Ripon by 6.20 special.

14. Route march towards Grevelthorpe and through woods. Bathing parade, missed it as warned for Canteen Corporal to 9.45.

15. Company and officers drill before noon. Parade at 3.50 for operations, left at 4.00 for Laverton arrived 7.00. Outpost all night.

16. Left Laverton at 6.30 for attack on 'D' Company beyond Kirby Malzeard, left there 10.30 back at camp 1.45, then warned for hospital guard. On at 5.45 pm till 6.00 am.

17. Off hospital guard 6.00. Morning off, afternoon company drill and issue of rifles, first evening out this week.

18. Extended order operations north of station, back at 4.30, walk by river.

19. Easy morning, visit of W. Slinger and friend till 9.00.

20. Sunday. Church parade in afternoon, walk round Littlethorpe in evening.

21. Bayonet drill before breakfast. Battalion operations to north of station. 'C' Company Spectators. Afternoon company and section rifle drill on parade ground.

22. Musketry, section and officers drill training before noon. Lecture by Captain Davis on musketry 5.30-6.30.

23. Musketry drill all day.

24. Inspection by Lt. Gen Sir Archibald Murray K.C.B., D.S.O. Afternoon attack practice north of station.

25. Battalion route march past right of Fountains through Sawley, back at 2.15.

26. Bayonet practice before breakfast, after cookhouse fatigue and issue of bayonets. Visit of N. Lightfoot and friends.

27. Sunday. Church parade at Trinity Church. In-lying picquet at 7.00 pm.

28. In-lying piquet. Bayonet drill before noon, rifle and fire drill after.

29. Bayonet fighting and drill before noon. Lecture by Captain Pringle after an incident of storming Port Arthur. Evening lecture by Captain Davis on war shot in the making.

30. Rifle drill before breakfast, after range practice. First class shot. Rifle drill afternoon on range, heavy thunderstorm, returned wet through, never forget Pringle the bully.

July 1915

1. Brigade route march through Markington, Normald Green, Burton Leonard, supposed 12^1/$_2$ miles, nearer 25, back at 2.00, inlying picquet.

2. Company drill, skeleton platoons, afternoon fire drill. Beat 18 hut. And pay.

3. Easy morning. Home on pass. Insurance paid up.

4. Sunday. At home.

5. At home.

6. To camp by 7.20 train after enjoyable holiday. Straight on parade, company drill. Afternoon bayonet drill and kit inspection.

7. Miniature rifle practice for company, instruction duties for self. Wet day

8. 15 mile route march by Haddock Stones, Sawly, Grantley, Clip and Thorn, back at 2.30. Easy after.

9. Kit inspection at 7.15, battalion parade at 8.55 for attack practice at Haddock Stones, back at 3.50.

10. Washouse fatigues etc., all morning. Brigade sports on racecourse.

11. Sunday. Drumhead Service on parade ground, took over orderly corporal's duties.

12. Orderly corporal for week, duties till dinnertime, then relived for musketry drill on parade ground at bottom of camp. Resumed O.C. duties at teatime.

13. Orderly Corporal. C Company and D Company left for night work at 3.00 and got back at 3.00 next day without me. Conducted 90 from station.

14. Orderly Corporal. Company back at 3.00.

15. Brigade route march left camp at 8.00, via Boroughbridge, self included, on to Staveley, Minskip, Bishop Monkton. Back at 3.30.

16. Orderly Corporal. Company out all day, back at 4.00.

17. Orderly Corporal. Visit of Transport Manager and J. H. Palin.

18. Sunday. Orderly Corporal. Cathedral parade, walk in evening.

19. Physical drill 6.45. Easy morning. Canteen Corporal at 12, Company left at 3.00.

20. Did nothing all day. Company returned at 3.30. Lecture by Captain Davis in Evening.

21. Musketry all morning and afternoon.

22. Brigade route march over eighteen miles by Brimham Rocks.

23. Review by Lord Mayor on Racecourse, presentation of T-boxes.

24. Kit inspection. Home on pass. Backdate of promotion to Lance-Sergeant.

25. Sunday. Back to Ripon by 8.00 train, arrived 11.00.

26. Company on duties. Field operations under Major Moore above camps, back at 1.30. Afternoon short route march towards Harrogate.

27. Musketry before noon, before breakfast. Afternoon, rapid practice on range.

28. Sick with eyes, afternoon standing by. Left camp at 11.45 for trench digging north of camp, back at 4.00 am.

29. Back at 4.00 am from digging. Kit inspection by Captain Kirton. 4.00 till 8.00 trenching.

30. Out at 8 to 12 trenching, evening 8.00 till nearly 1.00 am.

31. General fatigue, inlying picquet 7. Ripon feast of St. Wilfrid.

August 1915

1. Sunday, short drumhead service.

2. Musketry all day.

3. Up at 3 off at 4 trenching. Back at 10.00. Easy after.

4. To Bradford recruiting by 10.50 special. In Bradford 12.00. Lunch Valley Parade, march round and Peel Park. Finished 5.45 and to home.

5. At home. Parade at 5.30 round Whetley Hill etc., entrained at 7.30. Ripon at 9.00.

6. Easy morning, left at 12.00 for trenching back at 6.00.

7. Fatigues before noon, 12.00 parade for digging at Wormald Green range. Back at 8.00. In orders re. promotion to Lance Sergeant.

8. Sunday. Brigade church parade on Parade Ground. Address by Archbishop of York.

9. 9.00 physical drill under Sergt. Major Bilham to 12.00. After company drill and kit inspection.

10. Class 9-12, after, short visual etc.,

11. Class 9-12. Company at Bishop Monckton. Easy afternoon.

12. Short bayonet fighting before breakfast. Class 9-12. Brigade route march 13 miles, back at 2.00. Sergeant's Mess meeting.

13. Class 9-12. Firing practice on miniature range.

14. Class 9-10, then easy. Visit of wife and family and sister's party.

15. Sunday. Church parade to Y.M.C.A. hut. Band performance by East Lancs, Spa Gardens. Orderly Sergeant, evening.

16. Company and physical drill before breakfast. Class 9-1. Wet. Afternoon lecture by Captain Blagbrough in recreation room. On range signaling and recognition of targets.

17. As Monday before noon. Company on battalion drill at Studley Park, back at 1.30. Range instruction for all afternoon.

18. Snap shooting before breakfast. Self passed well. Class 9-12. Testing for rapid load afternoon.

19. Up at 4.00. Parade 5.00 for firing practice on new Ripon range. Passed 1st pr. W.O. 2nd. Back 12.45. After easy, photographed with company.

20. Easy before breakfast. 9.30 Firing back at 6.00.

21. Left for firing practice at 5.15, back at 12.30. Caught 3.50 train to Leeds, 5.50 to Bradford. Backdate of promotion to Sergeant.

22. At home. Back to Ripon by 8.00 train.

23. Left at 5.15 for firing practice, back at 2.45. Easy after.

24. Musketry before breakfast. P Class after 12.00. Musketry afternoon.

25. Last practice Physical Drill class. Afternoon bayonet fighting and Physical drill. Lecture in evening by Col. Tilney on finding way at night.

26. Battalion march to Newby. Self in charge of F men for visual training etc., back at 5.15.

27. Battalion left at 9.00 for field operations at Neby Park. Back at 5.00. Lecture by Lieutenant De Lissa on 'Discipline'. Sergeants Mess Concert.
28. Fatigues etc., Orderly Sgt.
29. Sunday. Orderly Sgt. Battalion Church Parade, Cathedral.
30. Musketry all day including Breakfasts. Orderly Sergeant.
31. Orderly Sergeant. Company firing on range, self instructing. Left at 9.30 back at 5.00.

September 1915
1. Orderly Sergeant. Company firing on range all day.
2. Easy day. Battalion on range. Left behind for orderly sergeant duty.
3. Another easy day as before.
4. Sergeant of guard 7.30 pm to 7.30 am.
5. Sunday. Off Guard at 7.30. Visit to Killinghall camp to see Bob. Enjoyable half day, back at 10.00.
6. Battalion left for firing practice at 6.15, back at 7.00.
7. Inspection by G.O.C. on parade ground. Afternoon Company drill.
8. Marking at Burton Leonard range for 18th. Back at 6.45.
9. Field operations and battalion drill at Hollin Hall.
10. Brigade field operations at Scarah Moor. Left camp at 8.00 back at 6.00.
11. Easy, waiting for orders home. Left Ripon 1.05, Bradford 2.50.
12. Sunday. At home.
13. At home.
14. At home.
15. Back at Ripon by 8.55 p.m. train, arrived 11.00.
16. Field Work with A Company above reservoir. After, lecture by Major Griffiths on parade ground.
17. Company drill and training practice on parade ground.
18. Fatigue work at transport shed.

Ripon. A youthful sergeant in full marching order.

19. Sunday. Church parade on Parade Ground. In orders for Sergeant A Company.
20. Removed to A Company. Medical inspection and company drill. Hut cleaning.
21. Short parade and hut cleaning. Easy afternoon.
22. Transport fatigues all day. Left Ripon station at 11.00 pm.
23. Pontefract 1.00 am, Swinton 1.50, Leicester 4.00, Banbury 6.00. Dinton 10.00 and to new camp.

NOTES

1. *A Ripon Record, 1887-1986*, Phillimore, Ripon Civic Society, 1986.
2. *ibid*.
3. *ibid*. The Radcliffe family had made their money in the Huddersfield textile industry, and the baronetcy was granted to Joseph Radcliffe for his exertions as a magistrate in putting down the Luddite risings in 1812.
4. I am indebted to the late Christopher J. Taylor, for the use of his grandfather's diary.
5. Sir Archibald Murray (1860-1945) was Sir John French's Chief of Staff. He was sent home after breaking down. His appointment as DCIGS was a consolation prize. He recovered to become Chief of the Imperial General Staff before being appointed to command British forces in Egypt in January, 1916. Although he re-organised the Canal defence system, he was replaced by Allenby and again sent home to be head of the army at Aldershot.
6. Taylor, *op.cit*.
7. Tony Miller, taped conversation with Steve Kerry, Bradford Industrial Museum
8. *ibid*.
9. Taylor, *op.cit*.
10. Officers' Records PRO WO/339.
11. *Yorkshire Observer*, 5 August 1915.
12. Information on Kennedy supplied by Colonel A. A. Fairrie, Curator of the Queen's Own Highlanders (Seaforths and Camerons) Museum, Inverness.
13. Walter Hare, taped conversation with the author.
14. Major-General Robert Wanless-O'Gowan (1864-1947), CB, CMG. commanded 31st Division throughout the War. He had served in the militia before joining the regular army (Scottish Rifles) in 1886. Married Alice Bland of Derryquin Castle, Co Kerry in 1887. He served in the Boer War at the relief of Ladysmith and was badly wounded at Spion Kop. He later commanded the 2nd East Lancs in India, and went to France as a staff officer with 5th Division in 1914. He was appointed to Command 31st Division at Ripon in August 1915.
15. *Yorkshire Observer*, 17 September 1915.

Pals striding out for the camera after a hot, dusty route march near Ripon. They appear to be carrying their No.1 dress.

Chapter Six

FOVANT

THE MAIN BODY of the two Bradford Battalions arrived at Dinton Station in a series of special trains after their overnight journey on the morning of Thursday, 23 September. They then marched the four miles to their new camp at Fovant. The Leeds and Durham Pals arrived the following day. They were to be at Fovant for two-and-a-half months and for most of that time believed they were going to France. If the outcome at the Battle of Loos had been different it is quite likely that would have been the case. Fovant was an isolated village in a valley near Salisbury and the traditional army training area of Salisbury Plain. The rolling countryside and chalk soil often reminded the Pals of the Somme in later years. After the Pals left, later units carved huge designs and badges into the chalk hillside, and these badges can still be seen today.[1]

The camp was built earlier in the year and first used by 26th Division, another Kitchener New Army Division. The 26th went to France 10 September as a reserve for the Battle of Loos, but never went into action before the battle was called off in October after the loss of 54,000 British casualties. The Pals were not too pleased with what they found at Fovant. The ground was muddy and it was difficult to keep clean. The huts were not as comfortable or as well equipped as at Ripon. Apart from one small public house and a Soldiers' Institute at the bottom of the lane leading to the village

Fovant Camp. Huts occupied by the Bradford Pals are on the right.

there was little to do by way of recreation. Unlike Ripon there was no town to walk round and the men soon got bored. Crown and Anchor games started up and the occasional rabbit hunt livened things up and added to the pot. Sergeant Harold Saville from Birkenshaw made his first diary entry at Fovant.

We have heard today that we are leaving for France in about five weeks. I have heard so many rumours that I do not know whether it is true. Anyway, we shall see. I have spent the evening from 6 o'clock until 10 playing solo. I have enjoyed it very much. It is the only way we have of passing the time here apart from sitting before the fire and listening to the cosmopolitan crowd of sergeants.

16/127 SERGEANT HAROLD SAVILLE M.M.[2]

The 93 Brigade Battalions were put together in four hutted units at the top of a hill looking across the valley next to the village. The Bradfords were sandwiched between the Leeds Pals and Durham Pals.

The pattern of activity at Ripon continued virtually unchanged, although a lot more time was devoted to shooting practice. Again the daily activity is detailed in the diary of Sergeant Herbert Taylor in Appendix B. The route marches continued as did the drilling, shooting practice and trench digging. The men were restive and bored and had almost come to believe they would never see overseas service. On several occasions troops on night marches got lost as their officers muddled map readings and geographical features. There was muttering in the ranks when it was noticed that both of the Pals' Colonels had a tendency to stay in camp during bad weather when the men were sent on route marches.[3]

Friday, 1 October. Brigade Day. Practising attack over moors and hills, climbing hedges and fencing, crawling under barbed wire, up hill and down dale. Returned 8.00 pm.   18/553 PRIVATE FRED CONQUEST[4]

Hitherto, the two battalion bands had been equipped only with drums and bugles, but at Fovant they finally received a full set of brass instruments – cornets, trumpets, trombones, clarinets, bassoons, French horns and euphoniums. Additional musicians were recruited and joined the Pals Battalions in Fovant – some in answer to advertisements placed in the musical and theatrical press, and others by word of mouth. Jock Ewart, (16/1723), the Bradford City and Scotland goalkeeper, was an extremely talented musician and joined the band of the 1st Pals as a cornet player at Fovant. Percy Bunney (18/1658) was a professional cornet player in the orchestra of the Ilford Hippodrome and found himself at Fovant after responding to an advertisement in *The Stage* magazine.[5] Nineteen year old Sam B. Wood from Stanningley was a solo cornet player at the Theatre Royal in Leeds when he joined the band of the 18th West Yorks with three other musician friends from Stanningley. All four were recruited by 18/1651 Sergeant Llewellyn Dixon, who probably got a bounty for doing so.

Llewellyn Dixon (clarinet) was Band Sergeant and Fred Power (18/636) Drum Sergeant, both old friends from the Bradford Alhambra. Sergeant Dixon had promised me Corporal's stripes and solo cornet position if I would join. He also recruited Willie Lambert (clarinet), Harold Bedford (Farsley Church

Entrance to Fovant Camp.

A bird's eye view of Fovant Camp.

Organist, who was to learn the clarinet) and Reg Wormald (French horn)
– all from the Stanningley area. Needless to say I did not get the promised
stripes. They already had a good solo cornet who was band cornet too, a
21 year old Kneller Hall man who came from Bradford City Police Force,
Corporal McLaughlin.

18/1655 Private Sam B. Wood[6]

Samuel Balmforth Wood (B.Mus., F.R.S.A.) – known as Sam B. – was
no mean musician. Within two years he was Bandmaster of the
Second Pals band at the age of twenty-five. In later years, he
achieved fame and distinction in the brass band community as a
composer and adjudicator in the Brass Band World Championships
at the Royal Albert Hall. He wrote the marching signature tune,
'West Riding', for the Championship winning Brighouse & Rastrick
Brass Band which they still use today. He also wrote a suite
'Bucquoy' and a march 'Le Fresnoy' as a tribute to his comrades in
the West Yorkshire Regiment. For many years he was music master
at Belle Vue Boys High School in Bradford and later at Morecambe
Grammar School. But his distinguished future was not known when
he and his friends arrived to a rather dusty welcome at Fovant and
discovered the transformation from civilian to military life.

We four Stanningley lads had arrived at Fovant camp about dusk and
after wallowing in the muddy camp lines trying to find out battalion,
tired and weary, we heard a band strike up. This roused our tired spirits
and we made our way to the sound of music. It turned out to be the 15th

Samuel Balmforth
Wood (B.Mus., F.R.S.A.).

West Yorkshire (Leeds Pals) band under a Mr Garside, with whom I had
often played professionally in Leeds, also Victor Marshall of Black Dyke who
came from Farsley, was in the band as solo cornet. At the end of the piece, with
happiness in our hearts, at locating someone we knew, we approached the
Officers' Mess outside which the band was playing. However our spirits were
very soon dampended for as we approached, although he recognized us,
Bandmaster Garside snapped out, 'What are you men doing here, clear out !' I
half remonstrated, but he certainly had no welcome for us, so we trudged away
feeling rather sick. At last we found our Quarter Master's billet hut, where we
were received very kindly, and they fed us and gave us a bed to sleep on.

18/1655 Private Sam B. Wood[7]

Sam described the culture shock of military life with the Pals at Fovant camp.

Morning came. The new environment was very exciting but bugles blew
much too early. After breakfast we met old friends, some very fed up with Army
discipline. They told us in no uncertain terms what 'Blankety' fools we were for
joining up. My school chum, Sam Cooper was on 2nd cornet in the band. I had
taught him, and he now put me wise as to what we were expected to do as
bandsmen. Up at Reveille, smartly make up the bed and out to the wash-house
where one could shave and splash about in the ice cold water. Then back to out
band hut for knife, fork and spoon. Breakfast of porridge and bacon, huge basins
of tea and chunks of bread. Dripping was also provided when we had a baconless
breakfast. One morning someone had made a mistake and gave us greasing fat!

Harold France, Bandsman.

Ugh! The cutlery did not half rattle on the tables and basins. After a couple of days my knife and fork had vanished, but my friend Sam Cooper soon 'won' me some more. He explained that this was a regular occurrence and that one had to replace any articles which vanished by 'winning' others when the owner was not looking. Sam had had six months training before I joined the Army. Our band practiced every morning, but as we had a lot of learners in the band these rehearsals were very boring to me and also to a cockney recruit, Peter Bunney, who had arrived from London the day after us. He was a good cornet player, and had come on the promise of a Lance Corporal's stripe straight from Ilford Hippodrome. We quickly became friends in distress and commiserated with one another at the cruel trick by which we had been lured into the Army.

18/1655 Private Sam B. Wood[8]

Berry of Hull, an enterprising firm of photographers arrived in the area in October to take photographs of the four Hull Battalions in 92 Brigade. Messrs Berry obviously networked well, for they took a splendid series of posed photographs of each unit in 93 Brigade as well as recording the Pals of Bradford, Leeds and Durham. Some examples are reproduced here.

In the middle of October, the Second Pals were joined at Fovant by their new Medical Officer, Lieutenant George Boyd McTavish, a Canadian. The Pals quickly took to him with great affection and gave him the nickname, 'Doc Mac'. The affection was mutual, as he wrote in a letter to a friend.

I've been real lucky – and am medical officer for the nicest bunch of boys you could meet anywhere. Am having just a fine time.

Dr G. B. McTavish, R.A.M.C. M.C. and two bars[9]

The doctor stayed with the 2nd Pals until the Spring of 1917, when he was struck down by serious illness after giving the Pals devoted and courageous service. By the time he left them he had been promoted to Major and been

18 West Yorks. Adjutant Captain Williams and R.S.M. Scott with Battalion HQ at Fovant.

awarded the Military Cross and two bars for going into No Man's Land to care for and rescue the wounded.

Dr George Boyd McTavish, from Winnipeg, Manitoba, was 31. Although 'Doc Mac' was a little older than his 1st Pals colleague Dr 'Paddy' Roche, he too had only recently graduated from Manitoba Medical College. He survived the war and became a much loved physician and surgeon in the northern outback area of Winnipeg. He was to serve again in the Canadian R.A.M.C. as a major for three years in the Second World War. He died in 1965 at the age of 82, having lived long enough to enjoy seeing his son made a judge. In his obituary, it was said he was the 'Albert Schweitzer' of the Canadian outback.[10]

Both Battalions contained a number of under-age recruits and no attempt was made to weed them out, even when the death of one produced evidence of his real age. Bill Brayshay (16/1391), was a strapping fifteen year old farm worker from Bradley near Keighley when he joined the First Pals at Skipton. He was only sixteen when he died of pneumonia in hospital at Fovant on 20 October 1915. His funeral was given full military honours on 23 October.[11]

There was one final visit to Bradford by the First Pals band for a week between 8-15 of November as part of a recruiting campaign in the city. Whilst they were there, they played outside the town hall around a mock tent guarded by sentries. On 11 November, they also played at the Scholemoor Cemetery funeral of a former Pal, Corporal J. G. Midgely. Midgley, a well qualified engineer, transferred to the Royal Engineers from Skipton because

Lieutenant John H. Robinson, 18th West Yorks and two sergeants loading a grenade launcher at Fovant.

of his technical knowledge. He was killed in a gas incident in France for which he was awarded the Distinguished Conduct Medal. Harold Saville described how an attempt was made to add interest to the endless shooting practice.

Monday, 15 November. Physical drill as usual in the morning. Went down to the range to fire Part IV. It was very interesting. They had two sections of four men who were supposed to be firing at each other but as that would be dangerous they fire at red tiles. They are arranged as below :

1	2	3	4	1	2	3	4	*Tiles*
1	2	3	4	1	2	3	4	*Men*

No 1 is supposed to be firing at No 5, No 5 at No 1. Therefore if 2 fires and hits his tile then No 6 is out of action and he gives his ammunition up to someone else. 16/127 SERGEANT HAROLD SAVILLE M.M.[12]

Towards the end of November a system of leave was introduced on a half company basis and a number of men did manage to make it home to Bradford, although the orders to embark for service abroad denied the opportunity to some.

The time at Fovant was used for another 'weed out' of the less fit and too old for foreign service. The too young were ignored. The most senior was Colonel Warden who relinquished his command of the 16th West Yorks on 5 December. He had taken over from Colonel Muller at Skipton, but now passed over command to Major H. H. Kennedy on a temporary basis. Major Kennedy took charge until the Battalion reached Egypt when it was expected a new Colonel would be appointed. Major Howarth and eight other officers left the 18th West Yorks and went to join the 20th West Yorks at Colsterdale, as did R.S.M. Turner. 16/19 C.S.M. Alfred Oddy was promoted to be Regimental Sergeant Major.[13] The 18th West Yorks Bandmaster Le Grove was another one left behind. He was an excellent bandmaster, but according to Sam B. Wood was rumoured to be approaching seventy. Sergeant Llewellyn Dixon, former clarinettist at the Alhambra Theatre took over the band.[14]

At the beginning of December the long waiting was finally over. Confusion and uncertainty as to the Pals destination continued to the end. On 29 November, staff at 31st Division HQ was warned that embarkation would begin for France on 9 December at Southampton and Folkestone, but within twenty-four hours this plan was rescinded. The change of plan was a direct result of the decision to evacuate the Dardanelles after the failure of the Gallipoli campaign. Kitchener returned to London at the end of November after inspecting the situation in Turkey, the War Cabinet resolved to evacuate the Dardanelles and alternative plans to cope with that decision now had to be put into place. It was clear that Turkish forces could mount a fresh threat on the Empire's life line, the Suez Canal. The Pals' destination was to be Egypt not France. Orders came to prepare to move out but no details were announced. On 2 December all leave was cancelled. Rumours flew that the Pals were destined for France, others said to Gallipoli. On Saturday, 4 December the Pals were paraded and issued with pith helmets and

Band of the 18th West Yorks at Fovant.

puggarees, but retained their normal khaki uniforms. On security grounds, no destination was announced. The men only discovered it was Egypt when they were on the high seas.

> *It was December when we left Fovant. It was snowing a bit and we were wearing pith helmets. We must have looked a comical lot in pith helmets. But anyhow, we used them when we got there. We'd all got gas helmets, everything ready for going to France and we just had to hand them in and just go. We didn't have lightweight uniform or anything, we just went as we were.*
>
> 16/853 PRIVATE FRED RAWNSLEY[15]

The final complement of the two Bradford Battalions leaving Fovant for Egypt was: 16th West Yorks: 29 Officers and 995 Other Ranks, (plus 18 horses and 55 mules). 18th West Yorks: 32 Officers and 995 Other Ranks, (plus 16 horses and 53 mules). The numbers included the Padre, Captain John Thornton, CF, and doctors McTavish and Roche. A nonconformist padre and a Roman Catholic padre attached to the 31st Division.[16]

Sunday was spent in a desperate cleaning up and packing exercise and Colonel Warden made his farewells and left the Battalion. He was not going with them and would be replaced by a new CO in Egypt. Just before midnight on Sunday, 5 December the men assembled in their companies and began the march to Dinton station.

Appendix A   Daily activity at Fovant Camp, 16th West Yorks

From the diary of 16/458 Corporal Herbert Taylor, 'E' Company, 16th West Yorks.
September 1915
24. Easy all day.
25. Cleaning up. Walk in afternoon. Wet night.
26. Church parade, Battalion Orderly Sergeant.
27. Physical drill, then easy.
28. On guard 7.30 (for twenty-four hours).

29. Off guard 7.30. Arrival of instruments.
30. Band practice all day.
October, 1915
1. Great Field Day.
2. To Salisbury, half day.
3. Sunday, Church parade.
4. Easy all day.
5. Easy morning, practice after.
6. Massed bands practice 9.45 to 11.00, afternoon same, retreat at 6.00.
7. Easy morning. Brigade away on last Friday's work.
8. Practice all day.
9. Practice morning, Tisbury after.
10. Sunday, Church parade, band in front to YMCA.
11. Practice before noon.
12. Easy.
13. Easy.
14. Practice before noon.
15. Practice.
16. Fatigues. Practice before noon. Visit to Tisbury, 5 sergeants.
17. Sunday. Church parade with band. Walk in afternoon, church evening.
18. Practice.
19. Easy.
20. Easy.
21. Easy before noon, practice after.
22. Easy all day till evening practice.
23. Funeral of Brayshay, D Company.
24. Sunday. Church parade cancelled owing to wet.
25. Practice all day.
26. Battalion Orderly Sergeant and practice in between.
27. Easy morning and afternoon. Officers Mess parade.
28. Easy morning and practice after.
29. Issue of rifles and bayonets.
30. Hut cleaning and practice in day.
31. Sunday, Church parade. Practice and digging.
November 1915
1. Shooting practice and digging
2. ditto.
3. ditto.
4. ditto.
5. ditto
6. ditto
7. Church parade.
8. To Bradford by 9.05 am train. Arrived Bradford 5.50 pm. Played in Town Hall Square.
9. Playing in Town Hall Square.
10. Playing in Town Hall Square.
11. Funeral of Corporal Midgley, Scholemoor.
12. Playing etc.
13. Funeral of Lance Corporal Halliday, Windhill.
14. Sunday. No Parade.
15. Back to camp 9.45 train. Arrived Dinton, 9.15.

16. Practice etc.
17. ditto.
18. ditto.
19. ditto.
20. Hut cleaning etc.
21. Church parade.
22. Practice etc.
23. ditto.
24. Massed practice before noon.
25. ditto.
26. ditto.
27. Visit to Tisbury with Bob.
28. Sunday. Firing on open range.
29. Firing.
30. Firing before noon. Funeral at Sutton Mandeville.
December 1915
1. Massed band practice before noon.
2. Practice, contrary orders re. leave.
3. Practice.
4. Mobilisation parade.
5. Sunday. Parade. Colonel Warden left battalion. Left Dinton at 1.30 am, 6 December.

Appendix B Officers of the 16th West Yorks. December 1915

	Appointed	Age
C.O. Major (temp Lt. Col). Walter Meredith Goodwyn	8.12.15	44
Second in Command Captain Humfrey Heyes Kennedy	3.12.15	33
Major Sydney Moore	26.11.14	38
Adjutant Captain Thomas Henry Russell	3.01.15	39
Captains		
George Stanley Blagbrough	23.09.14	34
Alan Clough	16.12.14	20
Frank Holmes	23.09.14	36
Robert William Hay Pringle	15.03.15	22
Henry Russell	29.11.15	38
Donald Smith	29.11.15	21
H.R. Watling	14.10.15	
Lieutenants		
Geoffrey Ambler Armitage	11.05.15	29
Sidney Leslie Frank Hoffmann	19.07.15	19
Frederick Robert Benson Jowitt	28.01.15	22
Owen Morgan	23.09.14	
Cecil Talbot Ransome	29.11.15	26
Frank Evan Russell	25.02.15	37
Robert Sutcliffe	19.07.15	34
Frederick Reginald Webster	19.07.15	37
Second Lieutenants		
John Speight Auty	29.04.15	31
F.O. Burnley	20.02.15	

	Appointed	Age
S.R. Cockrill	24.12.14	
W.F. Dawson	23.12.14	
Francis Martello Gray	16.05.15	
James Maximilian Harry Hoffmann	22.09.14	21
Charles Stuart Hyde	27.04.15	24
Charles Fraser Laxton	26.06.15	
Reginald Earle Laxton	26.06.15	
Sydney B. Newlands	18.05.15	20
P.C. Parker	26.06.15	
John Holdsworth Robinson	26.10.14	23
William Russell	01.06.15	37
Ralph Stead	03.04.15	30
Frank James Symonds	11.05.15	19
Quartermaster		
George Frederick Reynolds	24.10.14	40

Appendix C

Officers of the 18th West Yorks. December 1915

	Appointed	Age
C.O. Lt.Col. E. C. H. Kennard	20.07.15	40
Second in Command Major Albert William Robinson	15.03.15	36
Adjutant Captain Frederick Thomas Williams	01.08.15	24

Officers 18th (Service) Battalion (Second Bradford) at Fovant.
Back row: Capt. C.H. Keevil, 2/Lt G.F.D. Walker, Lt L.H. Bakes, Lt B. Hammond, 2/Lt H. Naylor, Lt M. Clough.
Second row from back: 2nd/Lt A. Doyle, Lt W.M. Wright, 2/Lt H.L. Dalley, 2/Lt S.H. Titford, 2/Lt A.H. Booth, Lt L.C. Watson, Lt J.R. Akam.
Third row: 2/Lt J.I. Wood, 2/Lt J.R. Thornton, 2/Lt W.J. Worsnop, 2/Lt C.M. Ray, 2/Lt F. P. Nowell, Lt O. Quitzow, 2/Lt W. Peace.
Fourth row: Capt. L.C. Baines, Capt. F.M. Horner, 2/Lt D.G.O. Hepworth, Lt H.E. Howarth, Lt H.E. Foizey, Capt. B. Tooke, Lt F.V. Robinson, Lt C. F. Cookson, Lt. A Cockerham.
Front row: Capt. F.T. Williams, Capt. D. Hellewell, Major Howarth, Lt-Col. E.C.H. Kennard, Major Robinson, Capt. C.S. Duckitt, Capt. J. Bland.

Captains

L. H. Bakes	01.12.15	
John Bland	01.09.15	46
Charles Stanley Duckitt	04.05.15	38
David Hellewell	04.05.15	
Francis Mariner Horner	04.05.15	37
Cecil Horace Case Keevil	01.10.15	34
W. H. Key-Jones	27.10.15	35
Bernard Tooke	02.10.15	28

Lieutenants

James Rhodes Akam	25.05.15	22
Morris Clough	26.05.15	23
Arthur Cockerham	03.04.15	39
Roland Sydney Cross	24.05.15	23
Harold Egbert Foizey	24.05.15	30
Alan Haworth	24.05.15	
Frank Victor Robinson	02.09.15	28
Frank Watson	01.08.15	
Lionel Cassels Watson	01.12.15	25

Second Lieutenants

Guy Johnson.Acheson	28.12.15	22
Allan Hodgson Booth	11.03.15	28
Harold Colley	02.04.15	24
Harry Leslie Dalley	25.05.15	
Robert Ivor Derwent	04.12.15	25
H.S. Naylor	25.05.15	
Francis Percival Nowell	09.06.15	21
Walter Peace	24.05.15	
C.M. Ray	26.04.15	
G.F.D. Walker	19.03.15	
John Leslie Wood	26.02.15	
John William Worsnop	06.04.15	22

Lieutenant & Quartermaster

Benjamin Hammond	11.03.15	

Dr George Boyd McTavish, wearing pith helmet, issued for tropics.

NOTES

1. The Fovant Badge Society does a good job now preserving the badges, and the area including the local pub is well worth a visit.
2. Sergeant Harold Saville M.M., first diary entry on 6 November, 1915. Diary kindly supplied by his family.
3. Notes by Brian Seekins from his father's recollections.
4. Fred Conquest. Diary at Bradford Industrial Museum.
5. Percy Bunney, notes kindly supplied by Martin Middlebrook.
6. Samuel Balmforth Wood, Personal notes and reminiscences kindly supplied by his son, Barrie Wood.
7. *ibid.*
8. *ibid*
9. G. B. McTavish, letter to a friend (12 January, 1916) in the Imperial War Museum collection, London.
10. Details of career in files of Canadian Medical Association, Ottowa. Information also supplied by W. A. B. Douglas, Directorate of History, National Defence, Ottawa, Canada.
11. Private Brayshay is buried in Fovant churchyard. His parents provided a civilian headstone unlike the other Commonwealth War Grave headstones in the same area. Unfortunately the grave became overgrown but it has recently been restored thanks to the Fovant Badge Society.
12. Saville, *op.cit.*
13. Conquest *op.cit.* Diary entry on 19 October re. Major Haworth and eight other officers.
14. Sam B. Wood, *op.cit*
15. Fred Rawnsley, tape with Steve Kerry, Bradford Industrial Museum.
16. Battalion War Diary.

Chapter Seven

THE MYSTERIOUS EAST:
EGYPT AND THE SUEZ CANAL

It was sand here, sand there, and more sand everywhere.
16/61 PRIVATE TIM WHARTON

THE MAIN BODY of the two Bradford Battalions, together with the Leeds Pals and the Durham Pals left Fovant Camp just before midnight on Sunday, 5 December 1915 so as not to be observed. They left in groups of two companies at a time, marching four miles to the main London and South Western Railway line at Dinton station. Here, no less than ten special trains set off at regular intervals during the very early hours of Monday morning to travel to Liverpool where they embarked on the Canadian Pacific liner R.M.S. *Empress of Britain*. For security reasons, the men had no idea where they were going.

The transport sections of the four battalions with their horses and mules had a much shorter journey to Devonport where they boarded the Federation Steam Navigation vessel *S.S. Shropshire*.

> *It was December when we left Fovant, and it was snowing a bit and we were wearing pith helmets. We must have looked a comical lot in pith helmets. We'd all got gas helmets, everything ready for going to France and we had just to hand them in and just go. We didn't have any lightweight uniform or anything like that, we just went as we were.*
> 16/853 PRIVATE FRED RAWNSLEY[1]

Tim Wharton, the stretcher bearer/bandsman who had bought his own drum, described the journey in his diary.

> *We left camp at Fovant at 10.30 pm on 5 December (Sunday) and arrived at Dinton Station at 1.30 am arriving at Liverpool Dock Station at 9.15 am. On emerging from the station we found ourselves alongside the boat that was to carry us to the land of the SPHYNX, PYRAMIDS, and after walking about some time we embarked on the good ship 'EMPRESS OF BRITAIN'.*
> 16/61 PRIVATE TIM WHARTON[2]

The *Empress of Britain* and her sister ship the *Empress of Ireland* were built at Govan shipyard in 1906 for the Canadian Pacific Line's trans-Atlantic route between Liverpool and Quebec. She had eight decks, and at 14,500 tons, was about a third of the size of the *Titanic*. With a service speed of 20 knots, she took six days to cross the Atlantic. Normal pre-war capacity was 1,860 passengers and crew. For many of the Pals this was their first sea voyage and for many, their maritime exploits had been limited to the rowing boats on Manningham Park Lake. Following the *Titanic* disaster in April 1912, passenger liners were required to carry sufficient lifeboats for their maximum

The **Empress of Britain.**

capacity. The *Empress of Britain* was equipped with 16 steel lifeboats 20 collapsible Englehardts 4 canvas and 2 canvas making a total lifeboat capacity of 1,960. There is no evidence that this lifeboat capacity was increased when the vessel was converted to be a troopship at the beginning of the war. The vessel was equipped with the Marconi wireless system for emergencies (although silence would have to be observed to avoid detection by German submarines) and each man had a life jacket. Presumably, the hope was that there would be time to call for help from the two escorting destroyers and torpedo boats which accompanied the *Empress* as far as the Atlantic. After that, the *Empress* was on her own. The men would have to take their chance in the water until rescue came – not an appetising prospect in the dark, cold December waters of the Atlantic. In the days before the convoy system, and obviously without radar and air support, there was little defence against a well aimed U-Boat torpedo other than a zig-zag course and speed. Private Laurence Greenwood, of the First Pals was a clerk in Brigade H.Q. and recorded the number on board as 145 officers, 41 Warrant Officers, and 4,352 men plus 300 crew. It was reckless to pack nearly 5,000 men into a single vessel with a lifeboat capacity of under 2,000 on such a long voyage.[3]

When the *Empress of Britain* edged away from the Liverpool quayside at 10.00 am on Tuesday, 7 December 1915, she carried nearly three times her normal peacetime capacity. On board were the four Pals Battalions of 93 Brigade, plus 31st Division's Pioneer Battalion (12th KOYLI), and a party from the Army Service Corps. The lower cabins had been cleared out to form large mess areas where the other ranks could sleep in hammocks suspended over tables and benches. The officers enjoyed cabins on the upper decks and excellent food. According to a Leeds Pals officer:

I really can hardly bear to think of the hardships (the men) are bound to go through during this voyage. They are packed absolutely like sardines right away below where on ordinary occasions, cargo and the steerage are.

LIEUTENANT S. M. BICKERSTETH (15TH WEST YORKS)[6]

Tim Wharton, normally a cheerful soul, was not impressed by the conditions or the food which seemed to consist mostly of inedible mutton stew.

We were herded together like as many pigs, and all through the voyage fed in a similar manner.

16/61 PRIVATE TIM WHARTON[7]

Fred Conquest was feeling unwell but was delighted to discover that he was luckier than most:

> *7 December. Sailed at 10.00 am. First day afloat not feeling well, being suffering from an inoculated left arm and an attack of influenza since 5th and swollen face since 1st. Pleased to say I have a nice bed. C & D Coys. (who were disappointed at not having leave) have had their luck returned, being the only ones on board with decent beds, the remainder of the Battn. And the 15th and 16th and Durhams, are all in hammocks & and in low stuffy places below, where they are crowded and very bad indeed. The boat is too crowded, about 5,000 soldiers on besides officers.*   18/553 PRIVATE FRED CONQUEST[4]

Tim Wharton had a home leave shortly before leaving Fovant – the result being a son he never saw grow up. Tim died of wounds on 29 July 1918. The infant son grew up – Tim's diary and drum became his most treasured possessions.[10]

> *We were escorted down the Irish Sea by two destroyers, and as the sea was on fairly good terms, everybody was in good spirits on the first day of our voyage.*
>   16/61 PRIVATE TIM WHARTON[5]

As darkness fell the escorting warships peeled away and the *Empress* sailed on through the St Georges Channel into the Atlantic. It was exactly seven months since the blue riband holder the *Lusitania* had been torpedoed by the U-20 in the very same waters with the loss of 1,200 lives.

The better informed may have pondered on the fate of the *Empress of Britain's* sister ship, the *Empress of Ireland*, which had sunk in only fourteen minutes in May 1914, with a loss of 1,014 lives after a collision with another vessel in the St Lawrence.[12] How could nearly 5,000 men possibly disembark in fourteen minutes if the U-20 or any of her sisters were lurking within torpedo range? It was not the most comforting thought as they struggled to sleep in swaying hammocks in the bowels of the ship.

> *What a different tale on the following day. On rounding the south coast of Ireland things became a bit rough and the effects of this soon became apparent to us, myself included, because I must confess that whatever my ambitions as a soldier are I am a rotten sailor.*   16/61 PRIVATE TIM WHARTON[6]

The stench of men being sea sick combined with primitive toilet arrangements was appalling in the confined space of the lower decks. A diet of boiled mutton for the main meal did little for the appetite. A number also suffered the after effects of the tropical injections on the day before sailing. The men had little space to move, and spent most of the time sitting at tables underneath their hammocks with their kit gathered around them.

An incident early in the voyage still caused resentment in the breast of one young under age soldier seventy-five years later. Private Sam Wainwright (16/402) and his mates decided to get some fresh air by squatting on the floor of an upper deck corridor. Shortly after Sam had got comfortable, the Commander of 93 Brigade Brigadier Kirk and his entourage came pounding down the corridor in a flurry of red tabs and highly polished boots on some urgent mission of command. 'The Brigadier kicked my legs and shouted, "Get out of the bloody way, soldier"'.[6] Sam was furious and wrote home to his brother detailing the incident concluding with 'Don't join the Army. They don't treat you with respect'. Sam's letter was subject to censorship and read by his Company Commander Captain Pringle. Sam was summoned by the Captain:

> Captain Pringle said, 'Look here, Wainwright, you can't send this. It will cause a lot of bother if it gets into a newspaper. It's insubordination to the Brigadier. You and I have a choice. I can either drop this letter quietly over the side of the ship, or I can put you on a charge. Which do you want?' Well, I told him to throw the letter away. It was quite decent of him really, because I could have got into a load of trouble.
> 16/402 PRIVATE SAM WAINWRIGHT[7]

Brigadier Kirk's short fuse may have been caused by stress and ill health. Although the Brigadier was only forty-nine, within five months he died from a heart attack shortly after the brigade arrived in France.[8] Fred Conquest recorded the daily routine on board ship of those who were well enough to fulfil it.

> This is our usual Daily Routine:
> Reveille 5.30
> Make up beds and stow hammocks
> Breakfast 7.10
> Physical drill in bare feet 8.30 to 9.00 o'clock
> Grand Inspection 10.00 o'clock
> Captain of Ship and Officers inspect everything.
> Dinner 12.10
> Tea 5.10
> Bedtime 8.00 o'clock (we usually turn in about 7.00 o'clock as there is nothing to do and we are very sleepy).
>
> Thursday, 9 December. Had an extra breakfast, Palethorpes sausages, and plenty, as many were poorly and couldn't eat. Not been sick as yet. Swelling in my right bottom jaw much worse. Don't know what it is, very painful. The tea is always putrid. I can drink very little of it. Sea fairly rolling all day, rocking the boat nicely. Sea getting rougher. Boat heaving sideways.
> 18/553 PRIVATE FRED CONQUEST[9]

Four days after leaving Liverpool, the *Empress of Britain* sailed through the Straights of Gibraltar under cover of night. There was a noticeable change as the vessel entered the Mediterranean, for even though it was December, the temperature rose and the sea was much calmer. The tedium of the day was relieved by the issue of beer at 3.00 pm although the men had to pay 4d (1¹/₂p) each, to purchase their allowance. Nevertheless, the next few days were far from uneventful as Tim Wharton recorded in his diary:

> From this point to the end of the voyage it was one series of exciting events. A certain portion of the men were told off last night to sleep on deck, in fact as many as could find room, and I can assure you there was no little competition for places as almost everybody favoured sleeping on deck to sleeping below because had anything happened during the night those below would have drowned like rats in a trap. On Monday, 13 December at midnight whilst going

full steam ahead we ran into another vessel.[18]
The collision had occurred with the French steamship *Dajurjura* which was on the regular mail run from Salonika to Malta carrying nearly a hundred passengers including the wife of the French Ambassador to Greece. Both vessels were sailing on a zig-zag course without lights as a precaution against submarines. The *Empress of Britain* hit the *Dajurjura* amidships bow end on cutting into the French vessel so severely that she sank within thirty minutes.

At first the *Empress* re-started her engines. Rather than endanger the lives of nearly 5,000 troops by stopping to pick up survivors, she prepared to move off leaving the French vessel to its fate. However, an escorting destroyer flashed the message, 'No danger, stand to and pick up survivors'.[19] Two French seamen were killed in the collision, but everyone else was picked up and by 1.20 am. The damaged, but still water-tight *Empress*, sailed on towards Malta. It was a reverse of the incident when the *Empress of Ireland* sank within fourteen minutes after a collision with the Norwegian collier *Storstad* in 1914. This knowledge prompted Tim Wharton to record,

> *It was an experience I shall not readily forget and had our boat been 20 seconds slower we should without doubt have suffered the same fate as our sister ship the* Empress of Ireland.   16/61 PRIVATE TIM WHARTON[20]

The *Empress of Britain* entered Valletta harbour in Malta fifteen hours later on the afternoon of Tuesday, 14 December. The Leeds Pals band played on deck and put on a show of imperial might as they entered the Grand Harbour. Sergeant Harold Saville was impressed with what he saw.

> *At about three o'clock in the afternoon we sighted Gozo island and about an hour later Malta. The first sight was absolutely magnificent. The first thing we noticed was the tents of the soldiers garrisoned there. The towers and castle-like structures with their coloured domes were shining in the sun. As soon as we got in the harbour mouth, we were surrounded by the Maltese boys in their little boats crying out for silver coins. If you drop them in the water near their boats, they dive in and catch them two or three feet below the surface. I was surprised to see the number of cruisers and battleships there were in the harbour, not to mention submarines, destroyers and innumerable steamers and moror boats. The thing we were able to interest ourselves with most was the method of coaling. The coal lighters were drawn alongside the vessel both port and starboard and the natives carried large baskets full of coal on their back. I saw one man carry a lump four men had to lift. We couldn't go ashore, so I didn't see much of the town. My only regret was that I did not get some lace for Florence and sisters.*   16/127 SERGEANT HAROLD SAVILLE M.M.[21]

Malta was the rendezvous point for meeting up with the transport sections of 93 Brigade who arrived on the same day in the S.S. *Shropshire*. The *Shropshire* sailed from Devonport on the same day the main body had left Liverpool. Each of the four battalions in the brigade started out with 18 horses (for the officers) and 55 mules for transport. Three officers and 102 other ranks formed each battalion's transport section on the voyage.[10]

The *Shropshire* was built at John Browns in Glasgow in 1911. The

Government met all running costs during her times as a troop ship, and in addition paid 15s 5d (77p) per head for each voyage to her owners, the Federal Steam Navigation Line of London. The Canadian Pacific Line received 17s (80p) per head for the *Empress of Britain*. At 12,184 tons, the *Shropshire* was not much smaller than the *Empress*, but she was nowhere near as fast with a cruising speed of only 13 knots as against 20 knots making her more vulnerable to submarine attack. As an extra precaution during daylight hours men were stationed a yard apart all around the deck to keep watch.[11]

Conditions on the *Shropshire* were extremely uncomfortable and even worse than on the *Empress of Britain*. There was much sea sickness, especially in the Bay of Biscay, and this wasn't helped by the overpowering stench of urine and manure from several hundred mules and horses. The animals undoubtedly suffered too. They had to stand throughout the near three week voyage and frequently slipped and fell in their own faeces as the ship rolled about. Over thirty animals were thrown overboard because of sickness and accidents during the voyage. Working with frightened animals on a rolling ship was unpleasant and dangerous with the real possibility of serious accidents and kicks.

It took three days to repair the collision damage to the *Empress of Britain* in Valetta and to re-supply and coal her. Whilst the officers were allowed to explore ashore the other ranks were confined on board throughout the three days. The men were kept occupied on fatigues loading stores and supplies that would be needed by the brigade in Egypt. There were the usual drills and exercises and in between times they were entertained with a daily programme by the band of the Leeds Pals. The Bradford bands' instruments had been stowed away so Sam B. Wood, the first cornet in the 2nd Bradford Pals, was an interested spectator.

I first heard 'Keep the Home Fires Burning' aboard ship and felt very homesick. I spent my time writing melodies of hymns etc., and poems, as well as making rough sketches of the passing coastline, Malta etc.,

18/1655 PRIVATE SAM B. WOOD[12]

There were also endless games of crown and anchor. For nonconformists such as Fred Conquest, games of chance were anathema, but he was certainly impressed with what he saw in the Grand Harbour and had no doubt that Britannia still ruled the waves. Malta was a hive of naval activity in what were to be the final days of the ill-fated Dardanelles campaign in Turkey.

We are in one of the finest and best harbours in the world It is a port for boats of every description. There are British Battle Cruisers, more still of French, one or two Russian and Japanese. There are several British torpedo boats and submarines and three fine hospital ships.

18/553 PRIVATE FRED CONQUEST[13]

The Pals sailed from Malta at 6.50 am on Friday, 17 December. Their presence and departure had almost certainly been noted by enemy agents and they soon felt the consequences. The short two and a half day run between Malta and the Suez Canal was a favourite hunting ground for the German U-Boats.

It was common knowledge that we should have to keep our eyes skinned as

German U-Boat preys on Allied shipping in the Mediterranean.

enemy submarines were on the look out for us and we were not long kept in doubt because the day after we left Malta one was sighted about 3.15 in the afternoon. Our ship's gun was immediately trained on it and we sent them a greeting in the shape of a shell which fell a little short. After a few minutes another put in an appearance, round went the gun and in a few seconds another shell was on its way. This fight between our gunner and the Captain of our ship and the submarine working for the chance to send 6,000 lives into eternity was one which left an everlasting impression on those privileged to witness it.

16/61 PRIVATE TIM WHARTON[14]

According to an officer in the Leeds Pals who was on duty as Orderly Officer, the torpedo only narrowly missed the troopship.

They had a shot at us but the torpedo missed us, the wash from our propellers helping to turn it away. LIEUTENANT S. M. BICKERSTETH, 15TH WEST YORKS[17]

If the torpedo failed to damage the *Empress*, it certainly damaged the trade of one of her crew who had a nice little sideline as the resident tattooist. Private Abe Nott (18/988) of the 2nd Bradford Pals had just received the first few punctures on his arm when the alarm went off. By the time the alarm was over he had changed his mind. Private Nott carried a small but indistinct black mark on his arm for the rest of his life. It was a reminder, he used to say, of the day when both a tattooist and a U-Boat failed to get him.[18] That the U-Boats failed was not for the want of trying. There was another near miss in the middle of the night.

In the early hours of the following morning another one was sighted. This time our enemy managed to discharge a torpedo at us which only missed us by 10 yards thanks to the successful way in which our ship was manoeuvred Our Gunner was forbidden to shoot as it was feared a panic may have been caused by the incident taking place so soon after the other and in the dead of night. We escaped further attention from our unwelcome visitor owing to our far superior speed which enabled us to soon get out of range.

16/61 PRIVATE TIM WHARTON[30]

The *Empress of Britain* arrived in Alexandria at 7.00 pm on Sunday, 19 December without further incident. The mails were disembarked but the men stayed on board because this was not their final destination. At 4.00 pm the following day, the *Empress* and the *Shropshire* sailed for Port Said. In the early light of dawn the Pals saw the impressive statue of Ferdinand de Lesseps, the instigator of the Suez Canal, gesturing towards Canal entrance.

After a dash through a dangerous part we arrived at PORT SAID at 6.00 a.m on Tuesday, 21 December. We anchored just outside the Suez Canal. We remained on board until the following day when we disembarked, and none of us were sorry to once more be on Terra Firma after 16 days of anxiety on board Most of us were very hungry and eagerly anticipating getting some decent food. We were formed up on the dockside and marched to our camping ground on the banks where after pitching our own tents we proceeded to settle down as best we could. It was sand here, sand there and more sand everywhere.

16/61 PRIVATE TIM WHARTON[31]

For the Pals Battalions of 93 Brigade, nine days made all the difference in gaining an extra medal. By arriving for active service and stepping onto foreign territory in a war zone on 22 December 1915, they qualified for the first of the three 'Pip, Squeak and Wilfred' Great War service medals, the 1914/15 Star.[29] 94 Brigade (the Accrington, Sheffield and two Barnsley Battalions) also served with 31st Division in Egypt but did not disembark at Port Said until the early days of January 1916. Although they arrived less than a fortnight after the Bradford, Leeds and Durham men (and the Hull Battalions in 92 Brigade), 94 Brigade missed the 31 December 1915 deadline for the award of the Star. The fact that they were on the high seas and had been attacked by torpedoes from probably the same U-Boats as 93 Brigade counted for nothing. The Sheffield City Battalion veteran Reg Glenn told the author that this omission always rankled with veterans throughout 94 Brigade in later years.[32]

*   *   *

The Pals Battalions of 31st Division were to be in Egypt for a little over two months. Their function as part of the Imperial Strategic Reserve was to defend the Suez Canal against attack by the Turks, and to help with the construction of a new defence system to the east of the Canal. In practice they saw no military action apart from the occasional accidental friendly fire incident.

The Suez Canal had been opened in 1869 as the long dreamed of link between the Mediterranean and the Red Sea. It had taken ten years to build and was 101 miles long. In the days of shipping and Empire it was the most vital communication link between East and West. Before the War the Turkish (or Ottoman) Empire included Palestine with only the Sinai Desert acting as a natural buffer between Turkish forces and the Suez Canal. Egypt was technically a part of the Ottoman Empire, but in practice it operated as a British protectorate. In January 1915 no less than 70,000 British troops were in Egypt, half of them to defend the Canal, and the 1st Australian and New Zealand Army Corps (Anzacs) were already in training for what became the Gallipoli (or Dardanelles) campaign in April 1915. The aim of the Dardanelles campaign was to seize Istanbul, knock Turkey out of the War, and free up a passage to the Mediterranean for the Russian fleet.

In February 1915 the Turks crossed the Sinai Desert and made a determined effort to capture the Canal but were repulsed after heavy fighting. In December 1915 when the Pals arrived, a small Turkish force under the German General Friedrich Kress von Kressenstein still lurked in the Sinai making nuisance raids. The importance of the Canal as a supply route to India, Australia and New Zealand could not be underestimated and its loss or disruption would be a massive blow to the Allied war effort. The worry now was that the evacuation of the Dardanelles after the failure of the Gallipoli Campaign would free up the Turkish Army to make another determined effort to capture or severely disrupt the Canal. Hitherto most of the defensive line had been on the west bank of the Canal, but a Commission under Major-General Sir Henry Horne recommended that the defensive line be built on the east bank far enough away for the canal to be out of Turkish artillery range. The Pals were to be part of the workforce and defence force needed to complete the construction of this programme.

The Pals spent their first few days in Egypt, including Christmas and New Year, encamped on the banks of the Canal next to Port Said awaiting the arrival of the rest of 31st Division. The pitching of tents was somewhat chaotic and not without incident. The 2nd Pals bandsmen had decided to stick together rather than to be with their Companies.

The bandsmen wanted to be together, so with much loud persuasion,

Alexandria quayside.

Sergeant Dixon, now in charge picked out three tents for the band. Someone 'won' a mallet and a box of tentpegs and we were soon installed. However we had unfortunately taken possession of tents in the Officers' lines. A kindly questioning voice was soon heard, 'What are those men doing in those tents?' With a little prompting Sergeant Dixon replied, 'I've claimed these three tents for the band, sir'. Alf Scott, the Quartermaster Sergeant and 'baby' brother of R.S.M. Harold Scott, had now appeared and roared 'Take the Bloody Band out and burn them !!!' Sadly we trooped away with our kits and had to find places with our Companies. Poor Sergeant Dixon! He was rather a frail person who should never have been in the Army but for being a fine clarinetist. He had to account for the mallet and box of pegs. The Quartermaster fired the question continually at him, 'You got a mallet and a box of pegs'. He must have been told this a dozen times, and we were all within earshot. It had a peculiar rhythm, and all through the war we chanted it whenever anyone lost anything. However, the bandsmen soon scrounged the missing articles, and Sergeant Dixon was half-forgiven.

18/1655 PRIVATE SAM B. WOOD[33]

On 23 December the 16th West Yorks came under the command of a new C.O. Lieutenant-Colonel W. M. Goodwyn, a forty-five year old Devonshire Regiment veteran of the Boer War. Colonel Goodwyn took over from Major H. H. Kennedy who had been in temporary command during the voyage.

On the same day, C Company, consisting of 216 men and six officers under the command of Captain Blagbrough, left Port Said to relieve the Gurkhas who were guarding the passing station at Ras El Esh.

The Suez Canal was 101 miles (160 kilometers) long, and with the exception of the lakes, the navigable width was never more than twenty-two metres. This meant that two average size vessels could not pass. Accordingly, passing stations had been built about every ten kilometers (six miles). The passing stations were about 300 meters long and provided places for southbound ships to pull in so as to let northbound ships pass. Ras El Esh was the first passing station on the Canal, fourteen kilometers south of Port Said, and vulnerable to any coastal attack by the Turks.

The remaining men of the 16th West Yorks and the 18th West Yorks had a relatively easy time whilst they waited for the rest of 31st Division to arrive. Physical drill took place every morning and afternoon with a bathing parade in the Canal, but Tim Wharton's hope and pre-occupation with getting some decent food was to be disappointed.

Our first day's food consisted of ships biscuits hard as stone & bully beef, so our expectation of a decent meal was hardly fulfilled.

16/61 PRIVATE TIM WHARTON[34]

Harold Saville soon noticed new companions he would be close to for the rest of the war.

The sand where we are encamped is full of ants and sand lice. We are getting lousy by now, but it does not matter. I am as happy as a mud lark. The only thing that bothers me is that I have not got a penny.

16/127 SERGEANT HAROLD SAVILLE M.M.[35]

Port Said, entrance to the Suez Canal.

After a couple of days the men did get paid and had an opportunity to supplement their meager diet.

> *After a few days we received our pay, 3s 6d (17p). No back pay as yet, but we felt rich, really rich. It was a great joy to supplement the rations at 7.30 on the morning. An enterprising Arab had set up a small brazier at the end of the lines on which he cooked the small Egyptian eggs, and one could get a small teacake with a fried egg on it for a penny ha'penny. We had hoped for a decent Christmas Dinner, but unfortunately on that day the biscuits provided were green mouldy and unfit to eat. We had to fill up with bully beef.*
>
> 18/1665 Private Sam B. Wood[36]

Attempts were made by the Nonconformist Chaplain to arrange some Christmas celebration and a decent Christmas meal for the men in 93rd Brigade – but at a cost.

> *Saturday, 25 December. Fine sunny day which makes it difficult to realize it is Xmas. 4 pm. About 500 Non-conformists had dinner at the Casino Palace Hotel, a first class place. We were charged 2s 6d [12½p] and had turkey and plum pudding which certainly made it feel more 'Christmassy' than anything although we did not get big portions as we do at home.*
>
> 18/553 Private Fred Conquest[37]

Tim Wharton was less impressed. His motivation for attending the dinner had more to do with hunger than religious observance.

> *Christmas Day was passed in a comparatively quiet way. A dinner was provided at the Casino Palace Hotel for Wesleyans and Nonconformists for which a charge of 2s 6d was made and in anticipation of easing my hunger I had my name entered on the list of those wishing to go, but am sorry to say it was a complete failure. I was a deal more hungry when I had finished than when I began.*
>
> 16/61 Private Tim Wharton[38]

Sam Wood and the band of the 18th were luckier than Tim on Christmas day, although they played for their supper.

We were ordered to play at the Officers' Dinner held at a large hotel in Port Said. After the performance we were given a slap up meal of all the left overs, chicken legs (in our hands) and Christmas pudding on plates.

18/1655 PRIVATE SAM B. WOOD[39]

Charles Pickworth, the extremely tall bass drummer in the First Pals band, was feeling extremely sorry for himself. He had gone to guard Ras El Esh with C Company, and it was a miserable Christmas Day. '25.12.1915. – Christmas Day. I have had no sleep for three days and only a biscuit for dinner.'[40] Three days later Private Pickworth complained in his diary that his face was covered in boils and sores which was extremely painful in the desert heat. For Sergeant George Ball, there was a succinct entry in his diary,

XMAS DAY. Church Parade. Passes from 2 o'clock till 9.30 p.m. Good time. Tea 1s 9d [9p] – French Picture Place 7¹/₂d [3p]. Five packets cigs from canteen profits. Spent up. Nearly lent N. 1/- [5p]. Everybody drunk.

18/605 SERGEANT GEORGE BALL[41]

Port Said was a bustling, noisy exotic port city where the Canal joined the Mediterranean Sea. It hummed with exotic activity and catered for the needs of (some you could write home about, some you couldn't) a large and transient population of sailors and soldiery whose numbers had dramatically increased with the war. It offered pleasures and dangers, and to most of the Bradford lads of 1915 it was totally different to any previous experience in their lives. It was a strange, bewildering place to a teetotal methodist like Fred Conquest. It was an assault on his senses and sensibilities.

Port Said is a strange place. The houses are all on the 'flats' system. They have straight roofs and from a distance of 200 or 300 yards it looks like a pile of unfinished buildings as though half built and then left. The lower classes keep goats and hens and pigs inside the houses. There are people of all races here, Arabs, Egyptians, French and many different coloured races, and from this fact naturally there are scores of types of dressing. Most of the inhabitants are very scantily clothed in dresses of gorgeous colours. In the streets men and boys pester you in droves hawking smallwares, cigarettes, oranges etc., All over the place are drinking Saloons, High Class with an orchestra under a verandha and lounges outside and very low class affairs. Nearly all shopkeepers speak English and many of them speak 7 to 10 languages. 18/553 PRIVATE FRED CONQUEST[42]

The Arab Quarter had a fascination for the soldiery.

We visited the city streets in the evenings. We were warned to go out with two or three others, side arms to be worn (bayonets) and not to visit Arab Quarters where the loose women were. There were many strange sights in the streets, conjurors, bird trainers, tumblers, all these performing on their own little carpets for a stage, and the trinket or fruit sellers with their trays in front of them. Also the money changers. These all formed a challenge to the rough lads from White Abbey, Bradford. One would be arguing the price of something, then with about a dozen pals gathered round, up would go the tray and all the

Char-Wallas plying their trade.

boys would grab anything that came their way and off like lightning before the screaming arab could complain to the military police.

18/1655 PRIVATE SAM B. WOOD[44]

Not surprisingly, the locals also got their retaliation in and there was a constant air of threat and danger to Port Said.

> *One afternoon later, I was having a swim near the canal entrance, where many creek-like shallows were to be found. A small rowing boat was coming my way and as it smoothly passed by, I saw to my horror it contained a dead soldier with his tongue almost cut out and hanging out of his mouth. He had been found in the Arab Quarter! I was almost sick at the sight.*

18/1655 PRIVATE SAM B. WOOD[45]

There was a hint of 'The Lord punishes all evil-doers' in Fred Conquest's diary,

> *Boxing Day. Two soldiers drowned while bathing. One soldier (K.O.Y.L.I.) found dead on sands. Believed to have been drunk and murdered by Arabs. We are not allowed to go in what is called the Arab Town which is a terrible place of vice and treachery, but the fellows slip in and have a lively time. The shops are open on Sundays as usual, the Sabbath is scarcely regarded here.*
>
> *29 December. A soldier of the E. Yorks died from cruel treatment of Arabs.*

18/553 PRIVATE FRED CONQUEST[46]

Illness was another very serious and real danger. Even though they had received two inoculations against enteric fever (typhoid) on the voyage, Tim Wharton noted in his diary that 16/845 Horace Seekins, and 16/846 Private William Heaton, had been admitted to hospital with the same illness, as were two men in the 18th Battalion.[47]

No doubt the fever was caught from eating food outside the normal ration issue to assuage a constant hunger. The Army authorities were aware of the problem, and Section Orders of 93rd Brigade detailed the official scale of rations to take effect as from 1st January 1916. There was a difference between what was available at Port Said and 'the equivalent' desert rations available in El Kantara.

19 – Scale of Rations

For all European Troops in Egypt with effect from 1-1-16 will be as follows:
Meat 1lb; vegetables ¹/₂ lb; salt 1 oz; bread 1lb; potatoes ¹/₄ lb; pepper ¹/₃₆ oz; tea ⁵/₈ oz; sugar 3 oz; mustard ¹/₅₀ oz; bacon 4oz; cheese 3 oz; jam lb.

Scale of equivalents

1lb meat becomes 1lb preserved meat; 1lb bread becomes 1lb biscuits or ³/₄ lb flour; ¹/₅₀ oz mustard becomes ¹/₈ oz curry powder; ¹/₂ lb fresh vegetables becomes

*¹/₄ lb fresh vegetables plus 2 oz rice and 3 oz potatoes and 4 oz onions.
Condensed milk at the rate of 1 tin per 16 men, in lieu of cheese ration.
C.A. Howard, Major, Brigade Major, 93rd Infantry Brigade.*[48]

Whether the men actually received all of what was still a very impoverished, and not particularly healthy, diet is doubtful, judging by their frequent comments and complaints about the food in their diaries and letters.

On New Year's Eve the 18th West Yorks left Port Said by train for a two-and-a-half hour journey alongside the Suez Canal to El Kantara nearly thirty miles to the south. It was to be their base for nearly two months until they left Egypt. Fred Conquest recorded his impressions of El Kantara in his diary,

Fri 31 December. Left Port Said at 8.45 am and had a pleasant journey in an open train along the side of the Suez Canal to Kantara. Arrived 10.00 am. Pitched tents 1 o'clock. We are camped on a sandy plane not far from the railway and Suez Canal. There are just a few remnants of buildings scattered about which are all that remain of Kantara which was a decent sized town until it was shelled by the Turks in the earlier part of the war. The few broken down places that are left bear evidence of this. It is very hot here through the day but comes cold at night. Camels are used a good deal for carrying water and supplies etc. The desert all around us is entrenched and dug-outs made. The 18th D.L.I. (Durham Pals) are close to us. The Leeds Pals are spread along the Canal side and the 16th (1st Bradford Pals) have remained at Port Said.

18/553 PRIVATE FRED CONQUEST[49]

Quartermaster Sergeant Joe Parker found himself on guard duty at the precious fresh water tank and met some of the Mysore Lancers who were also on guard duty,

Made friends with 3 sepoys and had a good day with them (Lator Singh, Rama and Kalas). Spent night in a homemade tent. Bitterly cold at night and warm during day.

CQMS JOE PARKER[50]

The rest of 31st Division arrived at Port Said on 5 January 1916. On the same

Port Said.

day, A, B and D Companies of the 16th West Yorks left Port Said and joined up again with C Company on their way to be near the 2nd Pals at El Kantara. The 16th had had an uncomfortable night.

> *On the night of the 4th of January we struck our tents in a drenching rain but luckily were able to sleep the night in some unoccupied tents nearby & on the following morning were astir by 4 o'clock getting ready for moving.*
>
> 16/61 Private Tim Wharton[51]

Both Battalions stayed in El Kantara or the nearby points 70 and 80 for the remaining eight weeks of their stay in Egypt.[52] El Kantara was the largest passing point on the Canal forty-five kilometres south of Port Said, halfway between Port Said and Lake Timsah. Before the war it was a small settlement and provided a small ferry service for an ancient camel route used by caravans travelling between Egypt and Syria. But as Fred Conquest recorded, it had been shelled by the Turks in 1915 and was now reduced to rubble.

The Pals pitched their tents on the bank of the canal, and for the first two weeks both battalions stayed in the immediate area providing guards for the Canal, digging trenches round the edge of the area, and helping to build a light railway. Light railway it may have been, but the rails (captured in German East Africa) were extremely heavy and Fred Conquest recalled in his diary how exhausted the men were carrying them. The food was still as bad as ever and hunger became an obsession. There was also a route march to 'toughen up' men who had been so recently confined to ship for over two weeks.

> *On the 7th we were paraded in full marching order and taken for a very gruelling march up the desert for about five miles. It was, under the circumstances the worst march I have ever done. The sun was scorching & the sand was very deep & consequently the going was very heavy. Several were compelled to fall out under the strain.* 16/61 PRIVATE TIM WHARTON[53]

But even though everything was exhausting thirsty work in the heat, there were a few bright spots. There was an endless procession of fascinating vessels from around the world including warships and large passenger liners where the passengers could help to brighten the Pals' day.

> *The passengers were mostly Americans as far as we could see, and later these good people proved to be very generous. As they passed by they threw into the water or right on to the banks tins of 50 or 100 Players or Capstan cigarettes which were soon retrieved. These well known brands were very welcome, as the smokers rations were named 'Red Hussar' or 'Beeswing' which were rather inferior. As I did not smoke, I was able to exchange my ration for money or chocolates which had started arriving from home.*
>
> 18/1655 PRIVATE SAM B. WOOD[54]

There were two other major bright spots. The first was the very welcome arrival of the first mail from home on 9 January. Several of the men received cakes or other food from home and it was shared out between them. Then, on the 11 January 93 Brigade held a Gymkhana and Sports.

> *The first event was a four legged race, the middle man to be turned about. I was in that, but we came in fourth just missing the prizes. Second there was a*

tug of war on mules which was very funny and won by 16th West Yorks. There was a relay race won by 18th Durhams. Then we had an exhibition of tent pegging with lance and sword by the Mysore Lancers. We had a Sack Race and a Boot Race. There was a Grand Kantara Derby for officers of 93 Brigade. Colonel Goodwyn of 16th came in third. Then there was a camel race by the Camel Corps... very interesting... about twenty ambling along in a bunch. Last there was a Musical Ride by the Mysore Lancers which was cleverly done without a hitch.

16/125 SERGEANT HAROLD SAVILE [55]

Norris Garside wasn't the only Pal to strike up a friendship with the Mysore Lancers. Sergeant Savile soon made some friends.

In the evening two Lancers came into our tent and we sang songs. I got them to write their names for me on the previous page in Hindustani and I have written their names in English underneath. Sergeant Syerhider and Corporal Mohammed Amom.

Native vendors were never far away.

16/125 SERGEANT HAROLD SAVILE[56]

A few days later, anticipating some of the culinary delights of Bradford in the late twentieth century, the extremely hungry Bradford Pals enjoyed a surprise feast.

In the evening our Mysore Sergeant Major came to see us and brought his orderly and his cook who carried some plates of curried rice and stewed goatflesh, also some native bread. They also got some stout. We had a scrumptious meal, in spite of the fact that everything was served with fingers.

16/125 SERGEANT HAROLD SAVILE[57]

Within a couple of days Harold arranged something in return.

The Lancers came down. The Sergeant Major's orderly and cook asked us to send to England for a signet ring each and wanted to give us a £ 1 each. We sent to Fattorini's for them.

16/125 SERGEANT HAROLD SAVILE[58]

One of the few other pleasures the Pals could look forward to at El Kantara in the Egyptian heat was bathing parade in the Suez Canal. The Battalion bands were used to play the troops down to the Canal where the 2nd Pals first cornet, nineteen year old Sam B. Wood, performed a remarkable solo worthy of inclusion in the Guiness Book of Records.

We frolicked in our 'birthday suits' and many of us were able to swim across the canal and back again. After a while the men in the companies were called out of the water to indulge in a short spell of P.T. As we had to play the troops back to camp we were excused the P.T. and while we were sat about – still in our birthday suits – we discussed the possibility of playing a tune with only our heads above water. We argued about it for a while but I was itching to prove it could be done.

It wasn't long before I was in the water with my cornet; the rest of the troops had by this time reached the banks and were taking a casual interest in the bandsman in the canal with his cornet. I took as deep a breath as possible and started to play a popular Sankey tune, second only to Colonel Bogey in popularity. The army words were 'When this blinkin' war is over'. The whole battalion immediately took up the second line, "Oh, how happy we shall be!"

I managed to finish the whole verse, although I must admit I was gasping at the last line. I was given a special cheer as I finished, and even the adjutant gave me a smile as I emerged, having proved it could be done.

18/1655 PRIVATE SAM B. WOOD[59]

Fred Conquest always enjoyed Sunday evenings in the desert at Kantara. He gives an evocative description of the events involving the Padre Thornton of the Pals and Padre Chappell of the Leeds Pals, and probably Sam Wood and his cornet, in his diary entry for 23 January.

On Sunday evenings we usually have a sing-song arranged by our Chaplain, and all the favourite hymns and songs are sung, with a cornet as accompaniment. We had an extra do last night. It sounds lovely and brings crowds of boys round. You can hear it such a long way on the sands. The following are examples of how appropriate the words are:

'Lead Kindly Light' – all the light we have is candles.

'Just as I am' – No Sunday clothes or anything special, just in the Khaki suit you have worn for over six months Sunday and weekday.

'Nothing in my hand I bring' – Most of the fellows may be broke, but there's no collection, everyone is welcome to come and sit on the sand and join in. The Reverend Gentlemen sit in the centre and tell a story or two. It is an

A hungry CQMS Joe Parker enjoyed a curry provided by Mysore Lancers, Lator Singh, Rama and Kalas.

acknowledged fact by officers and men that nothing at all carries our minds back to our dear homeland so vividly as the singing of all the old tunes. I have a lump in my throat, and I can put here with confidence that I enjoy them more than anything out here.

18/553 PRIVATE FRED CONQUEST[60]

Private Tony Miller had a less happy memory and Captain Charles Duckitt had a very narrow escape. No doubt there were jokes about the Captain's name afterwards but neither of the men involved thought the incident was funny, especially after a similar accident had result in a death in the Leeds Pals.[61]

We were practicing firing ball ammunition you know. The order from Captain Duckitt was 'Load, Fire, Release'. He was stuck out in front of me on horseback and he says whatever you do keep your fingers outside the trigger guard. I heard him say it, but me, instead of keeping my fingers outside the trigger guard it went inside and I pulled the trigger. I missed Captain Duckitt, but anyhow, he said, stand up the man that fired that shot. I stood up and I did 28 days field punishment for that, out in Egypt, and I came back under escort to France.

18/856 PRIVATE TONY MILLER [62]

Field punishment Number One consisted of being tied to a fixed object for up to two hours a day, which in the heat of Egypt, would have been even more unpleasant than usual. Two other members of the Pals suffered a similar punishment, but this time for stealing from the parcels of their comrades.[63]

The 'pleasures' of Kantara were shortlived for the First Pals. Apart from a small supply section that remained in Kantara, the whole battalion moved off seven miles east into the desert with their tents and full equipment on 19th January to Point 70. A few days later, half the battalion went further on to Point 80 with half remaining at Point 70. They were to be there for nearly six weeks.

Reveille at 6 o'clock. Paraded at 8-30 ready for marching out. We had absolutely full pack, blanket, ground sheet, and everything. It was the hardest work I have done in my life. We arrived here at Hill 70 at about 12-20 and got our tents pitched, after having a good can of tea and some stew. We saw three of the men from the outposts bring in five poor Arabs, mostly girls dressed in rags. It was very pitiful to see them. 16/127 SERGEANT HAROLD SAVILLE M.M.[64]

Point 70 and Point 80 were advanced defence post consisting of trenches and sand bags, with a further ring of smaller satellite outposts beyond them, and were in an extremely exposed uncomfortable situation. There were frequent sightings of Turkish cavalry scouts in the far distance, but the enemy never came near enough to be in firing range. The men soon discovered that high winds came in the night and their tents often blew down. The sand made it very difficult to get a proper purchase with their tent pegs.

Water was at a premium and brought in by camel and Sergeant Harold Saville noticed something that caused resentment in the other ranks.

As there was not much water we were not allowed any to wash in but I noticed that the officers had sufficient to have a bath in. I do not think that a real

British officer would allow his men to see a thing like that.

16/127 SERGEANT HAROLD SAVILLE M.M.[65]

The water situation improved when additional supplies arrived by camel train from Kantara, and the other side of other rank/officer relationships is shown in a diary entry by Charles Pickworth, the bass drummer in the band.

4.2.16 Defence work. Fell sick, sunstroke. Captain Russell very kind and made me a good tea.

16/213 PRIVATE CHARLES PICKWORTH[66]

The next three weeks were uncomfortable but uneventful other than the trial of two men caught stealing parcels, and a visit from the Commander in Chief in Egypt, General Sir Archibald Murray, 12 February.

He congratulated us on our happy appearance and the quality and quantity of our work.

16/127 SERGEANT HAROLD SAVILLE M.M.[67]

Happy appearance or not, there were cases of sickness, diarrhoea, and a number of men broke out in boils or had painful and severe dental problems. CQMS Joe Parker in the Second Pals was taken to the Casualty Clearing station with a displaced cartilage in his knee. He was transferred to Port Said for an operation at the 3rd General Hospital,

The finest hospital I have yet seen. 175 beds in one ward and spotlessly clean.

CQMS JOE PARKER[68]

The Second Pals were more fortunate than the First Pals and for the most part remained to guard Kantara on the Canal, but smaller parties did go out to Points 70 and 80 on a rota basis.

Trenches were dug, sand bags were filled and piquet guards mounted. There was the occasional football match with the two internationals, Dickie Bond and Jock Ewart playing on a pitch very different to Valley Parade. On 16 February Harold Saville went for a walk round the camp and everything seemed so quiet,

You could not tell that there was such an item as an enemy. If something doesn't happen soon this diary will not be worth reading.

16/127 SERGEANT HAROLD SAVILLE M.M.[69]

Five days later the First Pals did come under fire and made a very hurried retreat back to the camp from their digging operations. The fire was from a misdirected British artillery practice.[70]

The fact that the Pals were in Egypt for only two months was in part due to the fact that casualties in the evacuation of the Dardenelles were astonishingly low (only two wounded compared with an original estimate of 50%) and the Pals were becoming surplus to requirements.

There was also a positive reason for the move. Large events were afoot in Europe on the Western Front and the Pals were destined to be part of it. In December, 1915, an Anglo-French conference at Chantilly had decided on a new Allied offensive the following summer. The aim would be to push the Germans out of France and to win the war by the end of 1916. Shortly afterwards, Sir John French was replaced by Sir Douglas Haig as Commander in Chief of the British Expeditionary Force on the Western Front.

The failure of the Dardenelles campaign gave added weight to the voices of Haig and the new Chief of the Imperial General Staff, Sir William Robertson, who argued that the war could only be won on the Western Front. Detailed planning began for the joint Franco-British offensive in the Summer. On 14 February, Haig argued that British forces were 75,000 under strength in 39 Divisions and that it would take time to train any new troops for the offensive when they arrived.[71] The Franco-British plans were disrupted on 21 February, 1916 by a massive German attack on the French in the symbolic Verdun area. Additional British troops were now even more urgently needed on the Western Front and within days, 31st Division received orders to move to France.

On 29 February, Q.M.S Parker was still in the hospital in Port Said and was appalled to hear that 31st Division were to leave for France. There was every likelihood he would be left behind. He had been told his problem was cruciate ligament damage, that no operation would take place and he would have to rest. He appealed to the doctor to contact Major Albert Robinson.

Monotony something awful. Sisters very kind indeed. Heard that 31st Division going to France, so I appealed to the Doctor to let me go with them. Doctor saw the Major who after a bit of persuasion allowed me to go with them.

Q.M.S. PARKER[72]

Also on 29 February at only 24 hours notice, after nearly six weeks at Hill 70, the First Pals packed up and marched the seven miles to Kantara.

Bradford Pals officers visit the Sphynx. Captain Alan Clough, first left, Captain David Helliwell, second left, unidentified, Lieutenant Francis Horner, on right.

We set off from Hill 70 at about 3.30. My kit was fearfully heavy but when we got on the hard road within about a mile of camp it was alright. When we got to Kantara there was a great change. Lots more troops had come, there were camels galore. I heard that there were nearly fifteen thousand camels on the canal defences. We bivouacked on some very wet sand on the western bank of the Canal. Reveille was called at 3.30 a.m. and eventually we entrained in the same cattle trucks at about 9.30, arriving at Port Said about 11.00 and embarked on the SS Minneapolis *at 2.30 p.m. We prepared to leave at about 5.00 p.m. but owing to fouling the anchor of a British cruiser, we did not get clear of harbour until about 8.30 p.m*16/127 SERGEANT HAROLD SAVILLE M.M.[73]

It was 1st March, 1916. The First Pals' band played on deck as the *Minneapolis* left harbour. They were on their way to France.

C.Q.M.S. Parker, delighted to be re-united with his mates in the Second Pals, followed a few days later on the HMT *Ivernia*.

NOTES

1. Private Fred Rawnsley (16/853) taped interview with Steve Kerry, October, 1980, Bradford City Industrial Museum archive.
2. Kerry, ibid.
3. Private Tim Wharton (16/61). Diary in possession of family. Copy with author.
4. Private Fred Conquest (18/553) diary, in possession of the family.
5. For details of the Empress vessels see the book 'Forgotten Empress' by David Zeni, published by Halsgrove 1998.
6. Letter to his father, in Bickersteth Family War Diary (in possession of family). The actual numbers of troops on board, 145 officers, 41 warrant officers, 4,352 other ranks plus over 300 crew', was recorded in notes kept by 16/112 Private Laurie M. Greenwood, clerk to 93rd Brigade (kindly supplied by his family).
7. Wharton, op.cit.
8. Conquest, op.it.
9. Wharton, op.cit.
10. Information supplied to author by family. Private Wharton is buried at Longueness Souvenir Cemetery, St. Omer. He was 34.
11. Wharton, ibid
12. Zeni, op.cit
13. Wharton, op.cit
14. Private Samuel Fritz Wainwright (16/402), interview with author, July, 1991.
15. Ibid
16. The Battalion War Diary of the 16th West Yorks notes the death of Brigadier Kirk on 12th May, 1916. Brigadier General Henry Buchanan Kirk, son of Lt.Col. T.B. Kirk, had served with the Argyll and Sutherland Highlanders before the War and died at Le Treport hospital near Dieppe. He is buried in Le Treport Military Cemetery.
17. Conquest op.cit.
18. Wharton, op.cit.
19. Bickersteth, op.cit.
20. Wharton, op.cit.
21. Sergeant Harold Ireby Saville M.M., Diary.
22. Battalion War Diary, 16th West Yorks.
23. Information supplied by the National Maritime Register of Troopships, Greenwich.
24. Sam. B. Wood. Op. cit.
25. Conquest, op.cit.
26. Wharton. op cit
28. Bickersteth, op.cit.
29. Information supplied to the author by Abe Nott's family.
30. Wharton, op.cit.
31. ibid.
32. Reg Glenn (12/928) Sheffield City Battalion, 12 Yorks and Lancs, 31st Division, in conversation with the author 16th January, 1993.
33. Wood, op. cit.
34. Wharton, op. cit.

35. Wood. op. cit.
36. Saville. op.cit.
37. Conquest, opus cit.
38. Wharton, op. cit
39. Wood. op.cit.
40. Pickworth, op.cit
41. George Norman Ball, diary.
42. Conquest, op. cit.
44. Wood, op cit.
45. ibid
46. Conquest, op. cit.
47. Battalion War Diary, and Wharton diary, op. cit.
48. Section Orders, No III Section Canal Defence Force.
49. Conquest, op. cit.
50. Parker, Diary.
51. Wharton, op cit.
52. Battalion War Diaries.
53. Wharton, op. Cit
54. Wood, op. cit.
55. Saville, op.cit
56. ibid
57. ibid
58. ibid
59. Wood op.cit
60. Conquest, op. cit.
61. See *Leeds Pals* in this series by Laurie Milner.
62. Tony Miller, taped by Steve Kerry, 10/06/1981.
63. Saville, op. cit,
64. ibid.
65. ibid
66. Pickworth, op. cit.
67. Saville, op. cit.
68. Parker op.cit.
69. Saville. o.cit
70. ibid.
71. Haig Diary, 14th February, 1916 in The Private Papers of Douglas Haig, 1914-1919, ed. Robert Blake, Eyre & Spottiswood, 1952.
72. Parker op.cit.
73. Saville. Op.cit.

Dredger near Pals base at El Kantara.

Chapter Eight

FRANCE: THE WESTERN FRONT

March to June, 1916

A S THE BRADFORD PALS sailed across the Mediterranean, Falkenhayn's German 'mincing machine' was inflicting enormous damage on the French Army at Verdun. The original plan for a massive joint Anglo-French offensive with the aim of defeating the Germans and ending the war in 1916 was completely disrupted and had to be abandoned. As the French poured men into the defence of Verdun it became clear that any summer offensive would now have to be a largely British affair with a minimum of French participation. British and Empire troops manned eighty miles of the Western Front from the sea at Nieuport in Belgium almost as far as the River Somme in Picardy in France. The French Armies manned the rest for over three hundred miles to the Swiss border. Revised plans envisaged an offensive where the two armies linked up. The Bradford Pals were to be part of it and their destination on the front was the northern part of the Somme area between Albert and Arras.

HMT *Minneapolis* arrived in Marseilles with all of the First Pals and 197 of the Second Pals at 1.30 p.m. Sunday 6 March. Major Kennedy, with the two Transport Officers, Lieutenants Frank Russell (16th West Yorks) and Arthur Cockerham (18th West Yorks) and their two groups of thirty-three other ranks, arrived in Marseilles on the HMT *Northland* on the same day. Apart from the four chargers ridden by the two colonels and the second in command in each battalion, all the animals that had gone from England (plus camels that had been acquired in Egypt) had been handed over to 155 Brigade at Kantara. The two transport sections had a much easier time than on the way out.[1]

The food and accommodation on the Atlantic Transport Company's *Minneapolis* was much better than on the outward journey on what the men described as the 'Empress of Starvation'. Apart from a brief alarm about a fire, there were no U Boat scares and the journey was pleasant and uneventful. The former Red Star liner, *Northland*, had the unusual distinction of a name change in 1914 – her previous name, *Zeeland*, had been deemed too Germanic. Much to everyone's annoyance after the long sea voyage, the men were kept on board ship and not allowed to disembark until the following day.

Other groups from the Second Pals arrived on HMT *Ivernia*, HMT *Manitou* and HMT *The Briton* on the 11, 12 and 15 March respectively. No doubt they were glad to be on dry land again because the journey had not been without hazard. The *Manitou* had been in scrapes the previous April at the beginning of the Dardanelles campaign when a Turkish torpedo boat had missed her with three torpedoes off Smyrna.[2]

On 23 March, two weeks after landing the Pals in Marseilles, the *Minneapolis* was to be sunk without warning by a torpedo on a return trip from Marseilles to Alexandria. Fortunately very few were on board at the time and only twelve lives were lost.

HMT Ivernia.

Nor was the *Ivernia* invulnerable. The Pals may have been more nervous if they had known that Captain Turner, former master of the ill-fated *Lusitania*, was now skipper of the 14,000 ton Cunarder. The Pals luck held, but Captain Turner's didn't. *Ivernia* was torpedoed and sunk by the *U47* off Greece 1 January 1917 on a return run from Marseilles to Alexandia, carrying 2,400 troops of the Argyll & Sutherland Highlanders. Thirty-six crew and eighty-four soldiers died. *Ivernia* had the dubious distinction of having the tallest funnel (106 feet) ever installed on an ocean liner, and this may have made her more visible to the periscope of a U Boat.

HMT Manitou.

The food on the *Empress* may have been bad, but with a top speed of 20 knots she could outrun U Boats which had a surface speed of 17 knots. The *Minneapolis* and the *Ivernia* both had a top speed of 16 knots.[3]

The First Pals saw their first Germans 7 March when they disembarked. They experienced yet again that Army life often involved standing around waiting for something to happen.

Spent most of the morning walking about the quay, eating oranges and watching German prisoners of war doing work about the dock. They live and sleep in a couple of ships which are lying a few yards from ours. They are an extremely well made lot. I should think they must have been part of the Prussian Guard.

We were entertained by a little boy playing the cornet. Left the ship about

5.00 p.m. After a bit of a march around arrived at the station at 5.30. There were still some stores to get aboard so we did not set off until 7.30 p.m

We were fortunate enough to get into 2nd Class carriages. Our party consisted of the CSM, CQMS and D Coy Sergeants. We all went to sleep as soon as we got started as we could not see anything and we were all very tired.

16/127 SERGEANT HAROLD SAVILLE[4]

The journey north was extremely slow and circuitous with many stops and starts. As the train edged slowly northwards towards Paris, and then out again towards Picardy. Tim Wharton noticed the differences in landscape, but,

Far more dramatic was the number of women in black we saw as we passed through the towns and villages – a very serious sign of what war has meant to the home life of France, and it served to remind us of the serious work that was waiting for us.

16/61 PRIVATE TIM WHARTON[5]

It took over two days to reach Pont Remy where the Pals finally detrained at 7.00 p.m. on 9th March, 1916. The remaining groups of Second Pals followed in the next few days. They were less fortunate than the First Pals who had carriages. They had to make do with the famous 40 hommes/8 cheval trucks,

Cattle trucks. There were forty in a wagon or eight horses. We used to stop for meals and make tea from the engine. We had bully beef sandwiches. It were so slow you could get off't train, relieve yourself, and get on again.

18/1446 PRIVATE GILBERT ISLES[6]

Colonel Goodwyn the First Pals CO was unwell throughout the journey. He was taken off the train at Pont Remy and sent to hospital in Abbeville. The Battalion War Diary gives no details of his illness. Two weeks later it was reported that he had been evacuated to hospital in England. Major Moore took charge for two days until Major Kennedy arrived from Marseilles[7]. At the age of forty-five, Colonel Goodwyn was relatively old to command a front line battalion. Nevertheless he eventually recovered and returned to France in August, 1916 as CO of the 2nd Manchesters (to which Wilfred Owen was later attached). He survived the war and resumed a peacetime career with his old regiment, the Devonshires.[8]

Pont Remy is on the banks of the River Somme about four miles south east of Abbeville and was fairly close to Sir Douglas Haig's HQ at Mareuil. The surrounding villages were a hive of Army activity as a holding area. After detraining in the dark, the First Pals faced a seven mile march with full packs and equipment to their billets in Merelessart. It was a dark miserable march and they shivered in a blizzard as they marched.[9]

After gathering ourselves together we set off for our billets which we were told were seven miles away, and you will readily imagine after being so confined for so long we were very stiff and sore. We reached our appointed place just before midnight after one of the most punishing marches I have ever done. Our billet for B Coy turned out to be an old mill that had been standing empty since the outbreak of war, and we had to sleep on the damp brick floor. We were beginning to notice now what active service conditions were really like & I presume we shall yet be worse off.

16/61 PRIVATE TIM WHARTON[10]

The Transport Sections arrived the next day having acquired new animals to replace the ones left in Egypt. Looking after transport in what was still a largely pre-motor age was a formidable exercise. 'Farmer' Frank Russell and his thirty-three men in the First Pals Transport Section had care of two chargers, 15 draught horses, 9 pack horses, 20 draught mules, 4 Field Kitchens, 1 Officers' Mess cart, 2 water carts, 9 limbers and 1 maltese cart.[11]

Tim Wharton described the scene in Merelessart.

Most of our time is taken up with perfecting our bayonet fighting and marching to accustom our feet to the change from sand to hard stony roads, and many are the blisters that are prominent just now. The village where we are is Merelessart and is some few miles behind the first line trenches, but nevertheless near enough for us to hear the artillery shaking hands in Arras.

The sudden change from the great heat of the desert to the snows of northern France naturally was the cause of our doctor being very busy for some time, but no serious case has yet cropped up.

16/61 PRIVATE TIM WHARTON[12]

The rest of the Second Pals arrived in groups between 13 and 18 March and were based in the nearby village of Citerne.

They were certainly kept hard at it with drill, bayonet practice and no less than three route marches of over twenty miles. Groups of officers and NCO's were sent off for specialist instruction in trench warfare, including bombing, mining and anti-gas training, and a number visited the front line trenches in the Colincamps sector between Albert and Arras on the Somme.

Both battalions stayed in Merelessart and Citerne, until 25 March. They were better fed than in Egypt but they noticed the change in climate. The only tropical equipment they had been issued with was a pith helmet and puggarees. They were pleased to be wearing the heavy serge khaki which had made them sweat in Egypt but kept them warmer now as the snow continued to fall. Two bright spots were an inter-battalion football match 20 March, and receiving Christmas parcels from the Lord Mayor of Bradford belatedly on 24 March. A few lucky ones managed to get a few days home leave – with priority given to those who had missed the last leave at Fovant, – but instructions came to move forward to the trenches long before everyone was able to do so.

On 25 March, both battalions began a slow move towards the Front line. The long cross country march was done in stages over a number of days via Airaines, Vignacourt, Beauval, Beauquesne, Marieux, Louvencourt, Bertrancourt, Beaussart and Mailly Maillet.

Many of the men found the march extremely punishing and several dropped out including Norris Garside who was so desperate to stay with the Pals despite a cruciate ligament injury in Egypt. Norris struggled on and eventually made it back to the Pals after a further stretch in hospital. Fred Rawnsley also suffered in the march from Airaines to Vignacourt but revived somewhat later when he discovered that his fluent French brought a response.

Marched from Airaines to Vignacourt. Absolutely beggared. Big blister on heel. Got pally with a young woman in village.

16/853 PRIVATE FRED RAWNSLEY[13]

As they got nearer the front line they moved at night to avoid observation by enemy aircraft. They finally arrived at billets in Mailly Maillet just behind the front line on the night of 31 March. They were at the northern end of what is now known as the Somme in the Colincamps sector facing the Redan Ridge and the fortified village of Serre. Their baptism of fire came the same night with an artillery barrage on Mailly Maillet, but fortunately there were no casualties. Shellfire damage to the eastern end of the village church can be seen to this day.

Germans bombarded our billet. A good start. Enemy aircraft very busy.

16/212 PRIVATE CHARLES PICKWORTH[14]

They moved two miles up the road to Bus-Les-Artois on 3 April, and were cheered to receive a new set of clothing and steel helmets. Over the course of the next three weeks, the men were introduced to the front line trenches, sometimes in small groups, and sometimes at full company

31st Division men, Leeds, Bradford, Sheffield, Barnsley Pals, receive a warm welcome in France.

strength, and sometimes as part of a working party.

Diaries were now forbidden and letters were heavily censored, but fortunately for the modern researcher, some items still managed to get through. On 16 April, Charles Pickworth recorded in his diary,

Trenches for the first time. Very lively. Up to the knees in mud.

16/212 PRIVATE CHARLES PICKWORTH[15]

Charles was the tallest man in the First Pals and cut a splendid figure when he played the bass drum in the band. Up to the knees in mud meant it must have been very deep.

At the same time his band colleague, Bugler Vincent Phillips, smuggled a letter home to his family to record his first impression of the trenches.

It is surprising how used you get to the bullets flying over, but if you keep your head down, you are even safer in the trenches than in your billets. Of course you have only to stop one to get a knock out. They make it as comfortable as possible, we have fires every four or five bays. In our bay we had charcoal but no firewood and I didn't feel inclined to go across to the German trench and borrow some...We get cigarette and tobacco rations, 20 cigs and 1 oz bacca every week for the duration. Teetotallers cannot give their rum away as the Officer deals it out, not with a pint pot either. I am enclosing this in a chap's green envelope to be posted from Bradford as we can say practically nothing through our censor.

16/566 PRIVATE VINCENT PHILLIPS[16]

Both Bradford Battalions experienced a change of command in the first few weeks after their arrival in France with younger men taking over in each case. As we have noted, Colonel Goodwyn left the First Pals because of illness. Major Humfrey H. Kennedy stepped up to take over command with Major Moore who had joined the Battalion in the autumn of 1914 as his second in command.

The Second Pals also saw changes at the top within a month of their arrival in France. Colonel E.C.H. Kennard and his second in command, Major W.G. Johnson, were replaced by younger men on 17 and 18 April a few days before the Battalion took over a sector of the line for the first time. Both officers were sent back to England. No reason was given in the Battalion War Diary or in Divisional and Corps records. One can only speculate that Division had found them wanting given the strenuous nature of trench life. Both men were replaced the following day by officers with experience of the front.[17]

A number of men now began to receive specialist training and a Trench Mortar Battery was set up. Douglas Hunter (16/228) was one of them, and he was later awarded the D.C.M. in 1918.

By a strange coincidence, the Second Pals' new C.O. had the same surname as his predecessor although there is no known connection. Lieutenant Colonel Maurice Nicholl Kennard, M.C., was thirty-two years old and had been second in command of another 31st Division Pals Battalion, the 13th York & Lancs (1st Barnsley Pals) at Ripon and in Egypt. Maurice Kennard's family was well connected having made a fortune in

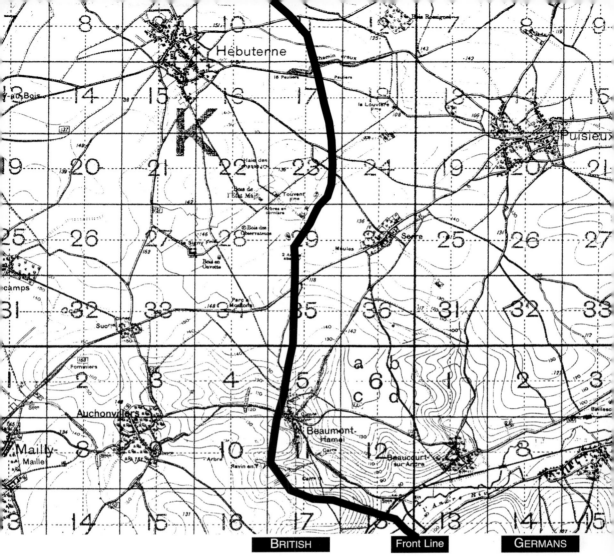

BRITISH   Front Line   GERMANS

banking in the eighteenth century and then married into the aristocracy with a country seat in Hampshire[18]. In 1902 the eighteen year old Kennard joined a good cavalry regiment, the 6th Dragoon Guards (Carabiniers), as a second lieutenant. By 1910 he had risen to be adjutant and was promoted captain in 1913. The outbreak of the war saw him in the thick of the action at Le Cateau. He was wounded at the end of October, 1914 in the Cavalry Division's desperate attempt to hold the Messines Ridge when he was awarded the Military Cross.[19]

By the summer of 1915, Maurice Kennard had recovered sufficiently to be promoted to Major and was transferred to be second in command of the 1st Barnsleys at Ripon. His experience of trench warfare would have been particularly useful in their training, but Barnsley miners must have been a new experience to an officer from the rather swell Dragoon Guards.[20]

The 18th West Yorks quickly became attached to their new C.O. and his

Captain F.T. Williams, Adjutant of the Second Pals, operating a sniperscope at Redan Ridge, May 1916. A complicated arrangement for operating a rifle in the trenches in safety. Manipulation of the bolt was achieved through transmission, via a series of levers. Thus reloading could take place without disturbing the laying of the weapon.

courage on 1 July at Serre was often recalled by survivors.

The new second in command, thirty year old Major Herbert Francis George Carter, had also seen his share of action and was to play a very significant part in the history of the Second Pals. He succeeded Maurice Kennard as C.O. on 1 July after the assault at Serre and commanded the Battalion until it was disbanded in February, 1918. He, too, had demonstrated his courage and in 1914 was the first officer in the K.O.Y.L.I. to be awarded the Military Cross [21].

Herbert Carter came from a military family (his father was Brigadier General F.C. Carter) and was educated at Wellington and Sandhurst. He had strong West Yorkshire connections through his mother, a Thornhill of Fixby Hall, Huddersfield. The Thornhills were Yorkshire gentry back into the middle ages. Their wealth grew in the industrial revolution when coal was found on their land between Huddersfield, Wakefield and Dewsbury.[22]

Carter joined the local Regiment, the Kings Own Yorkshire Light Infantry, in 1904 when he was eighteen. He served for a time in Crete and was clearly an able and intelligent young officer. He achieved rapid promotion to full lieutenant and was made assistant adjutant of 2nd KOYLI shortly after his twentieth birthday. His time in Crete gave him a taste for foreign travel and he pursued an unusual career leaving the Battalion to enlist on a language course. He served in Russia and Japan as an attaché at the British Embassies having become one of the Army's few first class interpreters in Russian and Japanese. There may have been connections with the Intelligence Service, and his post war service in

Vladivostok, where he helped to train the White Russian forces may have had more to it than linguistic fluency. He was also a gifted musician and artist, and it may be that his foreign travels developed his cosmopolitan taste for Turkish cigars and astrakhan collared overcoats.[23]

Carter, too, was well connected. His wife, Grace, was a Guinness and Carter was sufficiently well known to the Royal family for the King's personal secretary to write enquiring after his health when he was taken seriously ill in Russia in 1919. Sadly, Carter died of pneumonia in Russia in 1919 shortly before his daughter was born. Grace eventually re-married to Air Marshall Sir John Cotesworth Slessor, one of the architects of British air strategy during and after World War II.[24]

When war came in 1914, Captain Carter returned to join the 2nd Battalion KOYLI in Belgium, arriving at the front 25 October. Like Maurice Kennard, he took part in the desperate defence of the Messines Ridge. Casualties were heavy and within six days he was the only surviving officer in his battalion. He was mentioned in despatches and became the first KOYLI officer to be awarded the Military Cross 31 October.[25]

Carter was critical of lack of firepower on the British side (at that time there were only two machine guns per battalion, often obsolete Maxims) compared with the better equipped Germans. In November 1914 he wrote to a friend at Regimental H.Q. in Pontefract.

> *It is damnably frightening, but the excitement and comradeship is wonderful... My salaams to all and DO TRAIN SOME MORE MACHINE GUNNERS.*   Lt. Col. H.F.G. Carter, M.C.[26]

Carter was wounded at Hooge 17 November, 1914. His subsequent career reflects again the networking of the pre-war regular army. He spent time in Gallipoli as A.D.C. to General Hunter-Weston with 29th Division but returned to England when Hunter-Weston was evacuated out of Cape Helles with sunstroke and exhaustion in July, 1915. He joined the newly formed 31st Division at Ripon as a staff officer under the command of General Robert Wanless-O'Gowan who had been his Brigadier in Flanders. When the Pals arrived in France he had the advantage of being on the staff of his Divisional Commander and Corps Commander.[27]

Having arrived in France, the Pals now found themselves part of Fourth Army under Sir Henry Rawlinson. Fourth Army was divided into four different Corps with the Pals being part of VIII Corps (ultimately four divisions strong with nearly 40,000 men) under the command of Lieutenant General Sir Aylmer Hunter-Weston. The decisions made by Hunter-Weston, known to the troops as 'Hunter-Bunter', had a profound impact on their fate. To say the Pals were unfortunate in their Corps Commander is an understatement.

Gerald Brenan, an artillery observation officer with 31st Division, described how some of his men had to guard the Chateau of Marieux, Hunter-Weston's H.Q.

They were kept busy sweeping the drive free of wastepaper and cigarette-ends. Not quite the duties for which they had enlisted, but under many British colonels and generals there lay a fussy old maid and General Hunter-Weston was one of the worst for spit and polish.[28]

The debate on the competence of British Generals in the First World War has swayed backwards and forwards over the years. It has moved from a simplistic polarization between uncritical support and knee-jerk condemnation to a more pragmatic view that whilst mistakes were made, the Generals ultimately learned their trade and fashioned a more sophisticated and successful British Army by the end of the War. It is very easy to criticise with the advantage of 20/20 vision of hindsight and to ignore the difficulties facing the generals, particularly in the field of communications. There were indeed some first class British Generals, Plumer and Maxse spring to mind, but it is hard to find anyone with a good word to say for Hunter-Weston. According to Rhodes-James who wrote the major work on the Dardanelles campaign,

In many respects, "Hunter-Bunter" was a preposterous figure; fond of making dramatic entrances at staff conferences, rubicundly gruff, self-important and vain, he was something of a classic caricature of a British General at the beginning of the Great War, as one who served under him has commented, "he was a passionate believer in attack". "Casualties?" he once remarked, "what do I care about casualties"?[29]

The fifty-one year old 27th Laird of Hunterston on the Clyde coast was certainly adept at blowing his own trumpet. When VIII Corps was formed, Hunter-Weston used his own hunting horn device as the Corps insignia. He embellished the re-fashioning of his ancient mansion with the same device. His self-submitted entry to *Who's Who* is also revealing – it was six times longer than his fellow lowland Scot and Commander in Chief, Sir Douglas Haig – and full of exploits in the Sudan, India and the Boer War. What he did have in common with Haig though was that he was a prominent Freemason.[30]

Cuthbert Headlam, his Staff Intelligence Officer, was a close observer of Hunter-Weston. As a barrister and Clerk to the House of Lords, Headlam was a shrewd observer. In a series of letters to his wife he gave an insider's view of Divisional and Corps affairs. He had the advantage of a position that owed nothing to pre-war regular army service. He frequently questioned Hunter-Weston's sanity and gives an entertaining though somewhat disturbing picture of the General in action

H-W should retire to the H.of C.[31]*, but the lucky man must have the hide of an elephant and the vanity of a peacock.*

H-W is stark staring mad – sent an officer home 'on duty' to fetch his Xmas turkeys – then we prate on about economy and homilies are read to the men about waste. Futile little man. It is to my mind quite criminal that men like...our ass from here (Hunter-Weston) should be given commands. Why should good men's lives be sacrificed unnecessarily by putting them under incapable leaders?

Had a long talk with H-W last night – well that is hardly the right way of putting it – I went to him about one or two little matters and then he began a speech about the war, politics etc., which lasted for about half an hour. He is a tremendous windbag, talks very quickly and excitedly – he didn't say anything worth remembering.[32]

Officers' letters were uncensored. Unlike Private Sam Wainwright en-route for Egypt, Colonel Headlam's letters would not be dropped over the side of a ship. They were carried by King's Messenger.

One of the myths of the War is that most British Generals were cavalrymen[33]. Hunter-Weston's twenty year career in the Royal Engineers demonstrates the inaccuracy of the myth, although he commanded a cavalry column with much dash (and self-publicised derring-do in *Who's Who*) in the Boer War. Whatever doubts there may be about his judgement, there can be no question as to his personal bravery. At the beginning of the war he commanded 11 Brigade, the first brigade across the Aisne 13 September, 1914. Hunter-Weston personally tested out a bridge with cut girders and unexploded German demolition charges before allowing the Brigade to cross.[34]

Hunter-Weston's reputation for hands on driving of men led to him being given command of the 29th Division in the Gallipoli campaign in 1915. However, he was severely criticised both by historians and by the Royal Commission appointed to enquire into the failure of the campaign. The vagueness of his orders led to confusion and lack of direction when 29th Division landed 25 April, 1915. The infamous 'Casualties? What do I care about casualties?' comment followed a series of suicidal daylight frontal attacks in the early weeks of the campaign. He infuriated officers in his division when he told a brigade major that he was 'glad to have blooded the pups' when the newly arrived 156th Scottish Brigade suffered 50% casualties in its first action.[35] He was reputed to have awarded the Military Cross to an officer for

General Hunter-Weston

summarily shooting three men reluctant to go over the top.[36] There were echoes of this last incident in his speech to the Bradford Pals on the eve of the Battle of the Somme.

Ominously for the Pals, Haig's diary for 29th June, 1916 contains the comment, 'Hunter-Weston and the majority of his officers are amateurs in hard fighting and some think that they know much more than they really do of this kind of warfare.'[37]

Given this comment, it remains a mystery how Hunter-Weston

retained command of VIII Corps after the Somme. It was the Pals' misfortune to have him as their Corps Commander.

On Thursday 20 April, 1916, on the eve of the Easter Weekend, the 16th West Yorks took over sole responsibility for a sector of the Western Front for the first time. At 5.00 p.m. the Second Pals watched the 16th march out of the relative tranquillity of Bus-les-Artois. The 18th waited another four days before their turn came to enter the line.[38] The l6th's task was to relieve another of 31st Division's Battalions, the Hull Commercials (10th East Yorks), in the Colincamps sector on the Redan Ridge between the fortified hamlet of Serre and Beaumont Hamel.[39]

The Western Front had stabilised in October, 1914 with the Germans taking advantage of the high ground and usually having the better defensive positions. The German 26th (Reserve) Division had been responsible for this particular section of the line since October, 1914. By the time the Pals arrived in the Spring of 1916, the Germans had had over eighteen months to develop a formidable defensive network to complement their natural geographical advantage. British troops took over the sector from the French at the end of 1915 and found themselves occupying a series of poorly constructed trenches dominated from above by heavily defended German positions.

The Germans dug deep into the chalk to provide protection against any artillery bombardment; established a series of machine gun strong posts using triangulated cross fire which it would be impossible for any attacking force to avoid; and developed a three line trench system with tunnels to provide defence in depth. They cleverly positioned their front line in the dead ground just over the brow of the hill so that any attackers would be silhouetted against the sky line. To the front there was a deep stretch of barbed wire, whilst well behind the lines, often in the cover of woods, a powerful artillery force was assembled. The Germans were careful not to advertise the scale of their artillery capacity before 1 July, and the Pals found to their cost that British Intelligence had seriously underestimated the scale and power of these German batteries.

As the spring Maundy Thursday evening of 1916 closed in and dusk turned quickly to night, the First Pals faced a five mile trek through country lanes clogged with chalky mud. Their route was through the hamlet of Courcelles then up a hill to another abandoned hamlet, Colincamps. The hill out of Courcelles was under direct observation by the enemy for a stretch of over three hundred yards. They waited in Courcelles until darkness fell before entering a tunnel made of netting to cover the exposed section. There was a mixture of excitement and apprehension as they got nearer to the line and darkness fell. The netting tunnel gave a theatrical feeling of entering a dangerous and mysterious underworld fraught with hidden unseen perils. It was the moment they had been looking forward to for over eighteen months. Manningham Lane, the skating rink, the blue uniforms, all now distant memories. There were no spectators to cheer them or to make unkind remarks about chocolate soldiers. There was no Lord Mayor to praise their patriotism or to talk of Bradford's civic pride. There was no martial music to lift the spirits. This was the real war, and now they were to be responsible for a section of the Western Front.[40]

At the far end of Colincamps they took a right fork towards the Sucrerie, a pre-war sugar factory. A straight road, lined with the remains of poplar trees, now dropped down towards the recently begun Euston Road military cemetery. For some Pals this would be their ultimate destination on the long road from Bradford.

Just before the cemetery, a track branched off to the right curling behind the shelter of the sugar factory buildings and dropped down into the approach trench known as Sixth Avenue. It was another mile to the communication trenches Egg, Butter, Tournai and Freddy which led to the front line. It was a slow awkward dangerous business as the fully laden men edged forward in the dark. Their task was made more difficult by the atrocious state of the trenches which were flooded up to two feet deep in places, but by 11.15 p.m. the men from Bradford had taken over from the men from Humberside. The relief was completed with A Company (Captain Pringle), C Company (Captain Blagbrough) and D Company (Major Moore) in the front line, with B Company (Captain Holmes) in reserve.[41]

The Battalion War Diary records that the l6th's first night together in the trenches was relatively quiet. There was 'some shelling of trenches and a good deal of machine gun fire, but fortunately there were no casualties'.[42]

At dawn on Good Friday morning, the entire battalion took part in 'Stand To' for the first time together, manning the parapets of their sector of the line. It was a miserable wet morning. Through the rain and half-light the Redan Ridge loomed above them. They were conscious that the enemy was just 200 yards away up the slope. To the left was the

The Sucrerie near Euston Road, entry point for the communication trenches a mile behind the front line .

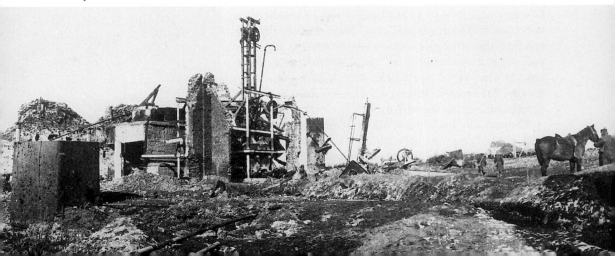

'Heidenkopf', or Quadrilateral, a German machine gun system bulging out of the line to allow enfilade fire across No Man's Land. Ten weeks later the Quadrilateral wreaked terrible havoc amongst the Pals.

Friday passed without casualties and with only intermittent artillery and machine gun fire, but working parties struggled on to clear drainage sumps in trenches which were little more than a wet morass.

Two important visitors, the divisional general, Major General Robert Wanless O'Gowan and Brigadier Henry Buchanan Kirk, arrived on the same day with an entourage of staff officers to cast their eye over the Battalion. There was much jumping to attention and saluting, and no doubt Sam Wainwright kept well out of the brigadier's way. It would be a long time before the Pals saw General Wanless O'Gowan in the trenches again. The Battalion War Diary records only one other visit in 1917, – although events made the Pals well aware of his existence. Brigadier Kirk was never seen again. The unfortunate brigadier died of a heart attack three weeks later. He was forty-nine.[43]

Brigadier John Darnley Ingles, commanding 93 Brigade.

Forty-three years old Lieutenant Colonel John Darnley Ingles was appointed as the new brigadier general to command 93 Brigade. He did so for the rest of the war. He was a driving professional soldier who had commanded the 8th Devons and been decorated with the DSO earlier in the war.[44]

Friday night saw the battalion's first patrol into No Man's Land – in torrential rain. Second Lieutenant Charles Laxton led eighteen men the full length of the battalion's front along the slope of the Redan Ridge, again fortunately without any casualties. Charles Laxton's brother, Reginald, was also serving as a lieutenant in the 16th West Yorks. The Laxton brothers had been commission from the ranks of the Leeds Pals at Ripon. They came from Batley where their father was in business as well as being Chairman of the local Conservative Party. The Laxtons were one of at least thirty sets of brothers in the two Bradford battalions. Such family bonds typified the special qualities of the Pals battalions, yet their vulnerability is also exposed. Reginald Laxton was killed six weeks later. Charles Laxton, the battalion intelligence officer, was severely wounded in both legs 1 July.[45]

The patrol's luck in avoiding casualties may have had something to do with the dreadful weather conditions which masked sound and made observation difficult for the enemy. Sensible Germans, given the chance, would have disappeared down their deep dug outs. The Pals passed the night as best they could, wet and shivering in their much less well equipped trenches.

One outcome of General O'Gowan's visit was the welcome arrival of Lieutenant Bickersteth of the Leeds Pals with a working party of sixty men to help with the drainage problem. Bickersteth described the conditions: 'The trenches are in a pretty rotten condition. There is about two feet of water in the front line trench and the communication trenches are not much better...(one can) find one's self sitting down in a hole about four feet deep full of water. I saw a fellow go right up to his chest and this is no exaggeration.'

The 16th's luck in avoiding casualties finally ran out on Saturday 22 April, forty-eight hours after their arrival in the trenches. The Battalion War Diary recorded enemy artillery was much more active with shrapnel and whiz-bangs. Private Edford Mackay (16/908), servant of the acting CO Major Kennedy, was the first casualty. He was severely wounded by shell splinters and died eighteen days later 10 May. Twenty-five years old Mackay was a warehouseman from West Bowling.[47]

On the same night, Sergeant John Burrows (16/920) of C Company was hit by shrapnel. After treatment by Dr. Roche he was taken to an Advance Dressing Station and then by horse ambulance to No. 29 Casualty Clearing Station at Doullens. A week later he was taken by train to No. 18 General Hospital in the huge base at Etaples near Boulogne. His Medical History Sheet gives a graphic description of his gradual deterioration – a fate shared with many thousands of British soldiers in the Great War. Under modern conditions it is almost certain that John Burrows would have survived. Comments in brackets are added for explanation.

Medical History Sheet, 18 General Hospital, Camiers
16/ 920   Sgt BURROWS John 16 West Yorks " C" Coy
Age : 28   Service : 1 year and 6 months
Injuries :   G.W. [gunshot wound] *Rt. Chest. Rt. Haemothorax* [bleeding into chest cavity]
History :   Wounded by a bomb 22/4/16 at Colincamps. Wound cleaned up under anaesthetic at 29 CCS
29.4.16   Admitted to 18 General Hospital. General condition, very good. Temperature, 100 degrees. Respiration rate 28. The patient has a septic wound about 1inch in diameter over the 8th rib. 2 inches below L of scapula. Has tyrnpanitic note over base of right lung with much diminished breath sounds.
04.5.16   X-Ray reports a foreign body lying in R chest & slight opacity on L side to suggest a haemothorax.
05.5.16   Patient had a slight attack of dyspnoea [breathlessness] *this morning which has passed off.*
07.5.16   7.30 p.m. while leaving his bed the patient had sudden very severe dyspnoea and became cyanosed [bluish coloration due to lack of oxygen] *and cold and sweating. Rales over L lung.* [abnormal sound from lungs, fainter and higher pitched than a wheeze indicating

moisture in lungs]. *Strychnine – Ether – Oxygen. Brandy – administered without improvement. R. chest was aspirated and about 25 oz. of blood stained fluid was withdrawn. No improvement followed.*
Patient died 8-30 p.m.

Signed C.V. Knight, Lt. R.A.M.C., 8 May, 1916
<u>*Post Mortem Findings*</u> *Perforating wound of the lowest lobe of the right lung on its posterior aspect. The foreign body had passed through the lung and had abraded the side of the body of the 5th dorsal vertebrae (spine) and had been deflected into the lower lobe again – where it was found. In addition, a small clot was discovered in the left pulmonary vein. Cause of death: Pulmonary embolism* [blood clot in lung blood vessel].
Buried, Etaples Military Cemetery, Plot V, Row C, Grave 10.[48]

At noon on Easter Sunday, intense artillery fire swept over the line for over half an hour. Lance Corporal Fred Slingsby (16/350) and Private Victor Smith (16/269) became the first Pals to be killed in the line, whilst Private Percy Blakey (16/820) was severely wounded and died the following day. Slingsby and Smith were buried at night in Euston Road Cemetery behind the Sucrerie. The battalion chaplain, the Reverend John G. Thornton, and the brigade Wesleyan chaplain conducted a brief committal service. Percy Blakey was twenty-five and worked at Manningham Mills. His brief funeral service was a far cry from the cheering crowds on Manningham Lane in September, 1914.[49]

The first letters of condolence were sent to their next of kin by Captain Blagbrough and Lieutenant Webster. The phrases were to become familiar but they gave what comfort they could, 'A cheery lad, worked like a Trojan, he was liked by us all, we feel his loss severely, none will die better or more honourably'.

Twenty-two year old Lieutenant Rhodes Akam, destined to die himself eight weeks later, wrote to the parents of twenty two year old Private James Fry (18/68), who died 28 April:

Your son was sitting in the trench when he was very badly hit by shrapnel and unfortunately did not recover from his wounds. If ever there was a plucky lad, he was one, and although he did not suffer, which I hope will be some little consolation to you in this great trouble, his end came very soon. During the time he was conscious he hardly ever murmured except to say, Tell mother I did my best, and he

Percy Blakey, killed 23 April, 1916.

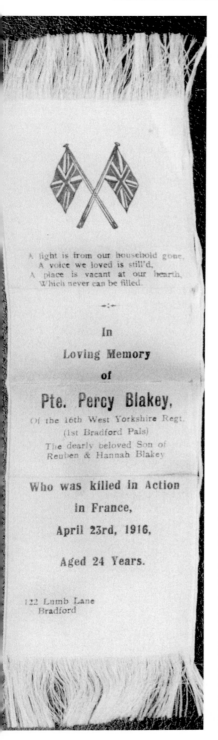

In

Loving Memory

of

Pte. Percy Blakey,

Of the 16th West Yorkshire Regt.
(1st Bradford Pals)

The dearly beloved Son of
Reuben & Hannah Blakey

Who was killed in Action

in France,

April 23rd, 1916,

Aged 24 Years.

122 Lumb Lane
Bradford

did. It is very hard for me to write to you, as words are so futile, but I hope that it will help you to know that we have given him a proper burial in a proper cemetery. Please accept my deepest sympathy for a good lad and one who did his best for his country.[50]

May saw both Bradford battalions rotating trench duties in the Colincamps sector on the Redan Ridge with other Battalions of 31st Division. The pattern was periods of five days in the front line, five days in billets at Bus-les-Artois, and then five days in reserve near the Sucrerie. Occasionally, small reconnaissance parties of three or four men led by an officer would explore No Man's Land to check the enemy's wire and to discover what they could about his defences. For the first time, a series of obituaries from the Pals began to appear under the title, Bradford's Roll of Honour, in the *Bradford Daily Telegraph*. There was a steady stream of casualties in both battalions, with the Second Pals suffering the most. The casualties came mostly from German artillery fire, but rifle grenades, and in the case of Private William Lassey, a sniper's shot, also took its toll. One particularly sad death was that of Private John Crossley (18/17) a twenty- nine year old widower who lived with his parents in West Bowling. He left four young children.

Between 17 and 24 May, the Second Pals had a lengthy tour of the trenches and suffered a number of casualties to artillery fire. Second Lieutenant Raymond Hummel was killed 19 May. He had been commissioned from the ranks of the Leeds Pals and came from a distinguished academic family, his brother and his father were professors at Leeds University. During the seven day tour casualties totalled nine killed and twenty six wounded.

One of the casualties brought the reality of war home to the Walden family of Barkerend Road, Bradford. Within nine days Mr and Mrs William Walden lost both their sons, twenty-two years old Ernest in the Second Bradford Pals, and twenty-three years old George who had joined the Royal Navy as a regular sailor in 1913. George was a gunlayer on HMS *Defence*, an obsolete cruiser based in the Mediterranean. In August, 1914, Defence helped to pursue the German ships *Breslau* and *Goeben* from Messina to the Dardanelles, an action which, in part, led to Turkey entering the war on the side of the

Central Powers. In January, 1915, *Defence* saw action in the North Sea in the Battle of Dogger Bank. George came home with exciting tales of the sinking of the German cruiser *Blücher*. No doubt enthused by his brother's stories, P.C. Ernest Walden decided it was more exciting to volunteer for the Second Pals than to be a police constable in the Bradford City Force. As Private Walden (18/357) he proved to be a good soldier, and was soon promoted to corporal.[51] At 8.30 p.m. on Monday 22 May, 1916, Corporal Walden, with Private Seed and Private Ferrand (18/252) (an old boy of Bradford Grammar School whose brother had joined the Leeds Pals), were detailed by Captain Keevil to spend the night in a listening post in No Man's Land on the Redan Ridge. Their task was to locate a sniper who had killed Private Lassey and wounded four of their comrades on the previous two nights.[52]

It was a real test of nerve for inexperienced troops in an uncomfortable, lonely position. In the darkness a scurrying rat could set tins rattling on the wire. In the early morning swirling mist could play tricks on tired eyes and look like an enemy patrol. A cough or clumsy movement could give their position away, and calls of nature had to be suppressed. There was an uncomfortable feeling that the Germans higher up on the Ridge knew exactly where they were. Two hours after the three men took up their post, an artillery bombardment from behind Pendant Copse raked the British front line from right to left and then back again. The *strafe* lasted an hour, wounding Lieutenant Quitzow and five members of a working party who were out at the wire.[53] When the bombardment stopped, Captain Keevil went up the sap to check on the listening post. He found Private Seed, half buried, badly injured and totally confused. There was no sign of Walden or Ferrand. Keevil led search parties until dawn for two nights but to no avail.[54] Ferrand's body was found by Private Arthur Wild 18/356 on 8 June when a new sap was being dug.[55] Ernest Walden was never found and his name appears on the Thiepval Memorial.

On 30 May, Mr and Mrs Walden received a letter of sympathy from Captain Keevil describing the circumstances of Ernest's presumed death, and saying, 'he has several times come under my notice for his coolness and courage'.[56] At midnight on the same day, unaware of his brother's fate, Able-Seaman George Walden sailed out of Invergordon harbour on HMS *Defence*. The Battle of Jutland was about to begin. The next day, Captain Poland on *Warspite* described the scene:

> I saw Defence *heading straight at the enemy, with a cloud of white smoke amidships and aft. She was banging away and going full speed, masthead colours and made a very gallant show. I saw three salvoes fall across her in quick succession, beauties. A flicker of flame ran aft along her forecastle head and up her fore turret, which seemed to melt. Then Whoof, up she went, a single huge sheet of flame, 500 feet high, mixed up with smoke and fragments. As it died down I saw her crumpled bow, red hot, at an angle of sixty degrees, and then she sank. I nearly vomited – God it was an awful sight. I couldn't get to sleep that night for thinking about it.*[57]

The Walden family had lost both their sons. There would be many sleepless nights in Barkerend Road behind drawn blinds.

Back on the Western Front, French pleas for support grew ever more desperate. On 26 May, 1916, Haig recorded in his diary.

General Joffre explained the general situation. The French had supported for three months alone the whole weight of the German attacks on Verdun. Their losses had been heavy. By the end of the month, they would reach 200,000. If this went on the French army would be ruined. He, therefore, was of the opinion that the 1st July was the latest date for the combined offensive of the British and French. I said that before fixing the date, I would like to indicate the state of preparedness of the British Army on certain dates and compare its condition. I took 1 and 15 July and 1 and 15 August. The moment I mentioned 15 August, Joffre at once got very excited and shouted that "The French Army would cease to exist if we did nothing till then". The rest of us looked on at this outburst of excitement, and then I pointed out that in spite of 15 August being the most favourable date for the British Army to take action, yet, in view of what he had said regarding the unfortunate condition of the French Army, I was prepared to commence operations on 1 July or thereabouts.[58]

Detailed work began on a revised plan for what was to become the Battle of the Somme. The target date was at first 25 June, later revised to 29 June. It finally took place 1 July, 1916. At a meeting of his army commanders at the end of May, Haig discounted any idea of ultimate victory in 1916 and stated that the offensive would have three objectives. First, to provide relief for the French at Verdun by drawing German troops to the Somme area, second to inflict losses on the Germans as part of the wearing out fight, and third to place the British in a favourable position for final victory which could be expected in 1917.

At first unaware of these momentous decisions, the Bradford Pals continued their rotation duties in the trenches.

Sir Douglas Haig

The months of May to June, 1916 were bad for the three Russell brothers, Tom, Frank, Willie and their cousin Harry. Captain Tom Russell, adjutant of the First Pals, left on the 20 May with an unspecified illness. Lieutenant Frank Russell, the transport officer, found that his service in Egypt had led to a flare up of malaria which he had caught in his days in the Norfolk Regiment in East Africa in 1898. He left the First Pals for England on 30 May. Lieutenant Willie Russell had transferred to the Machine Gun Corps in May, but was sent home sick in August, 1916.[59]

Their cousin Captain Harry Russell was killed when C Company HQ received a direct hit at noon on 10 June. Secondnd Lieutenant Reginald Laxton, brother of Charles Laxton the battalion intelligence officer, was also killed. Lieutenants Morgan and Davy were wounded as was 16/671 Corporal Robert Normington. The second in command of the

Battalion, Major Sydney Moore, was seriously wounded with his foot blown off. One wonders whether the various company and battalion headquarters were being scrutinized for movement by German balloon observers. For not many days previously Major Kennedy's Battalion HQ had been hit and the CO's servant killed.

Major Moore, a thirty-nine years old Inland Revenue officer from Bingley, had a dispute with the War Office about the cost of his artificial foot. He offered to pay the difference between the standard War Office issue prosthetic and a much better one costing £25. Despite a prolonged correspondence, he was told it was a case of either take it or leave it.[60]

In the meantime the build up for the great offensive continued and the detailed plans completed. The sheer size and scale of the movements must have alerted the Germans to what was afoot as troops, artillery, ammunition, supplies and equipment made dusty trails behind the British and French lines.

On 12 June, both Bradford battalions were relieved by East Yorks battalions from Hull and returned to their billets in Bus-les-Artois. Brigade instructions had been received as to the Pals' part in the coming offensive and the next week was spent in lectures to officers and NCO's as to the nature of their organisation and a study of the enemy trenches. Their preparations were interrupted by intermittent German shelling, and on 15 June three men in the Second Pals were wounded.[61]

A British force of well over 100,000 infantry was to attack on a sixteen mile front with a smaller French force attacking on the right on an eight mile front. The British aim was for the infantry to capture the Pozieres Ridge on a ten mile extent from the River Ancre in the north down to Montauban and the link with the French in the South. To the north of the River Ancre, Hunter-Weston's VIII Corps was to seize the German trenches on a three mile front and then dig in to form a flank guard for the forces pushing on further south. The Pals battalions of 31st Division were to be on the left flank of VIII Corps' sector. There was then a gap of a mile between the Pals and the Gommecourt Salient where General Allenby's Third Army was to mount a full scale diversionary attack. Behind the infantry, Haig optimistically arranged for three cavalry divisions to be in reserve under General Gough ready to exploit any breakthroughs and to capture Bapaume.

The attack was to be preceded by a massive artillery bombardment of the German wire and trenches commencing on 24 June. Five days later 31st Division's objective would be to capture the fortified village of Serre at the northern end of the Colincamps sector and to move on to the trenches to the south and east of the village beyond Pendant Copse a depth of over 4,000 yards.

It was a complicated task involving a series of four waves on a set timetable. It had to be understood, practised and rehearsed. It was also a formidable task with the Germans having ten machine gun posts facing

Sir Aylmer Hunter-Weston and his VIII Corps staff at Marieux, 24 June 1916. One week to go.

the attacking forces. One particular machine gun redoubt, the Heidenkopf (or Quadrilateral), could direct enfilade fire at the Pals from their right. It was essential that the neighbouring 4th Division put this redoubt out of action as soon as possible or the Pals attack would be extremely vulnerable.

On 20 June, apart from a small group left behind to carry rations, the Pals due to take part in the attack came out of the line and marched twenty miles west to Gezaincourt south of Doullens. The village was a pretty rural backwater similar to the villages near Fovant. It was thought to be safe and beyond the sight of German observation. Here they began brigade training with the Leeds Pals and Durham Pals. 94 Brigade (the Accrington, Sheffield and Barnsley Battalions) had been there the previous week. They were there for five days and their training was observed by the corps commander Sir Aylmer Hunter-Weston and the divisional general Robert Wanless O'Gowan.

Major Carter had gone ahead with some of the signallers to set up the arrangements at Gezaincourt. Tapes had been laid out to mark their

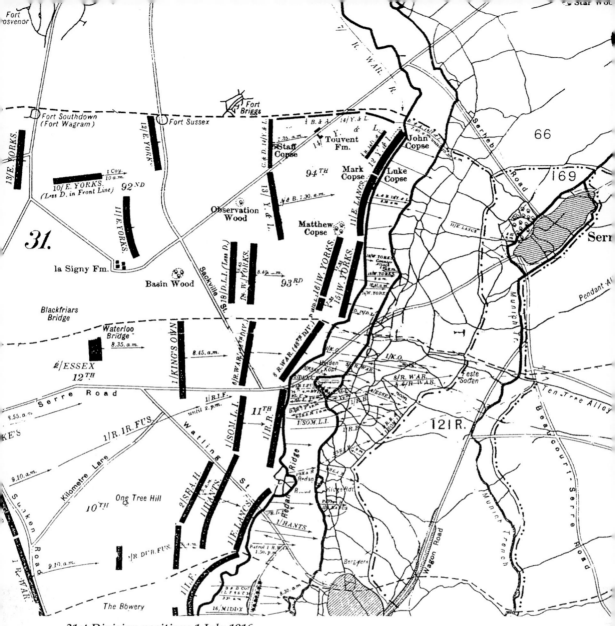

31st Division positions 1 July 1916.

objectives based on aerial photographs. The officers and NCO's having been shown models and maps of the area at Bus, now explained the plan in detail to the men. Movements were practised to conform to the timetable of the assault. Each man's equipment was checked and coloured tapes issued to be worn to match the objective each company was to take. Other colours were issued to wire cutters and mallet bearers. They were also issued with shiny metal triangles necklaces cut from biscuit tins to be worn on their backs to reflect the sun and allow observers to identify their progress. Time and again the movements were practised and timed with stop watches until the top brass was satisfied the men had got it right. They were like a well rehearsed football team practising set pieces without any opposition. The only thing missing was an enemy firing at them. That would come later.

The detailed local plan for the Pals was that two of 31st Division's brigades (93 and 94) were to be involved in the attack. The Hull Battalions in 92 Brigade would man the front line until the eve of assault and then remain in reserve. The two attacking brigades both operated on a two company front of 700 yards.

94 Brigade's front (led by the Accrington and Sheffield Battalions) was on the left running along the edge of four copses named 'Matthew', 'Mark', 'Luke' and 'John'. Their task was to capture Serre village and then to face north-east to shield the northern limit of the Fourth Army attack.

93 Brigade, on the right, also had a 700 yard frontage running south of the copses. Their task was to sweep round the southern edge of Serre village. They were then to swing left facing north east looking towards Puisieux au-Mont to extend the Fourth Army's protective shield. 4th Division would be on their right. The attack was to be in four bounds with four objectives, identified as the Green, Red, Brown and Blue lines. The men were to wear coloured ribbons tied to their shoulder straps identifying which wave they belonged to and what their objective was.

Two companies of the Leeds Pals wearing green ribbons were to lead the assault. They were allotted twenty minutes to capture and consolidate the fourth German line (the Green Line) which ran north to south across the road about 100 yards in front of the village. The German's had named the trench *Tubinger Stellung*. The Green Line was to be taken at 7.50 a.m.

The second wave, wearing red ribbons, consisted of two companies of the First Bradford Pals and the remaining Leeds Pals. Their task was to pass over the Green Line and then capture and consolidate the next

General Hunter Weston, before the Battle of the Somme, 29 June 1916: *'If we'd have had artillery like this at Gallipoli, we'd have got to Constantinople.'*
'The artillery let us down!' **General Hunter Weston, 2 July 1916.**

German trench (*Landwehr Stellung*) which ran south from the southern corner of the village (the Red Line). The timetable specified the Red Line was to be taken by 8.10 a.m., twenty minutes after the Green Line had been captured.

The third wave had more ground to cover. After passing through the Green and Red Lines they were expected to take their objective (the Brown Line) at 9.20 a.m. Wearing brown ribbons, their objective was a German trench running south from an orchard beyond the far end of Serre village in a zigzag pattern south to the rear of Pendant Copse. Three companies were allocated to this task, the two remaining First Bradford Companies and D Company of the Durham Pals.

The fourth wave consisted of all four companies of the Second Bradford Pals. They were to capture and hold the most distant objective, the Blue Line. This was a German trench running parallel to a track facing north east towards Pusieux beyond Pendant Copse. Their task involved a difficult swing to the left after they had crossed all the previously captured objectives. Their task was due to be completed at 11.00 a.m.[62]

The men were instructed to walk with their rifles at the port rather than to run and cheering and shouting was actively discouraged. In truth it would have been difficult to run because the men were so heavily laden with additional supplies, equipment and ammunition. They were told not to stop to assist casualties because that would hold up the timetable. Casualties, they were assured by General Hunter-Weston, would be well attended to by the stretcher bearers. Finally, Hunter-Weston pronounced himself satisfied and congratulated the men on their work.

Not everyone was satisfied. Brigadier Rees who took over command of 94 Brigade on 15 June tackled Hunter-Weston on two issues.

General Hubert Conway Rees.

> *One of my criticisms of the general plan of operations was that the time allowed for the capture of each objective was too short. I had a severe argument with Hunter-Weston before I induced him to give me an extra ten minutes for the capture of one orchard 300 yards beyond the village of Serre. I was looked on as something of a heretic for saying that everything had been arranged for except the unexpected, which usually occurs in war.*
>
> *There was no question of surprise. The enemy could hardly fail to know the extent of the attack and very little bombardment went on towards the north, between me and Gommecourt where a subsiduary operation was to take place. I suggested to Hunter-Weston that a number of dummy trenches might be dug to deceive the enemy and cause him to waste shells on the area. He congratulated me on the idea, but whether it was put into execution or not I don't know.[63]*

In fact whilst Rees got his ten minutes he didn't get his dummy trenches. German heavy artillery hidden behind Pusieux registered on 31st Division's trenches but bided their time until the assault came. When they

A cheer and a wave for the camera! British soldiers on the way up to the line.

finally unleashed their concentrated fire it was with devastating effect.

On 24 June, four days after the 16th West Yorks arrived in Gezaincourt, and only five days before the expected zero hour on 29 June, Major George Sutherland Guyon of the 2nd Royal Fusiliers arrived to take over command of the battalion from Major Kennedy.[64]

One can find no obvious reason for what appears to be a late decision to appoint a new commanding officer so near the launch of the offensive. There is no evidence of dissatisfaction with Major Kennedy by Division during the three months he had been in command. It may be something was noticed by Hunter-Weston at Gezaincourt. More likely, it may have been thought that Kennedy would be a natural successor to cover the loss of the First Pals second in command Major Moore on 10 June, and that Guyon was appointed because of his battle experience in temporary command of his old battalion at Gallipoli. He obviously had very little chance to get to know his new battalion in the remaining two days of training, but his function was to lead it into battle rather than to administer it.

Guyon, a forty year old regular, had joined the Royal Fusiliers in 1897 serving for three years in the Boer War where he was awarded five clasps. He then had a long spell in India before being promoted to Major in 1912. As second in command of the 2nd Royal Fusiliers, he was one of the first ashore and scaled the cliffs of X Beach in the Gallipoli landings 25 April, 1915. He then took temporary command when his CO became a casualty. No doubt these exploits commended him to Hunter-Weston, who was his Divisional General at the time.[65]

Guyon's battalion suffered terrible losses in appalling conditions throughout the early fighting at Cape Helles and later in the Suvla area. Guyon was wounded, but recovered and returned to take command of the battalion. At the end of October 1915 the unfortunate Major spent an agonising week in a dug out before he could be removed to hospital for an appendix operation. He was lucky to survive. By the time he was fully fit again the Peninsula had been evacuated and what was left of 29th Division had transferred to France.[66]

The two Bradford Battalions left the training area of Gezaincourt shortly after dawn Sunday 25 June. They followed the usual procedure of fifty minutes marching with a ten minute rest on the hour. As they passed through Sarton and Authie they saw the massive preparations for the 'Big Push' (as the forthcoming attack was referred to). They caught the feeling of excitement and anticipation that something really big was in the air and that they were going to be part of it. They then marched through the

artillery lines and were amazed at the power and volume of the barrage which had already begun aimed at cutting the enemy wire and pulverising their trenches. They arrived back in their familiar billets in the barns and stables of Bus-les-Artois at 2.00 p.m., 25 June, and began the count down of the hours to the expected zero-hour at 7.30 a.m. on Thursday 29 June.[67]

Major Albert Robinson of the 18th West Yorks had a stroke of luck and missed Serre. He was taken to hospital with pleurisy on 30 June.

As the waiting continued, the weather changed. Heavy thunderstorms led to flooding in the trenches and restricted the Royal Flying Corps who were 'spotting' for the Artillery. On 28 June with less than twenty-four hours to go, Haig and Rawlinson decided to postpone the assault. In Bus-les-Artois Brigadier Rees was unhappy with the way the news was announced: '*On 28 June it poured with rain all day and at about 4.00 p.m. a message was sent over the phone to say that the attack had been postponed 48 hours. I heard the news shouted down the village street, which was anything but desirable.*'[68] Zero-hour would now be 7.30 a.m. on Saturday 1st July.

The Pals consoled themselves that at least the artillery had more opportunity to blast the German wire and positions. The delay also allowed brigade to explore the strength of the German defences to see what damage had been done in order to pass more up-to-date information back to Colonel Craven in charge of 31st Division's Artillery[69].

Albert Robinson missed the attack on Serre through illness, but returned to play a prominent role in and after the war.

On the night of 28 June, the 12th East Yorks had launched a trench raid but failed to penetrate the German wire and retired with heavy casualties. The following morning volunteers were called for from amongst the Second Bradford Pals for a trench raid on the night of 29/30 June, to see if they could do any better. Forty-two bold spirits stepped forward. The party was led by Lieutenant Morris Clough together with Lieutenant Frank Watson (who was attached to the Light Trench Mortar Battery), Second Lieutenant John William Worsnop, Doctor George McTavish and thirty-eight other ranks. Whether it was prudent

Second Lieutenant 'Puff' Worsnop. Killed in the trench raid, 30 June 1916.

for Doctor McTavish to go, given that he would be needed when the assault began, is debateable but it was certainly brave.

The result was almost a complete disaster with very heavy casualties. It became clear that it was to be no cake walk on 1 July. The Germans were still there despite the barrage – they were alive and kicking extremely hard. Lieutenant Morris Clough managed to return despite being wounded and made a written report which is in the 18th West Yorks Battalion War Diary:

Party left our front line as scheduled 12.28 a.m., 30 June, 1916. Advance was slow owing to numerous shell holes and flares. Apparently our party was seen as soon as we had left our own trenches for they seemed prepared for us and we were met by bombs when between twenty-five and thirty yards from their trenches. They sent up a single green rocket and formed a barrage of hand grenades in front of us. The trenches seemed fairly knocked about, and the wire was cut where we were in sufficient quantity to allow the passage of troops. Their trenches seemed very full of men and apparently are very deep. Finding we could not get forward, I brought my party back as well and as soon as I possibly could. This took some two hours. As far as I can judge, my casualties at present are about 10 killed and 12 wounded out of 38 men and 4 officers. At present 2 officers, Lieut F. Watson and 2/Lt. Worsnop, are missing, I have been slightly wounded myself in two places.

Our H.E. shells were all dropping a little over half way between our line and the German line, and quite 20 yards short of their wire, and this was taking place during our scheduled hour for the raid. My watch was synchronized with an artillery officer sent by Colonel Craven. [70]

The number of dead rose to thirteen. On 30 June Private Joseph Tate (18/89) died of his wounds as did Private John Waddington (18/896). Lance Corporal Gradwell, thought to be missing, was in fact wounded and became the Pals first prisoner of war to be captured by the Germans. It is likely that Private Frank Sutcliffe (18/1196) was also captured. He is known to have died on 3 September and was buried at Miraumont Cemetery, then behind the German lines.[71] The bodies of Lieutenants Watson and Worsnop (friends from Bradford Grammar School days) were never found and their names are inscribed on the Thiepval Memorial. Private Jack Morris fondly remembered the diminutive twenty-three year old Second Lieutenant John Worsnop from Shipley many years later.

Second Lieutenant Leslie Dalley assisted in bringing in the wounded after the raid. He received the Military Cross for this action.

Before 1 July we used to go on working parties and we had a little officer, and of course route marches. He was going to be a curate at Low Moor Parish Church. They called him Lieutenant Worsnop and we called him "Puff" Worsnop with him being a little fellow. We used to sing, "A Little Child Shall Lead Them Gently on their Way", and he didn't mind. He used to smile when we sang it. Anyway we were going on a working party one night walking on duckboard, you know, sometimes they were all rotten or broken. He says, "Boys" he says, "I'm afraid I shall have to swear", he says, "I'm up to the balls in it". So anyway, poor little bugger got killed, he went on a bit of a reconnoitre the night before 1 July and got killed on that. That's when Mr. Worsnop got it.

18/911 PRIVATE JACK MORRIS[72]

Frank Watson's story had a sad twist. His body, and thus his uniform and equipment, was not recovered. A charge was made by a 'grateful' War Office to recover £ 3. 6s 2d (£3.30) from his estate (of £ 51) to cover the cost of his service revolver. In 1920 his wife, Winifred, wanted to re-marry a Mr. Arthur Chisholm, but had never received absolute confirmation from the War Office that Frank was dead. A prolonged correspondence ensued between Mr. Chisholm and the War Office. The War Office refused to give a categorical assurance as to the death of Frank Watson even though Lance Corporal Gradwell who was captured in the raid volunteered a statement that he had seen Lieutenant Watson killed. One hopes Winifred and Arthur found happiness.[73]

Two seventeen year olds were amongst the dead. Private Arthur Firth (18/1076) was a grandson of Alderman Firth of Leeds City Council, Private Kenneth Macaulay (18/835) was from Keighley. They must have been no more sixteen when they joined the Pals.[74]

Private John Waddington (18/896) aged twenty-eight was awarded the Distinguished Conduct Medal, second only to the Victoria Cross. The award was posthumous. The courageous Waddington died of his wounds 1 July as the major assault was being carried out.

For conspicuous gallantry during a raid. After a raid he repeatedly went back to search for missing officers and men. At much personal risk he brought wounded to our trenches.

CITATION, *London Gazette* 22 SEPTEMBER, 1916[75]

Captain Francis Horner of the Second Pals was Intelligence Officer of 93rd Brigade and wrote to Mrs. Waddington:

During the raid I acted as Receiving Officer. Your husband being one of the first to return to our line wounded, immediately volunteered to go back and search for his comrades. It was not until daybreak that he gave up the search after helping quite a number of our wounded to get back. On reaching the camp our Colonel [Kennard] met us and I brought to his notice the conduct of your husband. Never shall I forget the look in the Colonel's eyes as he said, Waddington, you are a splendid fellow.

CAPTAIN FRANCIS HORNER, 18 WY[76]

Sergeant Harry Dyson (18/261) was awarded the Military Medal. He risked his life again just over twenty-four hours later and was killed. Both he and John Waddington never knew they were to be decorated for their efforts to rescue the wounded on the night of 29 June. After the Somme, when Colonel Carter took over command of the 18th West Yorks, all the surviving members of the raiding party were presented with a Certificate of Merit designed by the artistic Carter, a practice of recognition he continued throughout his command of the Battalion.

The survivors returned in a shocked state to Bus. The Pals were now under no illusions about the expected strength of German resistance. The War Diary of the German 169th Regiment defending Serre carried the terse comment:

> *During the nights of 28./29 and 29./30., English patrols drive against S2 and S3; strength of the English detachments as established through prisoner statements in each case ;*
>
> *On 28./29.   at S2   14. Yorks and Lancs*
> *On 29./30.   at S3   18. West Yorks.*
> *Both drives repelled.*

WAR DIARY, 169TH REGIMENT (BADEN)[77]

NOTES

1. Battalion War Diary
2. See Robert Rhodes James, Gallipoli, p91 for a description of this incident. Several soldiers died by diving over the side when the Manitou was under attack.
3. Information supplied by the National Maritime Register of Troopships, Greenwich
4. Saville, op.cit
5. Wharton op. cit.
6. Gilbert Isles. Taped conversation with Steve Kerry, Bradford Industrial museum.
7. Battalion War Diary.
8. Officers Records PRO WO/339 and The Devonshire Regiment 1914-1918, C.T. Atkinson, 1926.
9. Battalion War Diary
10. Wharton, opus cit.
11. Battalion War Diary
12. Wharton, op.cit
13. Rawnsley, Diary, op.cit
14. Pickworth, op.cit
15. ibid.
16. Phillips, letter kindly supplied by family.
17. Battalion War Diary.
18. Burkes Landed Gentry
19. Information supplied by Major R.T. Morton, Regimental Secretary, The Royal Scots Dragoon Guards, Edinburgh.
20. See The Barnsley Pals in this series, Jon Cooksey.
21. History of the King's Own Yorkshire Light Infantry in the Great War, 1914-1918. Lt. Col. R.C. Bond, D.S.O., no date. Carter was recommended for the Military Cross by the C.O. of the Queen's Bays (letter quoted in above volume, p. 744).
22. Information supplied by Mr. Clifford Stephenson, Huddersfield.
23. Information supplied by Colonel J.S. Cowley, Regimental Secretary, K.O.Y.L.I. Infantry Office, Pontefract. Also PRO WO339 Officers' records.
24. Officers' Records, PRO WO/339. Carter's record includes a letter written on Buckingham Palace notepaper by the King's private secretary enquiring after Carter's health.
25. History of the KOYLI, op. cit p 744.
26. Ibid, p.743, letter written by Carter, 3rd, November, 1914.
27. Officers' Records, PRO WO339.
28. Gerald Brenan, *A Life of One's Own*, p202, pub. Cape, 1962
29. Robert Rhodes James, *Gallipoli*, p.210, Batsford, 1965.
30. *Who Was Who, 1929-1940*. p682.
31. Hunter-Weston was elected unopposed to the House of Commons as Unionist (Conservative) MP for his home constituency of North Ayrshire in October, 1916. He retained the seat until his retirement from Parliament in 1935.
32. The Headlam Papers, Durham Record Office, D/He 151. Letters of various dates in 1916 and 1917 to his wife. Lt.Col. Cuthbert Headlam was, G.S.O.3, G.S.0.2 and G.S.O.1 at VIII Corps, and later at G.H.Q. The Rt.Hon. Sir Cuthbert Morley Headlam (1876-1964), D.S.O., O.B.E., T.D., D.L., J.P., Clerk to the House of Lords 1897-1924. Conservative MP for Barnard Castle 1924-29 and 31-35, Conservative MP for Newcastle North 1945-51. Permanent Secretary to the Admiralty 1924-29.Rhodes James was a Clerk to the House of Commons in the 1950's, and it may be the 'one who served under him' was Headlam.
33. John Terraine in 'The Smoke and the Fire' points out that in July, 1914 there were eight field

marshals of whom only two were from the cavalry; eighteen generals included one cavalryman; twenty seven lieutenant generals had three cavalrymen ; of 114 major generals, eight from the cavalry.

34. See Lynne Macdonald, *1914*, p301, Penguin, 1987

35. Rhodes James, op.cit. p 231.

36. Claim made by John Laffin, but no source given, in *British Butchers and Bunglers of World War One*, p.51, Sutton, 1990

37. Quoted by John Terraine, in *Douglas Haig, The Educated Soldier*, pp.205/6. Hutchinson, 1965

38. Battalion War Diaries, 16th & 18th West Yorks.

39. ibid.

40. See Frederic Manning's autobiographical novel, *The Middle Parts of Fortune* (1929), later issued as *Her Privates We*, for a vivid description of the net tunnel near Courcelles.

41. Battalion War Diary, 16th West Yorks.

42. ibid.

43. ibid. Brigadier Kirk is buried at Le Treport Military Cemetery.

44. Brigadier General John Darnley Ingles CMG, DSO, DL (1872-1957) son of John Chamberlayne Ingles Deputy Inspector General of the Royal Navy. Educated at Cheltenham College and Westward Ho. Joined the Devonshire Regiment in 1894 and served in the Boer War where he was at the Relief of Ladysmith and Mentioned in Despatches. Mentioned in Despatches five times in the Great War. Retired from the Army in 1926 after commanding the 2nd Devonshire Regiment and lived at Totnes, Devon.

45. Patrol and weather conditions in Battalion War Diary. See *Yorkshire Observer* on 17 June, 1916 and 8th July, 1916 for details of Laxton brothers.

46. Letter from Lieutenant S. Morris Bickersteth to his father, 21st April, 1916, Bickersteth Family War Diary. My thanks to Laurie Milner, author of *Leeds Pals* for sharing his research with me.

47. Obituary and photograph, *Bradford Daily Telegraph*, 13 May, 1916.

48. Extracts from Sergeant Burrow's medical record in MH1O6/2307 PRO. I am most grateful to Julian Sykes for providing a copy of this document.

49. Battalion War Diary.

50. Letter from Lieutenant Rhodes Akam, 18WY, published in the *Bradford Daily Telegraph*, 2 May, 1915.

51. Corporal Walden is included in the list of police officers who had volunteered to join the forces in the *Bradford Weekly Telegraph*, 3 September, 1915.

52. Letter written by Captain Keevil published in *Bradford Daily Telegraph*, 7 June, 1916. Details of the Ferrand brothers in *The Bradfordian*, Summer Term 1915. School Magazine of Bradford Grammar School.

53. Battalion War Diary

54. Keevil, op. cit.

55. Battalion War Diary

56. Keevil, ibid

57. Poland, quoted in *The Sailor's War*, 1914-18', Peter H. Liddle, p. 113.

58. Douglas Haig, Diary 26 May. In *The Private Papers of Douglas Haig, 1914-1919*. Edited by Robert Blake. Eyre & Spottiswood, London, 1952.

59. Battalion War Diary, and PRO WO/339 Officers' Records.

60. Officers' Records, Sydney Moore, PRO WO/339. Correspondence in Moore's file.

61. Battalion War Diary 18WY.

62. 93 Brigade War Diary, WO95/2359.

63. Papers of Brigadier-General Hubert Conway Rees, C.M.G., D.S.O., Imperial War Museum Department of Documents (IWM 77/179/1).

64. Battalion War Diary

65. *The Royal Fusiliers in the Great War*, pp 89-105, H.C. O'Neill, Heinemann, 1922.

66. ibid. p.105

67. Battalion War Diary

68. Papers of Brigadier-General Hubert Conway Rees, C.M.G., D.S.O., Imperial War Museum Department of Documents (IWM 77/179/1).

69. 93 Brigade War Diary, WO95/2359.

70. Battalion War Diary.

71. Officers' Records. PRO WO339 Statement by Gradwell in Watson's file in 1920 identifies him as a Prisoner of War together with corroboration by other wounded soldiers in 1916. Frank Sutcliffe's details from Commonwealth War Graves Commission.

72. Private Jack Morris, tape with kind permission of Stephen Kerry, Bradford Industrial Museum.

73. Officers' Records. PRO WO339 Frank Watson, corroboration by other wounded soldiers in 1916.

74. Commonwealth War Grave Records confirms ages. Both on Thiepval Memorial.

75. Citation, London Gazette, 22 September, 1916.

76. *Bradford Daily Telegraph*, 24 August, 1916.

77. Extract from War Diary of 169th Infantry Regiment. Generallandesarchiv Karlsruhe 456 EV 42 Vol 108. I am grateful to Jon Cooksey author of the *Barnsley Pals* in this series for this information. The unit on 28 June was not in fact the 14 Yorks & Lancs, but on e of the Hull Battalions.

Chapter Nine

THE INTERNATIONAL SPORTSMEN

18/922 Company Sergeant Major Richard Bond
Bradford City and England

Welcome Bradford Pals, 31st Division. Dickie Bond. We've got him.
NOTICE PLACED IN NO MAN'S LAND, NEUEVE CHAPELLE, 18 JULY, 1916

'Dickie' Bond.

Sergeant Richard Bond of the Second Bradford Pals was better known as the Bradford City and England right winger 'Dickie' Bond and was a soccer superstar of international fame. He played more than 300 First Division games for City and won eight England caps at a time when international matches were few and far between. It was the golden days when City won the F.A. Cup and there were two First Division teams, Bradford City and Bradford Park Avenue. Crowds often topped the 30,000 mark. In 1911, a new F.A. Cup was made by Fattorinis of Bradford (the previous Cup having been stolen). By happy coincidence the first winner's name on the new Cup was Bradford City.

Forty years on, the *Telegraph and Argus* described Dickie Bond as,

The most famous figure in Bradford football history... a legend and an institution – the darling and idol of the Valley Parade crowd.[1]

In his playing days, he was,

The firebrand outside right with the face of a cherub who can do more to disturb the peace and harmony of a football match than a gang of suffragettes.[2]

When war was declared, professional football continued in England until the end of the 1914-15 season. But the war was to have a massive impact on both Bradford clubs. Donald Bell of Park Avenue became the only professional footballer to be awarded the Victoria Cross, although he was killed on the Somme before he knew of the award. The Scottish internationals Jimmy Spiers, scorer of the Cup winning goal for City (and awarded the Military Medal) and Bob Torrance who played in the Final, both died in the War. The former City captain and England international

Evelyn Lintott was killed at Serre with the Leeds Pals. City's Scottish international goalkeeper Jock Ewart joined the 1st Bradford Pals and was wounded at Serre. Dickie Bond fought at Serre with the Second Pals and became a Company Sergeant Major. Other City players, Irvine Boocock, Joe Linford, Harold Walden and Bond's inside forward partner, Oscar Fox, all joined the Bradford Pals.

In 1991 a surviving Bradford Pal, ninety four year old Sam Wainwright could still remember Dickie:

> *When he was playing you always expected something to happen. He was an entertainer and very exciting to watch. He was fast and very skilful. He used to talk to the crowd near the touch-line and take the 'micky' out of the opposing full-back by putting the ball between his legs.*

16/402 PRIVATE SAM WAINWRIGHT [3]

Dickie's talkative habits could get him into trouble. A lifetime's disappointment came in 1911. He was suspended before the Cup Final for replying in kind to 'improper language' from the Arsenal crowd. After scoring a penalty against the twenty stone Notts County goalkeeper Albert Iremonger, Bond expressed an opinion about the keeper's shape and skill. Although no match in speed, an irate Iremonger chased the diminuitive winger the length of the field to the delight of the Valley Parade crowd. On his first return to Preston, he retaliated to barracking from his former supporters by dropping his shorts. There is nothing new in football.

Evelyn H. Lintott.

Sam Raistrick (16/1742), a cook in the First Pals, was a great friend of both Jock Ewart and Dickie Bond. His son Bill (who served in the First War with the Lancashire Fusiliers) remembered standing behind the goals with his Dad and watching Dickie:

Oscar Fox

> *When he scored he used to say, 'Go on. Pick that one out'... I can see him now, rolling his sleeves up as he ran back. He was a right little live wire was Dickie.*

PRIVATE BILL RAISTRICK, LANCASHIRE FUSILERS [4]

In April, 1915, at the age of thirty-one, Bond joined the Second Bradford Pals with his centre forward team-mate Harold Walden. The *Weekly Telegraph* reported:

> *There can now be little doubt that others will follow their example and recruiting locally is certain to receive a fillip.* [5]

The following Wednesday, Park Avenue entertained City in a First Division 'derby' in the last match of the season before a packed crowd. At half-time,

> Quite a number of recruiting speeches were made, and the fact that Corporal Dickie Bond donned his military overcoat and cap and took part himself, saying a few words, aroused considerable enthusiasm.[6]

The result, Park Avenue 3 City 0, aroused less enthusiasm amongst the City supporters, but much was to happen before the two teams met again.

As a teenager Bond served in the Artillery before buying himself out of the army to sign for his home town team, Preston North End. His previous army experience, coupled with his age and the genuine respect in which he was held, accounted for his appointment to the rank of Corporal.

Inter-battalion football and cricket matches in 93 Brigade were fiercely competitive sporting occasions. The Bradford Pals had the edge in soccer but the Leeds Pals had it in cricket. The First Pals could field the City and Scotland goalkeeper Jock Ewart, his team-mate Joe Linford, and Abe Waddington who later played cricket for Yorkshire and England. Dickie Bond and Harold Walden were great friends of Jock Ewart, but it didn't stop them having blistering confrontations on the pitch. The Leeds Pals had former City captain and England international Evelyn Lintott, as well as Yorkshire and England cricketers M.W. Booth, Roy Kilner and Arthur Dolphin.

By the time the Pals reached France, Dickie was a Sergeant in B

Officers 18th West Yorks cricket team.

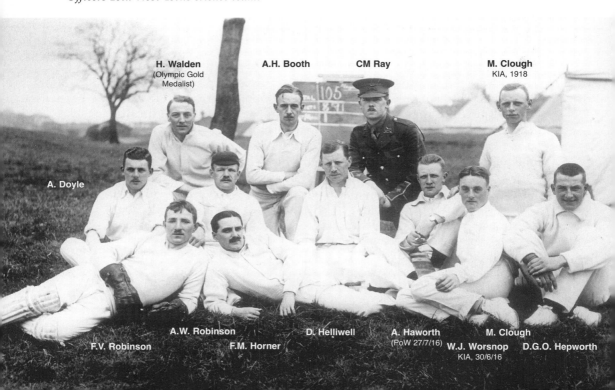

Company in charge of a Lewis Gun team. He survived the 1 July unscathed although his Lewis gun partner Dick Collins was severely wounded in the face.

Four weeks after the attack at Serre, the Second Pals re-entered the line at Neuve Chapelle. On the first night in the trenches, the Germans mounted a raid on the British lines killing ten, wounding thirty-six, and taking thirty-six prisoners. Sergeant Bond was captured in a dug-out as he was shaving.

As daylight came the 18th could see a wooden board placed in No Man's Land with the words:

Welcome Bradford Pals, 31st Division. Dickie Bond. We've got him.[7]

This would not be the last time that the Pals would come across Germans with excellent English, and an intimate knowledge of the city of Bradford.

Dickie Bond survived two and a half years in a prisoner of war camp, and two days after his return he played for City against Avenue in another local derby. He teamed up again with another ex-Pal Oscar Fox on the right wing. He stayed for three more seasons after the War, but his transfer to Blackburn Rovers in 1922 at the age of thirty-eight coincided with City's relegation from the First Division. His First Division career with City amounted to 473 appearances and ninety-six goals despite losing four years to the War.

He became a publican and later kept a fish and chip shop in Garstang before his death at the age of seventy-one in 1955. In 1948 he contributed a series of reminiscences to the *Bradford Yorkshire Sports and Football Argus*. Of his time at Valley Parade he was to write,

They were happy days that I spent there, I wish they were coming all over again.[8]

No doubt Bradford City fans would echo that last sentiment today.

16/1723 Private John Ewart, Bradford City and Scotland

'Jock' Ewart, the Bradford City and Scottish international goalkeeper, was more than a brilliant and entertaining international footballer. He was a talented musician and linguist able to play more than a dozen musical instruments and to speak several foreign languages. He also had an outrageous sense of humour, and with fellow Pal and international footballer Dickie Bond, he often enjoyed a night out on the town.

Jock was twenty-one years old when Bradford City signed him from Airdrieonians in May 1912 for a then record fee for a goalkeeper – £1,200. The fee came out of the profits of City's F.A. Cup win and another long cup run in 1912. He had already represented the Scottish League and went on to represent his country.[1]

He played nearly 300 games for City in two spells up to 1929. In 1922 the *Bradford Daily Telegraph* described him as,

A player of unquestioned brilliance. The only criticism levelled against him is on the ground of excessive daring, but this notwithstanding his judgement was seldom found wanting.[2]

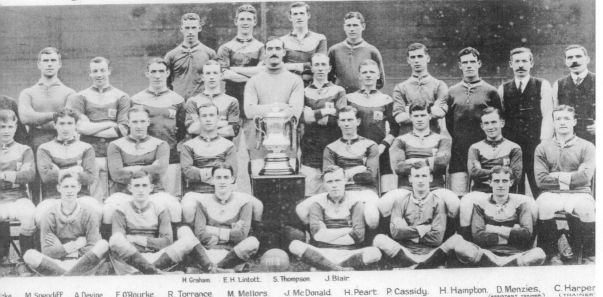

BRADFORD CITY A.F.C.

WINNERS OF THE ENGLISH CUP. SEASON 1910-11.

H. Graham. E. H. Lintott. S. Thompson. J. Blair.

rke M. Spendiff. A. Devine. F. O'Rourke. R. Torrance. M. Mellors. J. McDonald. H. Peart. P. Cassidy. H. Hampton. D. Menzies, C. Harper
(MANAGER) (ASSISTANT TRAINER.) (TRAINER)

O. Fox. W. Gildea. R. Campbell. J. H. Speirs. G. Robinson. D. Taylor. F. Thompson. F. Farren.

W. B. Walker. J. McIlvenny. P. Logan. R. Bond. J. Young. G. Gane.

Jock Ewart and Dickie Bond were great friends. Forty years later Dickie recalled Jock's penalty saving technique,

> In the art of ragging opponents I always say Jock was every bit as good as I was, and he had a way all his own when a penalty was given against City. He would come out to the spot and move the ball off it and ask who was taking the penalty, though he generally knew. Then he would turn to the kicker and say, "Ye takkin a penalty? Mon, ye couldna hit the stand". I always say Jock saved as many penalties for City with his tongue as he did with his hands.[3]

Critics of modern football will reflect not much has changed!

Jock Ewart (16/1723) joined the 1st Pals as a bandsman at Fovant in the Autumn of 1915 along with his friend Sam Raistrick (16/1742). Sam was in demand as a cook, whilst Jock became a cornet player and stretcher bearer. Sam's son, Bill, who had joined the Lancashire Fusiliers, moved in the same lively circle. Bill remembered some of Jock Ewart's antics in a conversation with the author,

> They were allus in't pub, Jock and Dickie and't rest on 'em. Jock were good mates wi' me Dad and they used to knock around together. He were a man's man were Jock, there were no edge to him. He were a reet good laugh. Ah once saw him knock a pint o' beer off't bar, catch it wi' his foot, and then flick it int' t'air and catch it wi' his hand – it were his party trick. He did it for bets. Dickie would take the money and they allus won 'cos folk

Jock Ewart.

couldn't believe he could do it. They 'ad a few too many once an't police come chasing after 'vem. Do you know what Dickie said to't police? He said 'We're ghost huntin' – it were in't paper that were – ghost huntin'. They got into trouble wi' t' Club for that. Ah don't know why me Dad joined up 'cos he wasn't much of a soldier. Ah suppose he went 'cos Jock went. ALL I got from him were a post card from Port Said. After't War me and me Dad used to go down to t' City and stand behind t'goal at Spion Kop end and Jock used to climb up't posts like a monkey when City were attacking. He'd say to me Dad, 'What do you think o' that, Sam ?' Eeh, he were gallus were Jock, reet gallus.[4]

For readers outside Yorkshire the word 'gallus' translates as 'amusing in a daring and eccentric way'. When Private Ewart got to France, he still entertained all around him. His fellow bandsman, bugler Vincent Phillips (16/566), wrote home on the 15 April, 1916:

It is surprising how used you get to the bullets flying over, but if you keep your head down you are even safer in the trenches than in your billets, of course you have only to stop one to get a knock out, ..but we got so used to it that Jock Ewart said the men in his bay were striking matches on the shells as they passed over.

16/566 PRIVATE VINCENT PHILLIPS [5]

In fact Private Ewart wasn't getting used to it. He suffered from shell shock and was in hospital by the time the next letter was sent. Vincent Phillips went on,

Sergeant Richard Bond, seated second left, Ripon.

> *Jock Ewart is in hospital. He doesn't take to this life, no chicken and Midland (Hotel) dinners here. He greatly misses Peter O'Rourke (the Bradford City manager). I know that Dickie sticks it much better than Jock.*
>
> 16/566 Private Vincent Phillips[6]

Private Ewart came out of hospital and returned to the First Pals in time for the Somme offensive. Throughout the 1 July, along with the other bandsmen/stretcher bearers, he pushed himself to the limit bringing in the wounded. But he was again caught by enemy artillery fire. This time he suffered a head wound and the shell shock came back.

> *He was sorely wounded, and at one time it was feared he was down and out for good. But he pulled through bravely.[7]*

He took a long time to recover in hospital, but in the last weeks of the war he was well enough to join the home based West Yorks 51st Training Battalion at Whitley Bay where he was again a member of the band.

The two Pal soccer internationals were eventually re-united at Valley Parade – Dickie Bond after over two years in a prisoner of war camp and Jock after a long spell in hospital. Their re-appearance for City in 1919, with fellow Pal Oscar Fox as Dickie's inside right partner, was an emotional occasion. Normal life began again but sadly Jock's neurasthenia contributed to an unstable life style which led to his premature death. There were two more highlights. He was capped for Scotland again and received praise for keeping a clean sheet in a 3-0 victory over the old enemy England in 1921. In 1923, after City's relegation, he was lured back to Airdrie. Airdrieonians had an exceptionally successful side and he won a Scottish Cup winners medal in 1924. In the semi-final, 'Jock Ewart miraculously saved a certain equalizer which earned him stitches in a head wound and a hero's ovation.'[8]

For four years Airdrie were First Division runners up. One of Jock's particular chums in the side was a "soccer all time great" – the tragic but gifted Hughie Gallacher. Like Jock, Hughie enjoyed a drink or more.[9]

By 1927 City had dropped into the Third Division North. They re-called the manager of their cup winning days, Peter O'Rourke, in a bid to restore former glories. O'Rourke's first act was to bring back Ewart and in 1929 City won promotion. Ewart moved on to Preston North End but retired in 1931 at the age of forty.[10] Within four months he faced disgrace. He was suspended for life and warned off all grounds by the Football Association for allegedly "interfering with the Bradford City-Bury match by offering payment to players".[11]

He became a publican, not the wisest of occupations. Happily, the F.A. lifted the suspension after a chance meeting with a Bradford journalist on a Glasgow station. Despite Jock's continuing good humour and charm, the journalist could see he was terminally ill with not long to live. The journalist interceded privately on his behalf to end the suspension. Shortly afterwards the journalist wrote Jock's obituary. In June, 1943 Jock died at the age of fifty-two.

> *He was one of the most spectacular goalkeepers in the Kingdom..... a*

gifted musician and linguist. As a man he possessed many endearing qualities.[12]

16/1188 Private Abe Waddington, Yorkshire and England

Shortly after 7.30 a.m. on the 1 July, 1916, twenty-three year old Private Abe Waddington of the 1st Bradford Pals was wounded and crawled into a shell hole for shelter in No Man's Land near 'Sap A' at Serre. As he came out of the dead ground from Rob Roy Trench on to the top of the ridge he was hit by shrapnel in both legs and in the hand.[1]

Inside the shell hole he found a scene of devastation. Bodies of dead and dying Leeds Pals and Bradford Pals lay scattered all around. As he gathered his breath and kept his head down to avoid enfilade machine gun fire from the Quadrilateral, he was astonished to discover that he was lying next to one of his cricketing heroes, Lieutenant Major (Major was a first name) Booth, the Yorkshire and England all-rounder.[2]

Lieutenant Booth was in charge of the Number 10 Machine Gun team in the Leeds Pals[3], but was grievously wounded. When Booth moved his team forward, he was hit by shrapnel. He had got up and tried to press on only to collapse again in agony. Only two of his gun team survived. Booth crawled into the shell hole where he later died in a distraught Abe Waddington's arms. Private Waddington was rescued by a stetcher party led by George Morgan, but Major Booth's body was not recovered until the following Spring when it was identified by an M.C.C. cigarette case presented to mark the England team's tour of South Africa. Booth now lies in Serre Road Number One Cemetery.[4]

Abe's widow, Doris, told the author that before Abe was rescued he watched the bodies of his recently dead comrades being eaten by rats. He clung on to Major Booth's body and screamed at the rats to get away. Mrs Waddington said the memory of this horrific event haunted him with nightmares for the rest of his life.[5] Yet by a strange paradox, the young private was to take Major Booth's place in the Yorkshire team and went on to play for England.

In Yorkshire, cricket was a religion and Major Booth was a power in the land. He twice took a 'hat-trick' of wickets. In 1913 he was one of the 'Wisden Five' and completed the 'double' of 1,228 runs and 181 wickets (the highest total in the country). In 1913/14 he was in the England tour team to South Africa. In the last golden summer of 1914 he took 7 for 21 against the M.C.C. at Lords, and in one of his last matches he delighted the Bradford crowd by hitting sixes over the grandstand into the football ground.[6]

Booth's death was a devastating blow to Yorkshire and its supporters. It also devastated his sister who could not accept that he was dead. After the war Abe Waddington visited Miss Booth in her Pudsey cottage, but to his distress was unable to

Abe Waddington.

convince her that Major was dead.[7] Until she died in the 1950's, Major's sister kept his room undisturbed and left a light burning in the cottage window in the forlorn hope that he would return.

The war brought an end to county cricket in 1915, but any Yorkshire supporter fortunate enough to be living in the Ripon area could delight in the inter-battalion cricket matches of 93 Infantry Brigade. It is doubtful if any other brigade in the British Army provided cricket of such quality or ferocious competitiveness.

The Leeds Pals had the stars with four current members of the Yorkshire team (three with Test caps), Major Booth, Arthur Dolphin, and the brothers Roy and Norman Kilner. Yet the Bradford Battalions also had extremely useful sides with players such as Tim Wharton from Undercliffe, and Major Albert W. Robinson from Park Avenue who played in that cradle of Yorkshire cricket the Bradford League.

The First Bradford Pals had a young left arm fast bowler who played for Laisterdyke in the Bradford League. He gave the big names an extremely hostile reception. They noted a fluent action, an ability to move the ball in the air and off the pitch, and an aggressive demeanour designed to intimidate even the toughest batsman. The name Waddington was remembered in 1919 when the Yorkshire team had to be rebuilt after the deaths of Major Booth and Alonzo Drake.

The young man had no doubt about his sporting talent (he played football as a reserve goalkeeper for Bradford City, and competed as a scratch golfer in the Open Championship). His impetuous assertiveness didn't always win friends in the Bradford battalion, but those who knew him well, such as the great Wilfred Rhodes would speak of the generous side to his nature.[8]

John McGrath, the last survivor of the Second Pals, recalled to the author, 'Abe was a bit of a wild man, always getting into scrapes.'[9] When Abe was brought in on a stretcher at Serre by young George Morgan, he was taken to the Aid Post at Basin Wood. George was not overfond of Abe and remembered him swearing and cursing at every bump of the journey. Private Waddington was not best pleased, and said so, when ordered off the stretcher by the hard pressed battalion doctor 'Paddy' Roche. He was told to walk to the Dressing Station at Colincamps.[10]

He was evacuated to England and after a lengthy stay in hospital was again passed fit. His experiences at Serre convinced him that the infantry was not the place to be. He transferred to the Royal Flying Corps and attained the rank of Sergeant by the time of his discharge in March, 1919. He returned home to work in the family fat refining business at Crossley Hall, and resumed cricket with Laisterdyke.

In the first summer of post-war cricket, Yorkshire needed replacements for two pace bowlers, Booth and Drake. The surviving Leeds Pals wounded at Serre, Roy Kilner and Arthur Dolphin, remembered the bowling of Waddington at Ripon. At the advanced age of twenty-six, Abe was called into the Yorkshire side half-way through the season. According to the club's historian, "he burst upon the scene like a fiery comet".

In just eight weeks he took over 100 wickets and helped Yorkshire win the championship. Only ten other players have taken over 100 wickets in their first season (Rhodes and Close are the other Yorkshiremen), but none has done so in less than half a season like Waddington. It was the start of a short, but highly successful, seven year career with the County. The championship was won on five occasions by what was probably the greatest side in the County's history.

It must be more than coincidence that the three former Pals, all wounded at Serre, Dolphin, Kilner and Waddington stand together behind the immortal Hirst and Rhodes in the photograph of the 1919 Championship winning team.

Waddington's success came from left arm medium fast bowling. His run up and delivery was described by the great cricket journalist J.M. Kilburn as the most beautiful classical action he had ever seen. A rhythmical curving run followed by a good length ball which could lift, move in the air, or cut away in both directions. The flowing style was accentuated by a penchant for monogrammed silk shirts with his initials. There was nothing shy or retiring about the Waddington style.[12]

The first dramatic season was followed by even more success in 1920. Four wickets in five balls against Northants and seven wickets in an innings three times. At the end of the season he had taken 140 wickets and was selected for the England team to tour Australia. Two Serre survivors, both from Bradford, Arthur Dolphin and Abe Waddington, flank the back row of a photograph of the touring team.

Although he had little success in the Tests, he topped the bowling averages for the tour as a whole. He never played for England again though this may have more to do with temperament than ability given continued success with Yorkshire. In 1922 he took eight wickets in an innings three times, and had astonishing figures of seven wickets for six runs as Sussex were bowled out for 20 at Hull.[13]

Yorkshire played to win and had little time for the public school niceties. Between 1922 and 1925 Yorkshire lost only six matches out of 122. Michael Stevenson recalled the legacy this produced. 'I vividly recall the apparent bitterness evinced against Yorkshire by the other counties with whom I contended as a struggling undergraduate at Cambridge. When one played against Yorkshire there was an edge, a feeling of being hunted. It was as if one were being psychologically intimidated.'[14]

Yorkshire were not always welcomed on other grounds. Even the good natured Roy Kilner was quoted before a Roses match – 'We say good morning' and after that all we say is 'Howzat'.[15] The volatile Waddington often said more, and it landed him in trouble.

In 1924 against Middlesex he was reported by the umpires because they claimed his attitude towards decisions incited barracking. Middlesex cancelled the fixture for the following season. Only a written apology by Waddington (insisted on by Yorkshire President, Lord

Hawke) saved the fixture. Against Surrey there was more bad feeling, with Waddington again at the centre of it.[16] A heavy fall damaged his bowling shoulder in 1923 and his career began to decline. In 1927, his last season, he scored a century before retiring at the age of thirty-four. He received a benefit of £1,000, a considerable sum at the time. His career record in seven seasons was a remarkable 831 wickets at a little over 19 each. The rest of his life was hardly quiet or retiring. He continued to get into scrapes. He combined the leadership of P. Waddington and Company with a lively social life in Bradford, including Bradford Pals Reunions.[17] The cavalier could be a puritan. When the President of a Bradford Golf Club told a smutty story in front of a lady, Waddington poured a pint of beer over his head[18]. The *Telegraph and Argus* contains numerous tit-bits about Abe's attitude to driving, the police, the licensing laws, war-time controls and the regulations in the fat refining business.Despite the scrapes, he maintained deep friendships with former playing colleagues. He was a pall bearer for Roy Kilner after the latter's death in 1928. The closeness of relationships was emphasized by Roy Kilner naming his son 'Major' after Major Booth. Booth had been Kilner's best man.[19]

Abe died in 1959. To Herbert Sutcliffe, 'Abe was one of my best friends and I found him a grand chap. He was generous to a degree'. To Wilfred Rhodes, 'he was a man of a most generous disposition'. For Maurice Leyland (who wore his Yorkshire cap when playing for England) 'Abe was, one of the finest sportsmen I ever met, and, probably the best left arm bowler of his kind I have ever seen'. J.M. Kilburn wrote in the *Yorkshire Post*, 'As a man he will be remembered for the strength of his friendships'.[20]

In 1953 there was a revealing episode. He travelled to Australia as a guest of the England team (captained by Len Hutton). The ship stopped at Naples, and accompanied by Hutton, Bill Bowes, Herbert Sutcliffe, Bob Appleyard and Johnny Wardle, he went to visit Hedley Verity's grave at Caserta. Verity, the greatest of Yorkshire's spin bowlers, had died of wounds after leading a company of Green Howards into action in 1943. Len Hutton placed a spray of white roses held together by a Yorkshire tie next to the headstone. Not a word was spoken.[21] M.W. Booth and the ghosts of Serre still stirred Abe Waddington's soul. He quietly left his most precious possession – his Yorkshire cap – on Verity's grave.[22]

NOTES

Dickie Bond

1. *Bradford Telegraph & Argus*, 10 September, 1955
2. Ibid.
3. Samuel Fritz Wainwright, 16/402. interview with author, July, 1991.
4. Bill Raistrick. Taped interview with author, 19th November, 1989.
5. *Bradford Weekly Telegraph*, 23rd April, 1915.
6. Ibid.
7. Private Herbert Bradley, 18WY. Taped conversation with Steve Kerry, Bradford Industrial Museum
8. Yorkshire Sports, 21st August, 1948.

Jock Ewart

1. See *Bradford City: A Complete Record 1903-1988* by Gary Firth, Breedon Books for full details of the Club's history.
2. *Bradford Daily Telegraph*, 8 January, 1922
3. *Yorkshire Sports*, 21 August, 1948.
4. Bill Raistrick, taped interview with the author, 19th November, 1989.
5. Bugler Vincent Phillips, letter in possession of his son Mr.S. Phillips.
6. Ibid.
7. Bradford Daily Telegraph, 8th January, 1922
8. *The Hughie Gallacher Story*, p19, by Paul Ioannou, Breedon Books, 1989.
9. Ioannu, ibid. Gallacher played twenty games for Scotland, scoring twenty-four goals, between 1924 and 1935. He later played for Newcastle United and Chelsea, scoring 450 goals in a twenty-four year career. He was idolised on Tyneside. Tragically he committed suicide under a train at Gateshead in 1957.
10. When another famous Scottish player, Alex James, left Preston North End to join the great Arsenal side of the 1930s, Jock Ewart played his violin on Preston railway station as part of the send off ceremony.
11. *Bradford Daily Telegraph*, 24 February, 1942.
12. *Bradford Daily Telegraph*, 25 June, 1943.

Abe Waddington

1. *Bradford Daily Telegraph*, Bradford's Roll of Honour Casualty lists, July, 1916.
2. Information supplied by Mrs. Doris Waddington, conversation with the author, 22nd May, 1989
3. Booth's responsibility based on copy of Brigade report on events of 1 July, 1916 by Brigadier-General J.D. Ingles, typed and retained in a scrap book by 16/112 Corporal L.M. Greenwood, M.S.M., Brigade Clerk. Kindly loaned to the author by his daughter-in-law, Mrs. L.W. Bentley.
4. Laurie Milner (author of the *Leeds Pals* in this series), kindly shared his research with the author.
5. Mrs. Doris Waddington, ibid.
6. Records contained in the Yorkshire County Cricket Club Yearbook, 1991. Individual match reports in the *Bradford Daily Telegraph*.
7. Mrs. Doris Waddington, ibid,
8. Wilfred Rhodes, quoted in *Yorkshire Post*, 28th October, 1959. Abe Waddington's obituary.
9. John McGrath, taped interview with author, ibid.
10. George Morgan, tape loaned to author by Malcolm Brown, ibid.
11. History of Yorkshire County Cricket Club
12. *Yorkshire Post*, obituary, 29th October, 1959
13. See *Yorkshire County Cricket Club Year Book, 1991*. His nephew, Keith Waddington, still has the ball with which Abe took seven for six.
14. Quote from 'Illy', page 24, by Michael Stevenson, pub Midas Books, 1978
15. Stevenson, ibid.
16. Y.C.C.C. Year Book 1991, ibid, for career details. *A History of Yorkshire County Cricket Club*, ibid, for details of Middlesex and Surrey controversies.
17. Keith Waddington, Abe's nephew remembers attending the Reunion with Abe. Interview with author, 29.7.1991.
18. Keith Waddington, ibid.
19. Information kindly supplied by Mick Pope, biographer of Roy Kilner, *The Laughing Cricketer of Wombwell*, Darf Publishers (1990).
20. *Obituary, Yorkshire Post*, 29th October, 1959
21. Sir Leonard Hutton, p.24, *Fifty years of cricket*, pub. Stanley Paul, 1984.
22. *History of Yorkshire County Cricket Club*, ibid.

Chapter Ten

SERRE

SATURDAY, 1 JULY, 1916

Good luck, men. There is not a German left in their trenches, our guns have blown them to Hell.
MAJOR-GENERAL ROBERT WANLESS O'GOWAN, G.O.C. 31ST DIVISION[1]
Battalion set off in good spirits. Wish I was going with them.
16/853 PRIVATE FRED RAWNSLEY, DIARY ENTRY, 30 JUNE, 1916[2]

Early on Friday afternoon 30 June, the corps commander, Lieutenant-General Sir Aylmer Hunter-Weston arrived in Bus-les-Artois. His retinue included the divisional general Robert Wanless O'Gowan. Hunter-Weston's purpose was to encourage the troops, and with characteristic modesty he had no doubt that he was just the man to do it. He had chosen to speak only to the Kitchener volunteers of 31st Division.

In a letter to his wife written that evening he gave his version of events.

Today I went round eight battalions of the New Army (31st Div.) that are to form part of my assaulting line. They have never yet been in battle and I therefore went and gave them an inspiriting address, with most excellent results. I felt I had got them. My other Divisions in front line are the 4th (with

my old stonewall 11th Infantry Brigade under General Prowse in first line) and the incomparable 29th. Of these I have no fear and as I could not address by word of mouth all 80,000 men I command, I had to content myself with messages to my Divisions to pass down to each officer, N.C.O. and man, and to devote my powers of speech to the New Blood.

A heavy task to speak to eight separate battalions and two machine gun batteries, over 8,000 men, in the open air. Fortunately my voice has stood the heavy strain, and I was given the power to strike the right note and to enthuse the men. It is a valuable gift to be able to speak fairly well.[4]

Whether the Corps Commander 'was given the power to strike the right note' may be judged by the comments of Private George Morgan of the 16th West Yorks.

He stood on a box and made a speech to us. He went on about having the true 'attack' spirit and the old words about fighting for Britain's honour came out. He said the

Lieutenant-General Sir Aylmer Hunter-Weston.

Germans were barbarians who didn't understand honour and it was the Germans who had started the war. We were to have no doubts in our minds about which side was fighting for a just cause. God was on our side and the only good German was a dead one... all that sort of stuff. He went on like that for some time. He told us not to worry because not even a rat would be left alive in the German trenches after our bombardment.

Then he said something which made us all very angry. He said anyone who funked the attack and didn't go forward would be shot on the spot. He said there would be plenty of military police about in the trenches and they had strict orders to watch for any shirkers. We felt sickened by this sort of talk. What sort of men did he think we were?

He said nothing about the trench raid the night before. We thought he must have prepared his speech days before. Anyway he then rode off to raise the morale of some other battalion They led us to believe it was just going to be a tea party. Some bloody tea party. 16/1205 PRIVATE GEORGE MORGAN[5]

Hunter-Weston's optimism about the impact of the artillery bombardment, 'not even a rat will be left alive' was not shared by his Divisional artillery officers. Lieutenant Harry Siepmann of the Royal Artillery was in charge of a battery of six 18-pounder guns which he described as being housed in six hollow cubes constructed of sandbags and steel girders, to a height of fully ten feet. Harry Siepmann's battery was located between the Sucrerie and Basin Wood immediately behind the trenches allocated to the Pals. He had a grandstand view of the events of 1 July. He recorded his opinion of the VIII Corps' artillery arrangements.

From a gunner's point of view, (the arrangements) were idiotic. In the first place, we were instructed to cut 'lanes' in the enemy wire by the use of low bursting shrapnel, thus advertising to the enemy the exact points at which the attack would seek to penetrate their defences.

In the second place, the ration of ammunition allotted to our battery for this purpose was 1,000 rounds, to be expended in the course of seven days. We knew well enough, to our cost, how desperately short the supplies of ammunition to the British Army were at that time. But we also knew that to cut a 'lane' with shrapnel (or, for that matter, with high explosives, which was scarcer still) was the most wasteful use to which ammunition could be put.

LIEUTENANT HARRY SIEPMANN, ROYAL ARTILLERY, 31ST DIVISION[6]

Lieutenant Siepmann was not the only person to believe that the artillery plan would advertise the exact point of the attack to the enemy. A more influential figure, Brigadier-General H.C. Rees, in command of 94 Infantry Brigade (the Sheffield, Accrington and Barnsley Pals) on the immediate left of the Bradford Pals in 93rd Brigade in the attack, complained vigorously to the Corps Commander,

A few days before the attack, I pointed out to General Hunter-Weston that the assembly trenches stopped dead on the left of 94 Brigade and that not a spade had been put into the ground between me and the subsidiary attack at Gommecourt. Worse still, no effort at wire cutting was made on that stretch either. A child could see where the flank of our attack lay, to within ten yards.

BRIGADIER-GENERAL HUBERT CONWAY REES C.M.G., D.S.O.[7]

Hunter-Weston whilst congratulating Rees on his observation,

He was extremely optimistic, telling everyone that the wire had been blown away, although we could see it standing strong and well, that there would be no German trenches and all we had to do was to walk into Serre.

BRIGADIER-GENERAL HUBERT CONWAY REES C.M.G., D.S.O.[8]

If the task was that simple, one is tempted to ask why the Corps Commander didn't offer to ride at the head of his troops and make a triumphal entry into Serre. No doubt the survivors of the trench raid the night before would have been happy to show him the way. Private Joe Macdonald (18/1346) was one of those survivors, but he was killed in the main attack on 1 July.

Nothing was done to follow up Rees' suggestion for dummy assembly trenches between Serre and Gommecourt. The German heavy artillery at Pusieux behind Serre did not disclose itself before 1 July and was able to register and focus all its power on 94 and 93 Brigades. Although Brigadier Rees was more enthusiastic about Hunter-Weston's oratorical powers than the men, stating it was a magnificent speech, he was still sceptical of its content.

'We had been informed on several occasions that the enemy had only fifty-five guns north of the [River] Ancre, a statement about which I was a trifle sceptical at the time; my scepticism was fully justified as the enemy were reported on the 3 July to have no less than sixty-six batteries in action behind Serre alone.'[9]

After Hunter-Weston's departure from Bus and as the time to move up to the line on that fateful Friday evening approached, the Pals gathered together quietly sitting in sections in the orchard and fields just off the road at the western end of Bus village. Two of the Leeds Pals, R.G. Potts and J.J. Ward sitting in the Church Yard, carved their names low down on the rear of the church tower. The carving survives to this day and the carvers survived. Both were commissioned later in the war.[10]

Last letters were written and requests made to visit relatives 'if anything happens to me'. One such letter was written by Lieutenant Robert Sutcliffe of the First Pals. The bespectacled Sutcliffe, a solicitor and former Yorkshire golf champion, was one of no less than twenty-four old boys of Bradford Grammar School serving as officers in the two Bradford Battalions.

Just a line to say I go "over the lid" tomorrow. My company are in the first line of attack and hope to do great things. We all naturally hope to come through all right, but of course, one never knows, someone's bound to go under and it's the only way to end the war. It's a great thing to be in, and I'm glad our division is one of the first chosen to go over.

LIEUTENANT ROBERT SUTCLIFFE, 16WY[11]

Thirty-one year old Second Lieutenant Ralph Stead, of C Company, was a schoolmaster at Paignton College in Devon and had joined the Pals at the

Leeds Pals graffiti on Bus Church.

suggestion of his friends the Russell brothers from Norfolk. He wrote to his parents on 28 June,

> My dearest Dad and Mother.
>
> The advance has come at last and early tomorrow we shall attack. I am in command of the front line of my Company and it is the very first line of attack. If I come through I shall be able to tell you about our part of the greatest battle that will ever be. If I should be killed you must not fret, as it is the finest death to die, and I have no fear of meeting it. I must stop now.
>
> With love, Ralph.

SECOND LIEUTENANT RALPH STEAD, 16 WY[12]

Corporal Harry Cockroft (16/1185) in C Company of the 1st Pals didn't write a letter. Instead he went looking for his brother Willie (16/1170). When he found him it was a happy meeting with a deal of good natured banter about Willie's yellow arm band. Willie claimed it was a new badge of rank as chief sanitary man. In fact it meant he was to be a wire cutter going in at the head

Aerial view of Bus-les-Artois looking east towards the German lines. Courcelles and Colincamps are in the distance.

of the first wave on the left flank of the First Pals. The yellow band had a sinister side to it. Should the wire cutter be killed or wounded, he would be easily identified and the implements retrieved to allow the wire cutting to be completed. Harry would be further behind in the second wave with the Number 6 Lewis gun team. The two brothers had no illusions about the danger. Their younger brother Tom had been killed in Flanders in 1915 serving with the Duke of Wellington's Regiment. They shook hands and wished each other luck. They never saw each other again. Harry survived and gained the D.C.M. for his courage at Serre. Willie, equally brave, became the second Cockroft brother to die.[13]

The band of the Leeds Pals, many of whom had played together in the Leeds City Tramways band before the war or as part of the orchestra at the Grand Theatre, contained musicians of the very highest quality. They now played a selection of music to pass the waiting time on the grassed area in the

middle of the village. The haunting intensity of one piece stayed in the memory of Private Bill Slater of the Second Bradford Pals for the rest of his life.

Although I cannot remember all the programme played on that lovely summer evening so long ago, I certainly have an abiding memory of one piece, Schubert's Unfinished Symphony. *Because of this, every performance that I have heard of it since takes me back to that evening in Bus, still quite clear, in my mind's eye, with all those Leeds and Bradford Pals sitting around on the grass quietly listening, and with all of them no doubt wondering, as I certainly did, what waited us at daybreak the following morning.*
                                      18/273 PRIVATE WILLIAM SLATER[14]

When the bandsmen finished their last item, they carefully stored their instruments away in their billet and quietly prepared for the change of role from musician to stretcher bearer.

Tim Wharton (16/65), the First Pals drummer who had bought his own drum because the army issue one wasn't good enough for him, now carried a stretcher. He was with his inseparable mate, the french horn player Corporal Franklin Morrell (16/811). Bugler Vincent Phillips (16/566) in B Company, was worried about his companion, Jock Ewart (16/1723) who played the clarinet. Jock had trudged up the road with him from Gezaincourt in a distinctly edgy state as they passed through the batteries. He was nervously chain smoking and had visited the local estaminet for rather more than his fair share of liquid refreshment. Jock, the Bradford City and Scotland goalkeeper, was known for reckless bravery when diving at the feet of centre forwards – but he had recently come out of hospital after being shell shocked a few weeks before. Just to be at Bus-les-Artois and then to march up to the line with the Pals surpassed any bravery he displayed on the football field given the shaky state of his nerves.[15]

Jock's Bradford City team-mate and fellow international, Sergeant Dickie Bond (18/922) checked and re-checked the mechanism of his Lewis gun with his partner Dick Collins (18/110) as the 18th West Yorks waited to follow the 16th out of the village. Dickie always admitted to a tightness in the stomach as the adrenalin began to flow before a First Division match. The familiar butterflies began again in Bus. At 5.45 p.m., there was an additional anxiety for one of the Second Pals bandsmen Corporal Percy Bunney (18/1658). Percy, a professional musician from Ilford, had joined the Pals in the Autumn of 1915 at Fovant in response to an advertisement by the Bradford battalion for bandsmen in *Stage Magazine*. He soon became friendly with two of the Bradford men, Private Bert Crimmins (18/313) and Private Arthur Wild (18/356).[16] Crimmins and Wild failed to show up for the 18th Battalion's 5.45 p.m. Roll Call, and their names were duly noted as absent by Lieutenant Thornton. The two men had been on carrying duties for several weeks including the previous night and had not been involved in the assault training at Gezaincourt. They had instructions to report back in time for Roll Call and had been warned to carry more supplies up to the line when the battalion moved off. Corporal Bunney was aware that Arthur Wild's nerves were in a bad state after being buried by a 'coal box' which had exploded next to him when they were digging a Sap on the Redan Ridge early in June, and he knew the two men had a reputation for liking a drink in the village estaminet which had done a roaring trade all week. Crimmins and Wild did eventually return to the battalion, in mid-July under arrest. They were shot as deserters on 4 September and their story is told in a separate chapter.

The First Pals bandsmen left ahead of the rest of the Battalion at 4.30 p.m. Charles Pickworth the bass drummer described what he saw.

> *30.6.1916 Left for the trenches at 4.30 for carrying. Eve of the Advance. Had rum just before entering the trenches. Shelled all the way down trenches, but the rum was working, and took little effect on my nerves. Arrived in trenches 9.30 p.m. prepared rations ammunition ready for the battalion which began to arrive after 1.00 a.m. July 1st. Nearly all trenches flattened out. We carried all supplies of ammunition, rum etc., I was about exhausted and deaf with the noise of the guns.*
>
> 16/212 PRIVATE CHARLES PICKWORTH[17]

The Leeds Pals were the first Battalion of the brigade to march out of Bus. Just before they were due to leave at 6.00 p.m., the air was rent by the sound of an explosion. One of the Leeds Pals had accidentally triggered off a bucketful of primed Mills bombs and rifle grenades. The man was killed and fourteen others were severely wounded. The Leeds Pals bandsmen, so recently playing the haunting melodies of Schubert, now found themselves dealing with casualties before their battalion had even left for the line.[18]

At 6.35 p.m. the First Bradfords followed the Leeds Pals out of Bus. A total of twenty-two officers and 675 men marched out along the road to Courcelles.

Ten per cent of the Infantrymen from each Battalion remained in Bus as a cadre to ensure the battalion could continue under the two second in commands, Major Kennedy and Major Carter. Specialists such as the signallers, clerks and the transport section also stayed behind. Fred Rawnsley, one of the signallers, watched his friends march off and noted in his diary, 'Battalion set off in good spirits. Wish I was going with them'.[19]

Adding his own personal word of cheer and encouragement was the Divisional General, Major-General Robert Wanless O'Gowan. He stood at the roadside at Bus with his staff. As the men marched past George Morgan heard him shout, 'Good luck, men. There is not a German left in their trenches, our guns have blown them all to hell'.[20]

When the 16th West Yorks reached Colincamps they were served with a hot meal of bully beef.[21] By now the early banter and nervous joking had worn off. They were tired and subdued as they moved off again just before 10.00 p.m. The British artillery continued to howl and scream over their heads. As they left Colincamps and neared the Sucrerie, a chill sobering sight awaited them. Near Euston Dump on the approach to Southern Avenue they had to pass Euston Road Cemetery. Casualties from the previous two months were buried there. Now, through the darkness the marching men saw the preparatory work of the Division's pioneer battalion, the 12th K.O.Y.L.I., several freshly dug mass graves ready for the next day. At Euston Dump the already heavily laden men were given even more to carry.

> *I picked a shovel because I thought it was not as clumsy and it was put through our equipment at the back. You couldn't walk, you know, in fact I think I was walking bow legged...I had so much weight.*
>
> 16/1205 PRIVATE GEORGE MORGAN[22]

The 16th West Yorks had come under sporadic enemy artillery fire as they left Colincamps. There were several casualties, including George Morgan's cousin, Sergeant Billy Morgan (16/8).

> *We were going down Sackville Street and they sent some shells over and somebody said, 'Billy Morgan's got it'. Now Billy was my cousin, he was my platoon sergeant, and as it happened it had blown his head... blown his head...right off..., all mutilated.* 16/1205 PRIVATE GEORGE MORGAN[23]

George felt sickened by what he saw. His friends didn't know what to say to him. There was nothing he could do but march on with tears streaming down his face. As the Pals trudged up towards the line, often flattening themselves to avoid enemy shell fire, the Corps Commander Sir Aylmer Hunter-Weston was in his château at Buquesne writing in his usual optimistic vein to his wife.

> *Tomorrow is the great day, and by this time tomorrow another great page in History will be turned. Everything promises well for the success of the great venture and never have I entered a battle with so many chances in our favour. The result is in the hands of God but I can say that all that can be done to ensure success has been done by Haig, Rawly and by my staff. Difficulties,*

disappointments, contretemps and heavy losses there are sure to be, but I rejoice in difficulties and pray God I may be given strength and judgement to put right the matters that require to be put right, as difficulties arise.

LT. GEN. SIR AYLMER HUNTER-WESTON, VIII CORPS[24]

It is difficult to know how the general could reconcile his 'not a rat left alive' to the men, with 'heavy losses there are sure to be' to his wife.

At 8.45 p.m. the Second Bradfords left Bus for the trenches. Private Bill Slater remembered the intensity of feeling as they followed the Leeds Pals and the First Bradfords in the march up to the line.

William Slater.

The feeling of comradeship among us seemed to grow as we marched forward into a common danger. In particular I have a lasting memory of the man who was closest to me as we marched. I was only eighteen at the time, having joined the army under age, and he was some years older than I. As he spoke to me, I became aware of a feeling of tenderness in him towards me, as though he sensed my fears and was trying to reassure both himself and me. "Don't worry, Bill", he said. "We'll be all right". And he spoke as gently as a mother trying to soothe a frightened child.

18/273 PRIVATE WILLIAM SLATER[25]

The march was a stop and start affair for the Second Pals. Despite the fact that there was a 'one-way' traffic system in operation, there was massive congestion in the communication trenches. The artillery barrage was not a one sided affair, and the two leading battalions came under enemy fire as they neared the front line. Stretcher parties evacuating casualties suffered by the Leeds Pals and 16th Battalion understandably ignored the 'one-way' system in Southern Avenue and slowed progress down even more even though the East Yorks retiring from the line stuck to the system. A sight of the casualties did little for the morale of these relatively raw soldiers. As twilight came and darkness fell, it must have been like travelling into Dante's inferno. The earth shook and the sky was lit up by the awesome power of the British barrage. On top of the ridge beyond Courcelles the road was exposed and open to enemy observation. A three hundred yard long canvas camouflage tunnel had been erected to avoid detection. As the men entered the tunnel, it seemed like the entrance to some sort of nightmare theatre. It took the Second Pals nearly eight hours to reach their positions in Dunmow and Landguard trenches at 4.30 a.m. The final stretch through the mud of the communication trenches had been particularly exhausting.

There had been no hot meal at Colincamps as they struggled through the village in the dark. Instead they took their first casualty. Captain Charles Duckitt, commanding D Company had had a near miss from a clumsy accidental shot from Tony Miller in Egypt. There was no escape this time and he was hit by a shell splinter. Captain Duckitt recovered and eventually returned to the battalion only to be killed at Gavrelle the following May. As the shout of 'stretcher bearer' rang out for Captain Duckitt, Lieutenant Whitaker took over command of D Company and led them into their positions in Dunmow Trench.[26]

A photograph of an artillery barrage at night on the Western Front.

The 93 Brigade battalions finally reached their assembly positions in the early hours of the morning 1 July. The Leeds Pals (15th West Yorks) in the first wave were in the Front Line, and in Leeds Trench just behind it, by 2.45 a.m. They were joined later at 5.30 a.m. by the 93 Light Trench Mortar Battery in Leeds Trench and in Sap A and Sap B. The First Bradford Pals (16th West Yorks) and D Company of the Durham Pals (18th Durham Light Infantry) in the Second Wave were in place in Old Monk Trench, Bradford Trench and South Monk Trench by 3.20 a.m. The Second Bradford Pals (18th West Yorks) forming the Third and Fourth waves were in Dunmow and Landguard Trenches by 4.10 a.m. The rest of the Durham Pals were in Maitland Trench by 4.50 a.m.

One Company of the Pioneer Battalion, the 12th Kings Own Yorkshire Light Infantry, were in Legend Trench at 5.53 a.m tasked with digging saps to link up with the German lines after a successful assault. 93 Brigade Machine Gun Company had taken up position in Legend Trench and Fargate Trench at 10.00 p.m. on the previous evening.[27]

Now the waiting began. George Morgan, grieving for his cousin Billy, remembered the waiting time.

> *I was afraid – everyone must have been afraid, but I was more afraid of showing it. I didn't want to let the side down. I hoped I would be able to do what I was expected to do.* 16/1250 PRIVATE GEORGE MORGAN[28]

George went on to describe waiting in the narrow and specially dug Assembly Trench.

> *We assembled in Bradford Trench, it was the trench we'd dug specially for assembly. There was nothing in this trench. I just put my shovel across it and made a kind of seat. Course I had to keep moving when anybody wanted to go past. It was very tense, in fact there was not much talking at all. I don't know what other people were thinking about. I were thinking about home, you know, my home. My thoughts were on home because I knew we'd have some., well, a lot of casualties really, although they'd told us we wouldn't and of course you wondered if it was gonna be you. Then we just had one or two bits of humour like when Dawson Horn came dancing down the trench. He was a right humorist was Dawson, and he came dancing down the trench laughing as usual and he said, "Ahhhh, we're looking forward to going over the top, and if I catch a little bow legged German", he says, "without rifle and bayonet won't I run the bugger round".* 16/1250 PRIVATE GEORGE MORGAN[29]

Sadly Private Dawson Horn (16/865) never found his little bow legged German, and after the assault nobody found Dawson. His name appears on the Thiepval Memorial.

The dawn came and it was a beautiful morning. But still the British artillery barrage screamed overhead crashing into the German lines. Watches were checked as the minutes ticked away. Company officers now came round with platoon officers to distribute the rum ration. George Morgan's company commander was twenty-two year old Captain Donald Smith who was accompanied by twenty year Lieutenant Frank Symonds. Although Donald Smith was very young he was a tough minded impressive figure with powerful connections in Bradford, and he had played Rugby Union for Batley RFC and the Yorkshire County team. He was a staunch lemonade Liberal and blue ribbon teetotaller. He had decided opinions about the size of the rum ration:

> Well, he was a well known teetotal advocate and he dished it out, you know, very very sparingly. Anyway Dawson wouldn't have any. He said, "I want to go over in my own senses", as if that drop of rum would have made much difference, it didn't. And they wouldn't give you anybody else's. So that was the last thing they did with us before we went over... our rum ration. What was left went down the sump.
>
> 16/1250 PRIVATE GEORGE MORGAN [30]

The sound of the barrage was terrifying but at least it offered comfort to the Pals that the Germans were taking a terrific pounding. The barrage, consisting of 18-pounders and 4.5 howitzers, was spectacular, but the German dug outs were sufficiently deep to provide protection for the defending troops. Nor was the German wire badly damaged. What damage there was left narrow lanes where attacking troops would be congested and make them an easy target. Where the British wire had been deliberately cut in the night, the same problem applied. Bridges laid across trenches for troops advancing from behind the first line had the same effect.

The Brigade War Diary records that from 7.10 a.m. German artillery was replying heavily on the British front line and assembly trenches with shrapnel. [31]

At 7.20 a.m. the Pals Battalions in 93 Infantry Brigade felt the ground shake as the Hawthorn Ridge mine was blown just over a mile away to the south beyond the Redan Ridge. A huge cloud of debris, earth, stones, and human remains erupted into the air. It was a moment captured for posterity by Geoffrey Malins in the film of the *Battle of the Somme*. It is repeatedly shown now in television news items and documentary programmes.

The blowing of the mine may have given the Pals a momentary encouragement, but in reality it was the final confirmation to the Germans, if any was needed, that the infantry assault was about to begin. The ten minute gap between the blowing of the mine and the start of the infantry assault was one of the critical factors in the ultimate failure of VIII Corps' attack, and the responsibility for that decision lay with the Commander of VIII Corps, Lieutenant General Sir Aylmer Hunter-Weston.

At 7.20 a hurricane trench mortar bombardment began, but it coincided

A battery of British field guns on the Somme front.

with the lift of the main artillery bombardment on the German front line. This too, sent confirmation to the Germans that the British assault was about to begin. After seven days huddled deep in their dug outs, the men of the German 169th Infantry Regiment prepared to climb up to the parapets to meet the Pals.

> *Now everyone knows that the hour of retaliation will soon come. Cartridges and hand grenade reserves are made ready and at 8.30 [7.30 British time] the alarm call 'They are coming!' is screamed in the dugouts.*
>
> OTTO LAIS, 169 INFANTRY REGIMENT[32]

At 7.21 a.m. the two lead platoons of the Leeds Pals climbed quietly out of their front line trench. Their task was to space out and then lie down on the tapes for the next nine minutes until zero hour came at 7.30 and to ensure that the succeeding waves behind them would follow in the correct direction. They had been seen and the two platoons climbed out into a devastating enemy artillery bombardment. They began to suffer casualties immediately, their only cover being the waist-high grass or shell holes created by the bombardment.[33]

At 7.30, the waiting time was over. The whistles blew and the heavily burdened men struggled to climb up the scaling ladders. George Morgan's platoon officer was twenty year old Second Lieutenant Frank Symonds. With Ralph Stead and Cecil Ransome, he was one of the Thetford Grammar School group set – all friends or relatives of the Russell brothers who had joined the Pals together at Skipton.

> *There was no lingering about when zero hour came. Our platoon officer blew the whistle and he was first up the scaling ladder with his revolver in one hand and a cigarette in the other. "Come on, boys", he said and up he went. We went up after him one at a time. I never saw the officer again. He was reported missing and his name is on the Thiepval Memorial. He was only young but he was a very very brave man.*
>
> 16/1250 PRIVATE GEORGE MORGAN[34]

Any thought of an orderly walk with rifles to the port to fulfil the plan to take over the German lines was quickly dispelled. What happened next was a

The ruined village of Serre and, inset, some of the Germans of 169th Infantry Regiment who defended it against the Pals battalions.

chaotic nightmare of noise, confusion, pain and death.

> *The German machine gun fire was terrible. Our colonel [Colonel Guyon] was hit after only a few steps along the trench. I helped to prop him up against the trench side. Then we climbed on to the top of the trench. I had not reached my full height when a machine-gun bullet smacked into my steel helmet. I felt as if I had been hit with a sledge hammer: it was completely smashed in.*
>
> PRIVATE W.H.T. CARTER, 16WY[35]

> *As soon as you attempted to get out of the trenches you were fired on. The trench was just a shambles and of course there was confusion. I always remember one chap, an officer called Captain Pringle. We never used to like him as he used to bark at us. He was waving his revolver about and shouting, he could have shot anyone. I got hit in the wrist... it was shrapnel. How I got out I don't know. We were hit by shells, snipers and machine guns. I got to the dressing station. I never saw the Germans. You can just understand when you are in a hailstorm and suddenly it all comes down.*
>
> PRIVATE GEORGE GRUNWELL, 16WY[36]

George Grunwell survived and lived for a further eighty years to become the last known original Pal from either of the Bradford Battalions.

George Morgan recalled the struggle to climb up the ladder and the impact and terror of going over the top:

I nearly fell back into the trench with the weight of the equipment. Well our orders were that we had to go in extended order about two yards between each man but when we got on the top the men were falling so rapidly that there was no extended order at all. Billy Booth was the man who went up before me and he was the nearest to me. He fell and he screamed "George, do help me"... and my second in command said, "Come on George, leave him, leave him, leave him. The stretcher bearers will see to him. Come on." So I went on and then he got hit and he fell and he said, "I got hit, George. Go on". He says "the 18th, the Second Pals'll be coming up, the next wave'll be coming up and they'll join you".

Well I went on a bit and I felt a right thud in my tummy here... and a piece of shrapnel had blown the pouch off, one of me pouches... and sort of burnt me a bit. It was red hot you see and it knocked me down. I thought well this is where I'm wounded but I wasn't. Anyway I fell in a shell hole and there was nobody there. I didn't even get to the wire. Well nobody came up, I laid in this shell hole and nobody stood up and there was nothing to be seen. Didn't know what to do with no officers, you see, with nobody to direct you or anything. I lay there for what seemed to be hours and then I made me way back and the trenches were full of wounded and dead.

I dropped into trench and I dropped into another Pal who was dead. He must have fallen back into the trench, he must never have gone up the ladder... I knew it were Norman Waddilove without looking at him because he had a silver bracelet on his wrist with his name on, but I knew it was him without looking at it because he looked as if he'd gone to sleep and that's how a lot of 'em were.

16/1250 PRIVATE GEORGE MORGAN[37]

Private George Gransbury (16/779) described what happened to Captain Pringle and Captain Donald Smith in a letter sent from hospital to his parents in Thornton. The letter was published in the *Yorkshire Observer* on 14 July.

Over we went and as we were the first the fireworks started. The Boches meant keeping us at long range and not caring to be gun fodder we knocked on and got about 100 yards and only about twenty-five of us were left in our company. Our officer was wounded and a corporal was in charge. Still on we went and began to miss each other. I dropped on Captain Pringle and dragged him to a shell hole in which were Captain D. Smith and Lieutenant R. Sutcliffe. A few privates filled up the spare places. I was creeping up the side of the crater to see what was going on when a high explosive dropped right on top of us. How I escaped God alone knows. Captain Pringle was blown from the opposite side on to the top of me and I was buried but could breathe. A lad helped me out.

16/779 PRIVATE GEORGE GRANSBURY[38]

The difficulty of knowing precisely what happened to Captain Pringle and to the others is shown by what could be interpreted as a contradictory report collected in hospital from Private Luther Horner.

Captain Pringle was wounded twice in the legs and shortly afterwards killed outright by shell fragments striking his face. He died less than an hour later.

16/694 PRIVATE LUTHER HORNER M.M.[39]

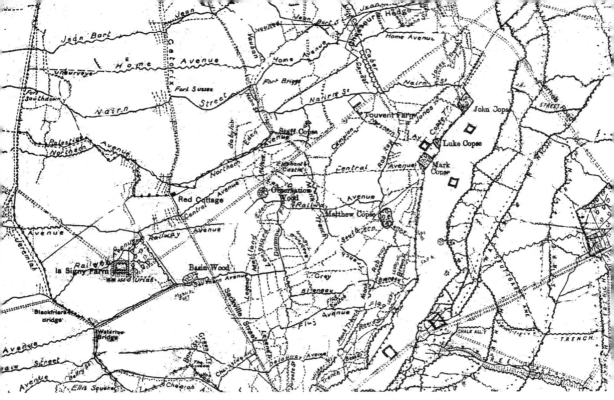

A trench map showing the British trench system in front of Serre. See aerial photograph on page 189.

There is a story that Robert Pringle's body was found twenty years later, but this seems unlikely because he is buried in Euston Road Cemetery which was used for casualties immediately after the battle. Bodies found later in the war, and in the years after the war, were buried in the Serre Road cemeteries close to where the bodies were found.

Captain Donald Smith's body was never identified and his father never accepted his death, but the bespectacled solicitor Robert Sutcliffe was brought in by stretcher bearers. He died five days later on a hospital ship crossing the Channel. He had amused George Grunwell and his mates at Skipton by getting his left mixed up with his right and nearly marching the platoon into the canal. In his last letter he wrote,

> We all naturally hope to come through all right, but of course, one never knows, someone's bound to go under and it's the only way to end the war. It's a great thing to be in.
>   LIEUTENANT ROBERT SUTCLIFFE, 16WY[40]

He was buried on the high Pennines amongst his nonconformist ancestors in the Chapel burial ground at Slack near Heptonstall.

The slight five foot five bespectacled figure of twenty-one year old Captain Alan Clough led D Company of the First Pals over the top. He looked, and indeed he was, an intellectual. He had abandoned his science Tripos at Trinity College Cambridge in order to join the Pals because he felt it was his duty to do so. His grandfather, Sir John Clough, had been a Liberal MP and his family were wealthy mohair spinners in the Worth Valley. Both his grandfather and his father were members of the Keighley Recruiting Committee and he felt a duty to set an example. In October, 1914, his Headmaster at Tonbridge School supplied a reference for young Clough to Colonel Muller.

Small in stature, a family trait, but in all respects most desirable as an officer. Afraid he is not.[41]

Afraid he may have been – but it was far from evident in Alan Clough's conduct. He was soon wounded but carried on leading his men and sending messages back to Battalion HQ in an astonishing display of courage. His first message was written when D Company had climbed out of Bradford Trench and given to one of the runners, Private Drake, to take back to Battalion Headquarters. It read:

To O.C. 16th West Yorks   No 10
From O.C. 'D' Coy
'D' Coy advancing. Casualties unknown
(Sgd) Alan Clough (Capt)
Place In front of Bradford trench   Time 8am   1/7/16[42]

What happened next is described in the contemporary evidence collected from the wounded as they lay in hospital after the battle.

I saw Captain Clough hit with a bullet in the wrist. He fell and got up again. He was hit later in the shoulder and then again in the body. He fell and got up three more times. I was hit and lay just behind him where he finally fell. He was still lying there when I got back into a Sap.

16/186 PRIVATE ERNEST WARHURST[43]

I saw Captain Clough hit three times. On the last occasion he failed to rise. He was 15 to 20 yards from the German trenches.

16/1401 PRIVATE JOSEPH SHELDON[44]

My Pal, Private Chambers, was Captain Clough's runner. When Captain Clough was wounded, Private Chambers returned to find Captain Clough writing another message with a map out. It was never finished.

16/125 PRIVATE FRED LEEMING[45]

Alan Clough's body was never found. His second in command Lieutenant John Holdsworth Robinson, took over command for only a matter of moments before he too was killed. His father Sir John Holdsworth Robinson was Chairman of the Bradford Chamber of Trade, and Chairman Citizen's Army League. Alan Clough and John Holdsworth's names are on the Thiepval Memorial.

Nineteen year old Private Harold Coe (16/130) was Alan Clough's observer. He had joined up with two friends from Pudsey, nineteen year old Norman Waddilove (16/313) (whose body was recognised by George Morgan) and twenty-one year old Squire Clough (16/707). Their families were part of the business and political establishment of Pudsey but all preferred not to have a commission. All three were killed on 1 July and their names appear on the Thiepval Memorial. Norman Waddilove's father, a textile millionaire, owned Claremont in Bradford which later became the home of the Pals Comradeship Association.

For the Second Pals in Dunmow and Landguard Trenches the waiting continued. They came under enemy shrapnel fire at 7.10 a.m., and the bombardment intensified ten minutes later with high explosive fire as well. They began to suffer casualties as the waiting continued. At 8.20 a message was received at Battalion Headquarters from Brigade that the 16th West Yorks were held up, an understatement if ever there was one, and ordering the 18th's C.O. Colonel Kennard to go forward to Sap 'A' in the front line to investigate. The Colonel was still making his way forward when the order was given for the 18th West Yorks to leave the trenches at 8.40 a.m.[46]

Lieutenant Harold Foizey was due to lead a party of bombers and quietly smoked a cigarette. Corporal Norman Goldthorpe was standing next to him and recorded what happened in his diary.

At 8.20, I remember saying a little prayer and just before we climbed out, our officer Lieutenant Foizey said "I know I will not come back". I told him to believe he would as I certainly believed I would.

18/251 CORPORAL NORMAN GOLDTHORPE[47]

After the order 'fix bayonets', came the blast of whistles at 8.40 a.m. and the 2nd Pals climbed out of Landguard and Dunmow trenches. Unlike the First Pals and the Leeds Pals, the Second had the initial advantage of dead ground in the first few yards when they left their trenches. Norman Goldthorpe's diary entry continued:

I scrambled out behind Lieutenant Foizey with his section of bombers... having not travelled more than thirty yards or so the section was reduced to four men. Lieutenant Foizey ordered his small party to take cover behind a small hillock whilst he went forward to see what was happening, but he was killed covering only a couple of yards.

18/251 CORPORAL NORMAN GOLDTHORPE[48]

Private Albert Hawkes (18/351) who was wounded, described how Norman Goldthorpe took Lieutenant Foizey's German trench maps, revolver, watch and Very light pistol and later handed them in after the battle.[49] Norman Goldthorpe was later commissioned and survived the war. In 1974 he made a final pilgrimage to France and wrote of Lieutenant Foizey in his old diary again, 'Fifty eight years to the day, on 1 July 1974, I was to stand beside his grave in Euston Road Cemetery and pay my last respects to a very gallant gentleman.'[50]

Bill Slater, who was in Landguard trench, described the initial moments of the advance:

For some reason nothing seemed to happen to us. At first we strolled along as though walking in a park. Then suddenly, we were in the midst of a storm of machine-gun bullets and I saw men beginning to twirl round and fall in all kinds of curious ways as they were hit, quite unlike the way actors do it in films.

18/273 PRIVATE WILLIAM SLATER [51]

About a 100 yards beyond Dunmow trench, the leading waves of the 18th West Yorks began to come under heavy enfilade machine-gun fire from the German machine guns in the Quadrilateral (Heidenkopf) on their right. They also caught up with their colonel who had gone on ahead of them to investigate what was happening at Sap A.

It was hell on earth. Everyone dropped flat on their stomachs. Colonel

A German shell lands close to the British front line.

> *Kennard was standing and carrying only a walking stick. He called out, "Come on boys, up you get", and began to walk towards the enemy.*
>
> 18/175 PRIVATE FRANK BURN[52]

The colonel walked forward into a hail of machine-gun, rifle and artillery fire and was killed almost immediately. Lieutenant Colonel Maurice Nicholl Kennard M.C. (three times mentioned in despatches, and wounded in 1914) was thirty two. His body too was never identified, and his name appears on the Thiepval Memorial. The 18th's Adjutant Captain Frederick Williams was with Colonel Kennard and was extremely fortunate to survive. The medical records in his file at the Public Record Office disclose,

> *Wounded in the right side of the head by a bullet which passed through the lobe of the ear close to the right external meatus pursuing its course through the posterior margin of the steroid mastoid. The right ear drum was perforated and there is facial paralysis on the right side. Suffers frequently from attacks of giddiness. All teeth to be removed. Hearing permanently impaired.*[53]

It is remarkable that Fred Williams recovered sufficiently to transfer to the Royal Flying Corps where he became Adjutant to 46 Training Squadron at Catterick. He was eventually awarded the M.B.E. for service with the R.A.F.

Captain Cecil Keevil, who had spent two nights searching No Man's Land for Privates Walden and Ferrand in May, had led A Company over the top from Dunmow trench. He was hit and seriously wounded. Like Fred Williams he never returned to the Pals, and he too transferred to the Royal Flying Corps as a navigator, only to be killed in 1917.[54]

Lieutenant Harold Colley, the Second Pals' Intelligence Officer who had taught the First Pals Officers German at Skipton was with Colonel Kennard and the Adjutant. He was less fortunate than Captain Williams. Private John

Harrison was interviewed in hospital in Boulogne:

> *I saw Lieutenant Colley lying on top of a shell hole, bleeding badly in the back. He asked for a drink of water and to carry him back to the trench. We did. We went on but returned later. We passed the same spot but couldn't find him. There were no stretcher bearers and I think he was blown up. They were shelling every inch of the trench, I don't know how we got back ourselves.*
>
> 18/1349 PRIVATE JOHN HARRISON[55]

Musketier Karl Blenk, one of the German machine gunners of the 169th Regiment, described the 18th West Yorks' advance through the already savaged Leeds and 1st Bradford Pals:

> *There was a wailing and lamentation from No Man's Land and much shouting for stretcher-bearers from the stricken English. They lay in piles but those who survived fired at us from behind their bodies. Later on, when the English tried again, they weren't walking this time, they were running as fast as they could but when they reached the pile of bodies they got no farther. I could see English officers gesticulating wildly, trying to call reserves forward, but very few came. Normally, after 5,000 rounds had been fired we changed the barrel of the machine-gun. We changed it five times that morning.*
>
> MUSKETIER KARL BLENK, 169TH REGIMENT[56]

Lieutenant Colonel Maurice Nicholl Kennard. C.O. 18th West Yorks killed in action 1 July 1916.

Bill Slater looked around and felt,

> *utterly bewildered by the noise and astonished by the sight of men spinning round and round after being hit. I quickly took shelter in a shell hole and began to feel a longing for death.*
>
> 18/273 PRIVATE WILLIAM SLATER[57]

Very few of the 18th Battalion got beyond their own wire, yet astonishingly, Lieutenant Rhodes Akam from B Company was seen to get through the German wire. Twenty-one year old Akam had played on the wing for Bradford Grammar School and scored tries in the inter-Pals rugby match at Birch Lane in April, 1915. He broke the rule about walking and followed his instincts to run full pelt at the enemy. He leapt over the first German line and was seen running towards the second line with a few of his platoon. Akam's brave little group was never seen again, and his name appears on the Thiepval Memorial.[58]

Right: *Aerial view of No Man's Land and German and British front line trenches at Serre. The four copse, Matthew, Mark, Luke and John can be discerned from the white chalk disturbances caused by German artillery fire. See map on page 184.*

The following November, Lieutenant Harry Siepmann, the Artillery observer who had watched the Pals' attack, interrogated a German prisoner who had been a sergeant in charge of a trench mortar battery on 1 July in front of Serre.

> *I cannot now remember the exact figures he gave me, but they were of this order: thirteen British infantrymen succeeded in getting down into the first line-trench, and one officer and two men actually got out of it and were killed before reaching the second line.* LIEUTENANT HARRY SIEPMANN, ROYAL ARTILLERY[59]

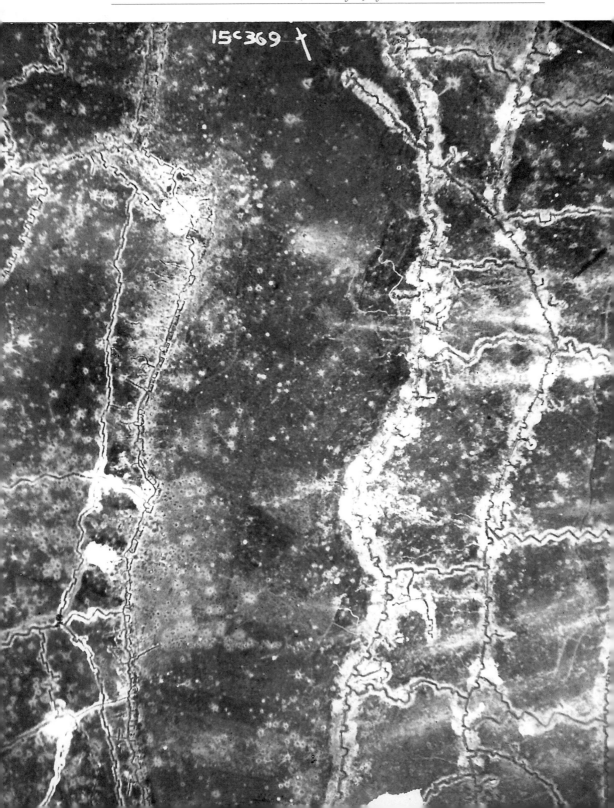

German machine gun team.

It seems highly likely that Akam and two members of his platoon were the men concerned. No medals came their way, but there can be no doubt about their courage and heroism.

Back at Division and Corps HQ the fog of war reigned. At first Wanless O'Gowan and Hunter-Weston were encouraged by what they heard. There is evidence that one man, Private Arthur Howard of the Leeds Pals, got beyond the first German trench and actually reached Serre village where he was fortunate to be taken prisoner. There were also rumours of a party of Durhams reaching Pendant Copse and some of the Accrington's reaching Serre, but there is no conclusive evidence for this and it seems unlikely.[60]

At brigade level the truth about the failure of the attack was more obvious. Brigadier Ingles and Brigadier Rees cancelled orders from General Wanless O'Gowan to send more troops from the reserve over the top. The fear now was of a German counter attack. German troops could now be seen quite clearly standing on their parapets firing into No Man's Land. They were expected to advance into the British trenches at any moment.

Brigadier Rees remained at Brigade HQ to co-ordinate events with Wanless O'Gowan who had now joined him. The Bradford's Brigadier, John Ingles, opted for the more hands on approach and went down to the trenches to take temporary command of the men who had scrambled or crawled back into the trenches. He ordered any men he found to go forward and man the trenches. George Morgan came across his agitated brigadier carrying an ammunition box,

He says to me get up to the front line and take this ammunition. Big box. I'd been carrying the wounded out and he grabbed a big box of ammunition and told me to get it to the front line. Thought the Germans might attack. If they had have done, you know, they'd have walked straight through the window. Practically no defence. 16/1205 PRIVATE GEORGE MORGAN[61]

Brigadier Ingles gave his version and recorded what he saw in the Brigade War Diary:

During my tour of the trenches between 10.00 am and 12.00 noon I found a considerable amount of congestion. Units had become much disorganised and the trenches were full of dead and wounded especially at the junction of MONK and BLENAU and MONK and FLAG, both of which points were under a very heavy shell fire from howitzers. The trenches at these points were demolished and men were retiring stating they had been ordered to leave the front line.They were easily stopped and on investigation I found that the front line was full of dead and wounded and being heavily shelled. With the help of Captain Jackson, 10th Easy Yorks, and Lieut Clark 18th DLI the men retiring were diverted into BRADFORD and DUNMOW and collected by Regiments. I could observe none of our troops advancing on right or left and the Germans were holding their front line in strength. Taking into consideration our heavy losses and the disorganisation resulting therefrom and the scarcity of officers and NCO's I decided that a further advance would be fruitless and ordered what officers and men I saw to man the trenches in which they were reorganised. This was about 11.00 am. I then returned to Brigade Headquarters.

BRIGADIER-GENERAL JOHN DARNLEY INGLES DSO, 93 BRIGADE[62]

In No Man's land the wounded lay out and found what shelter they could as the German barrage continued to rain down on them. Sam Wainwright (16/402) felt an almighty blow on his hip but saw no blood. He later worked out he must have been hit by some sort of flying debris. Whatever it was, it broke his hip. Despite being in considerable pain, he managed to crawl into a shell hole. He lay in his own private inferno until he was picked up by stretcher bearers in the night.[63] Survivors huddled into whatever cover they could get in No Man's Land. Bill Slater described what must have been the feelings of many:

As I crouched there in a shell hole I became so weary of the whole ghastly business that I began wishing that if I was going to be killed I could get it over quickly. I don't remember praying, although I had been a devout Anglo-Catholic before joining the army. I was more curious about death than afraid of it. Would there be a sudden blackness, like the switching off of a light and would one be aware that this blackness was death? As each approaching shell seemed likely to explode on top of me in the shell hole I braced myself to meet the threatened oblivion. What really frightened me was the possibility of being shattered by a shell but not killed outright, and then having to lie there unattended until I died miserably and painfully.

18/273 PRIVATE WILLIAM SLATER[64]

Many of Bill's comrades did come to such a terrifying and lonely end. Their bodies were either never recovered, or if they were, they now lie in an unmarked grave. But Bill was lucky and as time went by he gained a new determination to survive. 'I began to feel strengthened by the thought of how devastated my father and mother would be on receipt of such news.'[65]

As darkness fell, Bill and many others managed to crawl back into the relative safety of Dunmow trench. Private Dick Collins from Idle was less fortunate. He was in a Lewis gun team under the command of Sergeant Dickie Bond (18/922), the Bradford City and England footballer. As the Lewis gun team followed the infantry over, Dick was hit in the back by a piece of shrapnel. Sergeant Bond, after applying a field dressing to the wound, tried to reassure the young private by saying, 'You've got yours. You won't get another now.'[66] Unfortunately, Sergeant Bond's prophecy proved incorrect. Minutes after the gun team had pressed on and left him behind to wait for the stretcher bearers, Private Collins was hit again, this time by a machine gun bullet which entered the left cheek, went through his mouth and then passed out through the other side of his face. He lay unconscious in No Man's Land for two nights. Other survivors crawled past him and assumed he was dead. When he finally recovered consciousness he managed to attract attention. He was carried to the dressing station on a piece of trench duckboard because there were no stretchers available. Dick Collins was fortunate to survive. He faced months of agonising hospital treatment before being discharged from the army in 1918 as unfit for further service. In later years, he returned to Serre on many occasions with the Pals Comradeship Association. His final journey was in 1969. The surviving Pals led by George Morgan carried out his last wishes and interred his ashes in Serre Road Number 1 Cemetery.[67]

Sergeant Dickie Bond.

Others managed to make their own way to the Aid Post at Basin Wood. Somehow or other Corporal Albert Wood of the 16th West Yorks managed to get there himself. He was sickened by what he saw

> *I managed to crawl half a mile to Basin Wood where I saw the most horrible sight. Our M.O. [Captain Roche] was working at a trestle table in his vest, and bodies were piled like sandbags all around him.*
>
> CORPORAL ALBERT WOOD, 16WY, [68]

The two doctors, Paddy Roche attached to the First Pals and Mac McTavish attached to the Second Pals, worked ceaselessly to the point of collapse on their gruesome task at Basin Wood. The normally cheerful McTavish wrote to a friend afterwards:

> *Just a line as I'm in no mood to write a letter. Anyway I'm sure you don't want to hear much about what I've been seeing lately...I'll never forget July 1st as long as I live. It was an awful day.*
>
> CAPTAIN DR. G.B. MCTAVISH M.C. AND TWO BARS, R.A.M.C.[69]

At night when the last men had been attended to at Basin Wood, the two doctors led groups of stretcher bearers into No Man's Land to rescue the wounded. For their devotion and courage, both doctors were awarded the Military Cross. One of the saddest casualties brought into Basin Wood was Private Arthur Normington (18/1374) of Caledonia Street. Arthur

Normington was one of the older men in the Second Pals. He was the father of seven children and his eldest son was serving in the Army. He had worked at Illingworth's Mill in Wapping Road. Arthur Normington died of his wounds at Basin Wood. When the news of his death reached his wife, Eliza, she had a total breakdown. On 14 July she committed suicide by throwing herself in the canal. She was one more casualty of the Somme.[70]

The columns of the Bradford *Daily Telegraph* were to carry page after page of details of casualties in July, 1916. It is beyond the scope of this book to do other than summarise so many personal tragedies. There were many under age victims. Private Willie Whitaker (18/596) of Wyke had claimed to be nineteen when he joined the 2nd Pals in 1915. He died aged seventeen.[71] A number took a time to die. Company Sergeant Major Harry Pass (18/626), a former police sergeant at Baildon, had both his legs blown off on 1 July and died five days later.[72] A number of brothers were casualties. Private George Pennet (16/498) of the 1st Pals was severely shell shocked – his brother William (18/358) of the 2nd Pals was killed. Private Walter Johnson (16/1187) was so severely wounded that he was discharged from the Army in September as unfit for further service – his eighteen year old brother Arthur (18/875), another under age soldier, was killed. A friend writing in the *Yorkshire Observer* claimed that Arthur would have been awarded the D.C.M. if he had lived.[73]

After the battle, a concerted effort was made to discover what had happened to the missing officers. Staff officers visited wounded soldiers in hospitals asking for information, and their statements are included in short typewritten notes in the respective officer's file at the Public Record Office (now the National Archive). In Lieutenant Ralph Stead's file is the letter to his parents, 'If I should be killed you must not fret, as it is the finest death to die, and I have no fear of meeting it'. There is also a statement from Private Harry Laycock (16/550) who was receiving treatment in the military hospital in Etaples:

> *Lieutenant Stead was in C Coy. I saw him in the charge at Colincamps at 8.00 a.m. on July 1, 1916. He was wounded in the knee and was told to go back. He refused to go down and got up to lead the lads again but was shot down by MG fire. He was very young and very brave.* 16/550 PRIVATE HARRY LAYCOCK[74]

Although Harry Laycock recovered from his wounds and returned to the Pals, he was killed at Gavrelle 3 May, 1917. Whether Ralph Stead's parents ever heard the details of his courage it is impossible to say. His body was subsequently recovered and he is buried in Serre Road No. 1 Cemetery. For Harry Laycock there is an inscription on the Memorial to the Missing at Arras Cemetery.

In the Second Pals, Private Frank Smith was wounded but he tried to help Second Lieutenant Rob Derwent, the cub reporter son of the Managing Director of the *Bradford Telegraph*,

> *I helped a stretcher bearer bind up Lieutenant Derwent's wound which was just above the groin, shrapnel had gone right through and it bled a great deal. He had been wounded some hours and did not speak. He frothed at the mouth, folded his hands, stretched out his legs and fell away.* 18/1093 PRIVATE FRANK SMITH[75]

One of Rob Derwent's final reports had rhapsodized about how nine wickets taken by Yorkshire and England all-rounder Major Booth led Yorkshire to an innings victory over Sussex at Bradford Park Avenue in August, 1914. Booth died at Serre on the same day leading a team of bombers with the Leeds Pals.[76]

Drummer Charles Pickworth had carried rations into the trenches ahead of the assault troops and stayed in the front line as a stretcher bearer. In his diary he described what he saw until the surviving Pals were relieved four days later.

The First lot met with a murderous fire. It was a brave attempt. After the 18th [West Yorks] followed with the same result all battalions were collected together and an attempt made to rush them but they outnumbered us with guns, made it absolutely impregnable. We had our reinforcements up too late. Our machine gunners were nearly wiped out, all officers killed or wounded but two, stokes gunners suffered the same fate. Everything was disorganised. All available men was rallied including carriers for the last attempt, but officers could not be got to lead the men. The order was given to retire to third line defence. This was done well without much loss, this line to be held at all costs. The carriers had a rough time getting ammunition up. The enemy shelled us with tear shells. The band lost two men and a few shell shocked. This being done the wounded had to be fetched in. Our front line filled up with dead and wounded. This was a terrible job. The lads worked day and night under heavy fire from artillery and the snipers were very busy in all parts. The shelling continued but both sides busy with wounded and dead. The band was relieved on the fifth July to prepare for the battalion coming out tomorrow.

16/212 Private Charles Pickworth[77]

Lieutenant Harry Siepmann, the Artillery observation officer on the ridge near Basin Wood watched the carnage 1 July. He saw an amazing incident the next day.

The following morning I watched the German snipers picking off our wounded who had been caught in the wire. I also saw as brave an action as it is possible to imagine. Without any explanation as might have been given with a red cross flag, two men climbed slowly out of our front line. A stretcher was then passed up to them and they proceeded to carry it ploddingly into No Man's Land. Hundreds, perhaps thousands, of eyes must have been upon them, and all firing of any sort suddenly ceased. Complete, uncanny silence descended like a pall, as

The wrecked ground in front of the village of Serre after months of fighting over it.

the two men trudged steadily on and stopped beside a body lying on the ground. They lifted it onto the stretcher and plodded slowly back, the way they had come. The silence remained unbroken until they were safe, and then the war was resumed. LIEUTENANT HARRY SIEPMANN, ROYAL ARTILLERY, 31ST DIVISION[78]

Out in No Man's Land, in two separate positions, two of the First Pals dug themselves in to what shelter they could and waged a one man war. Using water and rations from the dead they stayed out in No Man's land providing covering fire with their Lewis guns. They moved at regular intervals to avoid retaliatory enemy fire and maintained a lonely protective vigil over the wounded and the men in the trenches behind them. Corporal Harry Cockroft (16/1185) and Private Tom Pearson (16/1154) were awarded the Distinguished Conduct Medal for their gallantry.[79]

Company Sergeant Major George Cussins (16/842) and Sergeant Ellison Murgatroyd (16/573) were also awarded the DCM for taking charge of the remnants of the First Pals after every officer had become a casualty. Ellison Murgatroyd, a commercial traveller, was later commissioned in the 16th West Yorks. Sadly, as Captain Murgatroyd, he was killed during the Great German Spring Offensive 26 March, 1918. George Cussins was promoted to Regimental Sergeant Major in the 16th West Yorks to replace RSM Alfred Oddy who was wounded at Serre. In February, 1918, like Ellison Murgatroyd, he was transferred to the Leeds Pals. He returned to the Bradford police after the war. Walter Hare remembered exchanging cheery greetings with him when he was on point duty at Drighlington cross roads, an easier task than re-organising the troops at Serre.[80] R.S.M. Cussins had written a kind letter to Walter's mother when Walter was captured in March, 1918 and Walter was glad to be able to thank him.[81]

The surviving Pals were brought together and did their best to man the shambles of a trench system. The bombardment gradually died away and was reduced to the occasional exchange of machine gun and rifle fire. Both sides were exhausted and the expected German counter attack never came.

Reinforcements arrived with Major Kennedy from the First Pals and Major Carter with the Second Pals. A gradual re-organisation took place with the

Durham Pals holding the front line, the Second Bradford Pals holding Monk Trench, the Leeds Pals holding from Warley to Dunmow trenches, and the First Bradford Pals manning Maitland Trench.[82]

The wounded and those who had taken shelter in shell holes gradually filtered back into the British lines when they could under cover of darkness, but the shouts and screams of the wounded who could not get back sounded across No Man's Land throughout the night. By 10.50 p.m. Major Carter reported to Brigadier Ingles that the 18th West Yorks were now 120 strong.

At one o'clock in the morning, 2 July, stretcher bearers arrived from the Hull battalions to assist the exhausted 93 Brigade men, and at 2.30 a.m. rations came with reinforcements of seventy-five men from each of the assaulting Battalions' reserves. Despite being wounded and losing blood, Lieutenant Peace of the Second Pals had been trying to hold things together in the trenches throughout the night with his Bradford Pal colleague Captain Francis Horner, the Brigade Intelligence Officer. Major Carter finally ordered Walter Peace to go off to hospital on 2 July. Lieutenant Peace was later awarded the Military Cross and returned to the 18th West Yorks after his recovery.[83]

By early morning 2 July, after receiving the reinforcements, Brigadier Ingles noted the strength of the First Pals as five officers under Major Kennedy and 155 men. The Second Pals under Major Carter had seven officers and 170 men. They continued to man the trenches through their exhaustion, shock and grief for the next three days.

It is difficult to be precise about the exact number of casualties given the chaos of 1 July. In the weeks before a number of men had been attached to the Machine Gun Corps and 93rd Light Trench Mortar Battery from both battalions. Their casualties were entered separately, although they could legitimately be described as Bradford Pals.[84]

The 16th West Yorks War Diary records twenty-two officers and 675 men went into action on 1 July. On 5 July it gives a figure of 527 casualties (75.6%). with eleven officers killed (one missing but believed killed) and eleven wounded, a casualty rate of 100%. In fact twelve officers died when Robert Sutcliffe succumbed to his wounds on a hospital ship 5 July. Lieutenants Jowitt and Webster were incorrectly reported as killed in the newspapers, although Jowitt was badly wounded and Webster unharmed in reserve. The other ranks figures were fifty-three killed, 149 missing and 303 wounded (a casualty rate of 74.8%). A revision based on War Graves Commission records reveals at least 155 dead (141 killed 1 July with fourteen dying of wounds in July). A number died after July, but it has not been possible to quantify this.[85]

The 18th West Yorks suffered 490 casualties (70.3%) 1 July, with twenty-two officers and 675 men going into action. The figure rises to 515 if the trench raid on 30 June is included. The break down is nine officers killed and thirteen wounded (100%), other ranks 118 men killed, 375 wounded. Again some of the wounded died after July.

Analysis of War Grave Commission data reveals the youth of the two Bradford Battalions. In 1916, ages were given for 221 of those killed in the other ranks. They were very young indeed. The largest single age group for casualties was age nineteen. A fifth (forty-four) of all casualties were under age when they joined up, and half (110) were twenty-two years of age or younger when they were killed. There are also two men in their mid forties who somehow got through the upper age limit. The ages given provides a profile of each battalion and also reflects the reluctance of married men to volunteer in 1914 and 1915.[86]

The First Pals' position as lead battalion is reflected in a higher deaths to wounds ratio because of their longer exposure to enemy fire and the added difficulties of bringing in the wounded. This also affected the recovery and identification of bodies for burial. In the First Pals, 122 officers and men are recorded on the Thiepval Memorial to the Missing compared with 74 in the Second Pals. The waiting mass graves at Euston Road were a dramatic reminder of reality to the marching men, but only a few of them are actually buried there. The majority are in 'unknown' graves in Serre Road Number One Cemetery on the front line, with others at Serre Road Numbers Two and Three, Railway Hollow Cemetery and Queen's Cemetery.[87]

A number were never found and still lie in what was No Man's Land to the west of Serre. In 1994 the identity disc for Private Harry Walker of the Second Pals was discovered after the ground had been ploughed. On 22 July 1916 a sad item had appeared in the *Bradford Daily Telegraph*, typical of many such notices placed in the *Telegraph* in the summer of 1916:

> WALKER *Private H. 42, Kingswood Street, Great Horton, of the 2nd Bradford Pals has been reported wounded, but no letter has been received from him since July 1st and any news regarding him would be greatly welcomed by his parents. Private Walker is 17 years of age and enlisted in April, 1915. He was prior to the War, a scholar at the Wesley Place Sunday School, Great Horton and was employed by Messrs Aykroyd and Grandage Ltd.*[88]

There are no reports of prisoners being taken from either battalion on 1 July although many relatives clung to the hope that their missing sons or husbands had been taken prisoner. The father of twenty-two year old Captain Donald Smith, the commander of D Company who was sparing with the rum to George Morgan and friends, was Councillor E.J. Smith. Councillor Smith was a powerful figure in Bradford Liberal politics and had contacts in the Cabinet. He was a prominent member of the Citizens' Army League and Chairman of the City Council Health Committee. He could not accept that his son had been killed and wrote several letters to the War Office on Council headed notepaper refusing to complete the arrangements for his son's estate.[89]

Many men of both battalions recovered and went back to the front, either to be killed or wounded again. Many were discharged as unfit for service and bore the pain and disfigurement of their wounds for the rest of their life. All had mental scars and lived with the pain, the memories and the nightmares for the rest of their lives. Doris Waddington, wife of the Yorkshire and England fast bowler Abe Waddington (16/1188), told the author that Abe often woke up screaming when he was troubled with nightmares of Serre.[90]

Casualties in the German 169th Regiment were considerably less. The 1st

Machine Gun Company of the Regiment recorded five dead and fourteen wounded out of a total of 149.[91]

The 1 July, 1916 was the most disastrous day in the history of the British Army with nearly 60,000 casualties. On the first day hardly anything was gained in the northern and central part of the line, but there was success in the south around Montauban where the Liverpool and Manchester Pals of 30th Division took all their objectives. The French to their right and 18th Division to their left also took all their objectives. The Somme Campaign dragged on to mid-November with a penetration of German territory by up to seven miles, but Serre did not fall. Total British losses were 240,000.

Some of the original Pals from 1914 and 1915 were casualties with other battalions during that campaign. The 20th West Yorks was made up of two companies from the original Pals as well as new recruits as a reserve Depot Battalion in 1915. A number of these men found their way to the Somme. Ten were killed with the 10th West Yorks at Fricourt on 1 July. A First Bradford Pal who joined in September, 1914, Private Frederick Rowland Wade (16/407), somehow found himself transferred to the Accrington Pals and was killed at Serre fighting alongside the Bradford Pals as 27302 of the East Lancashire Regiment. Five men from the 20th West Yorks were killed serving with the 9th Cheshires near Mametz. Eleven were killed serving with the 11th West Yorks and no less than fifty five were killed serving with the 12th West Yorks later in the Somme campaign.[92]

TABLE ONE. ANALYSIS OF AGE OF CASUALTIES WHERE AGE GIVEN Bradford Battalions. Men killed in 1916			
Age of casualty	16th West Yorks	18th West Yorks	Total
17	1	4	5
18	2	6	8
19	13	18	31
20	9	8	17
21	9	13	22
22	13	14	27
23	7	8	15
24	9	4	13
25	5	5	10
26	5	5	10
27	3	6	9
28	5	5	10
29	1	5	6
30	1	2	3
31	1	5	6
32	0	2	2
33	3	0	3
34	0	3	3
35	4	2	6
36	1	4	5
37	3	2	5
38	0	0	0
39	1	0	1
40	1	1	2
41	0	0	0
42	0	0	0
43	0	0	0
44	0	0	0
45	1	0	1
46	1	0	1
Totals	99	122	221

Thirty six years later, in 1952, many surviving members of the Pals eagerly sought out Robert Blake's newly published selection of Haig's private papers and diary. What they found led to great resentment and bitterness. Haig's diary entry for 1 July 1916 confirmed suspicions that their corps commander was out of touch with reality, and in one short painful phrase, Haig revealed his own ignorance of the Pals ordeal and heroism at Serre. Haig began with a sceptical dismissal of what must have been a typical piece of Hunter-Weston bluster over the telephone on the evening of 1 July:

> *Hunter-Weston said* [the VIII Corps] *began well, but as the day progressed, their troops were forced back into the German front line, except two Battalions which occupied Serre Village, and were, it is said cut off.*
>
> FIELD MARSHALL SIR DOUGLAS HAIG[93]

Hunter-Weston's comments were in fact nonsense. But then the devastating insult which was never forgotten or forgiven by the Pals. Haig went on, 'I am inclined to believe from further reports, that few of the 8th Corps left their trenches.'[94] Whether 'further reports' of nearly 4,000 casualties in the eight lead Battalions of 31st Division caused the Commander in Chief to revise his opinion we will never know. A charitable view is that Haig's comment had more to do with Hunter-Weston's credibility than the credibility of the Pals. Nevertheless the hurt was deep. In 1932, Sir John Edmonds had the advantage of hindsight and more 'further reports' when he produced the *Official History*. Dealing with the first day of the Somme, he produced a more fitting tribute to the tragedy of the Pals Battalions at Serre.

> *In 31st Division, the extended lines started in excellent order but gradually melted away. There was no wavering or attempting to come back. The men fell in their ranks, mostly before the first 100 yards of No Man's Land had been crossed. The magnificent gallantry, discipline and determination displayed by all ranks of the North Country Division were of no avail against the concentrated fire of the enemy's unshaken infantry and artillery whose barrage has been described as so consistent and severe that the cones of the explosions gave the impression of a thick belt of poplar trees.*[95]

Why, then, did the attack succeed on the British right flank in the South around Montauban and fail in the North on the British left flank at Serre? Both 30th Division on the right and 31st Division on the left consisted of New Army Pals Divisions. There is no reason to suppose the men of Leeds, Bradford, Durham, Accrington, Barnsley and Sheffield were any less determined or courageous than the men from Liverpool and Manchester.

A number of factors have been discussed and all have some weight. Hunter Weston's decision to blow the Hawthorn Ridge mine ten minutes before the attack, combined with his early lift of the main artillery barrage, certainly provided confirmation to the Germans that the assault was about to begin. They had enough time to come out of their deep dug outs to man the parapet in time to face the Pals. The un-destroyed machine gun nests at the Heidenkopf allowed deadly enfilade fire on 93 Brigade as the Pals went forward. But it is the author's view that it was the artillery on both sides, enhanced for the Germans with the presence of an open flank at Serre, that was the critical factor between the success of 30th Division and the failure of 31st Division.

As Brigadier Rees pointed out, the one mile gap to the left of 94 Brigade up to Gommecourt allowed the German artillery to concentrate its fire on 94 and 93 Brigades, effectively doubling its power. The Germans always knew where the open flank was going to be and built up their artillery strength behind Pusieux without disclosing its presence until the assault began. The British believed the Germans had fifty-five guns behind Serre when in fact they had sixty-six batteries. On the British side, as Siepmann said, there were insufficient heavy howitzers in 31st Division and the 18-pounders used to cut lanes in the wire were not effective. What few gaps there were in the wire simply created congestion and made the infantry an easier target for the machine gunners. Nor did the British barrage have sufficient penetration of the deep German defensive dug outs which a more powerful howitzer bombardment could have provided. At Montauban there was no flank gap and the heavy howitzers of the French Army on the right of 30th Division helpfully created massive destruction of the wire and defence works in front of the more fortunate Pals from Liverpool and Manchester.

Sixty years later George Morgan looked back and gave his thoughts on Serre: *'I wanted to go back, I always wanted to go back but I were always a bit scared of going alone. I joined our Association and we started having pilgrimages to France. We went to places... to me they're holy places. It was consecrated ground where we walked when we got to the Somme. I feel that they're there just the same as they were then. They're there just now like they were when they were killed. I feel that they're there at Serre. I feel something different when I get there.*[96]

NOTES

1. George Morgan on tape kindly supplied to the author by Malcolm Brown, quoting Major-General Robert Wanless O'Gowan, G.O.C. 31st Division.
2. Fred Rawnsley, diary in Bradford Industrial Museum.
3. Robert Nichols (1893-1944), *Eve of Assault : Infantry Going Down to Trenches*. Poem published in *Up the Line to Death, The War Poets 1914-1918*, Methuen (1964). Nichols served as an Artillery officer in 31st Division. He was a member of the Georgian poets, a friend of Brooke and Sassoon, and later a professor of English literature.
4. Letter to Lady Hunter-Weston, 30.11.16, in Hunter-Weston Papers NSS 48365, British Museum, Manuscript Library.
5. Private George Morgan, taped conversation with Malcolm Brown (1976), and kindly made available to the author.
6. Harry Siepmann. *Echo of the Guns: Recollections of an Artillery Officer 1914-18*, (Hale, London 1987).
7. Papers of Brigadier-General H.C. Rees, D.S.O., Department of Documents, Imperial War Museum.
8. Rees. Op.cit.
9. ibid.
10. 15/731 Robert Gowland Potts commissioned in 3rd Yorks and Lancs, 20th March, 1918. 15/938 John James Ward, commissioned in West Yorksire Regiment, 29th January, 1918.
11. Letter written by Robert Sutcliffe, published in *Bradford Telegraph*, 10 July, 1916.
12. W0339/3839, officers file, Lieutenant Ralph Stead. Stead joined the 1st Pals at Skipton after being commissioned from the ranks of the 19th Royal Fusiliers (Public Schools Battalion) in April 1915. He was a friend of the Russell brothers from Norfolk and recommended to Colonel Muller by Harry Russell (the former Conservative Party Agent in Bradford who became Adjutant to the First Pals).
13. Information supplied by Jack Cockroft, son of Harry Cockroft.
14. William Slater, notes kindly supplied by Martin Middlebrook.
15. Vincent Phillips correspondence in possession of family.
16. Percy Bunney, notes kindly supplied by Martin Middlebrook.
17. Pickworth, diary, op.cit
18. See Milner, *Leeds Pals*, op. cit. in this series.
19. Rawnsley, op.cit.
20. ibid.
21. Battalion War Diary
22. Morgan, op.cit.
23. ibid.
24. Hunter-Weston, op.cit.
25. Slater, op.cit. and Battalion War Diary.
26. Battalion War Diary
27. 93rd Brigade War Diary
28. Morgan, op.cit
29. ibid
30. ibid

31. 93 Brigade War Diary
32. Otto Lais, 169th Infantry Regiment. *Experiences of Baden Soldiers at the Front, Volume 1: Machine Guns in the Iron Regiment (8th Baden Infantry Regiment No 169)* by Otto Lais, G. Braun, Karlsruhe 1935. Kindly supplied by Andrew Jackson.
33. Milner, opus. Cit.
34. Morgan, op.cit
35. Carter, notes kindly supplied by Martin Middlebrook
36. George Grunwell. Taped interview with Steve Kerry, Bradford Industrial Museum.
37. Morgan. Op.cit
38. *Yorkshire Observer*, 14th July, 1916.
39. Robert William Hay Pringle reference in officer's file, PRO, WO339
40. *Bradford Daily Telegraph*, 10th July, 1916
41. Alan Clough, reference in officer's file, PRO, WO339
42. Battalion War Diary.
43. Alan Clough, reference in officer's file, PRO, WO339.
44. ibid.
45. Ibid
46. Battalion War Diary
47. Norman Goldthorpe, diary in Bradford Industrial Museum
48. ibid.
49. Officers Records, information as to fate collected from wounded other ranks. PRO WO/339
50. Goldthorpe, op. cit.
51. Slater, op.cit
52. Frank Burn. Taped interview kindly supplied by Steve Kerry
53. Williams. Officers records. PRO WO339/21554
54. Keevil, Officers records PRO WO339
55. Colley, Officers records PRO WO339
56. Quoted in Martin Middlebrook, *First Day of the Somme*, Allen Lane, 1971. I would like to thank Martin for so kindly allowing me to reproduce this quotation.
57. Slater, op.cit.
58. Akam, Officers records, PRO WO339.
59. Siepmann. Op.cit
60. See Milner, *Leeds Pals*, op.cit, Middlebrook, *First Day of the Somme*, op.cit. and Turner, *Accrington Pals*, op.cit.
61. Morgan Op.cit
62. 93rd Brigade War Diary.
63. Wainwright, interview with author, op.cit..
64. Slater, op.cit
65. ibid
66. Dick Collins, quoted in *Telegraph and Argus*, 28 June, 1966.
67. Morgan, op.cit.
68. Albert Wood, notes kindly supplied by Martin Middlebrook.
69. Dr. G.B. McTavish, letters in the Imperial War Museum
70. *Bradford Daily Telegraph*, 15 July, 1916.
71. ibid, 10 July, 1916
72. ibid.
73. *Yorkshire Observer*, 11 July, 1916.
74. Stead, officers' records, WO339.
75. Derwent, officers' records, WO339.
76. See Milner, opus cit.
77. Pickworth, op.cit
78. Siepmann, op.cit
79. *London Gazette*. 20.10.16 16/1185 A Cpl H. Cockroft D.C.M. For conspicuous gallantry in action. He held on to a position in No Man's Land under very heavy shell and machine gun fire with the only survivor of his machine gun team. When ordered to retire he got his gun back and` re-opened fire.
London Gazette 26.9.16 16/1154 Private T. Pearson D.C.M. For conspicuous gallantry in action. When he and one other man were all that remained of a machine gun team they continued to work the gun in No Man's Land under heavy shell and machine gun fire. When the other man was knocked out and he himself wounded, he continued to fire the gun single handed for an hour till assistance arrived.
80. *London Gazette*. 22.9.16 16/842 A CSM G. Cussins D.C.M. For conspicuous courage and ability throughout the campaign. He has shown admirable coolness and pluck in times of stress. He took charge when his officer was wounded and organised his line though wounded. He subsequently did valuable work as Regimental Sergeant Major.
London Gazette 20.10.16 16/573 Sergeant E. Murgatroyd For conspicuous gallantry in action. When his battalion had suffered severely he took charge of the men round him, and organised the defence with machine guns with great ability. He showed great coolness under heavy shell and machine gun fire.

81. Walter Hare, conversation with the author.
82. 93 Brigade War Diary.
83. ibid.
84. Battalion War Diary
85. *Soldiers Died in the Great War, West Yorkshire Regiment.*
86. Analysis of Commonwealth War Graves records.
87. ibid.
88. The disc was found by Paul Hughes of Bishops Stortford. Publicity in the *Telegraph and Argus* alerted Private Walker's nephew to the find. Harry Walker was fifteen when he enlisted and had gone to York where he joined the 3rd West Yorks as 19559 before managing to arrange a transfer to the Pals.
89. Donald Smith, Officers' Records, op.cit.
90. Mrs. Doris Waddington, conversation with the author, 22 May, 1989.
91. 169th Regiment War Diary, op.cit. quoted by Jon Cooksey in the *Barnsley Pals* in this series.
92. Commonwealth War Graves Commission records and Soldiers Died. Op.cit.
93. Robert Blake, Robert Blake, 'The Private Papers of Douglas Haig, 1914-1919', p. 153. Eyre and Spottiswoode, 1952.
94. ibid.
95. J.E. Edmonds, *Official History, 1916, to Jul 1,* (London 1932)
96. Morgan, op.cit

Lance Corporal John Willie Wooton after the war, wearing the helmet and tunic he was wounded in on the first day of the Battle of the Somme.

Chapter Eleven

AFTERMATH

Many a tear shed...many spent a restless night with shaken nerves.
DIARY ENTRY, 16/212 PRIVATE CHARLES PICKWORTH[1]

THERE WAS VERY LITTLE REST at first for the shattered survivors of the two Bradford Battalions as they finally made their way out of the line after four nightmarish days and nights, 4 July 1916. The remnants of the First Pals were in the support trenches at the rear and because of this were the first to be relieved (by 1/7th Worcesters of 48th Division). They were given a tot of rum before they began to move out in heavy rain at 5.00 p.m. They struggled back to Colincamps where they had a very welcome hot meal. The surviving members of the Battalion band, who had acted so heroically as stretcher bearers, were waiting for them at Colincamps. The bass drummer, Charles Pickworth, recorded in his diary the emotion of the occasion and how the band tried to lead and encourage the men. Major Kennedy walked rather than rode at their head with acting Regimental Sergeant Major Cussins at his side as they made a final effort to get to their billets.

Band met battalion out of trenches and played them to Louvencourt.
16/212 PRIVATE CHARLES PICKWORTH[2]

Somehow, the band found the strength to overcome their emotions and played. The familiar strains of the Regimental March, 'Ca Ira', echoed across the road back to Bus and Brigadier Ingles and General Wanless O'Gowan saluted them as they moved off. The men barely noticed. They trudged wearily as best they could for a further six miles (the War Diary states 'proceeded' rather than 'marched') to Louvencourt and to the relative safety of billets in barns and abandoned buildings. They finally arrived at 10.30 p.m.

Arrived in dark. Had a good night's rest, many a tear shed...many spent a restless night with shaken nerves. Day's rest, all parcels and letters of missing were shared out to remainder which caused most depressing sights.
16/212 PRIVATE CHARLES PICKWORTH[3]

The Second Pals had an even more difficult time because they occupied the front line. Their relief (by the 1/8th Worcesters of 48th Division) took place under the cover of darkness. The relief began at the same time as the First Pals arrived in Louvencourt – 10.30 p.m. The Second Pals were at the end of their tether and had a dreadful time splashing their way out of the line through Railway Avenue. Heavy rain had been pouring down throughout the afternoon and evening and at places the trenches were four feet deep in water. The journey was made worse by congestion as stretcher cases were still being brought out, and some of the equally weary and confused survivors of 94 Brigade (the Accrington, Sheffield and two Barnsley Pals Battalions) mistakenly drifted into Railway Avenue instead of their own exit line,

Northern Avenue.

When the Second Pals finally managed to stagger out of the trench system at Euston Dump it had taken over three hours to move less than a mile. It was decided to abandon their heavy sodden mud caked overcoats to lighten their load. They arrived in Bertrancourt two miles further on at 3.00 a.m. and received hot tea laced with rum. Louvencourt was finally reached after 4.00 a.m. 5 July. The men were given some hot food before finally being allowed to collapse into an exhausted disturbed sleep on bales of straw in a large barn.

The number of survivors of the assault on 1 July can be estimated at less than two hundred men in each battalion. To these must be added about another two hundred held in reserve but who were used as reinforcements to hold the line. There were also specialists such as signallers, clerks and members of the transport section who had remained behind at Bus-les-Artois.

There was no Reveille 5 July and the men were allowed to come to on an individual basis. No doubt the smell of hot bacon played its part. At 3.00 p.m. the 18th were paraded and addressed by their new C.O. Major Carter, and later both of the Bradford Battalions received an address from Lieutenant-General Sir Aylmer Hunter-Weston, the Commander of VIII Corps. Never at a loss for words, Hunter-Weston had a printed message distributed to all troops expressing his admiration for their efforts, and (now) telling them that they had had the most difficult part of the line to attack, but that 'Next time we attack, if it please God, we will not only pull our weight but will pull off a big thing'. The leaflet somehow found its way to his opposite number General von Stein of the German 14th Reserve Corps who had it translated and distributed to his own men with his own comments that 'the next enemy attack will, and of this I am certain, suffer the same fate as the first'. [4]

Hunter-Weston again revealed his self-congratulatory lack of imagination and self deception in a letter home to his wife.

> *The men are not the least bit down hearted at their losses, and are as fit and happy as can be, working away to clear the battlefield and getting ready for our next operations. I was of course disappointed that we did not get through, but not worried or upset. I had done my little best and was well repaid by the courage and discipline of the troops. Next time we'll succeed.*

LT. GENERAL SIR AYLMER HUNTER-WESTON. COMMANDER, VIII CORPS [5]

In London, thirty-one year old Corporal Harry Bateman (18/104) was far from fit and happy. He was in agony with shrapnel in his groin and was virtually unable to pass water. He was being prepared for his next operation. He was fighting for his life and his wife was called from Bradford to be at his bedside. She was told he was very weak from the loss of blood and that his leg would have to be amputated. The surgeon asked young Mrs. Bateman to tell Percy and to get him to sign the form. When she did Percy protested strongly and said he didn't want to lose his leg and he wouldn't sign. His wife did sign the form, but Percy died during the operation on 8 July. He did come home, to be buried in West Bowling Cemetery. His wife lived with grief for the rest of her life and Percy's two year old daughter never knew her father. [6]

In Louvencourt, as the Pals tried to recover and sleep, George Morgan remembered someone shouting out his name.

I said, Yes, I'm George Morgan. They said, Will you come with me? So I went with them to another village, I don't know which village it was and they took me into a little building and there was just a trestle table. There was Bill Kenny on this table, laid full length, and there was an RAMC man and a Catholic priest there. Billy says to me, "Hello, George, I'm glad to see you. Will you write that letter and tell my fiancée that I'll soon be home". I says, Yes, I will. I'll write and tell her. And the RAMC man shook his head as much as to say he'll never, never make it. He was paralysed from the neck down and they told me they'd administered the last rites. Anyhow, I wrote this letter to his fiancée.

16/1205 PRIVATE GEORGE MORGAN[7]

The village George visited was almost certainly Authie where the 31st Division Advanced Operative Centre was situated. It was two miles up the road from Louvencourt on the way to Doullens. Bill Kenny and Billy Booth the friend he had to leave behind are both buried in Doullens Cemetery.

On the same day, twenty-one year old Erich Weintz died of wounds received on the Somme in the base hospital at Etretat on the coast. He had found it more discrete to serve under the alias of Private Eric White (18/1039) even though he lived in Britannia Street, Shipley.

Whether the rest of the Pals were as fit and happy as can be is another matter, but Hunter-Weston had no more use for them in the immediate future. They were to be despatched to a quieter section of the Western Front to receive reinforcements and recover their effectiveness. On 6 July the two Bradford Battalions marched out of Louvencourt. They left the Somme on the same day that Percy Bateman died. They were to be away from the Somme for three months.

Percy Bateman

Led by their bands, the Pals marched for two days for thirty miles across the Somme back country to the rail head at Conteville, picking up a few reinforcements on the way. They received great kindness from the Royal Flying Corps at Candas airfield. The R.F.C. fed them and sent lorries back to Louvencourt and Bus to collect the abandoned overcoats and stores and before taking the items on to Conteville Station. On the 8 July, after what seemed like an interminable wait, the two Battalions entrained for a six hour journey north through the night towards the northern most part of France just to the south of the Belgian border.

The weary men detrained at Berguette in the flat marshy plain of the River Lys between St. Omer and Bethune. The only available refreshment was tea at a Y.M.C.A. stall which was paid for out of regimental funds. There was then a five mile trudge to temporary billets in twin villages (the 16th West Yorks at Busne, and the 18th West Yorks at L'Ecleme). A week was spent cleaning up and on skills training for replacement specialist units such as signallers, bombing, wiring, snipers, stretcher duties and the unglamorous but essential

Sanitary Squad.[8]

Back home in Bradford on 13 July, as relatives still tried to find out what had happened on the Somme, the *Yorkshire Observer* ran a ludicrous story claiming that Bradford troops had captured Serre. Under the heading 'Soldiers' Stories', the article was part of a regular syndicated series and carried all the hallmarks of the bombastic national jingo by William Beach-Thomas. The article quoted an un-named Bradford sergeant as saying,

> *The Germans put their machine guns into shell holes created by our bombardment and used them to deadly effect. But it was "better to be hit by a machine gun than an 18-pounder" and he was under the impression, like a good many of his fellows, that if we suffered severely the enemy had suffered a great deal more.*[9]

The true reality was the dreaded knock on the door from the telegram boy, and page after page of photographs and casualty lists in all the Bradford press throughout July and August reporting the deaths and wounds of Bradford soldiers. It is doubtful if any of the shattered survivors scattered around hospitals in France and England would take any consolation from the difference between a machine gun bullet and a shell.

On 14 July, the men were delighted to get new underwear. They enjoyed hot baths at Busnes and tried to rid themselves of lice. Two days later they moved nearer towards the front line, joining up with the rest of 93 Brigade at Robecque and then moving further forward together to Lestrem. Rather belatedly, and probably as a result of the casualties on the Somme, a few under age men were sent back to the Base Depot from Lestrem.

When the 18th West Yorks paused at Robecque, two dishevelled figures were marched up under Military Police escort and handed over into the custody of Regimental Sergeant Major Scott. They were Privates Crimmins and Wild who had disappeared in Bus-les-Artois on 30 June. They had been arrested at Vignacourt for desertion and their story is told in a later chapter. For the next twelve days, whilst the Battalion was out of the line at Lestrem, the two men were held under close arrest in the guardroom.

In the First Pals, somebody else was in trouble. On 14 July, Private J. Patchett (16/1501) had been tried by a Field General Courts Martial on the charge of wilfully disobeying an order when the Battalion was in Egypt. The Private had apparently refused to put a light out when he wanted to read a book in his tent at Point 70. He was found guilty and sentenced to two years hard labour. He was sent to Etaples to begin his sentence 28 July from the reserve line at Croix Barbee.[10]

Specialist training continued at Lestrem for both battalions and new officers were taken on the strength to replace those lost on the Somme, but there was still no large influx of reinforcements for the other ranks. On 20 July the Pals were inspected by the Commander of First Army, Sir Charles Monro, who, congratulated them on their smart appearance and remarked that he had no doubt whatever of their being 'just as steady under fire as they were on parade'.[11]

A week later, on the morning of 27 July, the 18th West Yorks marched out of Lestrem on a four hour trek south to Windy Corner in the Neuve Chapelle sector. They were to relieve the First Barnsley Pals in the front line. The main body of the 16th West Yorks followed and took over billets from the Accrington Pals at Croix Barbee with the task of manning seven sand bagged defence posts as a Reserve Defence Line. The Leeds Pals also followed to provide additional support.

Both Battalions were still at half strength.The 447 men of the 18th West Yorks who went into the front line had their numbers augmented by 160 men from the First Pals in what was designated X Company under Captain Blagbrough. Their destination was the Richebourg St. Vaast part of the line opposite and to the south of Aubers Ridge often disrespectfully known as the Pope's Nose on account of its shape.

The front line area covered what little ground had been gained in the first of three British offensives in the spring of 1915. Rotting bodies from the Indian Corps and the Seaforth Highlanders still littered the ground and it was a chilling place. Although it was now regarded as a quiet sector, the Barnsley Pals had suffered forty-eight casualties in their tour.[12]

The area was wet and marshy as part of the flood plain of the River Lys and shelling had smashed up the system of dykes and drainage. It was a land subject to mist and flood and because of the nature of the ground it was virtually impossible to dig trenches without them flooding to waist level. Although described as trenches, the front line was actually made up of a series of interconnected and often isolated breastworks and scattered posts built up with sand bags. The system was a product of the area's geography and was meant to provide defence in depth against a major assault, but it provided very little protection.

The First Pals in X Company were deployed on the right, whilst A Company was in the centre and B Company on the left. D Company held the strong point of Port Arthur in the centre and provided central support behind A and B Company. C Company provided back up in posts behind the others in front of Battalion Headquarters which was positioned in Forresters Lane. Lieutenants Humphries and Stephenson spread their specialist Lewis gun teams and signallers out between all the companies. The 12th East Yorks (Hull Sportsmen) were on their right and the Durham Pals were on their left.[13]

The Pals' positions faced south east. Behind the German lines they could make out the Bois de Biez and to the left the four miles long Aubers Ridge. Although the Ridge was at most only fourteen metres high, it gave the Germans an excellent observation point to watch for movement in the British lines. Probably aware of the relief that afternoon, the Germans decided to give the Pals a very nasty welcome.

At 9.30 p.m. the Germans began a heavy bombardment of the Pals' front line and kept up continuous machine gun fire on the parapet. Telephone communications were soon cut, and as darkness fell at about 10.15 p.m. German raiding parties broke into more than one part of the line occupied by B Company.

A Runner from D Company brought news of the attack back to Battalion

Headquarters. Shortly afterwards Private Herbert Riley (18/1015), who was further forward with B Company but had escaped capture was taken back to tell Major Carter what he had seen. According to Riley, who had escaped with a wounded corporal, Josh Lee (18/1152):

> *A minenwerfer had burst near a sentry post, and immediately afterwards the Germans came over, apparently twenty-five to thirty strong and dressed in black. He and Corporal Lee were in a dug out. A German threw a light on them and told them to put their hands up. The German was armed with what appeared to be a knob-kerrie or hand grenade and a revolver. Corporal Lee and himself made a dash for it and got away, the former being hit in the leg. When they left, the trench was held by Germans.*
>
> 18/1015 PRIVATE HERBERT RILEY[14]

B Company took the brunt of the attack. Total casualties from the raid and the barrage amounted to ninety (five officers and eighty five men) – which was a significant blow given the weakened state of the Battalions. A Company lost their C.O., Lieutenant Roland Cross, but otherwise they reported they were alright – including Crimmins and Wild, the two men under arrest for desertion. It might have been better for them if they had been in B Company. The other officer killed was Second Lieutenant Walter Rawleigh Humphries, the Lewis gun officer. Ten men were killed, thirty-four were wounded, and three officers and thirty-three men were taken prisoner. In X Company, from the 16th West Yorks, five men were killed and three were wounded in the barrage.[15]

The tall twenty-five year old Roland Cross was married and had been a warehouse salesman. Major Carter had recommended him for promotion to Captain and for the Military Cross for his work 2 July. Carter later certified Gladys Cross's widows' pension claim and pursued the award of the M.C. with a letter to the War Office – only to be told the award could not be made posthumously.[16]

Twenty-one year old Rawleigh Humphries had played Rugby Union for Bradford and Yorkshire. He had written to his family after the 1 July to reassure them he was alright.

> *I have come through the ordeal with hardly a scratch, my helmet saving me from several nasty wounds, both shrapnel and bullets. My men were absolutely fine. It is not wise to say anything about casualties.*
>
> SECOND LIEUTENANT WALTER RAWLEIGH HUMPHRIES, 18WY[17]

Four weeks later his luck ran out. His father wrote to the War Office from his home at Skipton where he was struggling to complete the forms needed to finalise his son's estate. 'I have done the best I could. I do not fully understand it. Second Lieutenant Walter Rawleigh Humphries was my youngest son from whom we all expected so much, and now that he is killed my heart feels broken.'[18]

Another whose luck ran out was Private Fred Jowett (18/450). He had survived taking part in the Trench raid 30 June, as well as the assault on 1 July, and received a 'Certificate of Merit' from Major Carter 19 July at Lestrem:

> *This soldier was one of the raiding party of June 30, 1916 in the Colincamps Sector. Being unwounded he helped to bring back two of his wounded comrades.*

> *On the night of 1 July, he also did good work in holding on to a post in our front line under severe shell fire.*[19]

One of the three captured Second Pals officers in B Company was twenty-five year old Lieutenant Lionel Cassels Watson from Heaton. Watson had joined the First Pals as a private (16/1045) in 1914. In civilian life he was an engineer and his commission with the 18th West Yorks was supported by references from Sir William Priestley, Liberal M.P. for West Bradford, and Dr. Keeling his old Headmaster at Bradford Grammar School. After his repatriation at the end of 1918 he was required, as were all captured officers, to give the War Office an account of his capture.[20]

Walter Rawleigh Humphries

> *Coming from the Somme front after our attack on July 1 '16 we took over on July 27th part of the line at Richebourg St. Vaast near Neuve Chapelle. Having suffered heavy casualties on the Somme we were holding the line very thinly, our company strength being less than half. On the night of the 27th the enemy put a very heavy barrage over our front line – this lasting about three quarters of an hour and a very large raiding party attacked and got into our trench. The attack was on about a two platoon front. The front line trench consisting of breastworks, badly in need of repair, afforded very little cover against the heavy & accurate barrage put up by the enemy. We were entirely outnumbered, having in the two platoons twenty-odd men,*

the estimated strength of the enemy being about one hundred and fifty. The attack was certainly a surprise, the enemy coming through their own barrage. I was unwounded but received many heavy blows about the back and neck when in the hands of the enemy in our trench. At the time of capture I was acting as second in command to Lieut. A.N. Howarth commanding B Coy.

LIEUTENANT LIONEL CASSELS WATSON, 18WY[21]

Lionel Watson had been badly shaken up on the Somme and clearly had a rough time in the Prisoner of War Camp at Guttersloh. His medical file carries a record of a mental breakdown which was treated by the camp medical officer.[22] His statement makes an interesting contrast with the note about the raid in the Battalion War Diary. Short of checking the German records, there is no way of confirming the numbers involved. Lionel Watson was captured with his company commander, Lieutenant Arthur Howarth. Howarth had joined the First Pals in September 1914. He was the nephew of the Lord Mayor of Bradford and came from a prosperous woolcombing family. In 1914 his father, who held the rank of Major and was a moving spirit in the formation of the battalion, had arranged a commission for him. He followed his father into the Second Pals when the First went to Skipton but his father stayed behind with the 20th West Yorks when the Pals went to Egypt. The third officer, Second Lieutenant Walton had been with the battalion for only a matter of days. The Germans, complete with their own telephone system, did not stay long. Private Gordon Chapman (18/1416) was one of the men captured. They took their prisoners and a Lewis gun and went as swiftly as they came. After his capture, he recorded in a diary what happened:

Arrived in the trenches at 4 o'clock in the afternoon. About 9 o'clock bombardment started and first shell half buried us. This lasted for about an hour & before we knew anything the Germans were on top and all around us. We were forced to give in for they were in big numbers and only three of us were left. Not a gun of any sort from our side was firing a shot. It's a wonder that any of us were alive for they could have killed every man. Our line was a mess and all we had to do was walk straight out. The raiding party brought a telephone over and were using it from our trench.

After being searched we were marched out of the trenches and one soldier gave me some bread. Saw Mr. Haworth at the dressing station and spoke to him but was told to "hold my tongue". On arriving at the hut we were surprised to find many more of our chaps there all having coffee and bread. Here we spent the night and marched away at daybreak.

Friday 28th July we had a two hour march in the early morning and then motored to Seclin. Spent two hours in a school room, then entrained for Douai arriving there at 4 o'clock in the afternoon. Same night the officer allowed us to write a letter home which arrive at F.G. 24 August. We all had beds or the first time since leaving England.

Gordon Chapman as a PoW.

18/1416 PRIVATE GORDON CHAPMAN[23]

A thorough debriefing of the survivors took place, and the acting adjutant,

Second Lieutenant Harry Dalley, typed up an account of the findings for the Battalion War Diary. Unfortunately, fatigue must have got the better of him, for the date heading is wrong by twenty four hours.

Further information of German raid on night of 28/29th July, 1916.

The enemy entered our front line in two parties; one near bay 80, and the other near Bay 100. The strength of each party was about 16, and the whole were in charge of an officer.

On entering the trench these two parties worked inwards, on uniting they left our line with several prisoners. Their arrival was very unexpected and rapid. It seems probable that they made use of the old trench from the SEVEN SISTERS to point S.5.c.40, and then parallel to our front line opposite S.11.1. They advanced under cover of the smoke from their bombardment and immediately after the lift.

Many of our men were surprised in their dug-outs, which were lit up with the aid of electrical torches carried by the enemy. The enemy were armed with revolvers and bombs. Our witness states that several of the enemy inflicted slight wounds on prisoners, presumably with the idea of preventing their escape. It is noteworthy that one of our men was bandaged up by a German, who had wounded him with a bomb and then a revolver.

Those of our men who were not taken prisoner did not throw bombs at the enemy, fearing that they should hurt our own men. Some of them, however, made us of their rifles.

Attached is the gist of a statement made by L/Cpl DENTON, "B" Coy.

He was taken prisoner in the trench, and taken about 300 yards towards the German line. He there knocked over his man and escaped, reaching our lines this morning at about 10 am. He was slightly wounded. He reports that Lt. Howarth, Lt Watson and 2nd/Lt Walton were all made prisoners.

The enemy had two parties each of about 16 or 17 men, with one officer, they cleared the trenches, and joining forces left our line with the prisoners.

He thinks the enemy stayed in our line for 20 minutes or half an hour.

Another man, who was left behind owing to his wounds, judges that they remained a quarter of an hour. It is reported that the enemy took away a box or two of machine gun ammunition (belts), and a Vickers gun.

It has been reported that during the above operations our own Artillery was firing very short, most of the shells bursting in or on our side of our wire.

A dead German was searched: the only thing that gave any information, however, was his pass for his leave from April 1916. He belonged to the 3rd ERSATZ Coy of the 248th ERSATZ BATTN RESERVE INF REGT. A belt was found in our trenches, belonging to a German reported to be wounded. This man apparently belongs to the 121st Regiment.[24]

Whoever the Germans were there can be no doubting the skill and professionalism in what was an immaculately carried out operation. The German connection with Bradford include a knowledge of Bradford football, and they were not above indulging in psychological warfare. The Bradford and England outside right Company Sergeant Richard Bond (18/922) was lathered up in his braces and shirt having a shave when the Germans burst in.

He was captured, but the Germans courteously allowed him to put on his tunic and dry his face. The next morning the equivalent of a modern tabloid headline was on a board posted in No Man's Land. Herbert Bradley described what the Pals saw the following morning.

> *First time in, Jerry came over and pinched some on 'em. They took that Bradford City footballer, Dickie Bond, he were taken. And then they put up a notice, did Jerries, it were tantalising. "Welcome Bradford Pals, 31st Division. Dickie Bond, we've got him."* 18/951 Private Herbert Bradley[25]

Reinforced by 120 men from the Leeds Pals, what was left of the 18th Battalion hung on in the trenches for another week. On the afternoon of 4 August, they were relieved and came out and spent five days in Lestrem.

On 10 August they went back into the line again at Festubert close to their previous tour for a prolonged spell of nine days. Although this was reputed to be a quiet sector, the enemy kept up an unpleasant level of sniper and artillery fire. Casualties were relatively light, with only one killed and six wounded. Sadly conditions had gone beyond the threshold of tolerance for one poor soul in the First Pals who committed a self-inflicted wound 12 August. His nerve had given way after two periods of intense enemy artillery fire.[26]

George Morgan remembered coming across Brigadier Ingles at this time in the line:

> *I was afraid many a time but I hoped it didn't show it. Now some did show it but I hope I didn't. No, I was afraid many a time and I always knew I'd either get wounded or killed because you had so many narrow escapes. I believe I saw the Brigadier three times in the trenches. He were walking on his belly nearly when I saw him. He shouted out to me once when we were at Neuve Chapelle and the trenches were rather shallow there – they'd been knocked in a lot you know. I were walking along this trench when a voice shouts, "Get down, man, get down. It's me they'll get, not you". And it was the Brigadier shuffling about on his tummy nearly. I know we got used to it.*
>
> 16/1205 Private George Morgan[27]

On 20 August, the Germans began a particularly hostile bombardment and blew a mine under a sap in the Givenchy area (probably as a diversionary tactic, but still quite a tunnelling achievement given the state of the ground). They immediately switched the bombardment to the 16th West Yorks section of the line at Festubert and tried to launch a raiding party on the Pals. This time the Germans were driven off.[28]

When the 18th West Yorks came out of the front line on the night of 18 August, Privates Crimmins and Wild were immediately placed under close arrest. They were told they would face a Field General Courts Martial on 21 August on a charge of desertion. The president of the Courts Martial would be the C.O. of the 16th West Yorks, Major Humfrey H. Kennedy.

NOTES

1. Pickworth, Diary, Bradford Industrial Museum.

2. Ibid

3. Ibid.

4. I am grateful to Jon Cooksey, author of *Barnsley Pals* in this series for allowing me to use his translation of General von Stein's response.

5. Lt. General Sir Aylmer Hunter-Weston, letter to his wife, Hunter Weston Papers, Mss 483655, British Museum Library.

6. Information, and photograph of Corporal Percy Bateman, supplied by his grand-daughter, Mrs. Rita Calam of Bradford.

7. George Morgan, talking on tape kindly supplied by Malcolm Brown

8. Battalion War Diary

9. *Yorkshire Observer*, 13 July, 1916. Sir William Beach Thomas (1868-1957) was one of only five journalists allowed to report on the Western Front and represented the *Daily Mail*. He later admitted to being deeply ashamed of what he had written in his autobiography,

   "A great part of the information supplied to us by (British Army Intelligence) was utterly wrong and misleading. The dispatches were largely untrue so far as they deal with concrete results. Almost all the official information was wrong. The vulgarity of enormous headlines and the enormity of one's own name did not lessen the shame".

10. Battalion War Diary.

11. Battalion War Diary. General Sir Charles Monro (1860-1929) conducted the investigation into the Dardanelles campaign which led to eventual withdrawal from the peninsula. Like Haig, he was an avowed 'Westerner' who believed that the war could only be won by destroying the German Army on the Western Front.

12. See the *Barnsley Pals* by Jon Cooksey in this series.

13. Battalion War Diary

14. Ibid. Corporal Lee survived, but Private Riley was killed at Gavrelle on 3rd May, 1917.

15. Ibid.

16. PRO WO339. Officers Records, R.S. Cross

17. Humphries, letter in *Bradford Daily Telegraph*, 10 July, 1916.

18. PRO WO339. Officers Records, W.R. Humphries.

19. Docement kindly supplied by family.

20. Lionel Cassells Watson. Officers Records, PRO WO339

21. Ibid.

22. Ibid. Written statement by L.C. Watson

23. Gordon Chapman, diary, kindly supplied by his son.

24. Battalion War Diary.

25. Herbert Bradley. Tape with Steve Kerry. Op.cit.

26. Battalion War Diary

27. George Morgan. Op.cit.

28. Battalion War Diary.

Chapter Twelve

SHOT AT DAWN

Sentence : To suffer death by being shot, with a strong recommendation to mercy on account of exceptionally good character.

These men are best forgotten.
      MAJOR-GENERAL ROBERT WANLESS-O'GOWAN. GOC 31ST DIVISION.

Not forgotten by those who loved him best.
- INSCRIPTION ON THE GRAVE OF 18/356 PRIVATE ARTHUR WILD, VIEILLE-CHAPELLE NEW MILITARY CEMETERY.

IN THE HALF LIGHT OF DAWN on Tuesday 5 September, 1916, Privates Herbert Crimmins (18/313) and Arthur Wild (18/356) of A Company of the Second Bradford Pals were marched out of a barn on the northern edge of Lestrem. It was a chill flat landscape close to the river Lawe between Bethune and Armentieres. The men were tied to posts three yards apart in front of the barn wall and blindfolded. White markers were placed over their hearts. At 5.51 a.m. they were shot by a firing party of their own comrades. The bullet marks are still on the wall of the barn. Mercifully, death was instantaneous and the officer was spared the *coup de grace*.[1]

Later in the day, the Commander of 31st Division, Major-General Robert Wanless O'Gowan, noticed that flowers had been placed on the men's graves. He was observed to kick the flowers away and express the view, these men are best forgotten, a sentiment later repeated to a full parade of the Battalion when the execution was announced.[2]

Major-General Robert Wanless O'Gowan

The event was not forgotten, indeed, it was bitterly resented. Seventy- three years later, the perceived injustice, the kicking away of the flowers, and the degrading effect on the participants in the firing party still provoked anger in the last survivor of the 18th Battalion, John McGrath (18/230). He recalled:

One of 'em...[the firing party]...went a bit doolally.. Y'know, wrong in't head. He committed suicide in Cleckheaton after t'war. The officer hit t'bottle and got an alcohol problem.
                          18/230 PRIVATE JOHN MCGRATH[3]

No doubt the other members of the firing party were distressed, for it was they who had placed the flowers on the graves. The affair was particularly difficult for Regimental Sergeant Major Harold Scott who had to take charge of arrangements because he had known Private Wild as a colleague in the Bradford City Police. It also caused anguish for the Pals' chaplain, Captain J.G. Thornton, a curate at Bradford Parish Church, who prepared the men for death and accompanied them to the execution.

Many years later, George Morgan commented:

They were sentenced to be shot, subject to Sir Douglas Haig. He could have said no, but he didn't. So they were shot. They didn't shoot any Australians. They would have rioted. They weren't like us. We were docile.

16/1205 PRIVATE GEORGE MORGAN[4]

George Morgan was correct about Haig's attitude. Although others lower down the chain of command helped to shape the decision ultimately taken by the Commander in Chief, Haig was personally required to confirm the death sentences. He did so 1 September choosing to ignore the court's strong recommendations to mercy. The execution was announced in Haig's General Routine Orders 10 September. Item 1782 records, The sentence of the Court was 'To suffer death by being shot'. There is no mention of the Court's rider, 'with a strong recommendation to mercy on account of exceptionally good character'. It is the author's view, after examination of the available evidence, that justice was not done in the case of these unfortunate men.

George Morgan was also correct about the Australians. The Australian Dominion Parliament's legislation ensured that their troops were exempt from capital punishment, much to the annoyance of the Commander in Chief. Haig repeatedly pressed the War Office to influence the Australian Government to introduce the death penalty. In a letter to the War Office on 27 July, 1917, Haig wrote:

The Australian Government can be assured that the power of inflicting the death penalty is very sparingly used. It is only in cases where the offence is of a very deliberate character and an example is urgently required, that such sentences are confirmed.[5]

It is interesting to test this definitive statement of Haig's position on Capital Courts Martial against the circumstances leading up to the execution of the two Bradford men. To say that the two men's conduct was 'of a very deliberate character' is too strong, though much was made of the term 'deliberate' as the papers were passed up the chain of command for confirmation by Haig.

However, there may have been other unspoken factors which played a part in Haig's decision. Haig's diary gives support to this view. First the entry 30 June, 1916:

The only doubt I have is regarding the VIII Corps [Hunter Weston] which has had no experience of fighting in France and has not carried out one successful raid.[6]

And then again, on Saturday evening 1 July, as thousands of men lay dead or in agony in No Man's Land, the ultimate slander which was never withdrawn:

I am inclined to believe from further reports that few of VIII Corps left their trenches ...the attack on the Gommecourt Salient... was of the greatest assistance in helping VIII Corps, because many of the enemy's guns and troops were employed against it, and so the VIII Corps was left considerably free...The VIII Corps seems to want looking after.[7]

Was it a case of 'an example is urgently required'? Did they pay the price for Haig's personal contempt for Hunter Weston? Were they, with a man from the Sheffield City Battalion, 'the example' needed to stiffen VIII Corps after 1 July? Was it that Hunter-Weston and Wanless O'Gowan were stung by the Commander in Chief and were trying to protect their own backs – for so far as is known the only executions resulting directly from the events of 1 July were the three men in 31st Division.

No doubt Hunter-Weston and Wanless O'Gowan could feel hot breath on their necks, and as we will see Major Carter was a man used to doing Hunter-Weston's bidding. Despite Haig's comments about the Gommecourt Salient, the commander of 48th Division at Gommecourt, Major General Stuart-Wortley, was dismissed 5 July 1916. In the event, Hunter-Weston was more fortunate and was simply moved to a quieter section of the line.

Whether the attack on Gommecourt was of real assistance to VIII Corps is debatable and has been discussed in an earlier chapter. Certainly Brigadier Rees in charge 94 Brigade on the left flank of VIII Corps would have disputed that view. But, even if one discounts the theory that they paid the penalty for Haig's unjustified prejudice against 31st Division, Crimmins and Wild were remarkably unlucky to be executed purely on statistical grounds. The 1914/15 Star medal rolls for all battalions of the West Yorkshire Regiment reveals a total of 109 cases of desertion (there were seven others in the two Bradford Battalions), yet only six other men were executed, and few could have had better character references than Privates Crimmins and Wild.[8] Maybe desertion at the time of a critical assault was likely to receive more severe treatment.

What then were the circumstances of the case?

Both men were amongst the first to volunteer for the Second Pals in February, 1915. Had they waited for conscription they would not have been on the Somme in June, 1916, or at Lestrem 5 September. Like the rest of their battalion they had progressed to France via Bowling Park, Ripon, Fovant, and Egypt.

Herbert Crimmins was thirty-two years old. He had been born in Pontefract and lived there until shortly before the war. According to his evidence at the Courts Martial he had five brothers serving in the forces, and his late father had served for twenty-seven years as a regular soldier. This military connection may have inspired him to volunteer to join the Pals.[9]

Arthur Wild was a twenty-four year old police constable from Wootton Street just off Manchester Road in West Bowling. As a policeman he was in a reserved occupation and under no obligation to join the Army. He was one of twenty members of the Bradford City Police Force who joined

18 WY at Ripon. Private Herbert Crimmins ringed. Sixteen-year old Ernest Brook kneels on left.

the 18th West Yorks together. One of the twenty was the City Force's Drill Sergeant, former Coldstream Guardsman Harold Scott who became the Regimental Sergeant Major of the Battalion.[10]

The reality of the Western Front soon hit the Battalion with a steady stream of casualties on an almost daily basis, mostly as a result of sustained artillery fire. Between 24 April and 10 June, nineteen men were killed and fifty-six were wounded.[11]

Crimmins and Wild were not alone in feelings of apprehension and fear. On 4 June, the day the battalion re-entered the front line, the War Diary records a self-inflicted wound by rifle fire.[12] Two events were to shake Private Wild.

The first was the deaths of Corporal Ernest Walden (18/357) and Private Claude Ferrand (18/252) in a listening post below the Redan Ridge 22 May. Arthur Wild and Ernest Walden had served together in the City Police as well as in A Company of the Second Pals. They volunteered together and had consecutive enlistment numbers.[13]

The second occurred in the early hours 8 June when Private Wild was digging a new Sap near to where Walden and Ferrand had been killed. As the party dug the Sap, they discovered Ferrand's body[14]. Shortly afterwards, as the digging continued, the enemy launched a barrage along the British line. Wild, probably disturbed by the discovery of Ferrand's body and the possibility of digging up his friend Ernest Walden, was severely shaken when a 'coal box' exploded next to him in the sap. Lieutenant J.R. Thornton (not to be confused with the Chaplain,

J.G. Thornton) helped to get Wild out. Wild was taken to the dug-out of his Company Commander, Captain Keevil, where he was given a drink of tea, and sent back to another dug-out to rest.[15] In his evidence to the Courts Martial, Wild explained what happened next :

> *I was excused after that from going into the front line trench for the rest of the battalion's tour in the trenches, On returning to hutments ...[at Bus les Artois]... I was excused working parties in the front trenches by my Company Commander. I did see the medical officer who gave me some pills and said I should be better in a few days. I saw the medical officer owing to being unable to stand the noise of shell fire when going up to the trenches.*
>
> 18/356 PRIVATE ARTHUR WILD[16]

On 10 June, Lieutenant Thornton took charge of a working party to move stores, water and ammunition from the light railway at Euston Dump up to the Assembly trenches at Basin Wood in readiness for the coming offensive. Wild, after two days' rest, and Herbert Crimmins were included in the ration carrying party. Wild was probably included in the carrying party because he was not thought suitable to be included in the training of the assault troops for 'the big push'.[17]

On the first nightly trek towards the trenches, Wild broke down under enemy artillery fire. Private Clifford Oram (18/47) later described Wild's condition to the Courts Martial.

> *I was in a working party along with Private Wild near Euston Dump when heavy shelling commenced. I then noticed Private Wild was bad with shell shock so I reported him to the officer in charge. By shell shock I mean that he was all of a shake and ducked and quivered at every shell.*
>
> 18/47   PRIVATE CLIFFORD ORAM[18]

Lieutenant Thornton immediately ordered Oram to take Wild back to the huts at Bus-les-Artois. Wild recovered sufficiently to make a successful return to the carrying party at the second attempt on the following night.[19]

On 20 June, the rest of the Battalion came out of the line before going off to the relative tranquility of Gezaincourt, twenty miles behind the line, for five days training in readiness for the offensive.[20]

Lieutenant Thornton's party stayed in the Colincamps sector and continued the nightly trudge from Bus to Euston Dump. During the day they had time on their hands and evidently slaked their thirst regularly in the bar of the Bus estaminet. The ration party must have become well known and welcome customers, as the long June days passed by. The bar still exists today and it's functioning in the Great War is a tribute to the tenacity of French free enterprise.

It was obvious that the stores build up was in preparation for a major offensive, and the Colincamps sector was humming with activity. When the great British artillery barrage opened up at 6.25 a.m. on Saturday 24 June, the sound of shells screaming overhead like express trains can have done nothing for Wild's nerves. On 26 and 27 June the men were drenched in heavy thunderstorms. When they reached Euston Dump, the sight of the K.O.Y.L.I. pioneers digging fresh graves in Euston Road cemetery must have filled them with less good cheer than could be found in the *estaminet* at Bus.

The rest of the Pals arrived back at Bus on Sunday 25 June[21]. The intention was for the attack to take place on Thursday 29 June.

As the rest of the Battalion slept in billets at Bus, Thornton's party plodded on with their nightly trek. The unnerving barrage continued to whistle overhead and the German response made equipment and ration carrying a hazardous task. Things became more difficult as heavy thunderstorms soaked the men and churned up the ground for three nights running on Monday, Tuesday and Wednesday.[22] Conditions became so bad that the offensive was postponed until Saturday 1 July.

On 29 June, as the exhausted ration party splashed up to Basin Wood for the nineteenth consecutive night, they could console themselves with the thought that having missed the training for the assault they would not be required to take part in it.

On the morning of Friday 30 June, their night's work completed, the ration party arrived back in Bus covered in mud and sweat. The village was a hive of activity as the Pals Battalions prepared to move up for the assault. At eleven o'clock, after a short sleep and cleaning up, Crimmins and Wild decided to slake their thirst in their favourite *estaminet*. At 12 noon they returned to the camp for their meal.[23]

What happened next is open to conflicting interpretation. In his evidence for the prosecution at the Courts Martial, Lieutenant Thornton stated:

> *About noon on June 30th the ration party were issued out with extra ammunition. The accused...(were).. .then present. The ration party were then warned not to leave camp. At 4.00 p.m....I received orders to parade at 6.00 p.m. to proceed to the trenches. On sending Sergeant Breen round to warn the ration party, he reported to me the absence of the accused. At 6.00 p.m. on calling the roll of the ration carriers, the accused (were) still absent.*

Lieutenant J.R. Thornton

LIEUTENANT J.R. THORNTON[24]

It should be noted that the lieutenant limited his orders to 'not to leave camps'. There is no mention of proceeding to the trenches until 4.00 p.m. However, the section corporal, twenty-two year old Tom Wise gave evidence and in one significant respect he differed from Lieutenant Thornton:

> *About 12 noon...I personally warned the ration carriers to parade for the trenches at 5.45 p.m. that night.*

18/1128 CORPORAL TOM WISE[25]

It seems extremely unlikely from this that Thornton's men were due to take part in the attack. The repeated use of the term 'ration carriers' implies that they were not assault troops, and they were not trained to do so. They were issued with extra ammunition, but as ration carriers, they could not carry the full equipment of the assault troops. They were due to leave Bus at 6.00 p.m. ahead of the rest of the Brigade to carry water and last minute items to Basin Wood. It is reasonable to assume they were to be held in reserve and would not be 'going over the top' at 7.30 a.m. on 1 July.

Again they had time on their hands. They also had money in their pockets, the Battalion having been paid up in full. One of the Durham Pals recorded the atmosphere at Bus:

> Our bank books were taken in and we were paid all our credit, which was substantial. Some of us had hundreds of francs, which immediately gave the impression to many of us that most were not coming back. The result was that the estaminets got most of it.
>
> PRIVATE R.T. TAIT, 18TH DURHAM LIGHT INFANTRY[26]

The temptation to ignore orders to stay in camp proved too great. At 2.00 p.m. the two men went back to the *estaminet*, whether out of habit or whether to build up dutch courage is unknown. They admitted spending the rest of the afternoon drinking.

When Crimmins and Wild were in the *estaminet* Lieutenant General Hunter-Weston, the Corps Commander, arrived in the village. The General had come to inspire his troops with a pep talk. George Morgan (16/1205) remembered what he had to say:

> Well he told us that there would be some casualties but we were certain to find very little opposition... and he also told us something we didn't like, that if any man hung back and stopped in the trenches that there'd be somebody there to shoot them... I resented the fact that we were being told that if there was any... anybody... any cowards amongst us, well what'd happen to us because it was the last thing in the world we thought of was dodging the column.
>
> 16/1205 PRIVATE GEORGE MORGAN[27]

Having satisfied himself that he had inspired his men, 'Hunter Bunter' went on to spread his message elsewhere. Most of the Pals settled down to write last letters or to listen to a concert from the band of the Leeds Pals. Two of the Leeds men carved their names on the base of the Church tower. In the *estaminet*, having failed to hear the General's fateful words, Crimmins and Wild were enjoying their last binge. They carried on until closing time when they staggered out and wandered off to a cornfield where they fell asleep.[28]

Crimmins outlined his version of events, later repeated by Wild, in evidence at the Court Martial:

> On June 30, 1916 about 11 a.m. at Bus les Artois. I and my friend Private Wild went out to an estaminet and had something to drink. I then returned to camp for dinner about 12 noon, and afterwards returned to the same estaminet where we had more drink and stayed until closing time. We then wandered along a road three or four miles and went into a cornfield and there fell asleep. When we woke up it was dusk and we were afraid to go back, and so went on to a village called Beauquesne.
>
> 18/313 PRIVATE HERBERT CRIMMINS[29]

Dusk was after ten o'clock, more than four hours after they were due to report for parade. Back at Bus, the parade duly took place at 5.45 p.m. When Corporal Wise took the roll call, the two absences were noted and reported to Lieutenant Thornton.[30] At 6.00 p.m. Thornton's men were amongst the carrying parties leaving Bus ahead of the assault troops. They were immediately followed by the Leeds Pals, with the First Bradfords marching out at 6.35 p.m. and the Second Bradfords at 8.45 p.m., followed by the Durham Pals.[31]

It appears from the men's evidence that when they woke up in a hazy condition they panicked. Crimmins admitted under cross-examination that he could walk, 'but the drink was in us'.[32]

In his still less than sober condition, former policeman Wild was probably aware that to be drunk on duty constituted a crime under the Army Act[33] and this would compound the offence of missing parade. In evidence Crimrnins admitted they 'were afraid to go back', whilst Wild stated,

> I was frightened of the consequences of my absence and also thought I would not be able to stand the noise of the guns.
>
> 18/356 PRIVATE ARTHUR WILD[34]

Alcohol clouds judgement and exaggerates emotions, be it sadness, happiness or fear. Fear leads to flight, and fly the men did. No evidence was given that they had a coherent escape plan. They claimed to have wandered off away from the gunfire in a confused panic. Ironically, they spent the night within a few hundred yards of Haig's Advance G.H.Q. at Val Vion château in Beauquesne.[35]

The men wandered around for the next three days. The level of activity and confusion behind the battle line enabled them to avoid immediate detection. By this time Wild had worked out a plan.

> I had a brother stationed at Vignacourt so I intended to go there, tell him everything and then give myself up.
>
> 18/356 PRIVATE ARTHUR WILD[36]

Here one must pause and consider whether this was true. It could be argued that the route of Beauquesne to Vignacourt was identical to that travelled by the Pals from the rail head at Pont Remy on their way to the Somme in March. This was not put to Wild at the trial, but if true, and it is a possibility, it undermines the men's defence that it was not deliberate desertion.

They finally reached Vignacourt on the edge of the battlefield area on 4 July, but did not find Wild's brother. The tired and no doubt hungry pair gave themselves up to Sergeant Reader of the Military Police at 1.00 p.m. They readily admitted being absent from 2.00 p.m. on 30 June.[37]

They were placed under close arrest and held in custody by the military police for the next eleven days. By this time, what was left of the 18th West Yorks had moved north near the Belgian border. The men were escorted back to their battalion 15 July and handed over at Robecque near Lestrem. Private Herbert Bradley (18/951) of the transport section was with his water cart when they returned. He remembered their dishevelled appearance and that they had lost their water bottles. He gave Crimmins a drink from his own bottle as the men awaited handover to R.S.M. Harold Scott.[38]

George Morgan (16/1205), who became a close friend of Harold Scott and his brother Quarter Master Sergeant Alf Scott (16/1027) in the Pals Comradeship Association after the war, recalled what he was told about the men's attitude when R.S.M. Scott gave them an extremely hot reception and warned them of the seriousness of their situation:

> *They laughed it off. They thought wandering away was just something or nothing... If it had been in England they would have got seven days CB.*
>
> 16/1205 PRIVATE GEORGE MORGAN[39]

It is difficult to know how genuine this attitude was, or whether making light of it was merely a cover for embarrassment when they came to realise the enormity of the battalion's losses on 1 July. As for the battalion, it was still in a state of collective shock and trauma and everyone was pre-occupied with pulling the threads together again.

For the next twelve days, whilst the battalion was out of the line, the two men were held under close arrest in the guardroom. But when the 18th re-entered the line in the Neuve Chapelle sector on 27 July they went into the trenches with the rest of the Battalion. On the first night a German raid resulted in eighty-two casualties, with thirty-six of the Second Pals taken prisoner. Captain Cross, the Commander of A Company was killed.[40]

If ever two men were unlucky not to be captured by the enemy it was Crimmins and Wild, for capture would have put an end to their problem. In the morning a taunting notice was seen in No Mans Land : 'Welcome Bradford Pals'.[41]

In later years, the *Telegraph & Argus* reported Herbert Bradley as claiming,

> *The two men had been given the option of going 'over the top' or being executed but the pair had opted to face the firing squad.*
>
> 18/952 PRIVATE HERBERT BRADLEY[42]

A recent study of all executions in World War One, *Shot at Dawn*, by Sykes and Putkowski repeats Herbert Bradley's statement, but makes the comment 'it would seem very unlikely'.[43] In fact Herbert Bradley was close to the mark, although his conclusion, 'the pair had opted to face the firing squad', is different to a more accurate and corroborated description he gave on tape and which will be quoted later. As a close friend of the two Scott brothers in the Pals Comradeship Association after the war, Herbert was in a good position to know what had gone on at Battalion Headquarters. Lieutenant (later Captain) J.R. Thornton was also close to Herbert Bradley and the Scott brothers as president of the Pals Comradeship Association.

Private Herbert Bradley

R.S.M. Harold Scott was a tall highly competent ex-Guardsman, a man of resource, initiative and presence who made the 18th West Yorks function like clockwork. He was aided in this task by his 'little brother' Alf Scott, the quartermaster sergeant, whom he had arranged to be transferred from the First Pals to work with him. The Second Pals were in awe of their R.S.M.,

> *Ooh, he were a proper soldier were Harold – talk about a sergeant major on parade. But he had it, for all we used to swear at him. He knew his drill you know, ooh, he did that. Ooh, he were a smart fella.*
>
> 18/952 PRIVATE HERBERT BRADLEY[44]

The German raid on the night of 27 July, in which the footballer Dickie Bond and thirty-five others were captured, resulted in the 18th West Yorks sending out a series of N.C.O. led three men patrols to probe the enemy's positions and to watch out for any signs of a repeat German raid.[45]

Despite his formidable exterior, R.S.M. Harold Scott was essentially a kind and considerate man who cared about the welfare of his men and he knew Arthur Wild from their days together in the police. He was under no illusions about the seriousness of their position, even if the two men themselves didn't fully appreciate the danger. He was concerned both for them and also for the potential damage to morale and reputation that a double execution would wreak upon his beloved Pals Battalion and the reputation of the City Police. He also had a natural revulsion for what he knew would have to be his own duties if executions were carried out.

After the war until his death in April, 1960, R.S.M. Scott kept silence even with his own family – although they knew he was troubled by what had happened. His sole confidant was his brother Alf. We now know that Harold Scott did his best to get the two men out of a desperate situation, almost to the point of putting his own position in jeopardy.

Shortly before his own death, 'little brother' Alf Scott confided in Harold's son-in-law, Jeff Mawby. According to Alf, the R.S.M. offered the men the chance to go on a three man N.C.O's patrol into No Man's Land. If they came back successfully they would have demonstrated courage which could help when they came to face a Court Martial, and no doubt remembering the fate of Dickie Bond and others, he dropped a hint that if they got captured by the Germans it could solve their problems. Sadly, said Alf, his brother's gruff insistent words, 'there's your rifle, there's your helmet, get yourselves out there', were not heeded.[46]

The two men did take part in wiring parties in No Man's Land, and according to Lieutenant Thornton in evidence for their defence, they behaved well[47]. But the offer to go on a three man patrol was declined. They could not believe that they were in serious trouble. As Harold Scott feared, the logic of Army discipline rolled on to its inevitable conclusion and the refusal was to cost the two men their lives.[48]

On 4 August, the battalion came out for five days relief in Lestrem, but on the 10th they went back into the line again at Festubert for a prolonged spell of nine days. Although this was reputed to be a quiet sector, the enemy kept up an unpleasant level of sniper and artillery fire. Casualties were relatively light, with only one killed and six wounded, but conditions had gone beyond the threshold of tolerance for one poor soul who committed a self-inflicted wound on 14 August.[49]

Crimmins and Wild came out of the line for the last time on the night of 18 August. They were immediately placed under close arrest and told they would face a Field General Courts Martial 21 August on a charge of desertion.

Again fate appears to have played a cruel hand to the two men. Before the 1 July, there is little doubt that Captain Cecil Keevil their company commander in A Company, would have been an automatic choice to represent them. Keevil was a caring conscientious officer (he spent two nights in May searching No Man's Land for three missing men, one of whom was Wild's friend Ernest Walden). As a successful barrister he would have been able to make the most of their case. Unfortunately for Crimmins and Wild, Captain Keevil was wounded 1 July. So far as is known none of A Company's other officers had legal training. Keevil's successor, Captain Cross, was killed 27 July. Lieutenant Thornton was a witness. It is not known who, if anyone, represented the men, and the phrasing of the Courts Martial transcript implies they represented themselves. Possibly as a policeman Wild thought he was capable of this, but it is doubtful if Crimmins was.[50]

The Field General Courts Martial was held 21 August at Loisir château to the south of Lestrem. The president, Major Humfrey H. Kennedy C.O. of the First Bradford Pals, had a reputation as a fair considerate officer. The other members of the Panel were Captain Jackson of the 10th East Yorks (the Hull Commercials) and Captain Hughes-Games of the Durham Pals. Although the men were tried separately, the two cases were dealt with on the same day and the prosecution evidence was virtually identical in each case.[51]

Papers relating to Capital Courts Martial Cases are subject to a seventy -five year rule in the Public Record Office (National Archive), and the author was able to draw upon these documents when they were released in January, 1992. Surprisingly, in otherwise very detailed material, the names of the prosecuting officer or any defending officer are not given. The usual procedure was for the prosecution to be carried out by the battalion adjutant and this unhappy task is likely to have fallen on the acting adjutant, Lieutenant Harry Dalley.

Lieutenant Dalley, a thirty-six year old wool traveller from Leeds, was commissioned from the ranks of the Leeds Pals in 1915. He took over as acting adjutant when Captain Williams was badly wounded 1 July. His brother-in-law, Sergeant Hugh Odgers of the Leeds Pals was killed 1 July.[52]

Both men pleaded 'Not Guilty'. The transcript of the evidence shows that both the prosecution and the defence were conducted in a low-key way. The prosecutor did not undertake a vigorous cross-examination of the men, and certainly nothing was made of their escape route.

The Prosecution produced three witnesses, Lieutenant Thornton, Corporal Wise and Sergeant Reader of the Military Police. Their evidence was brief and has already been quoted earlier in this chapter. The defendents chose not to cross examine the witnesses, although this is not surprising because Lieutenant Thornton and Corporal Wise later gave evidence for the defence. It is not clear who organised the defence, but clearly some thought had gone into calling witnesses. In his defence, Crimmins described the drinking session and the subsequent sleep in the cornfield:

> *When we woke up it was dusk and we were afraid to go back.* 18/313 PRIVATE HERBERT CRIMMINS[53]

He outlined their wanderings before concluding,

> *I am very sorry for what I did. I had not the slightest intention of deserting. My father has been in the Army for twenty-seven years and I have five brothers now serving abroad. I have been in the trenches both before and after this occurrence and tried to do my best.* 18/313 PRIVATE HERBERT CRIMMINS[54]

Lieutenant Harry Dalley. The formal phraseology suggests that Crimmins may at least have had some coaching to prepare his statement. His cross-examination involved only one question

> Question: *Did the drink you had so effect you that you did not know what you were doing from the time you left the estaminet until you reached the cornfield ?*

> Answer: *We could walk but the drink was in us.*[55]

Corporal Wise and Lieutenant Thornton, having given factual evidence for the prosecution, gave character evidence for the defence. The Court heard from Wise that,

> *The accused has been in my section since November, 1915 and during that time has given no trouble whatever with me. He has been a very good soldier, and very good in his work.* 18/1128 CORPORAL THOMAS WISE[56]

Lieutenant Thornton was equally generous:

> *The accused is in my company and I have known him for the last three months as a good character. I know of nothing against him. He has always worked well, and on a recent tour in the trenches went out on wiring parties and did his work satisfactorily.* LIEUTENANT J.R. THORNTON[57]

A formal statement as to character – 'Very Good' – was then read from Major Carter, comanding officer of the 18th West Yorks. No previous offence of any kind was recorded on his Field Conduct Sheet.[58]

At Private Wild's trial, the prosecution evidence was virtually identical. Wild's defence statement confirms the details given by Crimmins, but goes on to describe his shell shock and the search for his brother related earlier in the chapter.

When Wild was cross examined he answered,

I did not report sick after the explosion of the 'coalbox' as I was allowed to rest by my company commander.

18/356 PRIVATE ARTHUR WILD[59]

He also confirmed that he did not see the doctor after being made a member of the ration carrying party. Whilst this could be construed to suggest that Wild was exaggerating the degree of his shell shock, it could also be seen in his favour because he carried on when he was entitled to have reported sick.

Three witnesses gave evidence for the defence to support Wild's claim to be shell-shocked. Private Clifford Oram testified that on the ration carrying party,

Private Wild was bad with shell shock. I reported him to the officer who told me to take him straight back to camp. He was all of a shake and ducked and quivered at every shell.

18/47 PRIVATE CLIFFORD ORAM[60]

His Sergeant, who was working on the front line sap when Wild was first afflicted with shell shock described how,

the enemy sent over three minenwerfers which landed very close. I had to send Arthur Wild out of the sap as he was so shaken with shell shock.

18/1267 SERGEANT H. HUSTWICK[61]

Lieutenant Thornton confirmed Hustwick's statement.

Some coalboxes came near him [Wild]. *He was taken out with shell shock and I assisted to get him out. On another occasion whilst going up on a working party from Euston Dump, shelling was going on ...Wild... gave way completely, and I sent him back to camp at Bus. I reported the matter to the company commander* [Captain Keevil] *but do not know what steps he took.*

LIEUTENANT J.R. THORNTON[62]

Lieutenant Thornton went on to testify to Wild's character.

I have known the accused for nearly three months and he has never given any trouble except on the occasion in question. Recently he has been in the trenches again. He behaved alright in the support trench and on one occasion formed one of a wiring party when he did his job as well as anyone else.

LIEUTENANT J.R. THORNTON[63]

Wild's Corporal, Tom Wise, also added his support.

Private Wild is in my section and has been since we were at Fovant in November, 1915, and during the whole of that time I have found him a good worker and a good soldier.

18/1128 CORPORAL TOM WISE[64]

Again a formal statement as to character was read out from Major Carter – and again the character was described as 'Very Good'. This time, however, the dreadful crime of being 'Late on Company Parade' with a punishment of three days confined to barracks confirmed by Captain John Bland at Fovant was appended to Wild's Field Conduct Sheet.[65]

A reading of the Court Martial transcripts gives the impression that each case was over in little more than a quarter of an hour. There is no record of any summing up by either prosecution or defence, and one must assume that none were made.

After conferring, the Court was unanimous in finding the men guilty of desertion.[66] The Court then proceeded to pass the sentence of death, but in Crimmins' case,

> *With a strong recommendation to mercy on account of his exceptionally good character.*

In Wild's case,

> *on account of the nervous condition of the accused due to the explosion of a trench mortar projectile in the near vicinity of the sap in which he was working in the front line trench in the Colincamps sector in the early days of June, 1916.[67]*

In making these strong recommendations, the Court was certainly doing its best for the two men. The Court may have believed their recommendations would make it most unlikely that the death sentences would be carried out. They had good reason for such a belief, because official statistics show that only ten per cent of all death sentences were actually confirmed.[68]

Why, then, were the Court's recommendations ignored?

Over the next few days the Courts Martial papers made their way up the chain of command for observations from battalion, to brigade, to division, to corps, to army and finally to the Commander in Chief himself.

The first blow to the men's hopes, and one suspects to the Court's intentions, came the following day from their own battalion commanding officer, Major Herbert Carter. He did not directly address the question of the strong recommendation to mercy made by the Court under the Presidency of his fellow Bradford Pals C.O., Major Kennedy, but what he said when appending his comments to the papers did the men no good at all

First on Crimmins.

> *The character of this man from a behaviour point of view is good, from a fighting point of view, indifferent. From evidence gathered from his Company Sergt-Major, he was of a nervous disposition in the trenches, and not of much use...*
>
> *This soldier is a weak man, and as far as I can gather he has, in my opinion been led away (possibly under the influence of drink by Pte Wild. I think the crime was committed deliberately, nevertheless, as he has shown himself to be of a nervous disposition when in the trenches.[69]*

On Wild:

> *This man has always been of a rather lazy disposition, and one who needed driving the whole time to get the full amount of work out of him. Of his previous conduct in action I know nothing, except that he has never done anything exceptionally good. The case of shell-shock which is mentioned in the evidence was nothing serious, as I happened to be in the front line trench myself at the time. In my opinion, of the two men Crimmins and Wild, Wild was the stronger character, and I think undoubtedly deserted deliberately, with the sole object of avoiding further*

SCHEDULE.

Date 21st August 1916   No. CM 26

Name of Alleged Offender (a)	Offence charged	Plea	Finding, and if Convicted, Sentence (b)	How dealt with by Confirming Officer
Not more than six names to be entered on one form. 18/356 Pte Arthur Wild 18th W. York R.	Sec: 12. I (a) When on active service deserting His Majesty's Service	Not Guilty	Guilty. To suffer death by being shot with a strong recommendation to mercy on account of the nervous condition of the accused due to the explosion of the trench mortar projectile in the near vicinity of the Sap in which he was working in the front line trench in the COLINCAMPS section in the early days of June 1916	Reserved. J.D. Ingles Com'd 93rd Infantry Confirmed D. Haig 15.9.16

(a) If the name of the person charged is unknown, he may be described as unknown, with such addition as will identify him.

(b) Recommendation to mercy to be inserted in this column.

✕

J.D. Ingles   Brig. Gen. H.H. Kennedy Major
Com'd 93rd Infantry Brigade
Convening Officer   President.

SCHEDULE.

Date 21st August 1916.   No. CM25

Name of Alleged Offender (a)	Offence charged	Plea	Finding, and if Convicted, Sentence (b)	How dealt with by Confirming Officer
N⁰ 18/313 Pte. Herbert Crimmins 18th W. York. R.	Sec. 12. I (a) When on Active Service deserting His Majesty's Service.	Not guilty	Guilty To suffer death by being shot With a strong recommendation to mercy on account of his exceptionally good character Confirmed D. Haig. Gen¹ 1 Sep: 16	Reserved J. D. Ingles. Brig. Com'd 93rd Infantry Bri

Not more than six names to be entered in one form.

(a) If the name of the person charged is unknown, he may be described as unknown, with such addition as will identify him.

(b) Recommendation to mercy to be inserted in this column.

J. D. Ingles. Brig. Gen.
Com'd 93rd Infantry Brigade.
Confirming Officer.

H. H. Kennedy Major
President.

active service.[70]

One cannot doubt that these were honest opinions from a most competent professional soldier who was, in general, well respected by the men of his battalion. Carter was a highly intelligent man known for acts of kindness and sensitivity, yet these are damning comments and almost certainly led the High Command to disregard the Court's strong recommendation to mercy.

Nevertheless both the content and the system which allowed such comments are open to criticism. One is astonished that Carter submitted contradictory formal character evidence, 'Very Good', to the Court, and then followed it up with this subsequent material. He can hardly have known the men, and his later comments were based on hearsay evidence which was not tested by cross-examination in court. He joined the battalion as second in command from VIII Corps Staff, 17 April, 1916 and left for Gezaincourt 13 June, giving him only eight weeks to have any sort of contact with the two men before their offence.[71]

His comments on Wild are in flat contradiction to evidence given on oath to the Court by Lieutenant Thornton and Corporal Wise, both of whom worked closely with the men.

Major Herbert Carter.

Thornton concerning Wild:

> *'has never given any trouble...behaved alright in the support trenches...formed one of a wiring party when he did his job as well as anyone else.'*

Wise, who had worked with Wild since 1915. 'During the whole of that time I have found him a good worker and a good soldier.'

And how did Major Carter know that 'the case of shell-shock was nothing serious'? Lieutenant Thornton thought it was sufficiently serious to allow Wild to rest, and on the second occasion (when Carter was no longer in the area) to send him back to Bus. What is surprising is that neither the prosecution or the defence bothered to call the medical officer, Dr. McTavish, to give medical evidence. The key word used by Major Carter was the word 'deliberate'.

The word deliberate picked up its own momentum as the papers processed their way further along the chain of command. One wonders whether Major Carter, or his superiors paused to consider the contradiction between 'deliberate' and the comment that Crimmins was, 'a weak man...as far as I can gather...led away (possibly under the influence of drink) by Pte Wild' and, 'I think the crime was committed deliberately, nevertheless'. No benefit of the doubt here. Carter also introduced hearsay comments from Company Sergeant Major Charles Birkhill (18/875) of A Company that Crimmins was of a nervous disposition and not much use. This again contradicts Carter's written character evidence to the Court. One must conclude that there is basic injustice in a system which in effect was two trials – one at the FGCM where cross-examination could take place, and a second trial with closed written comments and opinions not open to scrutiny or cross-examination.

On the 23 August, the commanding officer of 93 Brigade, Brigadier General John Ingles received the papers. He gave his opinion that,

> *The state of discipline of the 18th Battalion West Yorkshire Regiment is good. I recommend that the extreme penalty is inflicted in that the crime was committed deliberately.*[72]

Ingle's praise of the state of the 18th West Yorks undermines one of Haig's stated criteria for the death penalty, that an example is urgently required, but he sharpened up Carter's use of the word 'deliberate'.[73]

We can only speculate why Carter and Ingles took the line they did in contradicting the Court's recommendation to mercy. It may be that their blood was still hot from the 1 July, and having seen so many good men go down saw no reason to help two men who had failed. Ingles was a tough 'hands on' brigadier who had been at the heart of things 1 July, and George Morgan remembered being virtually man-handled back into the line by the brigadier who was carrying ammunition boxes after the attack had failed[74]. But Major Kennedy had also been at Serre and still seen fit to recommend mercy. Had they been stung by Haig's known criticism of VIII Corps and were determined to show no sign of weakness to the High Command? Carter was a one time A.D.C. to Hunter-Weston, and there may have been 'private' conversations between them. Or could it be the most simple explanation, that in their eyes the men got no more than they deserved?

The papers passed up the line of command for comments and recommendations before arriving on the desk of the Commander-in-Chief.

On 26 August at 31st Division, General Wanless O'Gowan: 'I recommend that the extreme penalty be carried out as the crime was a deliberate one.'[75]

On 27 August, Lieutenant General Anderson of XI Corps: 'I concur.'[76]

On 28 August, General Haking, temporary commander of First Army. 'I recommend that the sentences should he carried out. The act was deliberate and the man was fully aware that he was avoiding danger by deserting at such a time.'[77]

Haking spoke with emphatic certainty even though he was not involved in the Somme. His nickname, 'The Butcher', came from the Australian General Elliott after the pointless waste of 7,000 British and Australian casualties at Fromelles in July, 1916.

With such a chorus, it is no surprise that the Commander in Chief confirmed the sentences on 1 September.[78]

But the question remains, was Justice done? Did the case merit a double execution based on Haig's two criteria of an example is urgently required, and the offence is of a very deliberate character? Readers must judge for themselves, although the author's view is that it is questionable at the very least.

On 1 September the duty signaller at 18th West Yorks, Private Bill Slater (18/273), received a signal confirming the sentence of death by firing squad. The battalion was seven miles away in the line at Le Plantin in the Festubert Sector, although they were due to be bussed back to Lestrem late at night on 3 September. R.S.M. Scott made the arrangements for dawn on the 5th September.[80]

When one leafs through the yellowing files in the calm and tranquility of the Public Record Office it is difficult to grasp the full horror of what took place at Lestrem at 5.51 a.m. on the morning 5 September, 1916. Life may have been cheap in the trenches, but there is no doubt that all who took part in that dreadful final ritual felt degraded. One member of the firing party totally lost his nerve after the event as Herbert Bradley later recalled on tape.

> *In't often we talk about it. See that lad there...[pointing at photograph] they called him Ramsden. He come from Cleckheaton, and that lad was in't firing squad. We never talk about it, don't put it down, owt like that..:'No,no,no. He were one, and he lost his nerve, aye, and he had to go down't line for a long time.*

18/951 PRIVATE HERBERT BRADLEY[81]

In fact, not only had Private Ramsden to go down the line, but according to John McGrath (18/232) he committed suicide after the war. He could not live with what he had been ordered to do, nor, according to John, could the officer in charge who turned to drink.[82] The Pals' chaplain, Captain John Thornton, who tried to give consolation to the men, never talked about the matter with his own family.[83] Young Richard Dalley was told by his mother never to ask his father, Captain Harry Dalley, M.C., the battalion adjutant, questions about the War.[84]

Afterwards, two simple wooden crosses were made by the battalion carpenters. Herbert Bradley remembered that 'Killed' was removed on an officer's instructions, and that the word 'Died' was substituted.[85]

Flowers were placed on the graves, but according to John McGrath they were kicked away by General Wanless O'Gowan with the comment, 'These men are best forgotten'. The phrase must have got back to Bradford, for Arthur Wild's family paid three pence a letter for an inscription on his grave which turns O'Gowan's phrase round and amounts to a statement of defiance: 'Not forgotten by those who loved him best'.[86]

The total cost, eight shillings and six pence, was no mean sum to pay out in the 1920's for an inscription the family were never likely to see.[87] The Wild family also entered his name into the Bradford Roll of Honour, alongside that of the brother he failed to find in Vignacourt and who served in the Machine Gun Corps.[88]

I certify that No *18/356* Private *A. Wild* ,of *18th W_d*

Yorkshire Regiment was executed by shooting at 5.51 a.m. on

September *5* 1916 at *LESTREM* .Death was

instantaneous.

J H Elyake
Capt R A M C
Medical Officer.

There is no such entry for Herbert Crimmins, nor is there any inscription on his grave.

Although the men were buried near the place of execution, after the war their bodies were moved to a new concentration cemetery. The two men lie near each other, but not side by side, in Vieille Chapelle New Military Cemetery. Near them is buried Private Haddock of the Sheffield City Battalion, also of 31st Division, who was executed 16 September after breaking down on the way to the line at Serre.[89] They are three more victims of 1 July, but are not included in the 57,000 casualties listed for that first dreadful day of the Somme offensive.

Did the double execution deter anybody else? Less than two months later one of the original lance corporals in the First Pals deserted.[90] This time there was no execution. It may be the corporal was fortunate in having Major Kennedy to submit a report on his character. Walter Hare of the First Bradford Pals recalled another example in the Autumn of 1916:

> We had an Irish lad with us. He went absent without leave for two days at Hebuterne. When he turned up again he got out of being Court Martialled by volunteering to go out on patrol to capture a German prisoner for information. He never came back. Whether he was killed or gave himself up, I just don't know. It's not right to call people cowards, it's just that we all have different limits on how much we can take, and unless you've experienced trench warfare you don't know what it's like. Those Generals should have spent less time in their fancy château's, and I know because I've seen them, and more time in the line. They might have been a bit more understanding then.

37468 PRIVATE WALTER HARE [91]

Walter's comments pose the question, when men are exhausted and at the end of their tether do they really give pause for rational 'deliberate' thought? To argue values and attitudes have changed and we shouldn't view 1916 through modern eyes is to disregard contemporary unease from First War veterans the author has met about the nature and processes of military justice.

The surviving Pals never forgot the executed men, but there was almost a conspiracy of silence about the event. They did not speak the men's names in Bradford, possibly for fear of hurt to relatives. With the release of the Courts Martial papers in 1992, the names are now in the public domain and have been published elsewhere.[92] Neither man had a wife or children. They were not heroes, but they were certainly not villains. If there was shame it was in the manner of their deaths. Snuffed out by order and shot by their comrades like beasts to the slaughter.[93] In a little over two years the war ended, but resentment lived on for over seventy-four years in the heart of one of those involved. When John McGrath discussed the matter with the author in 1990, his knuckles still went white with anger and he gripped his chair as he remembered what happened. [94]

> But who can judge him, you or I ?
> God makes a man of flesh and blood
> Who yearns to live and not to die
> Was scared as any frightened child,
> His knees were shaking under him
> his breath came fast, his eyes were wild.
> I've seen a hare with eyes as wild
> With throbbing heart and sobbing breath.
> But oh! it shames one's soul to see
> A man in abject fear of death.
> They shot him when the dawn was grey.
>
> Winifred Letts[95]

NOTES

1. WO 71/495 and 496, Public Record Office. Collection of papers relating to Capital Courts Martial of 18/313 Private Herbert Crimmins and 18/356 Private Arthur Wild. 5.9.1916. Death certificate signed by Captain H.E.P.Yorke, R.A.M.C. Captain Yorke was Medical Officer of the 13th East Yorks (T'others) in 92 Brigade, 31st Division. Papers released, January, 1992.

2. John McGrath, taped interview with author, 23rd March, 1989. An interview by John McGrath is also available on tape in the Bradford City Library Living History Archive.

3. ibid.

4. George Morgan, taped interview kindly loaned to the author by Malcolm Brown. Quoted in *Tommy Goes to War* by Malcolm Brown (p.236), Dent, 1978.

5. PRO WO32/5484 and WO 329/2655 and notes kindly supplied to the author by Julian Sykes and Julian Putkowski.

6. Haig Diaries, op. cit, Hunter-Weston and the majority of his officers are amateurs, 29 June, 1916. On 1 July, Haig expressed his disappointment in very direct terms to Hunter Weston by telephone.

7. Ibid. 1st July, 1916.

8. PRO WO 329/2655, analysis of 1914-15 Star Medal Rolls, West Yorkshire Regiment. Medals were withheld from survivors or next of kin if the soldier was found guilty of a serious court martial offence such as desertion. The reason for withholding medals was written in red ink in the medal rolls at Regimental Headquarters in York. Crimmins' and Wild's next of kin did not receive medals.

9. WO 97/4608 P.R.O. Service record of 8399 Private Alfred Crimmins, Yorks & Lancs Regt., (brother of Herbert Crimmins) provides family details. Herbert was the next of kin and the oldest of six boys living at Nag's Head Yard, Pontefract. Young Alfred enlisted in 1906 aged 15 years 9 months. Astonishingly he is recorded as only 4ft 61/2 inches in height and weight of 6stone 3 lbs. Both the Crimmins parents were shown as deceased. Information researched and kindly supplied to the author by Julian Sykes.

10. Wild appears in a list of seventy police officers of the Bradford City Police Force who had enlisted, *Bradford Weekly Telegraph*, 3 September, 1915. Twenty policemen in the list joined the 18th Battalion, but none are shown for the 16th Battalion.

11. Battalion War Diary, WO 95/2362 P.R.O., and in Prince of Wales Own Yorkshire Regiment archive, York

12. Ibid.

13. Ibid. Also list of police officers cited above. Obituary of Walden and letter by Captain Keevil in

Bradford Daily Telegraph, 7 June, 1916.
14. Battalion War Diary, op. cit
15. WO 71/496
16.Ibid.
17.Ibid.
18.Ibid.
19.Ibid.
20. Battalion War Diary, op. cit.
21. Ibid.
22. Ibid. Rain occured every day from 23 June to 29 June, with 6 mm on Monday 26 June and 8 mm on Tuesday 27 June (Rawlinson's War Diaries, quoted in Gliddon, *When the Barrage Lifts*, p 415, (Leo Cooper, 1990.)
23. WO 71/495 and 496
24. Ibid.
25. Ibid.
26. Private R.T.Tait 18th Durham Light Infantry (Durham Pals), quoted by kind permission of Martin Middlebrook in *The First Day on the Somme*, p. 103.Allen Lane, 1971.
27. George Morgan, tape supplied by Malcolm Brown, op.cit.
28. WO 71/495 and 496
29. Ibid.
30. Ibid.
31. PRO WO 95/2353, 93rd Brigade War Diary.
32. WO 71/495
33. Section 19(a) of the Army Act
34. WO 71/496
35. Ibid.
36. Ibid.
37. WO 71/495 and 496
38. Information supplied by Mr. David Bradley, son of Herbert Bradley, conversation with author, 28/4/91
39. George Morgan, op. cit.
40. Battalion War Diary, op.cit
41. Herbert Bradley, taped interview, Bradford City Museum Service Living History Archive, June, 1981.
42. Herbert Bradley, *Bradford Telegraph & Argus*, 27 June, 1981.
43. *Shot at Dawn*, Julian Putkowski and Julian Sykes, Wharncliffe (1989), p.122. Julian Sykes' great Uncle was Private Herbert Bedford Tidswell (40233) of the 18th West Yorks. Private Tidswell, from Sowerby Bridge, died of wounds on 13 November, 1916 and is buried at Couin. Corporal Thomas Wise (18/1128) who gave evidence at the Court Martial of Crimmins and Wild was killed in the same incident and is buried at Sailly-au-Bois.
44. Mr. Herbert Bradley, taped conversation in Bradford City Library sound archive, June, 1981. Herbert Bradley is quite explicit in this tape, and his version confirms Alf Scott's comments to Jeff Mawby that the men were given the opportunity to go on patrol. Herbert Bradley: *He (R.S.M. Scott) gave these two fellas...the chance to go over the top and give themselves up, be killed or taken prisoner, you see, but they wouldn't go, so they were shot.*
45. Battalion War Diary, op. cit.
46. Mr. Jeff Mawby, Harold Scott's son-in-law, and his daughter Mrs. Margaret Mawby, supplied this information to the author, conversation, 23/3/91. According to Jeff Mawby, Alf Scott said, Harold (R.S.M. Scott) told them to get captured, thus the R.S.M. was very much putting his own position on the line.
47. WO 71/495 and 496 op.cit.
48. Jeff Mawby, ibid.
49. Battalion War Diary, op.cit.
50. See section on death of Ernest Walden. Biography of officers of the 18th West Yorks in the February and March 1915 editions of *Bradford Daily Telegraph*. See also casualty lists in July, 1916 editions of *Bradford Daily Telegraph*.
51. WO 71/495 and 496
52. Information supplied by Mr. Richard Dalley.
53. WO 71/495 and 496
54. Ibid.
55. Ibid
56. Ibid.
57. Ibid.
58. Ibid.
59. Ibid.
60. Ibid.
61. Ibid.

62. Ibid.
63. Ibid.
64. Ibid.
65. Ibid.
66. Ibid.
67. Ibid.
68. See, *Statistics of the Military Effort of the British Empire During the Great War, 1922 (Part XXIII, Discipline).*
69. WO71/495
70. WO71/496
71. Battalion War Diary, op.cit.
72. WO71/495 and 496
73. WO 32/5484 and 329/2655 op. cit
74. George Morgan, op.cit.
75. WO 71/496 and 496
76. Ibid
77. Ibid.
78. Ibid.
79. WO 32/5484 and 329/2655 op. cit.
80. Letter to the author from Mr. Bernard Slater, son of Private Slater, (8/4/91).
81. Herbert Bradley, ibid, Bradford City Library sound archive.
82. John McGrath, op. cit.
83. Mr. John Thornton, son of Rev. J.G. Thornton, conversation with the author 28 March, 1991.
84. Richard Dalley, son of Captain F.L. Dalley, M.C., conversation with author, 1 February, 1992.
85. David Bradley, ibid.
86. The wooden crosses were eventually replaced by Portland Stone headstones by the War Graves Commission in the 1920's. Families had to pay three old pence per letter for personal inscriptions on the base.
87. The blow to widows of executed men was devastating financially as well as emotionally. The soldier's separation allowance ended with his death and no pension was payable. The widow had to throw herself on the generosity of the local Board of Guardians.

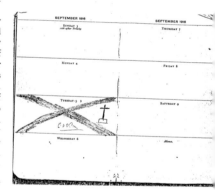

Sergeant Reader's diary with execution marked.

There was such a case in Keighley after the execution of Private Harry MacDonald of the 12th West Yorks on 4 November, 1916. Private MacDonald was the father of three children and his wife was pregnant. The Keighley Guardians awarded the maximum weekly allowance of 13/6d (equivalent of half the separation allowance) to Mrs. MacDonald and then championed her case for a pension. Philip Snowden, the Labour M.P. for Blackburn who was himself a Keighley man, took up the case in Parliament after the war, and Mrs. MacDonald eventually received a full pension. MacDonald deserted because of desperately sad personal problems in the marriage that he was too proud to disclose at his Court Martial. He had been invalided out with frost bite in Gallipoli, refused compassionate leave to see his ill wife, and then been badly shell shocked on the Western Front. Haig again personally confirmed sentence despite a strong recommendation to mercy by the court. The Commander in Chief arranged to be in London for the birth of his own child in March, 1918 less than a week before the expected German offensive. As recently as 1986, attempts to obtain a pardon for Harry MacDonald were turned down by the Ministry of Defence. (Correspondence held by Dr. A.J. Peacock, kindly loaned to the author).
88. 'Bradford's Roll of Honour', MSS. held in the Reference Section of Bradford City Library.
89. Vieille Chapelle New Military Cemetery, Graves 5/F/6. 5/F/9 and 6/F/5. See also *Sheffield City Battalion*, Ralph Gibson and Paul Oldfield, pub. Pen & Sword in this series, p. 175.
90. PRO, WO329 899/900, British Medal Roll and Victory Medal Roll.
91. Walter Hare, taped conversation with the author, 3 September, 1993.
92. Putkowski and Sykes, op. cit.
93. Mrs Margaret Mawby, daughter of R.S.M. Harold Scott, wished the author to emphasise the fact that the execution was 'under orders', and to point out how much distress compliance with these orders gave to her father.
94. John McGrath was still extremely angry and distressed about the incident when the author talked to him, taped interview, 23 March, 1989.
95. From 'The Deserter' by Winifred Letts in *The Poetry of War*, B.B.C./Longman (1990) p.127

Sergeant Reader, RMP, arrested Crimmins and Wild. He witnessed their execution.

Chapter Thirteeen

BACK TO THE SOMME

THE BRADFORD BATTALIONS stayed in the Neuve Chapelle sector until the 2 October. Throughout the late summer days of August and September, they alternated between manning the trenches in Festubert and Givenchy and with providing working parties to shore up precarious sand bagged defences or improve the road surfaces and drainage systems. They took a small but steady toll of casualties from enemy artillery and sniper fire, but also from illness and sickness. No significant reinforcements had been received and on 22 September the 18th West Yorks War Diary revealed a fighting strength of twenty-six officers but only 440 other ranks including specialist troops and the transport section.[1]

Both Battalion War Diaries reveal a steady stream of officers and men being evacuated for hospital treatment. The damp marshy atmosphere of the area and the death and detritus of the trenches was a breeding ground for mosquitoes and disease. The men suffered from general debility and exhaustion as well as fungal infections on the feet and in the crotch. Disease was spread by flies and the ever present lice and rats. Tuberculosis was to affect several men in the future, one of whom was Captain Charles Roche M.C., medical officer to the 16th West Yorks.

Charles Roche M.C. medical officer to the First Pals.

Conditions in the trenches at Neueve Chapelle were extremely uncomfortable whatever the weather conditions. Rain made it virtually impossible. Twenty year old Bernard Long, intelligence officer to the 16th West Yorks wrote home to his sister from his dugout in Festubert 1 September.

We are having it pretty awful here now. Simply flooded out – dug outs leaking and water running in through the doorway. I haven't had dry feet for a week. You had better send me a pair of socks or so. I shall not want my greatcoat. I bought a lining to my raincoat before I left Blighty. Cost me £2.10s 0d and will keep me warm through the winter. I am writing this letter to you in a dugout in the front line with my feet in a foot of water so you see we get used to anything. I'm waiting for the Colonel [Kennedy] to come back from his walk round so that we can come back together. He's awfully nice with me, sees that I change my clothes when I get wet and lends me breeches and underthings for a change.

SECOND LIEUTENANT BERNARD LONG, 16WY[2]

Bernard Long's C.O., Humfrey Kennedy, had been promoted to the rank of lieutenant colonel on 24 August. Captain George Blagborough, one of the original officers from 1914 and a master at Bridlington Grammar School, was promoted to major and appointed as Kennedy's second in command.

There was the relief of occasional stretches out of the line to clean up at Lestrem in the north, or at Gorre on the outskirts of Bethune in the south. Here there was always the prospect of getting a decent feed of egg and chips produced by an enterprising local, and the effect of this and a glass or two of wine had a positive restorative effect. Norris Garside had a favourite place in Lestrem.

In the old place once more and went to Madame's for our meals as usual.
Everyone supremely happy. 18/1145 CORPORAL NORRIS GARSIDE [3]

On 13 September, Bernard Long thanked his sister for a cake, told her what a difference it could make and how parcels were shared out in the mess. He also described the perennial but usually frustrated interest of the Tommies in the local young women.

Well thank you very much for the cake it was beautiful. I gave it to our mess of course (that's what everybody does) and the Colonel [Kennedy] was awful fond of it and in fact ate nearly half of it. We always had to leave some for him and the best of it is he didn't know it was my cake and had to ask the waiter where the dickens we'd got it from. They all like it in fact and I was half sorry I couldn't eat it all myself. The toffee is simply scrumptious and will last me a month. When we were back in billets we used to have some fun with the natives. The little kids used to come up and use the French phrases the Tommy uses. "No bon" (no good) "Na poo" (nothing doing or finished) "Compris?" (Do you understand?). The talk goes something like this between a soldier and a girl.

Soldier: Bonjour, Mamselle.
Girl: Bon jour M'sieur.
Soldier: Voos allie bon?
Girl: Tres bien M'sieur, et vous?
Soldier: No compris Mamselle but walk eh compris ce soir compris Mamselle?
Girl: Me no promenade M'sieur. Apres la guerre.
Soldier: You no bon.
Girl: Bonjour Monsieur.

And so the game goes on. The Tommies try hard but the girls won't have anything to do with any Anglais and they always say they will "Apres la Guerre". SECOND LIEUTENANT BERNARD LONG, 16WY[4]

Unfortunately, Bernard Long was sniped in the arm at Givenchy 20 September as he inspected a new German crater caused by mining. He was convalescent in England for nine months, but sadly he was killed in Flanders when serving with the 2nd West Yorks in August, 1917.

It was not all fun and cakes, and not everyone failed to achieve knowledge of the local female population. Officers' files reveal two sad cases of two original officers receiving extremely painful medical treatment for syphilis. One officer was discharged and his record states no pension was to be given and that he was likely to suffer permanent disfigurement. The man concerned was wounded on the Somme and was generally regarded as a good officer. From correspondence seen by the author, he was also a man of compassion towards his men. The tragedy was compounded because he was married with children.[5]

Another tragic case was revealed to the First War historian Dr. A.J. Peacock in the 1970's by a surviving member from one of the Bradford Battalions. The man concerned had arranged to do an interview on a tape which is now in a Cambridge archive. When Dr. Peacock arrived he was surprised to see several members of the old man's family sitting in a circle round the veteran. The man then confessed to Dr. Peacock and to his family that he wanted to unburden himself before he died. He claimed to have shot and killed one of his own officers. The man was under age when he enlisted and by his own admission was a poor soldier. He claimed to have been persistently bullied by an officer over a long period. A further incident occurred when they were alone together in a thinly manned section of trench. The young soldier finally snapped and claimed the officer was killed by a shell fragment.[6]

Alfred Bairstow.

The Second Pals came out of the line on 29 September after having what Joe Parker described as a rotten time with five killed and six wounded during their last tour in the Givenchy sector. After two nights in Gorre and two nights in an orphanage at Bethune they marched the eight miles to their old billets at L'Ecleme. Over the course of that few days they were joined by 252 re-inforcements.

The First Pals came out of the line at Givenchy 3 October and also made their way via Bethune to the original billets at La Miquellerie close to the Second Pals, and they too received re-inforcements of 150 men. A young twenty year old second lieutenant from Undercliffe in Bradford, John Lofthouse Stanley, also arrived. He was to play a significant role with the First Pals. After enlisting in the Territorial 6th West Yorks when he was eighteen, he was appointed orderly room sergeant in the 3rd West Yorks shortly after his nineteenth birthday. He was to become adjutant of the 16th West Yorks and be awarded the D.S.O. for gallantry at Gavrelle in May 1917.

Clearly something was afoot and 8 October both battalions marched to Lillers station. They travelled south to the railhead at Doullens and the Somme area again. There was then a ten mile march east to the picturesque little villages of Famechon and Thievre nestling in the wooded Authie valley. They were back in familiar territory and stayed in billets for eight days rest.[7]

As usual, Second Lieutenant Wilson and Quarter Master Sergeant Harry Drake (16/152) of the First Pals had gone on ahead to make the billeting arrangements in the Famechon. Harry Drake was the battalion translator. He had been a teacher before the war and was a fluent French speaker. He later wrote about how billeting was arranged, and of a strange experience when he fell ill and was cared for by an old Frenchwoman in Famechon in October, 1916.

The stay in Famechon lasted nine days. The time was spent training the

new men into the ways of the Battalion. Throughout October, a total of
five officers and 385 other ranks joined the 16th West Yorks as reinforcements. As already stated, in the same period the 18th West Yorks
received 252 additional other ranks. The Bradford Pals had taken a
battering on the 1st July but had maintained their identity on a much
reduced level for three months at Neuve Chapelle. Now the face of the
two Battalions was changing.[8]

One of the new men who joined the First Pals at Famechon was
nineteen year old Walter Hare from Cawood near Selby. It was the
author's good fortune to become a friend of Walter's and to visit the
battlefields with him on many occasions right up until his ninety-fifth
birthday. Walter recalled,

*The original Pals were very subdued and quiet at first, but they made me
welcome.They made me feel a real Bradford Pal, and I still feel that now. I
was proud to be in the 16th West Yorkshires then, and I still am today.*

37468 PRIVATE WALTER HARE, 16WY[9]

Walter, a Methodist teetotaller was put in charge of the rum ration. Both

Weary Pals at Sailly au Bois, November 1916.

battalions spent several days on an alternating basis in the Hebuterne section of the line just over a mile north of their original position at Serre. The trenches were those used by 48th Division 1 July when they had taken part in the Gommecourt diversion. Many of the bodies still lay in No Man's land.

A series of patrols were sent out in October to try to capture a German soldier for information. None succeeded because the wire was not cut, and on one occasion a patrol suffered several casualties. Walter Hare recalled how one of the new men avoided the same fate as Crimmins and Wild:

> We had an Irish lad with us. He went absent without leave for two days at Hebuterne. When he turned up again he got out of being court martialled by volunteering to go out on patrol to capture a German prisoner for information. He never came back. Whether he was killed or gave himself up, I just don't know.   37468 PRIVATE WALTER HARE, 16WY[10]

On 27 October, at Biersdorf camp near Cologne, Private Gordon Chapman (18/1416) was keeping a secret diary. He recorded it was three months to the day since he had been captured. 'Went to have a tooth out and had a terrible time. It took two of them to hold me down.'[11]

The Battle of the Somme was still continuing to the south of the Pals positions. On 13 November the Bradford battalions manned the front line at Hebuterne when an attack by the Hull battalions of 92 Brigade was taking place in yet another attempt to capture Serre. They were ready to move forwards should the attack succeed. The attack again stalled although there were signs of Germans beginning to crack. Joe Parker recorded in his diary.

> 13 November. Terrific bombardment commenced at 5.45 a.m. when attack opened. East Yorks went over later and got to German second line. German prisoners began drifting in – in tens and altogether 100 came in.
>   CQMS JOE PARKER [12]

Yet again Serre had proved a hard nut to crack, although the 51st Highland Division stormed through to take Beaumont Hamel further south. The Somme campaign closed down with the onset of winter. Gains to the depth of seven miles had been made but at a cost of nearly 420,000 British casualties. As a final sting in the tail, the 18th West Yorks suffered thirteen killed and twenty-one wounded on 13 November, whilst the 16th West Yorks suffered ten casualties. Their old artillery adversaries at Pusieux beyond Rossignol Wood still carried menace.[13]

Private Herbert Tidswell (40233) of Sowerby Bridge was one of the Second Pals who died of wounds on 13 November, 1916 and is buried at Couin. Corporal Thomas Wise (18/1128) who gave evidence at the court martial of Privates Crimmins and Wild was killed in the same incident. By strange coincidence, Private Tidswell's great nephew is Julian Sykes, co-author with Julian Putkoweski of *Shot at Dawn*.

Although the action slowed down with the onset of winter, the weather was as much of an enemy as the Germans. At the end of November, the 18th West Yorks War Diary recorded that sixty other ranks had been sent to hospital because of sickness.[14] There was a lighter touch on 9 December. At 12.30 p.m. as the rain poured down one German clearly had had more than enough in every sense of the phrase. The Battalion War Diary records that an enemy deserter was seen approaching along the Gommecourt-Hebuterne road and found to be under the influence of drink.[15] Joe Parker got a close look at him and took him into custody with Lieutenant Bowden.

Went into the trenches once more and in getting in got wet through. Pouring down. Went with Mr. Bowden to bring in a German deserter who was coming across No Man's Land. Got him to HQ after a bit of a struggle..

CQMS JOE PARKER[16]

When Christmas came, Norris managed to get a leave pass. After spending Christmas Eve in the Calais YMCA he got back home at 11.30 p.m. on Christmas Day 'to a great welcome'. On Boxing Day he went to see the Rugby League local derby in which Batley beat Dewsbury by 8 points to nil.[17] Joe was commissioned as a lieutenant in the First Pals shortly afterwards.

At Biersdorf near Cologne on Christmas Day, Private Gordon Chapman (18/1416) was a prisoner of war with some of the other Pals

'Pals in France' stretcher bearers at Sailly au Bois, November 1916.

Stretcher bearer in the Pals.

who had been captured at Neuve Chapelle. They worked in a mine and the manager, Pfeiffer, gave them a Christmas tree, some cigarettes and some schnapps. They had a whip round to buy a present for an old lady who occasionally gave them eggs and then they shared a Christmas pudding sent in a parcel from Bradford.[18]

In Bradford, many homes felt emptiness, pain and anxiety as Christmas 1916 arrived. The seven children of Arthur and Eliza Normington had lost both parents, at Serre and in the Canal. Percy Bateman's wife, and many others like her, did her best for a two year old daughter without a daddy. Councillor E.J. Smith, Chairman of the Health Committee, still believed his son Donald had simply lost his memory and would eventually turn up in a prisoner of war camp. In a further letter on City Council notepaper demanding more action from the War Office he wrote.

> There has been no proof of his death, and the absence of news from him may arise from loss of memory or other disability over which he has no control. I should be extremely obliged if you would kindly let me know what steps are taken when prisoners are returned in such a condition as to be unable to indicate their own identity, because I cannot help thinking that this is a case in point.[19]

NOTES

1. Battalion War Diary, 22 September, 1916.
2. Letter from Second Lieutenant Bernard Long (16WY) to his sister Ethel kindly supplied by his relative Valerie Hawgood. Although Lieutenant Long was only twenty, he had already graduated with First Class Honours in Science at Birmingham University. Valerie has published Bernard Long's letters and they can be obtained via Birmingham University.
3. Garside. Op.cit.
4. Long. Op.cit.
5. Officers Records WO339.
6. Information supplied by my good friend, and editor of *Gunfire* magazine, the late Dr Alf Peacock of York. The soldier concerned was only sixteen when he enlisted.
7. C.Q.M.S. Harry Drake in *Everyman at War* (1930) edited by C.B. Purdom. Harry Drake enlisted 9 September, 1914. Served with the First Pals as a corporal, sergeant, C.Q.M.S., and A/R.Q.M.S. throughout the battalion's existence. In February, 1918 he was posted as A/R.Q.M.S. to the 3rd Entrenching Battalion, but joined the Leeds Pals (15th West Yorks) in March, 1918 and survived the war. He was a teacher and fluent French speaker and acted as the Battalion translator.
8. Battalion War Diary
9. Walter Hare. Taped conversation with the author, 10 July, 1991.
10. Hare, ibid
11. Chapman diary. Opus cit.
12. Parker diary. Op.cit.
13. Battalion War Diary.
14. Ibid.
15. Battalion War Diary.
16. Parker. Op.cit.
17. Ibid.
18. Chapman. Op.cit.
19. Letter to the War Office, E.J. Smith. WO339 Officers files.

Chapter Fourteen

ROSSIGNOL WOOD

27th February, 1917

It should be made known to all ranks that if men are seen going over to the enemy they should be fired on at once, and that men who surrender without sufficient reason or desert to the enemy, will be tried after the war and shot.

TO ALL UNITS FROM FIFTH ARMY GENERAL STAFF.
Issued after 16th West Yorks attack on Rossignol Wood[1]

LIKE A DOMINANT QUEEN behind her Pawns, the brooding bulk of Rossignol Wood stood to the east of the German front line near Hebuterne at the northern end of the Somme. From the *Berg Graben* and *Zitzewitch Graben* (trenches) one could look south towards the killing fields of Serre two miles away. In more peaceful days it was the haunt of nightingales. To the Germans it was Copse 125, a place for hidden batteries to take a terrible toll of the Pals Battalions on 1 July 1916.

Today, traces of trench lines can still be seen criss-crossing the nettles and wood anemones. Shattered concrete pill boxes still defy the annual suffocation of nature and stand like discarded dragons' molars. There are empty gas shells, rusting trench tools, and the remains of a British infantryman's boot. If you find any of it, leave it where it belongs, for this is a special place. Here, in April, 1918, a fifty-four year old diffident short sighted priest added the Victoria Cross to his D.S.O. and M.C. Padre Theodore Bayley Hardy lay all day with a wounded man trapped on the wire below a German machine gun post, then crawled back for help at nightfall and led a rescue party to bring the man in. Here, the 'King of No Man's Land', New Zealand Sergeant Dick Travis, added the Victoria Cross to his D.C.M. and M.M. single handedly blowing away the massive *Berg Graben* wire and capturing two machine gun posts in July, 1918. Travis survived, but was killed the next day. And it was here, in the mud and darkness of early morning on 27 February, 1917, the 16th West Yorkshires were sent into a death trap. They suffered 226 casualties when they attempted to capture the wood as the enemy withdrew to the Hindenberg line. Seventy-eight men were killed or died of wounds (just over half the number lost at Serre), but it was a much reduced battalion and a two company attack. Forty-three casualties were original Pals, including 16/637 Sergeant Charles Farrar who had won the D.C.M. at Serre. Farrar lingered on to a painful death on 2 March.

For nineteen year old Walter Hare who had joined the Battalion at Hebuterne in September, 1916 it was, 'My first time "Over the Top". It was an absolute shambles of an attack and a useless waste of lives for nothing.'[2]

Readers must judge for themselves the competence of the Divisional Commander, General Robert Wanless O'Gowan who planned the attack. They may also consider what value the general who kicked flowers off the executed mens' graves placed on human life. For when it was learnt that sixty-five of the missing men were prisoners, a Divisional Court of Inquiry was convened. Major Humfrey H. Kennedy, second in command of the 16th West Yorks had held things together as acting C.O. after Serre, but he was reprimanded by General Wanless

O'Gowan, and told he showed lack of judgement for not shooting his own men in the back when he saw them surrender.[3]

The Pals were fortunate to have the humane Kennedy as an officer. There was mutual affection and respect between the tall genteel Scot and the Yorkshiremen he had known since Fovant. When challenged in his absence why he had not fired on his own men, Kennedy deflected the question by writing to the Court of Enquiry that the light was not good enough to distinguish what was going on.[4]

In the name of 'discipline, and for the sake of example', the same system which snuffed out the lives of Privates Crimmins and Wild at Lestrem expected Major Kennedy to dispose of sixty-five more. Included in those taken prisoner were (16/251) Company Sergeant Major Clarence Wilkinson a holder of the Military Medal, and (16/1185) Sergeant Harry Cockroft, awarded the D.C.M. 'for conspicuous gallantry' at Serre on 1 July.

When General Wanless O'Gowan presented Harry Cockroft with his D.C.M. on 7 November 1916, and told him he had seven days leave, he said, 'I can see in your eyes the urge to get back into action and get at 'em'.[5] In fact, Harry and the General lived in different worlds. Harry was grieving for the loss of his two brothers and recalled his one thought at the time was to get home to his wife and three year old son in one piece as soon as possible on the only leave he ever had. As we will see, the General would have been perfectly content to have seen Harry shot in the back by one of his own officers three months later.

The gulf of perception between the Major-General and the sergeant is not surprising. The 16th West Yorks War Diary records one visit to the trenches by General Wanless O'Gowan (12 June, 1917) after the Somme offensive – the 18th West Yorks Diary records none. Walter Hare, who was often at battalion Headquarters as a runner, only saw the General once – when the battalion was paraded at St. Eloi in March,1917 and Wanless O'Gowan complimented the 16th on their smartness. Many of the Second Pals remembered him from another Battalion parade when the execution of Crimmins and Wild was announced at Lestrem.

The winter of 1916/17 was the most severe since 1880. *The Times* reported the Household Cavalry infantry battalion had suffered heavy losses from frost bite.[6] On 9 February Sir Douglas Haig recorded 25 degrees of frost in his diary and noted that the sands at Boulogne were all frozen as the tide went out.[7] The only consolation for the two Bradford Battalions taking their turn in the line at Hebuterne was that the frozen mud was solid and at least gave a firm footing.

On the 7 January Walter Hare found that ice, like mud, produced its own sort of complications.

> *I remember being put on a charge at Rossignol Farm for not being shaved. We had come out of the trenches at Hebuterne the previous night, and the stream where we usually drew our water was frozen hard. When I told the officer that I could not break the ice he said, "What do you think your bayonet is for? Three days C.B." In fact, I didn't mind being confined to Rossignol Farm. It was a favourite billet with lots of straw and plenty of cover, and anyway there was nowhere else to go. I've been back to Rossignol Farm since: it looks just the same and the stream is still flowing.*

37468 PRIVATE WALTER HARE, 16WY[8]

Private Horace Wadsworth, who joined the 16th at the same time as Walter Hare in October 1916, found that shaving was the least of his problems and he was in no condition to stay at Rossignol Farm. The misery of the Arctic conditions compounded a severe attack of dysentry. His suffering was so intense that he was sent to the huge base hospital at Etaples. Horace was to be in and out of hospital until the end of the War. In May, 1918 he discovered there was no escape even there when enemy aeroplanes bombed and destroyed the hospital ward. Horace Wadsworth was not alone in his suffering. There were many other cases of dysentry, trench foot, pneumonia and general debility as stress and the appalling physical conditions took their toll.[9] The Canadian doctor attached to the Second Pals, Captain 'Mac' McTavish, was suffering himself. He wrote to a friend:

> *I have a cold that would choke a polar bear. Last November I caught a cold, or–*
> *at least a cold caught me, through no fault of mine. At the time I tried to get rid of*
> *it but no matter how deep mud I waded through or how much water there was in*
> *the trenches or how cold it was or anything else – that cold stuck with me. At last*
> *I resolved to let it live in peace. Well it did, but it wouldn't let me live in peace, in*
> *fact it tried to make me die in pieces. My cold stuck closer than a brother. I got a*
> *slight touch of 'flu that didn't frighten my cold a bit in fact it enjoyed the company.*
> *I coughed most of the day and to show there was no ill feeling most of the night too.*
> *The middle of Feb arrived. Time and again my Commanding Officer told me to go*
> *sick. Then he got one. I sent him to hospital and told him to go to the South of*
> *France. Well he got there, but before he left he made me promise that I would go to*
> *Hospital too.*   CAPTAIN DR. G.B. McTAVISH M.C. AND TWO BARS, R.A.M.C.[10]

In fact, Colonel Carter was extremely ill. It was several weeks before he was able to rejoin the Battalion and he missed the attack at Rossignol Wood. His replacement, Major Tilley of the 18th D.L.I., lasted a week before he too succumbed to illness and command was handed over to the 18th's adjutant, Major Albert W. Robinson, one of the original Pals from Bradford. Having spent time in hospital the previous October, Dr. 'Mac' was reluctant to go again. As we will see, he soldiered on for several more weeks until he finally collapsed in mid-March.

The two Bradford Battalions left Hebuterne and the Somme 6 January. They were to be out of the line for six weeks, a time to clean up, to recover, to take in new drafts, and to train. The two battalions moved in stages further away from the front, the first week to Sailly-au-Bois and Bayencourt, the next two weeks to Sarton and Authieule, and then after a twenty mile march the next three weeks were spent in the rear training areas around Autheux and Le Meillard to the west of Doullens.

Two of the 1 July D.C.M. winners, Tom Pearson and Ellison Murgatroyd rejoined the 16th Battalion at Sailly-au-Bois after enjoying a home leave in Bradford over Christmas. Corporal Pearson had been proudly escorted round the Town Clerk's Department by his father, and then received a rousing welcome at Messrs. Pickles and Rae, where he was presented with a gold watch and clock by his workmates. The newly commissioned Lieutenant Murgatroyd had married his fiancee Doris Smith at Burley Woodhouse. Sadly, the couple's married life was restricted to this one week of leave. Ellison Murgatroyd was killed at Moyenville in the German offensive of March, 1918.[11]

The New Year's Honours list also brought the announcement that Murgatroyd's old school friend at Bradford Grammar School, Charles Farrar (16/637), had been awarded the D.C.M. Sergeant Farrar, son of the Thornton quarry owner Alfred Farrar, had performed consistent good work throughout, and has at all times set a splendid example. Charles Farrar died of wounds a few weeks later after the attack on Rossignol Wood.[12]

The first six weeks of 1917 saw a massive induction of new drafts into both battalions, with new parties coming in nearly every day. No fewer than 418 other ranks and eight new officers joined the 16th Battalion from the 33rd Infantry Base Depot. Many of these men were conscripts. Over 224 of them are described as untrained, in the Battalion War Diary. There was also a smattering of more experienced men who had recovered from wounds. Some were original 16th men together with one or two former 18th men, but there were others from the Leeds Pals, the Leeds Bantams, the Sheffield Pals, and some regulars. The distinctly Bradford origin of the battalion was now diluted, even though most of the N.C.O.'s were still original Pals. There was still though a strong Yorkshire identity with most of the newcomers coming from the Leeds and York areas, although there were some former 4th Lincolnshire Regiment men.[13]

For the most part, the new drafts were made welcome by the surviving Pals. In a conversation with the author in 1990, Walter Hare, who joined the 1st Pals at Hebuterne in October 1916 recalled, 'I was proud to be in the 16th West Yorkshires then, and I still am today'.[14]

On 29 January, 1917, the 16th West Yorks came under the command of a new commanding officer. Forty-seven year old Lieutenant Colonel Albert Charles Croydon, M.C., D.C.M. arrived at Autheux to take over from the acting C.O. Colonel Major Humfrey Heyes Kennedy. Kennedy reverted to the rank of major and took over the post of second in command which had been vacant since the death of Major Blagborough the previous month.

The new colonel faced a formidable task – to weld a disparate mixture of the weary and the inexperienced into a fighting unit. He was a brave and experienced man well fitted to the task. He first joined the army in the Life Guards as an eighteen year old trooper in 1887, rising to company sergeant major before retiring on pension in 1909. He then became a clerk to the Haberdashers Company in London before volunteering again in 1914 and appointed regimental sergeant major to the 6th Lincolns. He was awarded the D.C.M. in Gallipoli in 1915, and commissioned in the 6th Lincolns. He was awarded the Military Cross for bravery in the same action in which Captain Percy Hansen won the V.C. at the Anafarta Ridge 9 August, 1915. The 6th Lincolns took severe casualties and were forced back when scrub and bracken were set alight by shell fire on Hill 70. Hansen and Croydon braved 30 feet high flames as well as enemy fire to rescue the wounded.[15]

Walter Hare remembers that the new colonel's insistence on drill and his fierce manner won him few friends at first. 'He used to enjoy himself making us drill when we came out of the line, when all we wanted to do was sleep.'[16]

Croydon's earthy language was disturbingly direct, but he eventually won grudging respect for his competence once the battalion had gone into action under his command. In the meantime, despite mutterings in the 16th about their new C.O.'s insistence on smartness and 'bull', both Bradford battalions welcomed the relief of being out of the line.

Lieutenant Colonel Albert Charles Croydon, M.C., D.C.M

Quartermaster Sergeants Stores beneath the civilian cemetery at Fonquevillers.

> *We are getting a rest after nine long months of front line work. The boys are enjoying themselves.*
>
> CAPTAIN DR. G.B. McTAVISH, M.C. AND TWO BARS, R.A.M.C.[17]

They enjoyed a mixture of training and recreation.·

> Only half each day devoted to work, the remainder (alternate morning and afternoon by half-battalions) to recreation, football, running, tug-of-war, bayonet-fighting, bomb throwing and boxing, in which all men took part.[18]

'Mac' described a typical day.

> *Up in the morning at 7.00 a.m. Saw the sick, lame, lazy and sinful – had breakfast at 8.30 – visited billets to see they were nice and tidy – had a class for one hour first aid – had lunch – went for a ride on my little horse, which is by the way the best little horse in Sunny France! Got back at 3.00 p.m. Went to see a football match against another battalion. We won. Came back – had tea – went to see a sick civilian, an old man – then to see an old lady who fell and broke two of her ribs – fixed her up – then visited the field ambulance – next had dinner – and after that I went to bed.* CAPTAIN DR. G.B. McTAVISH, M.C. AND TWO BARS, R.A.M.C.[19]

The sporting celebrities, Dickie Bond, Jock Ewart and Abe Waddington were no longer there to entertain the troops during the inter-battalion football matches. However, (18/230) Private John McGrath the l8th's inside right was a real survivor if ever there was one. John had been buried in a trench bombardment just before the attack at Serre, but had returned to the Pals in August after a spell in hospital at Etaples. He took a bit of a ribbing that his play was no longer up to scratch, but the truth was that he could no longer count on Dickie Bond's speed to make his passes look better than they were. But he was still glad to be back. John was to survive a further wound at Gavrelle, and then in 1986 he survived the tragic

Bradford City football stand fire. In the late 1980's he became the last survivor of the original Second Pals – and was still using an exercise hike in his bedroom.[20]

The 16th still had one sporting celebrity to boast about. 16/913 Sergeant Jack Manley, was a tough professional boxer and the North of England cruiser weight champion. He delighted the Bradfords, who made a few bob (or francs) betting on him, by making short work of the best challengers from neighbouring units. They were his last appearances in the ring – he was killed at Gavrelle a few weeks later. As well as enjoying recreation, both battalions commenced a new type of training.

In accordance with new system of platoon organization, under which platoon and company officers are entirely responsible for the training of their units, including bombers and Lewis gunners and rifle grenadiers. Work principally devoted to setting up drill, platoon drill, musketry and re-organisation of platoons, together with route marches.[21]

Platoon and company attacks were practised, and on 28 January the battalions received a visit from a general they really could respect, the commander of XIII Corps, Major-General W.N. Congreve V.C. The general was the V.C. father of a V.C. son (Major William Congreve V.C. was killed the previous July on the Somme). Like the Bradford Battalions, the general had little reason to admire Rawlinson's tactical awareness. On 1 July, XIII Corps made an early breakthrough on the right flank capturing Montauban and taking all their objectives by mid-morning. General Congreve immediately went to the front and saw the open undefended ground around Bernafay Wood, Trones Wood and Mametz Wood. He repeatedly pleaded on the telephone with Rawlinson to exploit the opportunity, but to no avail. By midnight the gap was closed. Rawlinson's caution lead to a massive cost later in July (including the loss of Congreve's own son).

As the Pals continued their training, they celebrated St. Valentine's Day with a Two company practise attack on a wood. The Durham Pals had taken part in an exploratory raid on Rossignol Wood, 19 December, so the Bradfords had a pretty good idea which wood it was they were practising for. Clearly something was in the air, and rumours began to circulate that the Germans were about to pull back. At Hebuterne strange sights and sounds were being reported from the German lines.

The Bradford battalions re-entered the line 21 February, 1917. The 18th took up positions opposite Gommecourt Park to the north, whilst the 16th on their right were opposite Rossignol Wood to the south. The positions were virtually identical to those held by 56th Division 1 July.

On the German side of the line, orders had been given to begin preparation for withdrawal to the Hindenburg line (the *Siegfried Stellung*) 4 February. Work on the *Siegfried Stellung* had begun the previous September when Hindenburg and Ludendorff took over the German High Command from Falkenhayn. Throughout the winter of 1916/17 the Germans had constructed a massive new defence line stretching over sixty miles from Soissons in the south, to Arras in the north. Engineers and surveyors selected the best possible tactical ground. Formidable switch lines with dense banks of barbed wire, 7,000 to 10,000 yards deep and containing a miriad of ingenious defensive devices, made the old Somme lines look like child's play. By straightening their line the Germans saved over thirteen divisions and shortened their supply lines.

The territory given up, over 1,000 square miles, amounted to ten times the territory captured by the Allies in 1916, but the Germans turned it into a waste land. Wells were poisoned, orchards destroyed, roads and bridges mined, buildings blown up, and booby traps laid everywhere for the unwary. The German withdrawal commenced on the night 23/24 February on 18,000 yards of Gough's 5th Army front from Warlancourt in the south through Pys, Irles, and Miraumont to Serre in the north. Serre, the village where the flower of northern youth had perished nearly eight months before, was given up without a shot being fired. On 25 February at 5.00 a.m. patrols of the Warwickshires nervously edged into Serre. They found nothing more than an empty pile of smoking bricks and shattered timbers. The Germans had simply stolen away in the night.

Paul Maze, an adventurous French interpreter attached to General Gough's staff, gave a graphic description of the entry into Serre:

> We walked on a while and approached some gaunt, shapeless trees rising above dismal ruins. We were on the outskirts of Serre. We went on carefully and came to a dug-out. I looked down through its gaping entrance and saw clods of mud freshly dropped from boots on every step. A smell of mildew rose from the bottom. All was still. Farther on we came to a shattered house, where I peeped through a broken window. Roof, bricks and furniture were as one. There was not a sound except the dripping of water from a beam punctuating the oppressive silence with a melancholy regularity. I had to pull myself together to advance a short way inside the village. I hated the look of it. Something was urging me to get out of the place, and quickly. Every yard I took forward marked a moment. Was I walking into a trap? I felt the enemy must be watching us all the time.[22]

The German withdrawal was planned with great thoroughness and skill under the code name 'Alberich' (the deceitful magical dwarf of the Nibelung Legend in the Siegfried Saga). The deceit was certainly effective: 24 February Haig was still uncertain of German intentions. Whilst he was certainly aware of the construction of the Hindenburg line, von Richthofen had given the Germans temporary dominance of the sky making it difficult for the Allies to confirm what was going on. As late as 25 February, after the German withdrawal had begun, Haig wrote in his diary,

> On the whole, such a withdrawal... [to the Hindenburg line] ...at the present

The torn up ground in front of Serre.

time seems to have greater disadvantages than advantages for the enemy... I agreed that Gough must push forward advanced guards to probe the enemy's front.[23]

The two Bradford battalions would take part in this probe. They were to find that Alberich was not only deceitful, but full of spite as well.

For the first two days after the Bradfords re-entered the line 21 February, enemy artillery, bursts of machine gun fire and sniper fire kept both battalions on their toes. They were very fortunate to suffer only one casualty between them. In the 18th Battalion War Diary, we note that companies were warned to keep a sharp look out in view of attempted enemy wire cutting. The Germans were still giving every impression of an active and continued presence.

At 5.18 p.m. 23 February, the 18th Battalion War Diary recorded smoke rising from the enemy line south of the Maze in Gommecourt Park, as if a dug-out were on fire. Artillery was informed and 18-pounders fired continually for several hours. A good deal of movement was observed at this point. A similar fire was observed at K.3.d.77 on which our 18-pounders fired.[24]

Smoke, and explosions in the enemy lines were again reported the following day, and at 11.00 p.m. Brigadier Ingles wired through that the enemy was thought to have evacuated his front line opposite V Corps, and ordered that patrols from the 18th Battalion should be pushed out to investigate.

Zero hour was set for 5.00 a.m. on 25 February, exactly the same time as the Warwickshires entered Serre. A Company and C Company formed patrols of two platoons strength under the command of Lieutenants J.R. Thornton and William Sleigh, with two platoons each from B and D Companies in support. Lieutenants Thornton and Sleigh were two of the four original officers to have celebrated Christmas with Dr McTavish and Colonel Carter. One of them would not return.

Withdrawal to the Hindenburg Line.

John Masefield, writing in 1917, stated it was doubtful if any part of the Western Front was stronger than Gommecourt. [25] The enemy line formed a sharp salient around the wood on the edge of Gommecourt Park. The salient pointed south west like an accusing finger towards Hebuterne where the British lines stood on a plateau.

From Gommecourt Park, the Germans had a perfect field of fire over a fifty yard width of barbed wire. Kern Redoubt, which included the Maze, was a fortress built into the centre of the salient with no less than twelve machine gun posts. There were similar fortress strong-points at Nameless Farm, Sixteen Poplars, The Z and The Little Z. Two hundred and fifty yards behind to the East was the most formidable strongpoint of all, the Quadrilateral. It is still possible to make out the trench lines today.

Even in daylight, it was impossible for the British to make out much detail of the

German lines amongst the shattered trees of Gommecourt Park. What they could see were decomposed bodies from 56th Division's ill-fated attack on 1 July still lying out in No Man's Land, or hanging on the German wire like grotesque scare-crows. For original Pals like Harry Cockroft, who had lost a brother at Serre, this must have been a sickening reminder of lost comrades just two miles away to the south.

By 25 February, a thaw had turned the ice hardened ground back into sticky chalky mud again. The mud seemed to have the ability to penetrate every human crevice and piece of equipment. In the chill misty darkness of early morning, the 18th Battalion's patrols edged nervously into this formidable and unpleasant landscape. Number 2 Platoon of A Company entered No Man's Land opposite the Mouse Trap, the most westerly tip of the entire Western Front. Their objective was to enter the northern edge of the salient by traversing round in a north-easterly direction. Lieutenant Thornton, accompanied by a bombing party, led they way.

With the German withdrawal, remains of those killed in previous attacks were retrieved.

As soon as the first patrol entered No Man's Land, a Very Light was fired by the enemy at Four Tree Sap. With their hearts pounding, the patrol froze, but they were certain they had been seen. After the light died down they pressed on, entering a deserted German trench about 100 yards north beyond the point of the salient. As they penetrated towards the second line they came into contact with a German post, but after a bomb fight, the enemy fled. Lieutenant Thornton detailed small parties to explore 'Fin', 'Field' and 'Fish' trenches, traversing South across the tongue of the salient. All three trenches were found to be deserted.

After another brief bombing exchange and another quick disappearing trick by the German bombers – Thornton's patrol met no more opposition as they moved further south. But within minutes the enemy began to shell his own front line heavily. It now became clear that the few Germans they had met were observation parties waiting to alert the artillery when the British entered the line. After enduring forty-five minutes of heavy shelling, and after failing to make contact with any of the battalion's other patrols, Thornton decided to return. He had got as far south as a point opposite 'Yiddish' Trench and identified the place where smoke had been seen over the last two days. 'This I found to be a burning dug-out, the wood around the entrance being charred.'[26] It was confirmation that the enemy had indeed abandoned the old front line.

Fortunately, Thornton's patrol suffered no casualties. A patrol from C Company led by Second Lieutenant Staff was also fortunate to come back unscathed having come under heavy machine gun fire. The sensible decision to retire was made when Staff discovered that crawling through mud had put his men's rifles in a useless state when they tried to respond to an enemy machine gun. Lieutenant William Sleigh's patrol was less fortunate. They followed Thornton's men into the salient but branched off north across Gommecourt Park. They survived a bombing exchange 200 yards into the enemy line, but five men were wounded by the artillery bombardment. Sleigh ordered most of the patrol to retreat back to the British lines with the wounded. But accompanied by an original Pal, Private John Collinson (18/1491), and Privates Langdale and Sykes, Lieutenant Sleigh decided to continue into Gommecourt Park. They were never seen alive again, though their bodies were later recovered and they lie together in Sailly-au-Bois Cemetery. The Lieutenant was only twenty-two, and his men were twenty-two, twenty-one and twenty-seven respectively: four young men dead and two more widows to mourn.

The last patrol to return under Lieutenant Priday got lost in the heavy mist, but fortunately they encountered no enemy troops. They eventually managed to find their way back through an artillery barrage without any casualties bringing back a collection of enemy hand grenades as trophies. Whether they paused to consider whether the grenades were booby traps is not recorded.

The intelligence collected by the patrols was passed back to brigade. Brigade then gave orders for the 16th West Yorks to move forward at 6.30 a.m. 27 February to occupy Rossignol Wood, half a mile beyond the German third line, and to push patrols forward beyond the wood to the enemy artillery positions with a view to capturing the batteries if they were still in position.[27]

A number of lessons had been learned since the 1 July debacle, and the tactics employed at Rossignol Wood were different to those used eight months before. The attack commenced in the dark fifteen minutes before dawn, yet one crucial factor was still the same. Infantrymen were sent into a frontal attack on a well defended strong point over open ground with the minimum of cover. No attempt was made to flank round the wood and to attack it from the rear. The parameters of the 16th West Yorks' attack were the arbitrary ones of the Hebuterne-Pusieux road (the 'Sunken Road') to the south and the Hebuterne-Bucquoy road to the north – tidy lines on a map but the antithesis of the more subtle tactics adopted by the Germans in their Spring offensive of 1918.

Once again the Germans were to get the better of things, and once again they were able to dictate the course of events. They knew the British would come, and they set out to inflict the maximum damage using the minimum number of troops. Again a few troops with machine guns were able to wreak havoc on infantry advancing over open ground. It is also significant that no fewer than 418 draftees joined the 16th West Yorks in the six weeks immediately before the attack. Over a hundred joined in the week of the attack. Half of these on the eve of the assault.[28] Many took no part in the training exercises. Walter Hare, who joined in September, claimed to have fired only five rounds before arriving in France. They neither knew, nor were known, by their battalion officers and N.C.O.s. Yet, in some cases within a few hours of their arrival, they were expected to take part in an attack which began in the dark.

The attack was to be on a two company firing line basis, with A Company on the right and B Company on the left. C and D Companies followed in support.

In the early hours of the 27th, Colonel Croydon set up his Battalion Headquarters on the edge of the British Front line in Woman Street trench. The second in command, Major Kennedy, together with the signals officer, the intelligence officer and the doctor, Captain 'Paddy' Roche, went forward to set up an advanced post at the Crucifix crossroads three hundred yards beyond the German third line, and halfway to Rossignol Wood. They rolled out a wire to maintain telephone contact with the Colonel.

A and B Companies went clear of the unoccupied enemy third line in the darkness at 5.30 a.m. and then on into the new No Man's Land. They deployed by platoon sending scouts on ahead to probe the enemy positions. The scouts soon reported back that the southern edge of the wood was still occupied by the enemy.

On his own initiative, Major Kennedy ordered Second Lieutenant Ballantyne, with No.5 Platoon of B Company on the extreme left of the advance, to move further to the north along *Pionier Graben* communication trench to the high ground above the Wood in an attempt to flank round it. They got to within fifty yards of the enemy wire in front of the wood when they were attacked by rifle fire, and then driven back down *Pioneer Graben* towards the crucifix by a German Bombing party. Kennedy sent forward his own bombing party in support, who in turn drove the Germans back 150 yards before establishing a block at the junction of *Moltke Graben* and *Pionier Graben*. Heavy machine gun fire from the north of the wood pinned B Company down and they were unable to make further headway.

The atrocious conditions underfoot now played a part in what was to become a disaster for the 16th West Yorks. Arthur Pearson, a stretcher bearer in the Leeds Pals and a survivor of Serre, recorded:

> Those trenches were a wet, squelchy, sticky mess. Mud was knee deep in the communication trench. Consequently the Bradfords, who should have gone over before daylight, couldn't get through the mud so it was daylight when they climbed out to attack. Jerry had left a few machine gun posts manned and the poor old Bradfords got the lot, they were cut down before they got far.
>
> 15/711 LANCE-CORPORAL A.V. PEARSON, 15WY[29]

The Germans throughout Rossignol Wood were alerted by the activity to the north and opened fire with machine guns across the open space to their west. 600 yards away A Company took the full blast of this fire just as they topped the ridge facing the wood. They took casualties but pushed forward to the southern edge of the wood. The wire was so thick in front of the wood that the only way in was by the enemy's communication trench. Here they again came under heavy enfilade machine gun fire and both the company commander Captain Armitage and his second in command Lieutenant Knight were killed instantly.[30] George Armitage, an old boy of Bradford Grammar School and son of a city mohair merchant, was one of the 16th's few surviving original officers, having been in the reserve at Serre. Colonel Croydon and Major Kennedy both wrote extremely kind letters to his widow which went beyond any formal expression of condolence.[31]

Lieutenant Tucker, and five of the original First Pals N.C.O.s (Company Sergeant Major Wilkinson, Sergeants Farrar and Cockroft, all of whom had been decorated for gallantry at Serre), now took the lead moving from shell hole to shell hole in small rushes. They were supported by 16/1025 Sergeant Stanley Barnes who had 'been promoted after good work on 1 July', and 16/214 Sergeant William Denison who was 'popular, and all his platoon had plenty of confidence in him'. 16/351 C.S.M. Clarence Wilkinson, M.M., got into the wood and was fortunate to survive. He spent the rest of the war in a German Prisoner of War camp. At the subsequent Court of Enquiry Captain Parker, the 16th's Adjutant, described Clarrie Wilkinson:

> He joined the 16th the same time as myself in September 1914. Commenced as a private and rose through all intermediate ranks to C.S.M. through sheer merit. A man to be trusted, the Coy, especially the older members would have followed him anywhere. All had every confidence in him as C.S.M. A man without fear.
>
> CAPTAIN P.C. PARKER M.C., 16WY[32]

16/637 Sergeant Charles Farrar D.C.M., led No. 4 Platoon on the right of the attack. They were unable to get through and were pinned down in shell holes south west of the wood. Charles Farrar was severely wounded and died two days later.[33] 16/1185 Sergeant Harry Cockroft D.C.M., going ahead of the main body of troops, managed to get his Lewis gun team into the edge of the wood. As they entered the wood they came under machine gun fire. The men on either side of Harry Cockroft were killed instantly, but he was saved by a slight mound in front of his head which took the bullets. Cockroft's team lay out for several hours before being surrounded and forced to surrender. As they were led to the rear of the German lines, they passed a German machine gunner. Harry was astonished to see that the man was chained to his gun and was puzzled as to whether this was a punishment or some form of fanaticism. In fact it was a method of moving the gun. Lieutenant Tucker was wounded, whilst Sergeants Barnes and Denison were taken prisoner.

From Battalion H.Q. in Woman Street, Colonel Croydon tried to piece together what was going on. He established that A Company had got to the southern edge of the wood and tried to enter by the enemy trenches. Not surprisingly the enemy machine gunners had positioned themselves for this:

> The enemy opened heavy machine gun fire which enfiladed these trenches, and killed, wounded and made practically the whole of these three platoons casualties, the fourth platoon took cover in shell holes in the open, and rejoined the battalion at night. The company commander [Captain Armitage] and the second in command are missing, two platoon commanders were wounded, one, Second Lieutenant Tucker, managed to get out of the wood and reported himself to me at night. No message reached me from this company after 6.00 a.m. I sent my two Vickers guns to take up a position in the enemy third line. The Vickers and Lewis Guns greatly

Trench map section showing the British trenches in front of Hebutern.

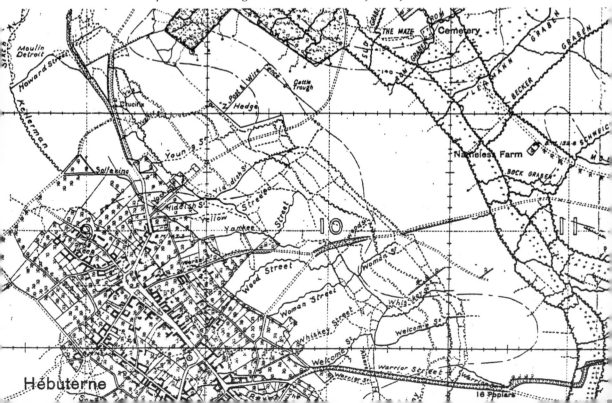

assisted in keeping down enemy fire, and were in position about 42 hours. On the night of the 27th I relieved the companies in the front line, sent forward rations and water, ten boxes of S.A.A. and ten boxes of bombs.

LIEUTENANT COLONEL A.C. CROYDON M.C., D.C.M, 16WY[34]

Unlike the colonel, Private Walter Hare had a worm's eye view, and it lasted for nearly three days. For Walter, the 27 February was 'my first time over the top, and I'd only fired five rounds before I arrived in France'. As a staunch Methodist, Walter had refused the customary rum ration.

We had no idea what our objective was. I expect the officers knew, but unfortunately we soon lost some of the officers. I pressed on over our wire which had not been cut, then across 'No Man's Land and to the enemy wire which was still intact. We were now having casualties by enemy machine gun fire but we kept moving forward as best we could. I got to the enemy's front line where there were a few dead Germans. There was a wood in front of us with a lot of enemy machine guns. We got bogged down, but Lieutenant Wilson wanted us to press on in spite of the machine gun fire. A corporal from another mob had got mixed up with us and he said we should stay where we were, and so we obeyed him because we thought his was the best advice.

Seventy-four years to the day later, Walter could still remember the sensation of lying in the mud as the bullets whistled over his head wondering if he was going to survive.

It was a case of, in Bruce Bairnsfather's immortal phrase, "If you know a better 'ole go to it". We were now in the Germans' support line and the machine guns had the exact range so we laid behind the trench and made ourselves a bit of cover. We hung on there for the next two days and nights without food or water, and our ammunition was getting short too. The attack seemed to have come to a halt, and it seemed as though we were the only ones left. But we stayed on and then on the third day the 'powers that be' must have realised we were still there because they heard us firing. We were very low on water and ammunition. 'Lefty' Crowther managed to get across to us by dodging through the shell holes with the orders to retire to our own lines which we did, thankfully. He brought a petrol can full of water which we were very pleased to have. We called him 'Lefty' because he seemed to have two left feet when we were on parade, but oh he was a grand fella. It's a great shame that he was killed later on. Eventually we moved to billets at Rossignol Farm, which was a favourite billet. We had a roll call of course, and we realised that we must have had a lot of casualties, and realised that we had been very fortunate. What a useless waste of life for nothing. 37468 PRIVATE WALTER HARE, 16WY[35]

Walter Hare, four days in No Man's Land.

'Lefty Crowther' was not alone in volunteering to bring in the isolated men. (16/568) Sergeant Albert Sands' efforts would have been recognised by at the least a Military Medal if an officer had witnessed what he did. As it was he received a Mention in Despatches. From his description of events to his son, the well known television actor Leslie Sands, it is almost certain that Albert Sands brought in the mortally wounded Sergeant Charles Farrar D.C.M. and Private Walter Higgins (16/208). In a letter to the author, Leslie Sands described his father's story.

My Dad took one pace forward,'568, Sergeant Sands, Sir!' He was issued with a pouch of hand-grenades and his comrades wished him luck. Then it was over the top through the barbed wire, and a long crawl on his belly across No Man's Land.

When he reached the emplacement it had three occupants, all of whom had enlisted with him. One man was dead, another badly wounded and the third fainting from terror and exposure. My father immobilised the Lewis gun, dumped all his heavy gear (for which he was later castigated), and took the wounded soldier across his back and, with the man who could still walk clinging to him for support, began the long and perilous trek back to the front line. When he staggered down into the trench, the man on his back was dead too. The officer shook him by the hand, and gave him a measure of rum. I have his (M.I.D.) certificate in front of me as I write.[36]

Although Albert Sands faced the heartache and privation of seven years' on the dole when he came back to Barkerend Road after the war, he lived to see his son Leslie achieve fame as a television actor and playwright. In the three days that it took to extract the survivors the Germans disappeared and abandoned the wood. Arthur Pearson of the Leeds Pals helped in this sad task,

There were not many unwounded survivors, and we SB (stretcher bearers) were attending to their wounded and carrying them down to the First Aid Post. All night and every night this went on the whole time we were in the line.

15/711 Lance Corporal Arthur Pearson, 15WY[37]

Operation Alberich achieved its purpose. The 16th West Yorks suffered 226 casualties: seventy-eight killed, eighty-three wounded and sixty-five missing. Forty three of the casualties were original Pals, many of them N.C.O.s. Another grievous blow had been struck at the heart of the old Battalion. When one remembers that this was essentially a two company action, with nearly all the casualties in A and B Company, then the scale of losses approaches that of 1 July.

During the l6th's attack, the 18th had been on stand-to in the old British lines behind the 16th in readiness to give support if necessary. Nerves were taught, and were not helped when one of the recent draftee conscripts committed a self-inflicted wound.

During the afternoon of 28 February, Brigadier Ingles gave orders for the 18th Battalion to attack the wood the following morning. He later postponed the order for a further twenty-four hours The level of casualties had clearly shaken Divisional Headquarters. It was decided to move up a heavy howitzer to give artillery support to smash up the German wire, and for the 18th D.L.I. to work towards the *Garde Stellung* in a pincer movement beyond the left flank of the 18th West Yorks towards a German strongpoint north of the wood. 'If only' is an easy phrase with the benefit of hindsight, but one is tempted to ask why these steps had not been taken in the first place during the 16th West Yorks' attack.

At 7.00 p.m. on the 28th, the 18th West Yorks began to filter through into the old German lines to relieve the 16th Battalion. By 4.00 a.m. 1 March the relief was complete.

Lieutenant Owen Morgan, one of the few original officers from 1914, with a platoon from D Company and a party of bombers, relieved Major Kennedy in his exposed observation post at the Crucifix. Apart from occasional sniper fire, all was quiet until 8.15 a.m. when Morgan reported seeing a group of Germans coolly sauntering across the skyline and away from the wood towards Pusiuex.

As work began to consolidate the old German trenches, the 18th came under heavy artillery fire. The enemy had the exact range of where their old front line met the Hebuterne-Bucquoy road. Six more men were wounded and four killed

Albert Sands, Mentioned in Despatches.

(including an original Pal 18/135 Corporal Bill Oyston). In many ways William Wadsworth Oyston was a typical Pal, young (only twenty), from an unremarkable yet 'respectable' background, but with sufficient achievement and idealism in his short life to mark him out as a thoroughly solid decent citizen for the future. He went to Grange Secondary School before joining the staff of the Prudential Assurance Company. He was a founder member and patrol leader of the Y.M.C.A. Boy Scout troop and a Sunday School teacher at Great Horton Wesleyan Church.[38]

On the morning of 2 March, the order to attack the wood was postponed yet again. Instead, two platoons from A and B companies of the 18th West Yorks were given the unpleasant but necessary task of clearing the bodies of men killed on the 1 July from the 56th (London) Division still lying in No Man's Land between the two old front lines. Graves were dug near the junction of Watson and Revel trench to the east of Hebuterne in the old British second Line.

At noon three man patrols were sent along the old German communication trenches to probe the edges of Rossignol Wood. Whilst the patrols encountered sniper fire, and one man was killed, fires were seen to be burning at four points along the northern end of the wood. It was obvious that the Germans were about to evacuate the wood, and orders were given for it to be occupied that night. Strong patrols were sent forward under cover of darkness and at 8.30 p.m. they entered the wood without opposition. To the north of the wood, the 18th West Yorks and the 18th D.L.I. followed in closely after a creeping barrage to capture a German strong point on the *Garde Stellung*. They took twenty-four prisoners and two machine guns. But in the wood itself, most of the birds had flown.

As usual the 18th's Medical Officer, Dr. Mac, despite a temperature of 103, had gone ahead with the advance parties into Rossignol Wood. He described his latest adventure in his own racy inimitable style:

We had a rather wet muddy time but before we came out – we once again started the ball rolling – Of course Fritz says he retreated, of course he did but it was because he was pushed – we visited a little village [Gommecourt] that he had held and made faces at us for a long long time. Another battalion relieved us and took over Fritz's dwellings. We went out for a rest but had to go back to take over some more of Fritz's line – of course we had a great time – such mud – as the boys said – they wished he had taken his trenches with him.

Bill Oyston, killed 1 March 1917.

Well the next few days and nights were rather strenuous – still we had a real good time – we were chasing Fritz out of a line he had held since he sat down in 1914. The night before we came out again for a rest we took or at least occupied a wood that he had held with machine guns. We sent patrols out – most of them came back with good reports – a couple were 'sniped' – another found a bombing post that Fritz had for fear of trouble – for some reason he had left it. They threw his bombs away and reported. In a few minutes we had strong patrols out – and a little later we got word we owned the wood.

    I went over right away – and the rest of the battalion followed. I had picked out a dug out to live in, looked around for spoils – put a notice up to the effect that I owned the home – then went scouting around to see what I could find. When I came back I found two guards on my abode. I said 'Well, what are you doing? – "Oh, we belong to the party that are watching the dugouts to see that no Germans come out – Our orders are that if we hear a noise we are to throw these bombs downs" – "Oh I see. I'm glad you didn't come while I was down there." The joke was that I had got ahead of our search party – still if I hadn't have come out when I did the joke might have been on me.[39]

Mac's letter was written on 17 March 'In a cosy little cot, in a cosy little room, in a cosy little hospital – somewhere in France'. It was his last 'adventure' with the Pals. The delightful Canadian doctor who served the Second Pals so well collapsed with pneumonia when the battalion came out of the line 4 March. Sadly for the Pals, when Mac recovered he was transferred to the 99th Field Ambulance Unit in 33rd Division. He added two bars to the Military Cross he had won at Serre and was promoted to the rank of major. He returned to rural Canada where for many years he practised as a much loved doctor. The citation for his second bar gives the measure of the man.

<u>Major George Boyd McTavish, M.C. and Bar, M.D., R.A.M.C.</u>

    For conspicuous gallantry and devotion to duty west of Villers Guislain from September 19 to 27, 1918. He worked for eight days and nights, refusing to be relieved, walking constantly through heavy barrages and machine-gun fire, organizing bearer squads on the whole divisional front. Although gassed, he still carried on, and saved the life of an officer who was knocked over by a shell when he was talking to him, holding an artery until help came, he himself having been knocked over by the same shell.

                                             Lond>Gazette, *March, 1919.*

One of the last of the original Pal Officers, Lieutenant J.R. Thornton, was one of the last to receive care from Dr. Mac. The Lieutenant, having survived Serre and the Gommecourt Park patrol, was 'sniped' in the wood as his patrol captured twenty prisoners. He was piggy-backed out to safety by his orderly, 18/175 Private Frank Burn. These two men epitomised the spirit of the Pals. Their friendship, regardless of rank, continued after the War. They were President and Chairman of the Bradford Pals Old Comradeship Association leading pilgrimages to France together for over fifty years.

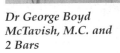

Dr George Boyd McTavish, M.C. and 2 Bars

    The battered and weary 16th Battalion had to stay in support in the old British trenches for three nights until the evening of 2 March when they were relieved by the First Barnsley Pals. They marched off to billets at Coigneux to clean up and rest. When the roll call was taken they realised the full severity of their losses. The 18th Battalion followed them out of the line into billets at Bayencourt when the Barnsleys moved further forward on 4 March.

    Whilst telegrams of congratulation arrived at 16th Battalion's H.Q. on the capture of the *Garde Stellung* from General Gough at Fifth Army H.Q. and from General Wanless O'Gowan at 31st Division, the Battalion was astonished to find that the same General O'Gowan had ordered the setting up of a Court of Enquiry as to why sixty-five of their men were missing.

The Court of Enquiry met 15 March under the Presidency of Lieutenant Colonel Stapledon, C.O. of the 10th East Yorks, and with two other officers as members, Major Currin D.S.O., a forty-four year old South African of the 13th Yorks and Lancs (First Barnsley Pals) and Captain Moxey the twenty-two year old machine gun officer of the 12th Yorks and Lancs (Sheffield Pals) as members. There is no doubt about the courage of Currin and Moxey. Major Currin was awarded the D.S.O. for rescuing a large number of wounded 1 July at Serre. Later, Captain Moxey would be awarded a posthumous George Cross as an R.A.F. bomb disposal officer during the Battle of Britain in the Second World War.[40]

Nevertheless, the Court of Enquiry in the Field was hardly a model for justice. The sixty-five missing men were not in a position to be represented, nor, of course, could they give evidence or cross-examine any of the witnesses. The most damning evidence, that of Second Lieutenant Tucker, was hearsay and would not have been admitted in a court of law. Major Humfrey H. Kennedy, a most important eye-witness, had already left the 16th West Yorks and gave only written evidence. He had no opportunity to refute the subsequent criticism made of him by the divisional general. It is unlikely that Major-General Wanless O'Gowan was much troubled by any such doubts or considerations.

Written character evidence of the missing N.C.O.s was submitted. If for no other reason, we should be glad that the Court of Enquiry took place, for it allows us to see the Pals' admiration and affection for their missing comrades. Yet how demeaning that it should have to be done. Brief extracts as to each character reference to the Court of Enquiry make the point.[41]

16/351 C.S.M. Clarence Wilkinson, M.M.

A man to be trusted...the men would have followed him anywhere... a man without fear.
16/208 PRIVATE WALTER HIGGINS

Possessed of high courage...a splendid example to the men... encouraging them during a hostile bombardment.
SECOND LIEUTENANT J.M. BARROW, 16WY

It was only a question of time before he received some other decoration..., the most fearless man and the finest leader of men I have met.
CAPTAIN P.C. PARKER M.C., 16WY

He always displayed great coolness and carried out his duties in a fearless manner... a clean,keen sportsman with a high sense of character.
16/19 R.S.M. ALFRED E.ODDY

16/1185 Sergeant Harold Cockroft, D.C.M.

I have been with him many times under heavy fire and he was very cool..excellent work and bravery on 1st July ...the men had the greatest regard for him
CAPTAIN P.C. PARKER, M.C., 16WY

Difficult to find any soldier more devoted to duty than he....by his coolness inspired his men... his familiar figure and cheerful smile are missed by all
16/566 SERGEANT ALBERT SANDS, M.I.D.

Of the stoutest character, honourable, highly efficient, possessing every quality which goestowards making the true British soldier... under fire I envied his coolness... his loss is felt severely... I feel sure that whatever became of him he gave a good account of himself
2ND LT. ELLISON MURGATROYD, D.C.M., 16WY

16/214 Sergeant William Denison

He was cool under heavy fire...well educated...took a prominent part in raising

concerts...a good N.C.O. in full control of his men
CAPTAIN P.C. PARKER, M.C., 16WY

His platoon had plenty of confidence in him.
16/208 PRIVATE WALTER HIGGINS

16/1025 Sergeant Stanley Barnes

A well educated man...executed his duties in a calm deliberate manner...a capable N.C.O of bright cheerful disposition... a good clean character
16/19 R.S.M. ALFRED E. ODDY

The Court heard five eye-witness accounts from survivors of A and B Companies. All confirmed the heavy casualties suffered as they were pinned down by heavy machine gun and shell fire huddled in shell holes in front of the German wire. 'A heavy fire was kept up and it was practically impossible to move'. They also agreed on the confusion and breakdown of communications at that point of the action. Private Walter Higgins, who was in a shell hole with the mortally wounded Sergeant Farrar on the right of A Company, witnessed a group of men surrender after enduring two hours of heavy fire.

Three or four men crawled out and put up their hands and shouted 'Kamerad' and 'Adolph' and ran towards the German lines without their rifles. The Germans then ceased fire and about twelve more men went over on my left. About an hour afterwards I heard voices from the rear which I did not recognise saying 'Come on, lets get up both together'. Three men then came towards me with their hands up shouting 'Kamerad'. They asked me to go with them. I refused. They then walked straight into the German lines. I do not know the names of any of the men I saw going across. They were all men of the new draft. I did not see any N.C.O.s going across.[42]

As we have seen nearly 100 new drafts had arrived in the week before the attack, half of them on the eve of the attack. It should have been obvious that to pitch such men into action with an unfamiliar unit so soon was asking for trouble. No fewer than twenty-seven of the sixty-five missing men joined the battalion in the fortnight preceeding the attack. Second Lieutenant Stanley then gave hearsay evidence of an interview between the wounded Second Lieutenant Tucker and Colonel Croydon on the night after the attack. It was this interview which almost certainly led to the Court of Enquiry. Tucker stated that he and his platoon were in a series of shell holes which were being heavily enfiladed with rifle and machine gun fire.

He dug a shallow trench connecting the shell holes up with one of the enemy communication trenches to enable his party to get cover. He crawled up this trench and was wounded. On reaching the communication trench he gave the signal for his men to follow and saw Sergeant Denison and the remainder of his platoon, about fifteen, proceeding towards the German Lines with their hands up crying 'Kamerad'. Second Lieutenant Tucker stated that he was then again wounded and remained in the trench until dark. SECOND LIEUTENANT J.L. STANLEY 16WY[43]

It is significant that the men had been pinned down under heavy enfilade rifle and machine gun fire for a considerable period, that there had been no communication between Tucker and Denison. Neither Denison or Tucker were able to give their own version of events or be questioned about what happened.

Lieutenant Stanley, the 16th's adjutant, gave written evidence of Major Kennedy's report of seeing ten men surrender near *Pioneer Graben* trench from his position at the Crucifix. When asked by Colonel Croydon why he didn't fire Kennedy had stated that the light was not good enough to distinguish whether the men were British or German, but that they disappeared in a dip near the German lines.[44]

The Court gave its opinion that there was no direct evidence to show what had become of the majority of the men, and also accepted the appalling situation faced by the 16th, 'that both Companies came under heavy machine gun fire, and it was practically impossible to move and impossible to get up to the wood'. Yet having admitted the difficulty of establishing exactly what had happened in such a chaotic situation, and confirming the inexperience of many of the men who had taken part in the attack, they came to the questionable decision to condemn Sergeant Denison unheard, and to conclude that he, was responsible for the surrender of his party. They passed no opinions on Major Kennedy's actions.[45]

One must assume that this conclusion was reached on the hearsay evidence of Lieutenant Tucker's interview with Colonel Croydon. Character evidence in Denison's favour was discounted, yet such was the substance of that evidence that it is worth repeating:

> I have no reason to doubt his courage at any time... cheerful and high spirited...and I do not remember observing any traces of fear in his demeanour.
>
> SECOND LT. J.M. BARROW, 16WY

> I regarded him as being one of the best N.C.O.'s in the Battalion. He never failed to be a good example to his men.
>
> 16/19 R.S.M. ALFRED E. ODDY

> He was popular, and his platoon had plenty of confidence in him.
>
> 16/208 Pte. W. Higgins

General Wanless O'Gowan, signed and endorsed the findings of the Court, but went beyond the Court's findings by adding a further comment about Major Kennedy on a matter of opinion rather than fact.

> I consider Sgt Denison was responsible for the surrender of his party. I am further of the opinion that Major Kennedy showed lack of judgement in not firing on this party.[46]

If the Major-General had taken the trouble to visit the Crucifix, it would have been obvious to him that it would have been completely impossible for Kennedy to see Denison's party who were on the extreme right of the attack. Whoever Kennedy did see, it certainly wasn't Denison. General Wanless O'Gowan, the General who kicked the flowers off executed men's graves, was now reprimanding an officer unheard for failing to shoot men in the back whom it was impossible to see from Kennedy's position.[47] Not only was the finding and confirmation against the missing men, and the subsequent criticism of Major Kennedy, against natural justice, but it would appear to be unlawful. The 1914 *Manual of Military Law* (Rule of Procedure 124f) lays down that:

> Whenever any inquiry affects the character or military reputation of any officer or soldier, full opportunity must be afforded of being present throughout the inquiry.[48]

The procedure also laid down that individuals had the right to make additional statements, and if they felt their character or military reputation was being impugned, they had the right to cross-examine witnesses.[49] This could not be done for Sergeant Dennison, and it was not done for Major Kennedy.

After the Inquiry, Fifth Army General Staff circulated the following message to all units, including the four Australian Divisions who were of course exempt from the death penalty:

> During recent fighting an N.C.O. and a party of fifteen men of a battalion which was heavily engaged deserted to the enemy. These men were seen crossing over to

the enemy with their hands up and without arms, but were not fired on by our troops. It should be made known to all ranks that if men are seen going over to the enemy they should be fired on at once, and that men who surrender without sufficient reason or desert to the enemy, will be tried after the war and shot.[50]

The statement turned out to be no more than rhetoric, and no action was taken against the men after the war. Good sense prevailed, all the survivors of the Prisoner of War camps including Sergeant Denison received their medals and none were treated as deserters. Denison had no problems of acceptance from his own comrades and he was an active and welcome member of the Pals Old Comradeship Association.

But there was to be no happy homecoming for four of the captured men. Private Albert Calvert (16/381), an original Pal, survived the end of the war but sadly died in Germany two and a half weeks after the Armistice. He is buried at Stahnsdorf Cemetery between Berlin and Potsdam. Private Walter Wilks (33061) died in hospital in Mons two months after his capture. Private Harold Walker (32894) died in Berlin in August, 1917, and Private Joseph Lynch (34004) died in Hamburg in October, 1917.[51]

Exactly why Major Kennedy left the 16th West Yorks in March, 1917 to rejoin his own Regiment, the Seaforth Highlanders, is not known and one can only speculate as to why Colonel Croydon had been appointed over his head after several months in command of the battalion. There may have been tension between two such very different characters. Kennedy, as President of the Field General Courts Martial, had unsuccessfully made a 'strong recommendation to mercy' plea in the judgement on the two executed 18th men. The plea did not coincide with the attitude of his superiors up the chain of command, and now came the Rossignol Wood affair. Was he judged to be 'too soft' by 31st Division? Whatever the truth, the departure of this humane officer was much regretted by the rank and file. He was, said Walter Hare, 'a decent man, approachable, you could talk to him'.[52]

Major-General Robert Wanless O'Gowan, visited the Bradford Battalions' front line trenches only once in 1917. Yet he was mentioned in despatches six times, granted Orders of Chivalry as a Companion of the Bath and a Companion of St. Michael and St. George, the Croix de Guerre avec Palme, the Belgian Ordre de la

Rossignol Wood today looking from Major Kennedy's position at the Crucifix. Owl Trench Cemetery in distance on the right.

Courrone, and the 4th Class Order of Vladimir with swords. He died at the age of eighty-three at his Surrey home in 1947 after retiring from the Army in 1926.[53]

Major Humfrey Heyes Kennedy transferred to the 15th Scottish Division where he was promoted to Lieutenant Colonel in command of the 8th Seaforth Highlanders. There was no Order of Vladimir, just the standard 'trio' of the 1914-15 Star, British Medal and Victory Medal. But he did win the affection and respect of his men. He was killed by a stray shell after personally leading his battalion into action at Chazelle Noyant 29 July, 1918. He was thirty-six. He is buried in Raperie British Cemetery to the south of Soissons.[54] And today in the Hebuterne sector? To the north of the village, within yards of the road to Fonquevillers, it was possible until recently to stand inside the concrete observation point where Lieutenant William Sleigh and his patrol left the British lines for the last time to cross No Man's Land into Gommecourt Park. The hessian pattern from the sandbags was still visible in the concrete on the outside of the post, and from the inside one had a concentrated view across to the Mousetrap and to the site of the Kaiser's Oak. Sadly, modern farming demands have removed it. Now Friesian cows munch contentedly amongst the dips of the old trench lines which are still visible. At Rossignol Wood there is a brooding stillness. The trees stand tall again. Visitors rarely come for it is off the beaten track away from the better known Somme landmarks. At the crossroads, Kennedy's post, the wayside Crucifix is long gone. But down the hill along the Pusieux road there is the Cross of Sacrifice at two small cemeteries. Rossignol Wood Cemetery is the first and Owl Trench Cemetery is just a few yards further on.

Rossignol Wood Cemetery contains German and British dead. The British graves stand mute testimony to the fact that nothing had been learned on the 27 February. They are men of the North Staffords sent into a similar ill-prepared attack two weeks after the Pals. The Pals' graves are in Owl Trench Cemetery. Captain George Armitage, Lieutenant Knight and forty-four men of A and B Company lie together in a mass grave made from a German trench. With them are seven unidentified KOYLIs of the pioneer battalion of 93 Brigade, tough little miners from Dewsbury and Wakefield. Without Lefty Crowther, Albert Sands and Humfrey Kennedy the cemetery would have been much bigger.

NOTES

1. PRO WO95/2362 A/740/381/1
2. Walter Hare, taped interview with author, 10/9/1989.
3. PRO WO95/2362 Proceedings of a Court of Enquiry in the Field on the 15th March, 1917 by order of Major General R.Wanless O'Gowan C.B., attached to 16th W.Y.Battalion War Diary.
4. Ibid
5. Letter from Mr. Jack Cockroft to the author, 16/9/90.
6. Colonel Repington, *The First World War*, 1914-18, Constable, 1920.
7. Haig Diary, 9th February, 1917
8. Walter Hare, op. cit
9. Horace Wadsworth, taped interview with author, 19/11/89. Horace was indeed fortunate to survive the bombing at Etaples, casualties totalled 182 killed and 643 wounded. The enemy target was the railway viaduct over the River Canche which carried over 100 troop trains a day, but in fact one of the base hospital wards was hit causing a major outburst of 'Hun Atrocity' stories in the press. Page 1974 of the *I Was There* series has a photograph of the funeral of a nursing sister killed in the raid.
10. Letter from Dr. G.B. McTavish, M.C. and 2 Bars, to Miss Maud Colville, 7/2/17, in the Imperial War Museum.
11. *Bradford Daily Telegraph*, 3/1/17
12. Ibid
13. PRO W095/2362. Analysis of drafts based on casualty figures attached to Court of Enquiry and also in *Soldiers Died in the Great War, 1914-19, The Prince of Wales Own (West Yorkshire Regiment)* pp 103/107.
14. Hare, op. cit.
15. Information supplied by Captain A.R. Smith, Curator of The Lincolnshire Regiment Museum.

16. Hare, op.cit.
17. McTavish, op. cit.
18. PRO WO95/2362. Battalion War Diary.
19. McTavish, ibid.
20. John McGrath, taped interview with author 23/3/89
21. PRO WO95/2362
22. Paul Maze D.C.M., M.M., *A Frenchman in Khaki*, Heinemann (1934). Maze, a French citizen, was special assistant to General Hubert Gough. Gough was one of the few senior generals to regularly get to the front line, and Maze was often used to gather intelligence in this way. Maze was the first man to be awarded the Military Medal when it was instituted in 1916.
23. Haig Diary, 25/2/17
24. PRO W095/2362
25. John Masefield, *The Old Front Line*, Heinemann, 1917.
26. PRO W095/2362. Details of patrols based on reports contained in Battalion War Diary. Casualties from *Soldiers Died in the Great War.*
27. Ibid
28. Ibid.
29. Pearson, Arthur Valentine, (15/711, 15th West Yorks, Leeds Pals), *A Leeds Pal Looks Back*, unpublished manuscript in Leeds Local History Library, circa 1961.
30. PRO W095/2362
31. *Bradford Daily Telegraph*, 9/3/17
32. Based on evidence at Court of Enquiry and subsequent casualty lists.
33. Cockroft, op. cit.
34. Lieutenant Colonel A.C. Croydon PRO WO95/2362
35. Hare, op. cit

Carter Kendal (right) captured at Rossignol Wood in a PoW camp.

Wounded Pals recovering at Suffolk six months after the Somme.

Walter Hare with the author at Rossignol Wood, 1992.

36. Leslie Sands, letters to the author 26/4/91 and 14/5/91. Quote from Leslie Sands' autobiography, *Tuppence for the Rainbow* pub. Bradford Libraries and Information Service (1990).

37. Pearson, opus cit.

38. *Bradford Daily Telegraph*, 9/3/17.

39. McTavish, op. cit. 17/3/17

40. Captain Currin later became C.O. of the 5th Leicesters. Squadron Leader Eric Lawrence Moxey was awarded the George Cross, the highest award for gallantry for bomb disposal work on 27 August 1940 at Biggin Hill Aerodrome, Kent. The citation reads, 'The KING has been graciously pleased to approve of the posthumous award of the GEORGE CROSS to: Acting Squadron Leader Eric Lawrence MOXEY (73498), Royal Air Force Volunteer Reserve. On the 27 August, 1940, it was reported that two unexploded bombs were embedded in an aerodrome. Squadron Leader Moxey, a technical intelligence officer employed at the Air Ministry, immediately volunteered to proceed to the site and remove them, though from the nature of his duties he very fully aware of the risk entailed in such an operation. One of the bombs exploded causing his death. On many occasions Squadron Leader Moxey has exhibited similar complete disregard for his personal safety". *London Gazette* 17 December, 1940.

41. PRO WO95/2362 Court of Enquiry. Evidence as to character. Op. cit

42. Ibid.

43. Ibid

44. Kennedy's evidence to Court of Enquiry, confirmed in his letter of sympathy to Mrs. Armitage (*Bradford Daily Telegraph*, 9/3/17).

45. Findings of Court of Enquiry. Op. Cit. PRO WO95/2362

46. Wanless O'Gowan, Note attached to Court of Enquiry, op. cit.

47. A site visit confirms Kennedy's view.

48. Manual of Military Law, 1914, Rules of Procedure, 124 f.

49. Ibid

50. PRO W095/2362 : H.Q. Fifth Army General Staff A/740/381/1, 29 March, 1917.

51. Albert Calvert, a wool warehouseman, died on 28th November, 1918. He is buried in the Berlin South-Western Commonwealth War Grave Cemetery, Plot 11. Row C. Grave 12.

52. Hare, op. cit.

53. Who Was Who, 1897/1980.

54. Battalion War Diary, 8th Seaforth Highlanders, 29 July, 1918. Lt. Col. Kennedy is buried at Raperie British Cemetery, 1VA D1, Villemontoire.

Appendix A: **The Colonel**

Lieutenant Colonel Humfrey Heyes Kennedy, 1882-1918

Humfrey Heyes Kennedy joined the Seaforth Highlanders in 1900 and served as a young Second Lieutenant in the Boer War, winning the Queen's Medal with five clasps. He was promoted to full lieutenant in 1908, and in 1912 was employed with the West African Frontier Force. He returned to Europe on the outbreak of war and after service with the Seaforths in Flanders was promoted to captain in November, 1914. He was promoted to major in the autumn of 1915, and transferred to be second in command of the 16th West Yorks at Fovant as they prepared to move to Egypt in December, 1915. A tall, genteel Scot, he continued to wear his own Regimental trews and glengarry. He was respected and liked by the rank and file in the Bradford Pals, He was, according to Walter Hare, 'a decent man, approachable, you could talk to him'.

Writing home to his parents in August, 1916, twenty year old Second Lieutenant Bernard Long, newly appointed intelligence officer to the 16th West Yorks, mentioned Kennedy with great affection,

Humfrey Heyes Kennedy.

> *I am writing this letter to you in a dugout in the front line with my feet in a foot of water, so you see we get used to anything. I'm waiting for the colonel to come back from his walk round so that we can come back together. He's awfully nice with me sees that I change my clothes when I get wet and lends me breeches and under things for a change.*
>
> SECOND LIEUTENANT BERNARD LONG, 16WY

Kennedy was kept in reserve at Serre, but moved up to the line to take over command when Colonel Guyon was killed. He held the battalion together as acting C.O. until Colonel Croydon's appointment in January, 1917. In August, 1916 he had the disagreeable task of presiding over the Field General Court Martial of the two 18th Battalion men charged with desertion. On the basis of the evidence, the Court had no alternative but to find the men guilty. However, the Court did add, 'with a strong recommendation to mercy'on its judgement. He left the West Yorks in March, 1917 after the Rossignol Wood attack. His humanity and decency undoubtedly saved lives at Rossignol Wood although he was criticised by the divisional general, Robert Wanless O'Gowan. Although there is no direct evidence, there may have been some tension between Kennedy and Croydon, men of very different backgrounds and approach, particularly after Kennedy had been in charge of the battalion for six months after Serre. Kennedy returned to his own regiment and eventually took over command of the 8th Seaforths in the 15th Scottish Division. He was killed by shellfire after leading his battalion into action at Chazelle Noyant near Soissons on 29 July, 1918 .He is buried in Raperie British Cemetery. He left a widow who lived in Dorking.

Appendix B: **The Pacifist Hero**

<u>16/1185 Sergeant Harry Cockroft, D.C.M.</u>
Harry Cockroft was awarded the Distinguished Conduct Medal for gallantry at Serre. He was captured during the attack on Rossignol Wood on 27th February, 1917 and spent nearly two years as a prisoner of war. For the first six months Harry was held in temporary accommodation and made to work as a labourer behind the enemy lines in France. When he finally reached a permanent prisoner of war camp at Gustrow near the Baltic coast towards the end of 1917, his weight had dropped to six and a half stones from his normal twelve stones. At one point, he and his comrades ate a dog shot at the perimeter fence by the guards. It was only when he reached Gustrow was he able to send a field service card to his family. On 17 July, 1917, the *Bradford Telegraph* had reported that Harry was killed in action after having been reported missing in March. His mother, already grieving for the loss of two other sons, was the only member of the family who refused to accept that he was dead. One can imagine the family joy when Harry's card finally arrived. At the outbreak of war, Harry Cockroft was twenty-six years old and married with a baby son. He was employed as a paviour at the Highways Department of Bradford Corporation. The family lived in Great Horton where Harry was an active member of the Working Mens' Club and a staunch home and away supporter of Great Horton Cricket Club in the Bradford League. He was also a committed life long supporter of the Labour Party. Harry was one of five brothers. The four older boys all volunteered together in December, 1914, with Harry and Willie (16/1170) joining the First Pals. A younger brother, Tom, was killed in Flanders in 1915 serving with the Duke of Wellington's Regiment. Harry joined C Company, and was soon promoted to corporal in the Number 6 Lewis gun team. After Serre he was promoted to sergeant, and the citation for his Distinguished Conduct Medal for 'conspicuous gallantry in action' on 1 July states:

> *He held on to a position in 'No Man's Land' under very heavy shell and machine gun fire with the only survivor of his machine gun team. When ordered to retire he got his gun back and re-opened fire.*
>
> The London Gazette

In fact, starting from New Monk Trench, Harry lost most of his section before he even got to the front line. Somehow the two survivors managed to get Number 6 gun over the parapet and into a shell hole twenty yards into No Man's Land. After firing a few rounds, the gun's cartridge guide spring broke. With great determination and courage Harry managed to replace it under intense enemy fire.

Later in the morning, still under heavy shell and machine gun fire, they were ordered back into what was left of the front line to prepare for an enemy counter attack. They hung on until late afternoon before being ordered back to Monk Trench. They held this exposed position for four days covering the rescue of the wounded and again guarding against counter-attack. Harry's companion, Sergeant Ellison Murgatroyd (16/573), was also awarded the D.C.M. On 1 July, the Lewis gun section had fort-nine casualties out of a total personnel of fifty-six.

When Harry was finally relieved he discovered that his brother Willie, a wire cutter, was missing. Willie's body was never found, and his name appears on the Thiepval Memorial.

When Harry returned from Germany for Christmas in 1918, he was determined never to do manual labour again. He was made a foreman on the roads by the City Corporation in 1919, and later became Highways Superintendant in Oldham.

The War profoundly affected his thinking, and he developed strong pacifist views. Uniformed organisations were anathema to him, and he forbade his son Jack to join either the Scouts or the O.T.C. when Jack went to Bradford Grammar School. Any bitterness felt towards the Germans after the death of his brothers disappeared and he corresponded with one of his German prison guard for many

Sergeant Harry Cockroft, D.C.M.

years. Young Jack was encouraged to take part in a school exchange visit with a German student by his father.

At the appalling Rossignol Wood Court of Enquiry, Major Kennedy was found in his absence to have 'lacked judgement' for not shooting his own men in the back. But one good thing emerged. The Pals gave character evidence for their missing comrades. Harry's companion at Serre, Lieutenant Ellison Murgatroyd, D.C.M.,by now commissioned from the ranks, spoke up for him.

Sergeant Cockroft is of the stoutest character, honourable, highly efficient, and possessing every quality which go towards making him the true British Soldier. He always remained unperturbed under the most trying conditions and under fire. I have often envied his coolness

LIEUTENANT ELLISON MURGATROYD, D.C.M, 16WY

Sadly, Ellison Murgatroyd did not survive the war. He was killed in the German Spring Offensive of March, 1918.

Harry Cockroft lived on to enjoy a happy retirement in a thatched cottage in Suffolk. He became indispensable to village life as secretary of the football club, cricket club and village gala. His teetotal habit mellowed and he enjoyed a lunchtime half-pint in the village pub. A surprising request by the Conservatives to be their local organiser caused some agitation, but there was one habit he could not break – he continued to vote Labour in a true blue Tory seat. He died in 1955 at the age of sixty-seven. Seventy years on, Serre again dominated Cockroft family thoughts. It was right and proper that Harry's son Jack should play the part of the Sergeant in the local Amateur Dramatic Society's production of play *The Accrington Pals*. Harry Cockroft was in many ways a typical Bradford Pal, of humble origin, yes, but none the worse for that, and a man of ideas, character, ambition and substance.

Chapter Fifteen

GAVRELLE AND OPPY WOOD

3 May, 1917

Way down in Oppy Wood, up to your neck in mud,
Be sure it is no fun, to go and strafe the Hun;
All you can think of at night is old Fritz's Very Light,
Minnies dropping, machine guns popping,
All the Front s alight I
The whizz-bangs as they fall, what memories they recall,
Your sure to change your smile,
They're dropping all the while ;
And then the officer will meet you,
With a tot of rum he'll greet you,
And he'll say "Mate – retaliate -
With a Mills's Number Five I[1]

Sung to the tune of 'Back Home in Tennessee' by Sergeant Albert Sands (16/568), in his post-war career as a musical hall entertainer. Sergeant Sands took part in the attack at Gavrelle as a member of the 16th West Yorks.

*   *   *

THE TRAGEDY AT SERRE 1 JULY, 1916 dominates the public memory of the Pals Battalions. The events of 3 May at Gavrelle and Oppy Wood are often overlooked, and yet the casualties were truly terrible, and proportionately greater. The number of 18th West Yorks men killed at Gavrelle was exactly the same as at Serre.

In the two weeks that followed the attack on Rossignol Wood, what was left of the 16th relaxed, cleaned up and slowly recovered in billets at Rossignol Farm near Bayencourt. Whilst there must have been tensions in Battalion Headquarters when it was known there was to be a Court of Inquiry, for the rank and file Rossignol Farm was,

> *A favourite billet. The house was occupied by the officers and servants, and we, the other ranks, were in the farm buildings which were dry and comfortable, with usually plenty of straw to add to the comfort.*
>
> 37468 Private Walter Hare, 16 WY[2]

New drafts, now mostly conscripts, continued to arrive from the West Yorkshires' No. 33 Infantry Base Depot at Etaples. 179 men and six officers swelled the numbers again to replace the losses at Rossignol Wood. There were also two notable departures in early March. Dr. George McTavish was suffering from pneumonia and was sent to the base hospital at Etaples. Major Humfrey Heyes Kennedy also made his farewells to the men he had known since Fovant. He moved on to the 15th (Scottish) Division before the Rossignol Wood Court of Inquiry met. For Private Walter Hare, the delights of Rossignol Farm were cut short on the first morning back when he fell for a crafty ploy from his Company Commander, Captain Greenwood. Maybe Walter should have remembered the old army saying, 'never volunteer for anything. We paraded as usual on our first morning out and after our Captain of C Company had inspected us he gave an order: 'Anyone whose uniform is so bad that he needs a new outfit, one step forward, march!' Six of us were sure that we needed some new clothes so we obeyed the order. The next order was, 'Right turn, quick march. Here is your fatigue party, Sergeant'. We were taken to a waiting lorry and the Sergeant agreed that we could not make our uniform any worse so we were suitably dressed for coal fatigue We were taken to the railway yard at Doullens and put to work filling sacks with coal which were destined I believe for the Field Kitchens. We had finished our task by mid-day so we were allowed to go into the town with orders to be back at 2.00 p.m. sharp.

Doullens was a long way behind the line and it looked to be going on as normal. I found an estaminet and had egg and chips, a nice change from bully beef stew. I also bought one or two silk cards to send to Emily, my girl friend and who later became my wife. But I never did get a new outfit. In fact I was still wearing my old uniform when I left P.O.W. camp in Germany at the end of the war.   37468 PRIVATE WALTER HARE 16WY[3]

This was not the last 'run in' Walter had with Captain Greenwood, but Walter ultimately got some satisfaction in the end in his tussles with authority.

There was no relaxation for the Second Pals, even though they too were out of the line in billets nearby at Bayencourt. After three days cleaning up and training drill, one platoon was detailed to help with woodcutting at Authie, whilst another platoon escorted German prisoners back to the cages. For the rest of the battalion orders came for a duty which must have brought back haunting memories of 1 July.

On the 8 March, the Second Pals spent four days converting the railway line from narrow gauge to standard gauge at Euston Dump. A few hundred yards away they could see the ruins of the Sucrerie and Colincamps. Nearby was Euston Road cemetery where the Bradford Battalions had marched past freshly dug graves on the way up to the line on the eve of assault 30 June. Just a mile away, in the old No Man's Land, they were aware that the bodies of many of their comrades were now being recovered and buried, for the most part into what is now named Serre Road No 1 Cemetery in what was No Man's Land, but also in Queen's Cemetery, Railway Hollow Cemetery and Serre Road Numbers 2 and 3. It was a sickening and gruesome task. Some of the 18th West Yorks joined with a number of the Leeds Pals to take part in the search. Some bodies were identified, including the Yorkshire and England cricketer Major Booth. He was identified by an M.C.C. cigarette case presented as a memento of the tour of South Africa. Recovery of identified bodies ended the hopes of some families who for months past had been advertising in the *Telegraph and Argus* for news of their missing relatives. But for the most part the bodies were too far gone for recognition or identification. The only consolation for the Second Pals working party was that they were out of the elements for ten days in hutted accommodation at Courcelles.

On 18 March, the two Bradford Battalions left the Somme area for the last time. Orders came to march north to Bethune by a roundabout route, keeping well clear of the immediate area of Arras where preparations had begun for the opening of a new offensive on 9 April. The two battalions, along with the Leeds and Durham Pals, marched together in easy stages taking over a week to complete the march to Bethune. The men enjoyed the beautiful rolling Artois countryside well away from the front as they looped west beyond Doullens and then north via St. Pol to Bethune. At night billets were found in neighbouring pairs of villages, the 16th West Yorks at Terramesnil, Autheux, Barly, Nuncq, Conteville, Bethonval, Belval and Auchy Au Bois, whilst the 18th West Yorks stayed at Sarton, Longuevillette, Neuvillette, Sibiville,

Valhuon and Ligny lez Aire.[4]

Whilst the French as a nation were grateful for British involvement in the war, it was inevitable that the impact of hundreds of thousands of troops, with a constant demand for billets, produced tensions in the Artois back areas as local people struggled to keep their farms going. Walter Hare, still in the same filthy uniform after the coal fatigue in Doullens, experienced a sample of this.

> *I rather enjoyed this march. It was a nice change from the trenches. We did it in short stages and had quite a lot of stops for rest. I think it was at Bethonval that we were billeted with some of the inhabitants for a night. Smithy, a friend of mine, and I were given the stone floored back kitchen to sleep in, with no blanket and not even a rug to lay on. French hospitality?*
>
> 37468 PRIVATE WALTER HARE, 16WY[5]

Efforts were made to keep good relations with the local people. Colonel Carter made a point of personally inspecting all billets before the Battalion moved off to ensure they were left in good condition. Men reporting sick to the M.O. were given the unwelcome job of cleaning up any mess found in the billets – a First War symbiotic solution. No doubt this was regarded as an incentive to avoid reporting sick, although it seems a little hard on the genuine cases.[6]

Although the winter of 1916/17 had been the hardest for over twenty years, and there were still flurries of snow, signs of Spring raised morale. It was good to be out of the Hebuterne mud, and of course nobody was shooting at them. Charles Carrington, a young subaltern in 48th Division, had been near the Pals on the 1 July north of Serre. He gave a classic description of such a march. It evocatively captures the atmosphere of the long trek to Bethune:

> *The column starts with correct drill movements marching 'at attention'. As soon as the rhythm is established and the human caterpillar acquires momentum the word is passed to march 'at ease'. Men sling their rifles, open their coat collars, tilt back their caps... and become human again from the waist up. Talking is allowed and friends look over their shoulder to exchange a word with friends in the rank behind. A blue cloud of tobacco smoke rises and thickens, and before long someone begins to whistle... This the sergeants encourage because it maintains the rhythm and ensure that the men still behave like automata from the waist down. If we sang on the march in the morning, the*

songs are gay and ribald, and it's more than likely that the company humorist has composed some topical verses to that song about the idiosyncrasies of the colonel. The nearest officer pretends not to hear, while he concentrates on memorizing it, so that he can give a spirited rendering of it in the mess that evening. Just when the language grows a little too free and the officer is wondering whether to take official cognizance of it, the word comes down the column – 'March at attention!' We are passing through a village where another regiment has its headquarters, and its quarter guard 'pays the proper compliment' by turning out and presenting arms, to which we reply, giving eyes right' by platoons. This is a bore, but it is only for a moment and is in a curious way enjoyable. This is our display of pride, our publicity, and we are ready to show them what good soldiers look like."[7]

The Bradford Pals certainly sang as they marched. One song from the 16th has survived in the papers of Private Horace Seekins (16/845).

> *I'm a bob or two in credit, some one said it,*
> *So here's to a good old time.*
> *I've got a new shirt at that; the other was full of chat.*
> *There's a few things missing, but I'm hoping and wishing*
> *They'll turn up in my small kit.*
> *My boots want mending, so the Quarter's sending*
> *Me up with a nice little chit.[8]*

Quartermaster Alf Scott always produced his usual magic. However difficult the circumstances, the Scott brothers always ensured the Second Pals were fed. Carrington described the organisation and paraphernalia involved.

> *The day wears on. Three spells of marching have brought us seven or eight miles and we halt for our dinners. A battalion of 800 men makes a column a quarter of a mile long, not counting the transport, sixteen limbered wagons, and two smaller vehicles called Maltese carts which trail behind. All these are loaded to overflowing with the official stores of the battalion and with everything that the Quartermaster has been able to scrounge in addition. With the transport are four cooking stoves on wheels, the field kitchens, in which dinners are being stewed in dixies as we go along. Behind them march the company cooks, stoking or stirring as they go, the only men in the battalion whose clothes can never by any force of discipline be kept clean. At the midday halt the 'cookers' come trundling up from the rear and are greeted with cheers. Again the orderlies for the day are called out, the dixies now full of stew, are carried to platoons while the men line up to fill their mess-tins, and each produces his own knife and fork. There may be green vegetables in the stew and there may be half a loaf of bread for each man, or 'two between five', and what is left he will keep for his tea. Every officer sees that his men are fed before going to his own mess, a picnic party set out under a tree by the officers' servants.*
>
> *There may be stragglers, or men who are about to straggle. That man who reported sick this morning but was sent by the doctor to 'light duty' looks as if he is going to faint. Though his mate on one side carries his rifle and his mate on the other holds his arm, he breaks step and throws everyone behind him out of step. 'Left-right left-right', bellows the sergeant. 'Pick it up there'. The subaltern, not so heavily loaded as his men, carries someone's rifle – out of bravado carries two rifles and the captain is just about to put the sick man on the 'company horse' when he is sent for and has to ride away to the head of the column. Everyone consults to get the sick man along because 'falling out on the march' is a military offence.... When at last we reach the billeting area in the dusk, no*

one notices that our rifles just slide off our shoulders as we order arms. Six hours
marching has brought us only fifteen miles, but we were up two hours before the march
began and there is much more to be done now we have arrived. [9]

So it was for the Pals on their seven days march through Artois as the snow showers
alternated with Spring sunshine on the circular route to Bethune.

The l8th West Yorks' delight increased when they reached Bethune 25 March. They
were accommodated in the town in the comparative luxury of Feuillade Barracks. The
16th, no doubt muttering about other's good luck, had to march on for a further two
miles nearer to the front line. They had to make do with billets at Beuvry on the La
Bassee road.

Bethune was still relatively unscathed and lay five miles behind the front line at La
Bassee. Before the war it was the prosperous centre of the coal mining area of the Lys
Valley. Apart from two brief days in Bethune in October, it was the first time the
original Pals had been near a European town for any length of time since leaving
Ripon sixteen long and eventful months before. Those careful enough not to lose too
much at Crown and Anchor had the pleasures of the town close at hand – estaminets
with 'erfs' and chips, bars with 'van blong et rouge', silk cards to send home to
sweethearts and family – and other, more dubious pleasures which were the subject
of heavy warnings from the M.O., Dr. Paddy Roche, and the new M.O. with the 18th
West Yorks, Dr. Alexander. War was also declared on the men's closest companions,
the lice. Candles were run up the seams of uniforms accompanied by the satisfying
pop of exploding chats. At last there was a chance to get a proper clean up.

Another cause for satisfaction on the day of arrival was the announcement that
Lieutenant Norman Priday of the 18th had been awarded the Military Cross for his
patrol work at Gommecourt and Rossignol Wood. The Pals were also delighted to find
themselves temporarily attached to the 62nd (West Riding) Division. Their arrival
meant that Bethune had become little Yorkshire, with no less than 15,000 Tykes
outnumbering the local residents. 62nd Division had been formed out of the reserve
battalions of the Territorial 49th (West Riding) Division under the command of a
former Gallipoli commander (and Yorkshireman) Major-General Walter Braithwaite.
The Division had yet to take part in a major offensive. Its brigades of KOYLI's, Dukes
and West Yorks eagerly pressed the Pals for details of the front. In turn the battle weary
Pals wanted to catch up with gossip of home from the Leeds and Bradford West Yorks
Battalions of 185 Brigade (the 2/5th, 2/6th, 2/7th and 2/8th West Yorks).[10] The original
Pals were delighted to recognise a few familiar faces. One of them, Jack Morris
(18/911) had been wounded at Serre on the 1 July. Quartermaster Sergeant Alf Scott
and Private Frank Burn (18/175) had helped to put his stretcher in the ambulance.
After two operations and a spell in England Jack was now back in Bethune with the
2/8th West Yorks. More wounds were to follow, but it was not the last reunion for Jack,
Alf and Frank. They were lifelong friends in the Pals Comradeship Association and
were still going back to France together in the 1970s.[11]

According to the Battalion War Diaries, the Pals were on standby reserve in case of
an enemy attack at La Bassee. Battalion Orders for 24 March made clear that on arrival
in Bethune,

All G.S. limbers loaded with S.A.A., grenades and mobilization stores will be kept loaded.
Water bottles must be filled and water carts re-filled, and the Battalion prepared to move
without additional transport at six hours notice under the orders of G.O.C. XI Corps.[12]

In practice, they were cards up the Commander in Chief's sleeve for two possible areas
of activity. As reserves from the 5th Army, their ultimate destination, either Arras or
Flanders, was to be determined by the outcome of strategic decisions at the very

highest level. This is made clear in Douglas Haig's diary entry for 12 March.

As to the British Army, my plan...is...to continue to make all preparations for attacks by 1st and 3rd Armies, keeping adequate reserves available either to support my 2nd Army (Ypres) or to exploit the success of our attacks near Arras. These reserves are obtained from the 5th Army.[13]

Haig had long been planning an attack in the north in the Flanders salient, but the new Prime Minister, Lloyd George, was equally determined to clip Haig's wings after the losses on the Somme and to subordinate him to the French commander, Nivelle. It was decided that priority be given to a French offensive on the Aisne in April with the British playing a supportive role at Arras. In the meantime, the Pals had come to one of the quietest sectors of the Western Front, as Walter Hare and his chum Smithy soon found out when they nearly walked into the German trenches. The scene could have been entitled 'Innocents Abroad'

Walter Hare.

We eventually landed at Beuvry which was a very quiet place and we had a good rest. One Sunday after Church Parade Smithy and I went for a long walk. We were suddenly halted by a soldier in a side trench just off the road who asked 'Where do you think you're going ? 'Just for a walk', we said. He told us that he was in the front line and 100 yards away was the enemy, and the village ahead we could see was La Bassee. I asked why it was so quiet and so different from the Somme. He seemed to think that there must be some arrangement, that if we did not shell La Bassee, they would not shell Beuvry.

37468 PRIVATE WALTER HARE, 16WY[14]

Battalion activity was largely restricted to weapons training and route marching, although according to Walter Hare the 16th were delighted to find that there was no space large enough for Colonel Croydon to indulge in his passion for Battalion drill.

There was plenty of time to enjoy Bethune, and a good time was had by all. A favourite rendezvous point was the impressive Belfry in the Grand Place. Much wine was drunk, many eggs and chips consumed, and as for the M.O.'s warnings, well, there is no evidence, nor shall we enquire. Professional photographers plied a prosperous trade both in studios and on the steps of the beautiful church of St. Vaast. Silk postcards and studio portraits were sent photographs home to family and friends.

Young Ernest Brook (18/761), an original Pal who avoided going over the top at Serre because his mother made a formal complaint that he was under age now rejoined the Battalion from the base at Etaples. He confirmed his return by getting a grim fierce looking studio portrait taken in full combat equipment with his mates.

Colonel Carter arranged for a series of group photographs of the 18th Battalion to be taken on the Church steps including all the officers with their French translator and two stray dogs the Battalion had adopted as mascots. Apparently the dogs attached themselves to the Battalion at Hebuterne and followed them everywhere. Perhaps the most appealing photograph is of the fearsome R.S.M. Scott

Officers of the 18th West Yorks on the steps of Bethune Cathedral, April 1917:

Front row: Captain Duckett, Major Robinson, Lieutenant Colonel Carter M.C., Lieutenant Dalley M.C. (Adjutant). Captain Peace M.C.

Second row: Lieutenant Stephenson, Captain Stanley (Padre), Lieutenant Whitaker (behind), Lieutenant Morgan, Second Lieutenant Jermyn (behind), Second Lieutenant Priday M.C. Second Lieutenant Daws, Lieutenant Leslie Wood, Second Lieutenant Hepple (behind) Second Lieutenant Bowden (behind) Lieutenant Clough, Lieutenant Frank Robinson (behind), Captain Alexander (Surgeon), Second Lieutenant De Lacy, Lieutenant Hammond, Second Lieutenant Clarkson, Captain Cockerham

Six standing at the back: Second Lieutenant Harris, Second Lieutenant Masefield, Lieutenant Toison (interpreter), Second Lieutenant Staff, Second Lieutenant Townend.

Lieutenant Colonel Carter and R.S.M. Scott in Bethune with HQ staff.

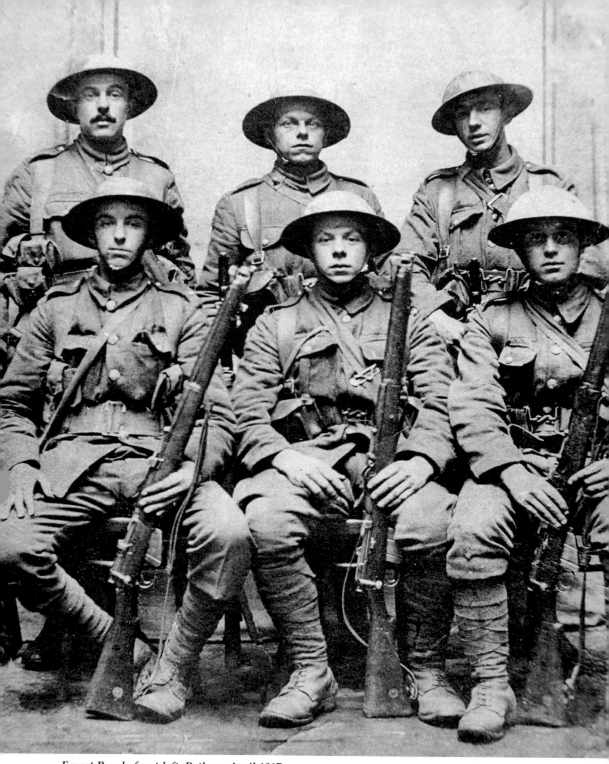

Ernest Brook, front left. Bethune April 1917.

with two other Warrant Officers tenderly posing with two French kiddies. The Belfry was to survive the 1918 offensive, but sadly the great medieval church of St. Vaast was reduced to rubble.

Seventeen days of comparative bliss passed by in a flash. Walter Hare enjoyed himself. 'I hoped we could stay there for the duration, but we were soon on our way to the Battle of Arras.'[15] On 12 April, three days after the start of the Arras offensive, 93 Brigade received orders to move south again. Their respite had lasted but a few short weeks. It might have been quiet in Bethune but in that time two events had taken place which shaped the world for generations to come. On the 11 March the Tsar of Russia abdicated, and on the 6 April the United States of America entered the war.

The Battle of Arras, launched in a snowstorm on Easter Monday 9 April, 1917, was essentially an attempt to divert German attention away from a much larger attack by the French under General Nivelle further south on the Aisne. According to Nivelle, his offensive would be the 'decisive blow' which would win the war. Haig was extremely sceptical, but as we have seen had to fall in with the plans

RSM Scott makes friends with the locals at Bethune. Corporal Garside, behind.

agreed between Lloyd George and the French. The Arras offensive, planned on a fifteen mile front from Vimy Ridge in the north to Croisilles in the south, would attempt to tie up German reserves to allow Nivelle a better opportunity to deliver his promise. For Haig it was more than this, it was a chance to break the Hindenburg line and take the strategically important town of Cambrai.[16]

Initially, the Battle of Arras promised the illusion of success. The Canadians spectacularly stormed Vimy Ridge, and the British achieved a rapid penetration of five miles either side of the Arras to Cambrai road. They had taken the Germans by surprise by assembling and then emerging from a network of underground wine storage tunnels and sewers under the city. On 12 April, General Allenby, commanding the 3rd Army, believed the breakthrough had come and ordered that, 'He wishes all troops to understand that the Third Army is now pursuing a defeated enemy and that risks must be freely taken'.[17] On the previous day in Bethune, the Pals had received orders to prepare to move south in readiness to give support. Allenby, believing in the breakthrough, sent in the cavalry only for them to be mown down at Monchy-le Preux. The German defence in depth system soon got to grips with the advance, and as the Pals moved south towards the thunder of the guns, it became clear that the breakthrough was an illusion. By the 14 April, Allenby's determination to push on, despite horrific losses and dreadful conditions of swirling snow in which units lost touch with each other, brought written protests from three of his divisional generals. Haig called a halt until there should be an improvement in the weather.

Nivelle's offensive finally began 16 April after several postponements. It was an unmitigated disaster. The Germans had full knowledge of the details of the attack, and within days it ground to a halt with over 200,000 casualties. Far from being the 'decisive blow' which would win the war, the Nivelle offensive nearly broke the French army as unit after unit began to mutiny and refuse orders to attack. Nivelle was eventually dismissed and Petain appointed to try to repair the damage.

As the situation on the Aisne grew more desperate, Haig reopened the offensive at Arras on 23 April. The spectacular gains of the opening phase of the battle were not repeated. Attrition once again became the order of the day and the Pals were to be part of this process.

At 6.00 a.m. on 12 April reveille was blown for the 18th West Yorks for the last time at Feuillade barracks. It was to be a busy day for everyone, especially Quartermaster Sergeant Alf Scott and his brother Harold, the Regimental Sergeant Major. The Transport Section under the genial giant Captain Cockerham were also early risers. Herbert Bradley and his chums in the section were all still original Pals from 1915. Battalion Order No. 67 shows how the 'Scott Machine' clicked into gear. No doubt anyone not wishing to have breakfast must have been genuinely sick.

> 6.00 to 7.30. – cleaning up of barracks, Breakfast 7.30, Sick Parade 7.30. Both blankets will be carefully rolled in bundles of 10, labelled, and delivered to Q.M.'s stores by 7.30 a.m. Officers' valises and Coy mess boxes will be sent to Q.M.'s stores by 8.30 a.m. Officers' Mess Cart will report at H.Q. Mess at 9.00 a.m. Maltese Cart will report to Medical Inspection room at 8.30 a.m. Coy Limbers will report at Q.M.'s stores at 8.30 a.m. for ammunition and Lewis guns, and pack ponies will be provided for 3 Lewis gun handcarts. The three handcarts will be allotted to D Company whose fourth gun and

Second Pals at Bethune. Captain Morris Clough (third from right, front row) has a distinctly 'Bairnsfather' look.

ammunition will be carried on C Coy's limber.[18]

The 18th paraded in full marching order at 9.55 a.m. for roll call. At 10.15 a.m. Colonel Carter, resplendent in astrakhan collared greatcoat and his favourite brand of cigar in hand, rode to the head of the Battalion. A quick nod to R.S.M. Scott, the ex-Grenadier Guardsman's word of command boomed down the length of the column, and they were off, determined to put on a good show for the locals and any 62nd Division men who happened to be watching. They had enjoyed their stay in Bethune, recovering in body and spirit. As the band struck up the lively strains of the regimental march, 'Ca Ira', the locals could be forgiven for thinking that this well known French Revolutionary song was some sort of tribute to their hospitality. The Pals, probably unaware of this, would no doubt have endorsed the sentiment if they had known.

At the same time similar scenes took place at Beuvry as the 16th moved out. An unusual feature of the march was that the Battalions now marched in threes rather than the usual fours, although no reason was given for this.[19] Over a period of two days the Bradford Battalions marched twenty miles due south to the Frevillers area just to the north of the Arras to St. Pol road. Here, two more weeks of intense training followed for the whole of 93 Brigade. Then on 28 April, the Brigade marched ten miles west toward the line, staying in huts in the Ecoivres support area five miles behind Vimy Ridge. Nearby, the twin towers of the ruined Abbey at Mont St. Eloi dominated the skyline. Dominating the sky were the constant comings and goings of triplanes of No 8 Squadron of the Royal Naval Air Service at Ecoivres airfield in a field just below the Abbey.

As a branch of the Royal Navy, the R.N.A.S. jealously guarded its independence, and the pilots at Ecoivres were a particularly lively bunch. On one occasion, when they weren't wearing their customary naval uniforms, two naked pilots leapt out of a swimming pool they had built using a tarpaulin to chase off an enemy plane. They returned to the pool 'mission accomplished'. The C.O. of No 8 Squadron, the 'Mad Major' Chris Draper, often flew between the twin towers of the Abbey as a stunt, and in the 1950's he was arrested after flying under fifteen bridges on the River Thames past the Houses of Parliament.[20] But perhaps the most famous pilot at Ecoivres was Raymond Collishaw, the third highest scoring British ace.[21]

The Pals were fascinated by the unusual tri-planes, and many of them envied the pilots who never had to foot slog it in muddy trenches. Yet in reality 'Black April' of 1917 had been a terrible month for the British pilots. A new German Ace, Baron Manfred von Richthofen, in command of *Jasta III* dominated the skies. He became a household name as the Red Baron with his Flying Circus. The faster more manoeuverable Albatross D.III aircraft gave the Germans air superiority over the Arras battlefield. The R.N.A.S. Sopwith tri-planes were the only aircraft capable of matching the Germans, and a heavy burden fell on the Ecoivres pilots to maintain an Allied air presence over the trenches. Indeed, after complaints by von Richthofen about the strength of the Albatross, the German aircraft designer Anthony Fokker observed the R.N.A.S. in action over the trenches to the north of Arras, and went on to design his famous Dr.I tri-plane with which von Richthofen is now more famously associated.

But the Pals had little time to watch aerobatics. Within twenty-four hours, and after a gap of nearly two months, they headed for the trenches again. At 8.00 p.m. on 29 April, 93 Brigade marched past Ecoivres airfield to relieve what was left of another unit with Naval connections, the Anson and Howe Battalions of 188 (Royal Marine) Brigade of 63rd Royal Naval Division, who were in the line at Gavrelle.[22] It was a long trek by what is now the D49 road to Gavrelle. Vimy Ridge loomed five miles ahead of them on their left as they made their way forward through Neuville St. Vaast, Thelus and Bailleul and then beyond Vimy to Hill 80. The sight of German observation

Band of the 16th West Yorks at Bethune. Charles Pickworth with leopard skin and Tim Wharton on his left.
Bandsmen in their role as stretcher bearers.

balloons gave the Pals an uncomfortable feeling that the enemy was fully aware of their movements.

The relief, completed in darkness at 2.25 a.m. on 30 April, was not easy. The Germans, aware of the relief, greeted the Pals with heavy shell fire as they moved into the line. Twenty men were wounded and seven killed including Private Charles William Burley (18/1320), an original Pal from 1915. Another original (16/840) Corporal Henry Roberts suffered a shattered elbow. He returned to the line as an officer with the East Yorks and won the M.C. four days before the end of the War.[23] Within three days the Bradford Battalions went 'over the top' again.

The second phase of the Battle of Arras opened on 23 April. The sweeping gains of 9 April were not repeated and the nature of the battle changed into a weary slogging match with every yard of territory bitterly contested. The British tactic now was to keep pressure on the Germans with a series of local attacks to 'tidy up' the line, and also to take pressure off the French who were in a sorry state after the failure of Nivelle's offensive on the Aisne. Some of the most bitter fighting took place in the ruined village of Gavrelle to the east of Vimy Ridge on the northern edge of the battlefield. On the 23 April the village was captured by the Royal Naval Division, but for the next six days of attack and counter-attack it changed hands several times. By the night of 29 April a thoroughly weary Royal Naval Division had managed to establish an outpost line of sorts beyond the village, but they had taken heavy casualties and were glad to be relieved by 93 Brigade. Able Seaman Downe of the Anson Battalion described the scene.

> *What a shambles! Dead in every bay. Eleven and Twelve platoons had been terribly battered by the barrage. I found eight men, the survivors of the platoon, clustered in the bay... discussing not the war, but the question of rations and water...our rations had not arrived on the previous day. In the early hours of the following day the West Yorkshires took over the trench, and our heavily depleted company trudged wearily back to Roclincourt.*[24]

German observation balloon.

By strange co-incidence one of the most gallant members of the Royal Naval Division to be relieved by the West Yorkshires later had a strong West Yorkshire connection himself. Surgeon McCracken, D.S.O. and Bar, of the Hood Battalion became a much loved G.P. in the Bronte village of Haworth near Keighley after the war. McCracken had tended the stricken poet Rupert Brooke en route to Gallipoli. At Gavrelle he was recommended for the Victoria Cross for rescuing 120 officers and men under heavy shell fire, although the award was the D.S.O. The recommendation came from his C.O. Commander Arthur Asquith, son of the Morley born former Prime Minister. Asquith again recommended McCracken for a V.C. at Passchendaele. Asquith was asked, however, to alter his recommendation to a Bar to McCracken's D.S.O. It then became apparent that Arthur himself had been recommended for the V.C. and that if both names were sent forward from the same battalion, neither would get it. Asquith's reply was characteristic of him: McCracken's name must go forward. They both got bars to their D.S.O.s.[25]

The two Bradford Battalions took up positions in a line running north to south over

Hill 80 north west of Gavrelle village. On the right, the 18th linked up with the Leeds Pals around the eastern edge of the village. On the left, the 16th linked up with the 13th East Yorks (T'Others) of 92 Brigade. The Durham Pals were in support behind the two Bradford Battalions. Small parties were pushed forward to take over outposts around the northern edge of the village.[27] General Ingles at 93 Brigade Headquarters was concerned at the extensive length of the line taken over by his Battalions, more than a mile and a half from the edge of Oppy Wood in the north to beyond Gavrelle in the south.[28] The Brigadier's concern increased on 30 April, when he received a 'Warning' Order from 31st Division for an impending attack by the Brigade. The order gave objectives for the attack but as yet no date. The attack involved two other Divisions (the 2nd in the North and the 9th in the South) in addition to the 31st.[29] On the face of it, the objectives appeared to be relatively straightforward, and as defenders of the High Command have frequently pointed out lessons had been learned from the fiasco of 1st July.[30] This time there would be no lengthy preliminary bombardment to alert the enemy, although three 'feint' barrages were to take place for short periods on 1 and 2 May. The advance would be under cover of a carefully calculated creeping barrage and would take place in the dark. 93 Brigade were to attack and occupy the German first and second lines beyond the villages of Oppy and Gavrelle. They were then to construct machine gun strong-points beyond the second line in readiness for any counter-attack. The plan involved a four wave attack, with the first wave taking the first enemy line, the second and third waves pushing on to the second line, and the fourth wave mopping up before joining the men already in the second line.[31]

The Divisional Order (No. 137), with its subsequent additions and alterations, makes fascinating reading and in its thoroughness it is an impressive document. It runs to several pages detailing such items as rations, casualties, burial of the dead and salvage arrangements. The order also reveals the attitude of the Divisional Command to the rank and file soldier. No doubt General Wanless O'Gowan must have grunted with approval as he read the section on stragglers.

Stragglers Battle Straggler Posts, each consisting of one M.M.P. and 3 men will be established at... N.C.O. in charge of Post will be responsible for:

Taking full particulars of all stragglers before sending them into Advanced Dressing Station, so that evidence may be forthcoming if disciplinary action is subsequently taken.

Taking particular notice of stragglers without arms or equipment and recording whether in his opinion such stragglers are justified in being so deficient.

Collecting the arms and equipment of men too exhausted to carry them and giving certificate to that effect to the men'.[32]

Pity the poor straggler. No doubt the exhausted men were duly grateful to receive their certificates.

At 2.00 p.m. 1 May, thirty-six hours after getting into the line, the four colonels, Croydon and Carter of the Bradfords, Taylor of the Leeds and Cheyne of the Durhams, were called to 93 Brigade Headquarters to be given details of the attack. Again no time or date was given and it was not until 3.20 a.m. 2 May that Zero Hour was announced for 3.45 a.m. on the following day.[33] What had appeared to be a straightforward plan turned out to be extremely complicated in order to accommodate the artillery schedules of neighbouring divisions. There were to be involved manoeuvres in the dark with the 16th West Yorks moving to the left in front of the Durhams, and the 18th having to split in two to fill the gaps left by the 16th on the left and to link up with the Leeds Pals on the right. The men were stretched out over a very wide frontage and were expected to cover a distance of between 800 and 1,000 yards to reach the second objective. The planners failed to anticipate, or chose to disregard, that the attack would

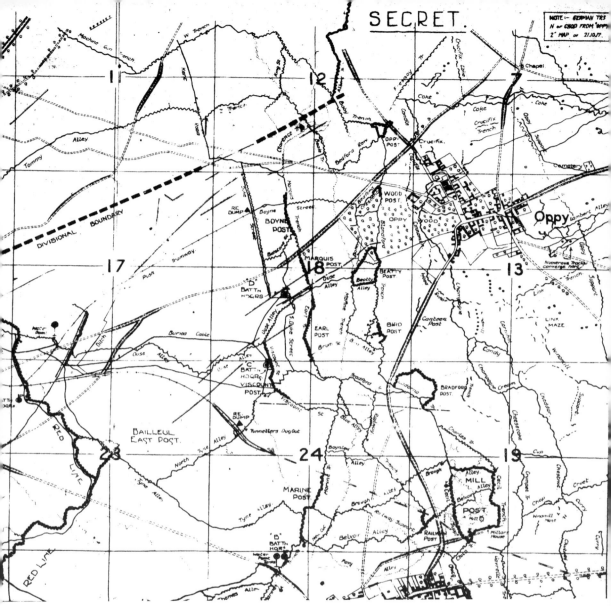

Trench map from 18th West Yorks war diary dated April 1917.

take place in bright moonlight with the men making easy silhouetted targets for the enemy machine gunners.

Colonel Carter's post attack report succinctly set out the complications and problems facing the Pals: 93 Brigade's attack was divided into two halves, the RIGHT (or Southern) and the LEFT (or Northern) attack. The barrage of the left attack was only to move at the rate of 100 yards in four minutes, so as to conform with the brigade on the left attacking OPPY. The barrage on the right was to advance at the rate of 100 yards in 2 minutes so as to conform with Brigade on the right. The Battalion was divided up for the attack into two half-battalions, one-half on the left of the 15th West Yorks, and the other half on the right of the 16th West Yorks, who were respectively on the right and left of this Battalion. The Battalion frontage was bounded on the NORTH by a line between B24 Central and B19 Central and on the SOUTH by a line running

E. and W. through C.25b93...

> I had thus a Battalion frontage of 900 yards, involving (with a double-company front in four waves) a company frontage of 450 yards, and a platoon frontage of 225 yards. Estimating platoon strength as an average of thirty, including officers and N.C.O.s, this would have meant an extension of sixteen yards if normal formation had been adopted. I therefore decided that instead of the first wave being in two lines there should be only one, which reduced the extension to eight yards.
>
> LIEUTENANT COLONEL H.F.G. CARTER, M.C., 18WY[34]

Such complications meant it was easy for things to go wrong and for communications to break down. In such circumstances the Pals were extremely vulnerable to an enemy counter-attack.

At 9.00 p.m. 1 May, the first of the British 'feint' barrages screamed over the Pals' heads, provoking an immediate and very accurate response from the enemy. As everyone kept their heads down, a few brave souls led by Second Lieutenant Bowden went over the top to put pegs out in readiness for tapes to lead to the forming up lines on the following night. [35] Whether the Germans were aware of the pegs is uncertain, but the 'feint' barrage did alert them to the possibility of an impending attack. Heavy enemy shelling continued throughout what must have been an extremely uncomfortable night for the Pals. Both Bradford Battalions suffered casualties (ten killed and a greater number wounded), and one poor man in the 18th was so terrified that he was driven to commit a self-inflicted wound.[36] On 2 May, more 'feint' barrages followed at 4.00 a.m. and 4.00 p.m., provoking yet another massive response from the enemy.[37] Whatever benefit may have been expected from the feints, no account seems to have been taken of the effect on our own troops. The predicable enemy response made it virtually impossible for the Pals Battalions to get any rest in the thirty-six hours preceding the attack. At Serre, the men at least had a hot meal and arrived in the trenches relatively fresh on the eve of the assault. At Gavrelle they endured three days and nights of poor food, fatigue, tension and constant enemy shelling as the minutes dragged by towards zero hour at 3.45 a.m. on the 3 May.

At 10.30 p.m. 2 May, Lieutenants Bowden and Dams of the 18th West Yorks again went out into No Man's Land, this time to lay out tapes leading to the Assembly positions. Signallers followed with their telephone cables and by 11.15 p.m. communications centres had been established.[38] Despite the dangers of the impending attack, it must have been a relief for the men to at last get moving towards the assembly positions. Their relief was quickly tempered by apprehension. At midnight the clouds lifted and bright moonlight began to illuminate No Man's Land[39]. The Germans must have had a perfect view of British silhouettes as the Pals moved into the assembly positions. As Lieutenant Bowden finished laying out the tapes ready for the attack in No Man's Land, his heart must have sank:

> Soon after I had finished taping, an enemy aeroplane flew low over the line and fired some white lights along the tape. It is fairly evident that the enemy knew we were making an attack, as he shelled the trenches where our men were assembling so heavily that getting into position on the tape was badly delayed. The aeroplane which I mentioned earlier must have seen the tape. Owing to the bright moonlight any movement was seen.
>
> LIEUTENANT C. H. BOWDEN, 18WY[40]

It was extremely unusual for an aeroplane to fly at night in the First War. The fact that it did, reveals the brightness of the moonlight and the high state of alert on the German side. The Germans clearly knew something was afoot, and the white flares would give their artillery a perfect bearing on the attack when it came. Colonel Carter's report after the attack graphically details the course of events as the 18th moved into position:

> *Owing to my dispositions in the line, a good deal of side-slipping and manouevering had to be done in the trenches to allow my men to come up and get out on to the tape. By 12.30 a.m. both my companies (A and B) had passed by Battn H.Q. at B.3O.a.89 ready to move into the trenches vacated by the 16th West Yorks. All men had been issued with haversack rations, bombs, rifle grenades, flares, etc.*
>
> *1.15 a.m... The moon was very bright up to 3.15 a.m., and at 1.15 a.m. I went up personally to superintend the getting-out of the left companies (A and B) on the right of the 16th West Yorks. Owing to the moonlight a certain number of men on the right must have been seen, and came under heavy machine gun fire. I then ordered the companies to move out at a point further down the line which was not then covered by machine gun fire.*
>
> *2.00 a.m... At 2.00 a.m. the enemy put up a barrage lasting until 2.20 a.m. which did a certain amount of damage in our trenches and killed and wounded some of my men who were just about to move out and line up.*
>
> *3.00 a.m,... At 3.00 a.m. an S.O.S. call went up on the left (to the N.) in the direction of OPPY WOOD, and a heavy enemy barrage with machine gun fire came down from 3.00 to 3.17 a.m. The men, however, did not hang back, and I myself saw them crawl out and get into position quite unhesitatingly and fearlessly under heavy barrage, in some cases even treading over the dead bodies of their comrades in doing so.*
>
> *3.20 a.m...By 3.20 a.m. B Coy reported in position, and in five minutes 'A' Coy were also in position. At 3.40 a.m. C Coy were reported in position, and I heard later through the 15th West Yorks that D Coy were in position, the runner from D Coy being slightly wounded and coming in later.*
>
> *The lining-up on the tape had certainly been delayed slightly owing to the moonlight and the machine gun fire and artillery fire which resulted, the enemy barrage from 2.00 a.m. to 2.20 a.m. and 3.00 a.m. to 3.20 a.m. being very severe; but I am satisfied that the whole of the Battalion was in position by 3.40 a.m.*
>
> LIEUTENANT COLONEL H.F.G. CARTER, M.C., 18WY[41]

The 16th had also taken heavy punishment from the enemy artillery barrages. They had other problems too, which were to prove of the utmost significance: on the left flank they failed to make contact with the East Yorks of 92nd Brigade.[42]

At 3.44 a.m., a minute before zero hour, the British barrage broke out to provide a curtain of fire ahead of the men. 93 Brigade War Diary, recorded the barrage was, 'Simply magnificent'.[43] Promptly at 3.45 a.m., having endured so much already, the Pals leapt up and moved towards the German lines. Fortunately the moon was now obscured by cloud, but the pitch darkness, combined with a ground mist and smoke from the barrage, made it difficult to keep contact on such a widespread frontage. The complexity of the plan led to the 16th and 18th men getting mixed up and losing their sense of direction.[44] Despite the problems, most of the 16th made relatively good progress behind the creeping barrage at a pace of 100 yards every four minutes. By 4.00 a.m. the first wave reached the first German line – only to find it lightly held and largely deserted apart from a few corpses. A few prisoners were taken and sent to the rear.[45] As the first wave stayed to mop up the first objective, the second and third waves continued to press on to the second German line behind the cover of the barrage. Captain Parker, in charge of D Company of the 16th West Yorks reported: 'Upon our approach the enemy was seen to leave his trench in large numbers, and retire in disorder. Our men fired at them inflicting many casualties.'[46]

Sergeant Albert Sands (16/568), who had been Mentioned in Despatches at Rossignol Wood, leapt down into the trench and charged into a dug out with a German pistol he had just picked up. His son, the actor Leslie Sands, recalled what happened next in a letter to the author, and illustrates how the brutality of war, kill or be killed, can affect otherwise loving and good natured men.

A young German was huddled, petrified, against the opposite wall, his rifle on the floor at his feet. As my father entered he pulled a photograph from his breast-pocket and held it out in silent supplication. It showed his flaxen-haired wife and their young son. My father took pity on him and jerked his head towards the open air. The man fled, and my father went on to search an inner compartment. He told me: When I went further on inside to look round, I felt a funny feeling and suddenly had to look over my shoulder and there he was, coming at me with a bayonet in his fist grinning all over his face. I shot him dead, Les, on the spot. And then I kicked his face in, for being what he was.[47]

Sergeant Jack Manley (16/913), one of the original Pals, was a tough hard stoker at Whitehead's Mill in Laisterdyke. Boxing under the name of 'Stoker Manley', he was the professional Lightweight Champion of Yorkshire at a time when professional boxing was a much bigger more popular sport than it is now.[48] His brother, also a professional boxer, had been killed earlier in the war. Jack was wounded at Serre but quickly recovered and rejoined the Battalion. Now he led the charge into the German second line. He was less lucky than Albert Sands and it was to be his last fight. Walter Hare was with him:

I was with C Company for this attack, with the first wave. I was on the extreme left of the wave – and I noticed there was no other battalion on the left of me, just a big gap. Captain Ashforth was with us, he was a big chap and he seemed to be a capable officer.

We managed to get to the enemy's front line, and then to the support trench. As we got into a communication trench and went round a traverse, with Sergeant Manley in front of me and a Corporal behind me, there were two rifle shots. Sergeant Manley was hit right through the head and fell down dead, right in front of me. The Corporal was wounded in the arm. It's strange really, but he laughed and waved his arm at me and said, "I've got a blighty – I'll see you in York". How they missed hitting me I don't know. The Corporal began to move back and told me to move back too as we seemed to be isolated with no other of our troops anywhere near us.

37468 PRIVATE WALTER HARE, 16WY[49]

16/913 Sergeant Jack Manley. Yorkshire Lightweight champion.

Back in the first line it had become apparent that the German decision to abandon their trenches in the face of the Pals' attack was neither cowardice nor lack of fight, it was simply good tactics in expectation of the British attack. According to Second Lieutenant Walton of the First Pals, there were dead Germans in the trench, but there were also what appeared to be dummies giving the impression that the trench was more heavily defended than it really was. Shortly after 4.00 a.m. German artillery began to fire on their own front line trenches with absolute precision. What had been a captured German trench became a death-trap, and casualties began to mount.[50]

Daylight began to break at 4.20 a.m. Further forward in the German second line, the initial euphoria of Captain Parker the commander of D Company was beginning to wear off. He saw that behind him the first wave was taking a terrific pounding from the German artillery. His group was also coming under sniper fire from the rear, suggesting that either the mopping up operation had not been completely successful, or that somehow the enemy had worked round behind him from the left. As visibility improved, so Parker's anxiety rose. He realised that no contact had been made with the East Yorks on the left and that he was isolated in an extremely exposed position with an open flank. Parker had about eighty men of his own company, a few from A Company with a wounded Captain Illingworth, and a few more from B Company along with Captain Ashforth of C Company who was also wounded.[51]

Parker pushed his Lewis gun teams well forward to provide cover, and the men began digging desperately to deepen and consolidate a very shallow trench. It was a well nigh impossible task given the numbers of the men and the chalky nature of the ground.[52] At 5.00 a.m. Parker still retained some optimism judging by his initial reaction when a party of Germans was sighted, but this optimism was quickly disabused.

> *The enemy was seen approaching our trench from half right in extended order. Their strength was approximately 100, and they appeared to be in three waves. We thought they were coming to surrender and waved our arms for them to come on. Whereupon they opened fire as they advanced, we retaliated with Lewis guns and Rifles. Many of the enemy fell and the remainder fell back in disorder.* CAPTAIN P.C. PARKER, M.C. 16WY[53]

The mixed force of Pals suffered casualties in the attack. Nevertheless, they inflicted heavy casualties on the enemy and succeeded in driving them off. Sergeant Agar of A Company was seen to wipe out about sixty of the enemy with his Lewis gun.[54] Shortly after the attack was driven off at 5.00 a.m. four of the Second Pals arrived carrying in the heavy figure of Captain Duckitt, one of the original Pals, who was badly wounded in the leg.[55] The men continued digging for a few minutes until they were again pinned down by heavy machine gun fire and forced to dive for cover. At 6.00 a.m. the enemy were seen to wave a blanket at two German aeroplanes which then flew low over the Pals, obviously observing for the artillery. The remaining Pals had a distinct feeling that the vultures were hovering over them. Sure enough, they came under artillery fire, and an attempt to signal to the rear for support with a rifle shutter ended rapidly when it was riddled with bullets.[56] The failure to link up with the East Yorks towards Oppy Wood, and to link up with anyone on the right, had now become of the utmost significance. Both flanks were in the air and the Pals faced yet another heavy counter-attack on their right flank. Further casualties were suffered, including Captain Illingworth who was severely wounded. At the time it was thought that Illingworth had been killed, but it was later discovered that he survived and was a prisoner of war in Germany.[57] The three senior surviving officers decided the time had come to cut their losses and to get away before they were completely wiped out. Parker, later to be awarded the Military Cross for his part in the action, described what happened:

> *At 7.35 a.m. the enemy came over in waves on our right flank and the M.G. fire on our left front and right near became intense and we had many casualties. For about ten minutes we held the enemy off with M.G. and rifle fire, but the enemy continued their advance in considerable strength. I held a hurried consultation with Captain Duckitt of the 18th W.Y. and Captain Ashforth, and we decided it was best to withdraw from the left, as in a few minutes we should have been completely cut off. Word was passed on from the left and the withdrawal completed, the men extending out as they ran. Heavy M.G. fire was opened from both flanks and front as we withdrew to our original front line, which we commenced to man, and I then reported the circumstances to my C.O.*
> CAPTAIN P.C. PARKER, M.C., 16WY[58]

Captain Charles Duckitt was a Bradford man, and at forty, one of the oldest men in the

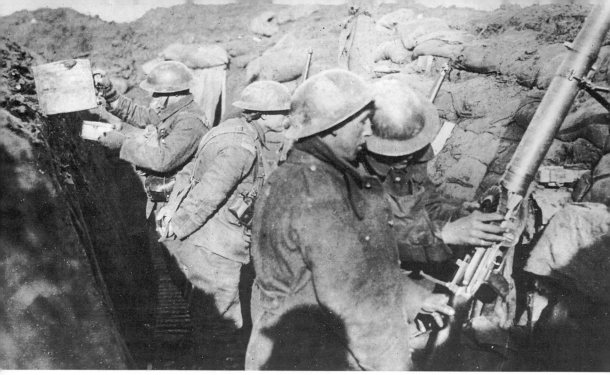

Lewis gunners, men of the 31st Division at Oppy Wood.

Second Pals. His large familiar cheery figure made him a popular officer. Duckitt, and the men carrying him in, were an easy exposed target. Sadly, they were killed in the retreat. The Captain's body was never identified and his name appears on the Arras Memorial.[59] When Captain Parker and what was left of the men eventually reported back to Colonel Croydon, they discovered that 16th Battalion H.Q. no longer existed. They found the Colonel holding on to an improvised line with a small mixed force just beyond the railway to the north of Gavrelle village. Whilst Parker had been hanging to the captured bit of Windmill support trench in the German second line, things had gone badly for the rest of the two Bradford Battalions.[60]

At 3.45 a.m. at 16th Battalion Headquarters, Colonel Croydon had been pleased with the way his men had gone forward in good order, keeping close up to the creeping barrage at a distance of about sixty yards. To follow a creeping barrage was a real test of nerve. The theory was that the curtain of fire wiped out the opposition, but it was not uncommon for shells to drop short – in modern parlance 'friendly fire' or 'Blue on Blue'.[61] It was just as well the 16th Battalion had got off on time, for within four minutes of zero hour the entire British front line and the assembly points came under retaliatory heavy shell fire. Battalion Headquarters also came under heavy machine gun fire from both the left and the right. It became apparent to an alarmed Colonel Croydon that the East Yanks on his left had been held up, and that a gap was rapidly opening up on the left flank.[62] It was obvious that Battalion Headquarters would be vulnerable to an enemy counter-attack coming down the trench system from the north, and that the Pals who had gone forward in the advance could be cut off from the near. Croydon realised that the whole of 93 Brigade faced a potential disaster and quickly wired an S.O.S. back to General Ingles. The Brigadier responded by ordering the Durham Pals to re-inforce the Bradfords, but it took time for this to be carried out and offered no immediate respite to the West Yorks in their exposed position.[63]

Croydon ordered his young adjutant, Second Lieutenant Joseph Stanley, to take two parties of bombers made up of battalion signallers, runners and servants to block the trench and to prevent any such happening.[64] Although not an original member of the Pals, the young second lieutenant was a Bradford man from Undercliffe. He joined the Bradford Territorials (lst/6th West Yorks) as an under age private and served in Flanders in April, 1915. By the time he had reached nineteen, the legal age for foreign service, he was a sergeant. He was commissioned shortly after his twentieth birthday and joined the First Pals on 1 October 1916. His ability was soon recognised and he was given the responsible role of adjutant.[65] On 3 May,1917, the twenty year old Stanley displayed leadership and courage of the very highest order. His battalion, along with the Second Pals and the Leeds Pals, suffered terrible casualties, but without him it is likely they would have been totally wiped out. What was a desperate situation would have become a total disaster. The colonel's decision to send Stanley's party to block the trenches to the north was quickly justified. Shortly after 4.00 a.m. an enemy party was seen coming down Wood trench from the direction of Oppy Wood – behind the advancing British infantry's open flank – and heading straight for Battalion Headquarters. German air superiority, which allowed for unchallenged observation, was paying off on the ground as well as in the air. After letting them pass, Lieutenant Stanley jumped over the parapet and bombed them from behind, breaking up the counter-attack and taking eighteen prisoners.[66]

For the first time in the battle, Colonel Croydon made contact with troops of the East Yorks on his left shortly after 6.00 a.m. – but in far from desirable circumstances. They appeared from the north – driven back down the trench system by a massive enemy counter attack from Oppy Wood. This was part of the same counter attack faced by Parker's group who were out at the second objective up towards Link Maze. Colonel Croydon, ably assisted by Private Fred Hallam (43484), got hold of the retreating men and posted them in shell holes to make a further line of defence behind the old railway line which ran diagonally across the trenches north of Gavrelle village.

For a second time Stanley and his team of 'amateur' bombers performed heroics saving the situation in Wood Trench to the north of Battalion H.Q. group. They again climbed out of the trench and worked their way round over the top to attack the enemy from the rear. When they ran out of Mills Bombs, Fred Hallam again come to the fore, volunteering to run the gauntlet under heavy fire to get a further supply. He scrambled back to Battalion H.Q. over the top and was in the open dodging bullets for over 100 yards before returning weighed down by a fresh supply of bombs.[67] Hallam succeeded in getting back to Stanley's group and joined in another bombing attack. More prisoners were taken, making a total of fifty, and the bombers managed to inflict heavy casualties as the enemy were forced to retire back again towards Oppy Wood. Stanley was wounded in the last exchange, but when he got back to Battalion H.Q. he insisted on staying when the wounded were being evacuated during a brief lull in the fighting.[68] Like Lieutenant Stanley, Private Hallam was in the drafts joining the Pals to fill the Somme gaps in the Autumn of 1916. Both were decorated for gallantry for their parts in breaking up the enemy counter attack. Joseph Stanley was awarded the D.S.O. and Fred Hallam the D.C.M.[69] It is no exaggeration to say that most of 93 Brigade would have been wiped out if they had failed. Stanley survived the War, but was severely wounded and invalided out in October, 1917. Like many others he had a shortened life, dying at the early age of forty-four in 1941. The citation for his D.S.O. reads:

> *For conspicuous gallantry and determination during an enemy counter-attack. By his fearlessness in leading a bombing attack under very heavy fire he completely frustrated the enemy's attack upon our trenches, cut off their line of retreat, and captured eighteen prisoners with the aid of two of his bombers.*

LONDON GAZETTE 18TH JULY, 1917

For Fred Hallam who bravely supported his young officer, the citation to his Distinguished Conduct Medal read:

43484 Private F. Hallam, For conspicuous gallantry and devotion to duty. During a hostile counter-attack he showed marked bravery and initiative in collecting and re-organising a number of men belonging to other units. He subsequently displayed splendid courage and ability in assisting his adjutant to form and lead a bombing party. He fetched the bombs himself, at immense personal risk under heavy fire over an exposed distance of 100 yards. LONDON GAZETTE 18TH JULY, 1917

For a short while things quietened down as the enemy infantry retreated back towards Oppy Wood. Croydon took stock of the situation knowing that what was left of his small force of odds and ends was still in an extremely vulnerable position. As we have seen, Captain Parker's group re-appeared and confirmed what Croydon had already guessed – that the advance had failed. But he still had a duty not to abandon the attacking waves who had gone out at 3.45 a.m. and felt he must provide cover for them as they straggled back. Even more vital from a strategic point of view, he also had to do what he could to stem any German attempt to breakthrough and re-capture Vimy Ridge. That this was a real possibility is revealed in Divisional records.

8.38 a.m. Divisional instructions – GAVRELLE to be held and if the enemy effect an entrance they are to be driven out. 3.50 p.m. Division telephone to say a Staff Officer is coming round to give Corps Orders to dig 3 lines and wire 3 lines because there is every indication that the enemy is going to make an attempt to take VIMY. [70]

During the lull Croydon managed to get the wounded out and got the remaining men to begin to consolidate the shell holes ready for another attack. He again wired brigade

The attack at Gavrelle.

for re-inforcements. Brigadier Ingles, in turn, wired Division who replied that the 12th Yorks and Lancs (Sheffield Pals) from 94 Brigade was coming up to give assistance.[71]

Battalion signallers and runners are often forgotten in the descriptions of infantry attacks. Yet their role was essential and extremely dangerous. Telephone cables were continually destroyed by artillery fire, but signallers had to keep going to patch up the lines regardless of the enemy barrage. In the 18th Battalion, Colonel Carter issued his own 'Certificate of Merit' cards to the signallers, to the runners and to Regimental Sergeant Major Harold Scott[72]. Signal Sergeant George Halstead (18/407) was later to receive the Distinguished Conduct Medal for his part in the Gavrelle affair.

For conspicuous gallantry and devotion to duty. He continually went out under very heavy fire in order to repair and maintain communications.

London Gazette, 9th July, 1917[73]

Lt Joseph Stanley DSO, age 19.

Communications were a continuous problem and breakdown of communications played a significant part in many of the disasters of that terrible war. As the 'Fog of War' descended, Brigade and Divisional H.Q. could only grope with tactics for lack of accurate information. It was not until after the Gavrelle offensive that Walter Hare saw his first primitive wireless set, 'a massive heavy affair with a giant accumulator – it took a bit of shifting'.[74] At 8.00 a.m. Colonel Croydon finally managed to make contact with Colonel Carter whose 18th Battalion Battle H.Q. was a few hundred yards further south close to the main Gavrelle-Arras road. The two Bradford C.O.'s agreed on the desperate nature of the situation and that machine guns should be pushed towards Hill 80 on the left to prevent a flanking attack from the direction of Oppy Wood.[75] No sooner had Colonel Croydon returned to his position, where the men were still trying to consolidate shell holes, than they again came under even more heavy artillery fire.

This made the position untenable, so I decided to withdraw my small force (which was becoming very weak owing to heavy casualties), slowly, to a better position in rear of Railway, selected by Lieutenant Colonel Carter. I then sent the men back, two at a time, to the new position, where they dug themselves in on a front of seventy yards.

On arriving at this position I was knocked down and struck on the helmet by the burst of a shell, which gave me slight concussion. I was taken to Colonel Carter's dug-out where I had to rest, leaving Colonel Carter temporarily in command of the situation.

At the end of four hours I had sufficiently recovered to resume command. We then received reinforcements from the D.L.I.

Lieutenant Colonel A.C. Croydon D.C.M., 16WY[76]

As we have seen, the Second Pals also had an extremely sticky time after the launch of the attack at 3.45 a.m. Colonel Carter described the start of their attack:

(ZERO)...the whole line moved straight forward, keeping close to the barrage at a distance of about sixty yards. At this time the moon had set and it was extremely dark. One could hardly see a yard in front of one for smoke and dust.

Within thirty seconds of our barrage starting, an extremely heavy enemy barrage of 8-in. 5.9, and lighter caliber came down on our front line trenches, and continued incessantly until 12 noon. Machine guns from all directions also opened fire almost simultaneously with the enemy barrage.

Lieutenant Colonel H.F.G. Carter, M.C., 18WY[77]

One of the first to be hit was Private John McGrath (18/230), whose arm was shattered by shrapnel. John survived the war, and in 1986 survived the tragic Bradford City fire. At the time of his death in 1990, he was the last known survivor of the original Second Bradford Pals.[78] Despite other early casualties, the 18th attack pressed on, and Colonel Carter outlined its progress:

> In most cases on the left the two objectives seem to have been reached by those whose business it was to get there, but owing to the heavy enemy fire, especially from machine guns, these lines were considerably depleted by the time they had reached the second objective. So far as I can see, touch had not been kept too well. This, I think, is easily accounted for by the extreme darkness, and the mass of smoke and dust from our own and the enemy barrage, and the extremely wide extension. Two consecutive casualties in the line left the men 24 yards apart, which would easily explain loss of direction and touch.
>
> LIEUTENANT COLONEL H.F.G. CARTER, M.C.,18WY[79]

The dust was produced by the enemy barrage hitting the bricks and masonry of ruined buildings in Gavrelle village. An aerial photograph taken 24 April kept as a scrap-book souvenir by the Brigade Clerk and former First Pal, Corporal Laurie Greenwood (16/112), shows most of the village buildings still with a fairly substantial structure. However, by 3 May, the buildings had been reduced to the heaps of rubble now depicted in the Royal Naval Division Memorial at the western entrance to the village.[80] As the 18th tried to press on through the darkness, blinding smoke and dust, they now came under machine gun fire,

> On the right the right-half Battalion did not seem to have got very much further than the first objective. In one or two cases they were held up by wire, but were mostly wiped out by machine gun fire before they reached the first objective.[81]
>
> As the leading troops became more extended, a new problem reared its head and finally brought the advance to a halt. Enemy troops captured in the early stages of the attack now began to realise how exposed the Pals were. In the initial stages the attack seems to have been a success, but it failed through lack of driving power, as our men took quite a number of prisoners, and others were about to give themselves up until they realised that they had no more waves coming over, and that the few oddments of men in the trenches were the only ones they had to deal with. This at once altered the situation, and our men were practically surrounded in many cases.
>
> LIEUTENANT COLONEL H.F.G. CARTER, M.C.,18WY[82]

A few members of the 18th did manage to get through to the enemy second line and went on to capture the Windmill, the final objective and the pivotal point of the attack. As at Rossignol Wood two months before, the thrust of the final attack was led by a small body of seven original Pals from different companies who by some strange co-incidence now found themselves together again. The Windmill changed hands no less than six times during the course of day, but its first capture was accomplished by a tiny but incredibly courageous group consisting entirely of 1914 and 1915 Bradford volunteers. Their efforts epitomise all that was best about the original Bradford Pals.

At the front was Lieutenant Frank Robinson, the Bradford and Yorkshire County Rugby player. With him was Company Sergeant Major Percy Nicholson (18/149), acting Company Sergeant Major Arthur Tyne (18/94), and the Lewis gun team of Corporal William Palframan (16/1107). When they got to the Windmill they found any further progress blocked by uncut wire four yards deep.[83] According to Company Sergeant Major Tyne:

> Casualties were caused by being sniped in the rear. Whilst holding the trench the Boche massed in great numbers on the ridge slightly half right. The German trenches were not good trenches, but there were a lot of machine guns there.

18/94 C.S.M. Arthur Tyne [84]

As the Germans launched their counter attack the outnumbered seven knew they would have to retreat. Lieutenant Robinson was killed as he struggled to destroy one of the German machine guns.[85] Further back the German prisoners turned on their out-numbered captors and over-powered them. The leading waves found themselves coming under fire not only from the front but also from the rear as newly emboldened ex-prisoners re-joined the fight. Those few members of the 18th who did reach the second objective found very little cover, just an extremely shallow trench.

> *It was impossible to lift one's head above it for machine gun fire.*

18/94 C.S.M. Arthur Tyne[86]

The tables had turned and several of the Pals were now taken prisoner. A bad situation now became critical. The 16th to Colonel Carter's left came under heavy counter attack from the direction of Oppy Wood to the North, and contact was lost with the Leeds Pals on the right. At 5.05 a.m. a runner appeared at Carter's H.Q. with a message from Colonel Croydon – the l6th's situation was desperate and could re-inforcements be sent? All the hard-pressed Carter could do was wire on the 16th's message on to brigade.[87]

> *Isolated groups began to re-appear at Battalion Headquarters and confirmed the extent of the confusion and exposed nature the Bradford Battalions. Just before 6.00 a.m. Second Lieutenant Harris of A Company came back with twenty men and ten prisoners, but reported that the advance parties of the West Yorks were surrounded.*[88]

An alarmed Carter went forward to investigate the situation for himself and discovered that his anxiety was well founded. Only two of his machine gun teams were still active, and his front was in an extremely vulnerable position.[89] At 6.08 a.m. a massive German barrage smashed into Gavrelle village, an almost certain prelude to a German counter-attack. Five minutes later a runner managed to get back with further dismal news, this time from Company Sergeant Major Nicholson (18/149) of D Company, reporting that all the officers were missing, the majority of the men were casualties, and that the C.S.M. was himself wounded. At 6.20 Carter returned to Battalion H.Q. and reported by wire to Brigadier Ingles how disorganised and serious the situation was. He emphasised the need for reinforcements to be placed on Hill 80 to prevent the expected enemy counter-attack outflanking him and reported that he had lost touch with the Leeds Pals on the right.[90] Just as Stanley and Hallam of the 16th had made a timely contribution further to the north, now another of the original Pals played a key role in averting complete disaster. Corporal Willie Palframan (16/1107) had joined the First Pals but was later transferred to the 18th. With his Lewis gun team, he had gone over the top with B Company at 03.45 a.m. and managed to get to the Windmill with Lieutenant Robinson. Two hours after the start of the attack, Willie and a few of his team managed to fight their way back to the start line with their precious Lewis gun and set up a defensive position.

Corporal Greenwood, Brigade clerk.

At 06.10 a.m. Corporal Palframan sent a runner back to H.Q. and asked for orders. When told to 'hold on', he did so with a vengeance. He held on to his exposed forward position throughout the morning and on into the afternoon stopping several attempts by the Germans to force a breakthrough. His determination bought time for the consolidation of other defence positions further back, and for the Durham Light

Infantry to bring up fresh troops as reinforcements. Corporal Willie Palframan was awarded the Distinguished Conduct Medal. His citation read:

> *When all his officers and his company sergeant-major had become casualties, he was isolated with a few men from the remainder. He held on, organising fire from a Lewis gun, and sending back valuable information to battalion headquarters. When subsequently outflanked he fought his way back with great skill and determination.*
>
> LONDON GAZETTE 18TH JULY, 1917[91]

Just before 7 o'clock Second Lieutenant Dams, who had laid out the tapes for the attack, also managed to get back to Battalion H.Q. The young officer was extremely lucky not to be a casualty and his experiences reflected the see-saw nature of events. During the attack, he had got close to the Windmill and taken a few prisoners. He was then taken prisoner himself when the enemy counter-attacked but managed to escape during a barrage and collected ten Pals stragglers on the way back.[92]

The only contact Colonel Carter had with the Leeds Pals to his right was a desperate S.O.S. signal at 7.32 on the power buzzer. The only possible response was to pass it on to Brigade – the Bradfords were in no position to do anything else but cling on to their own precarious position.[93] As we have seen, at 8.00 a.m. the commanding officers of the two Bradford battalions did finally manage to link up their remaining troops to form a defence line around Hill 80. No sooner was this achieved than Colonel Carter was in sole command of the mixed force. A severely concussed Colonel Croydon was carried into Carter's dug-out. Carter's next trial was to discover that wires to Brigade had been cut and he had to resort to sending a sketch of his disposition by pigeon.

The enemy barrage continued throughout the morning, although by 9.30 a.m. the situation improved with the arrival of re-inforcements from the rest of the 18th D.L.I. According to the Battalion War Diaries, a number of enemy prisoners were killed by their own barrage before it was possible to evacuate them to the cages. By early afternoon both sides seemed to have exhausted themselves although German shells continued to smash into the British positions. Whilst there was real concern on the British side that the Germans were attempting to re-take Vimy Ridge, this now seems unlikely. Brigade records describe reported German infantry numbers as about four hundred men in each attack[94]. It seems more likely that the German infantry were being used to capture the strategically important Windmill and, in combination with the German air force, to probe British positions looking for signs of weakness. Their reports would then lead to accurate artillery fire on the British positions. The apparent ease with which the German air force used spotter lanes further underlines their dominance of the air after 'Black April'.

By 3.15 in the afternoon the position appeared to have stabilised although the two Bradford Battalions were now in a severely weakened state. Apart from Battalion H.Q., only fifty men and two officers (Lieutenants Dams and Harris who had put out the tapes) of the 18th's original numbers were available to hold the line. Brigade orders were received to consolidate the remaining troops under one command and at 4.15 p.m. Colonel Carter was re-called to give a full report to Brigadier Ingles. Colonel Croydon, by now recovered from concussion, took charge of what was in effect a composite Battalion of the survivors of the two Bradford Battalions and part of the D.L.I.[95]

The survivors, no doubt in a state of exhaustion, passed a fairly quiet night according to the 16th's War Diary. But they then had to hang on to their positions well into the night of 4 May before being relieved by the second Barnsley Pals. No explanation is given for this thirty six hour delay in relieving troops who were clearly at the end of their tether. One must question whether the delay was sensible on either pure military terms or on grounds of compassion to the battered remnants of the West Yorkshire battalions, or whether it was a case of it being simply impossible to get the Barnsleys into the line any sooner. Walter Hare remembers the exhausting five mile trudge back along the main road past the Point du Jour towards St. Catherines near Arras. Men had been posted every fifty yards to stop the retiring troops from falling asleep on the line of march.

We went independently down the Gavrelle/Arras road to a bivouac camp at St. Catherines. I remember that there was a letter and a parcel waiting for me. A Sergeant who saw me told me to dump my equipment in a bivouac and go to the cookhouse for some breakfast. I woke up about four in the afternoon and the sergeant who had spoken to me was still around and asked if I was alright. I told him I was O.K. and had been

Gavrelle looking East towards the windmill. From Laurence Greenwood's scrapbook.

asleep since about eight in the morning. He told me I had been asleep since eight the previous day and that he had been told to let me sleep! We collected our packs and then had an identification parade. It was then that I realised we must have had a lot of casualties...I thought it would be a long time before we would be able to go back in the line. What a hope. Within a week we were back at Gavrelle.

37468 PRIVATE WALTER HARE, 16WY[96]

Walter was right about the casualties. The two Bradford Battalions suffered nearly 600 casualties on 3 May. In the 16th, ninety-one men were killed or died of wounds, 151 were wounded and seventy-two (many of them wounded) were taken prisoner. In the 18th, 106 men died, more than at Serre on the 1 July, 103 were wounded and seventy-five taken prisoner including the recently returned young Ernest Brook.[97] Over forty of the dead were original Pals who had joined in the heady recruiting days back in Bradford. Three of the 18th's seven remaining original officers were killed: the jovial burly Captain Charles Duckitt who narrowly escaped Tony Miller's clumsy mistake in Egypt had recovered from his wounds at Serre but his luck finally ran out at Gavrelle. Captain Bernard Tooke, another old boy of Bradford Grammar School, and Lieutenant Frank Robinson the Yorkshire Rugby player from Thornbury were also killed. The three men were close friends and appear in several photographs together. In the group photograph of the 18th Battalion officers taken at Fovant in September 1915, Tooke and Robinson stand immediately behind the seated Duckitt.

The Leeds Pals also suffered terribly with 174 killed and about 200 hundred others either wounded or captured.[98] One Leeds casualty epitomised the close links between the three West Yorkshire battalions. Lance Corporal George Ferrand (15/325), missing presumed dead, was Mentioned in Despatches for his part in the Gavrelle attack. Ferrand was a Bradford Grammar School old boy. Like Evelyn Lintott the Dudley Hill teacher and football international, he had joined the Leeds Battalion because its recruiting campaign was further advanced than that in Bradford. His younger brother Claude (18/252) did join the Second Bradford Pals and was one of the earliest casualties when he was killed in May 1916 in an incident which led the unfortunate Arthur Wild to lose his nerve.

After the attack Divisional staff analysed reports from 93 Brigade and its four battalions. An unsigned analysis, probably written by the Divisional Intelligence Officer, is contained in the 31st Division papers at the Public Record Office (National Archives).[99] The unknown author pulls no punches in his damning criticism of the flawed nature of the operation. He is critical of the hurried nature of the preparations, the fact that the troops used in the assault had to get to the line by double marches rather than by bus, that they spent forty-eight hours prior to the assault constructing support trenches and dumps and were far from fresh when they went into the line. He complains of inadequate artillery preparation and support, again due to the hurried nature of the attack. He states the difficulties posed by the wide frontage of the attack on a downward slope after formation and assembly in full moonlight. He states that the assumption that the West Yorks faced exhausted enemy troops was wrong: fresh troops had already taken the place of the men who had been fought to a standstill by the Royal Naval Division and actually outnumbered the attacking British troops. His most telling comment could be applied to strategy in all the great British offensives in the early and middle stages of the Great War.

The power of the defensive compared with the offensive was very much brought home to one in this attack... the effective fighting force of a division in the defence is double its effective strength in offensive operations... it is thought that an attack requires a local

The attack at the windmill.

> *majority of 4 to 1 to be successful unless one can make certain of breaking down the enemy's morale by artillery fire.[100]*

Yet again the Bradford Battalions had been given a near impossible task. Throughout the report there is no criticism of the troops themselves, indeed there is frequent praise for their bravery and determination. The Divisional analyst finally concedes that:

> *In any case, it was made quite clear that our attack formed part of a very extended operation and that if it failed its object would be gained to a large extent if it diverted the enemy's attention from more important operations further south.[101]*

There was no major breakthrough further south. The first day of the Somme is burnt into the imagination and folk memory of our country, especially in the North. But the emotional significance of the 1 July should not be allowed to overshadow the enormity of the casualties suffered by the two Bradford battalions in the forgotten action at Gavrelle.

NOTES

1. Information supplied to the author by Mr. Leslie Sands, and contained in his autobiography, opus. cit.
2. Walter Hare, taped conversation with author.
3. ibid.
4. Battalion War Diaries PRO WO95/2362
5. Walter Hare, ibid.
6. Details in Battalion Orders, contained in 18th West Yorks, Battalion War Diary
7. Charles Carrington, *Soldier from the Wars returning* , Hutchinson, 1965.
8. Song in the papers of Private Horace Seekins (16/845) kindly supplied by his son Brian Seekins.
9. Carrington, ibid.
10. 62nd Division later took part in the Cambrai offensive in the Bourlon Wood area in November, 1917, where they suffered very heavy casualties.
11. Telegraph & Argus, 1st July, 1976
12. Orders, 18th Battalion War Diary
13. Haig Diaries, p.212, 'The Private Papers of Douglas Haig' edited by Robert Blake, Eyre & Spottiswood, 1952.

14. Walter Hare, ibid.

15. ibid.

16. Haig's diary entry for 24th April, 1917 indicates his determination to break the Hindenberg line and to capture Cambrai.

17. General Edmund Allenby, Order of the Day to 3rd Army, 12th April, 1917.

18. Battalion Order No. 67, 11th April, 1917, 18th Battalion War Diary.

19. 16th Battalion War Diary, 12th April 1917. It may be that narrowness of the road could have influenced the order.

20. Chris Draper recorded his rather eccentric career in an autobiography, *The Mad Major*, in the 1950's (no date).

21. Lt. Col Raymond Collishaw D.S.0. & Bar, D.S.C., D.F.C., recorded 62 victories, a total exceeded only by 'Mick' Mannock (73) and Billy Bishop (72).

22. The Royal Naval Division was an unusual formation created by the then First Lord of the Admiralty Winston Churchill in September 1914. It consisted mostly of members of the Fleet Reserves who were surplus to immediate naval requirements. Although they came under Army control in 1916, they retained many of their naval traditions including the use of Naval rank.

23. 18th Battalion War Diary gives casualty details. Harry Roberts was evacuated to a hospital in Manchester where he refused to have his elbow broken and re-set. His therapy included needlework. He was awarded the M.C. as a Lieutenant with the 1st East Yorks at Limont Fontaine on 7th November, 1918 for, fine and determined leadership when the advance of his battalion was held up by machine gun fire. He took command of two platoons and led them forward, working round the enemy's flanks and causing him to retire and abandon his machine guns. Later he led another attack on a single machine gun. (London Gazette). Harry told his sisters that he got his medal 'for getting the rations up to the front line'. The citation is in the possession of his niece Mrs. Hadwen.

24. Able Seaman Downe, M.M., of the Anson Battalion, article, *In the Hell that was Gavrelle* pp 1127-1131, Volume Two, in the I was There series, Hammerton, 1939.

25. Material supplied by Mr. Colin Casson of Haworth, Quotation from The Times obituary notice of Brigadier Arthur Melland Asquith, 26th August, 1939, written by Major General B.J. Freyberg, V.C.

26. Walter Hare, 27th October, 1990 at Gavrelle.

27. Battalion War Diaries.

28. WO 95/2359 93rd Brigade War Diary.

29. 31st Division (Warning Order) No. 137, 30th April 1917. In 31st Division War Diary, PRO WO 95/2342

30. Terraine, in his biography of Haig, makes much of the thesis that the Generals learned from their mistakes. This is now a commonly held view amongst First War historians and a much needed revision of the 'Lions led by Donkeys' school of criticism. However, it is still legitimate to ask how quickly did they learn and what was the cost of their learning ?

Men of the 31st Division at Roclincourt, April 1917.

31. WO 95/2342 Additions to Minutes of Instructions in connection with 31st Divisional (Warning) Order No. 137, 30th April 1917.

32. Ibid

33. WO 95/2359 93rd Brigade War Diary.

34. Report on Operations on 3rd May, 1917, Lt.Col. H.F.G..Carter, 18th West Yorks. Appendix in WO 95/2359 93rd Brigade War Diary.

35. Battalion War Diary

36. Ibid.

37. Ibid.

38. Ibid

39. Ibid.

40. Bowden's report, appendix in Battalion War Diary.

41. Carter's Report, WO 95/2359

42. Report on Operations on 3rd May, 1917, Lt.Col. A.C. Croydon, 16th West Yorks. Appendix in W0 95/2359, 93rd Brigade War Diary.

43. WO 95/2359

44. Carter, ibid.

45. Ibid.

46. Parker, Appendix 'D' in WO 95/2359

47. Sands, op.cit.

48. Obituary of Jack Manley, Bradford Daily Telegraph, 1st June, 1917. Sergeant Manley lived at 33, Raglan Terrace, Thornbury. He featured in a photograph in the Telegraph in February, 1915 with his father and five brothers, all of whom had 'joined the colours'. One brother, also a professional boxer, was killed earlier in the War.

49. Walter Hare, ibid.

50. 16th Battalion War Diary contains a full report by Lieutenant Walton. The discovery of 'dummies' is a clear indication that the Germans fully expected the British attack and that they conducted an extremely skilful policy of defence in depth.

51. Parker, ibid.

52. Ibid

53. Ibid.

54. Ibid

55. Ibid

56. Ibid

57. Battalion War Diary

58. Parker, ibid.

59. Battalion War Diary

60. Croydon, ibid

61. Ibid

62. Ibid.

63. 16th Battalion War Diary

64. Ibid.

65. Lieutenant Stanley's service record, citation for the D.S.O.,and other documents kindly supplied by his daughter-in-law, Mrs. Margaret Stanley. Stanley was also Mentioned in Despatches.

66. Citation to D.S.O., Supplied by Mrs. Margaret Stanley.

67. Citation to Distinguised Conduct Medal : 43484 Private F. Hallam, London Gazette 18.7.1917.

68. 16th Battalion War Diary.

69. See citations above.

70. WO 95/2359 Brigade Advance H.Q

71. Battalion War Diary

72. See illustrations. Citations kindly supplied by R.S.M. Scott's daughter Mrs. Margaret Mawby, (18/1144) Lance Corporal Percy Garside's son Mr. Stuart Garside, and (20/97) Private Richard Hopkinson' s son, Mr. Richard Hopkinson.

73. Citation for D.C.M., London Gazette, 9th July, 1917.

74. Walter Hare, op. cit.

75. Carter, op. cit..

76. Croydon, op. cit.

77. Carter, op.cit.

78. Until shortly before his death, John was still used an exercise bike every day.

79. Carter, op.cit.

80. Photograph in scrap-book kept by Corporal Greenwood's daughter, Mrs. Bentley.

81. Carter, op.cit.

82. Ibid.

83. Eyewitness reports contained in appendix to 18th Battalion War Diary.

84. Tyne, Battalion War Diary

85. Ibid.
86. Ibid.
87. Battalion War Diary
88. Ibid
89. Carter, op.cit.
90. Battalion War Diary
91. Citation, Distinguished Conduct Medal, 16/1107, Corporal W. Palframan, London Gazette, 18th July 1917. Details confirmed in 18th Battalion War Diary.
92. Dams' Report in Appendix to 18th Battalion War Diary.
93. Battalion War Diary
94. Report by General Ingles in Brigade War Diary and 31st Division Papers, op. cit.
95. Ibid.
96. Hare, op. cit.
97. Casualties listed in Battalion War Diaries. Numbers killed confirmed in *Soldiers Died in the Great War*.
98. See Laurie Milner, The Leeds Pals, in this series.
99. 31st Division Papers, ibid.
100. Ibid.
101. Ibid.

18th West Yorks at Ripon. Lieutenant F.T. Williams (Adjutant), Lieutenant H.L. Dalley, Lieutenant C. S. Duckitt.

Chapter Sixteen

THE LONG SLOG

May, 1917 – February, 1918

GAVRELLE WAS THE LAST TIME the Bradford Pals went over the top together as an attacking force. In the thirteen months after their arrival on the Western Front, the two Battalions had suffered nearly three thousand casualties. One more effort was made to capture the Windmill position beyond Gavrelle by the Durham Pals, 18 May, with the Bradford Battalions in the trenches behind ready to give support should the attack succeed. The effort failed, the Arras campaign subsided, and the focus of attention moved away to other parts of the Western Front, first to the north of the Pals in Flanders, and later to the south of them at Cambrai.

On 7 June nineteen massive explosions thirty miles to the north across the Belgian border were heard in England. It signified a switch of tactics and direction to Flanders and away from Arras. The capture of the Messines Ridge in Belgium by Plumer's Second Army was a spectacular success. Eight miles of German trenches were stormed after a series of mines were tunnelled into place under the German lines.

At the end of July, the Paschendaele campaign opened to the east of Ieper. It was to last until mid November. Over a three and a half month slog, British forces captured seven miles of Flemish mud and slime at a

Mont St Eloi. Chris Draper used to fly through the Abbey towers.

cost of at least 265,000 casualties. On 20 November, Third Army launched a massive attack with 378 tanks at Cambrai. The early results were spectacular but flattered to deceive. The Germans counter attacked and regained most of the ground. Both sides lost 40,000 men.

The 16th and 18th West Yorks were fortunate to be spared these two offensives, although a number of recovered Pals were involved with other Battalions. For the next nine months the two Bradford Battalions continued to have trench tours in quieter sectors. They stayed in the area to the east and north east of Arras with a base camp at Mont St. Eloi and Roclincourt and in the trenches at Gavrelle, Vimy, Givenchy, Arleux and Mericourt. No offensive major activity took place other than the occasional raid by both sides but there was always the 'daily hate' at Stand To. The main cause of casualties was continuing artillery activity and illness. It was physically unpleasant and uncomfortable but for the most part quiet. A great deal of work was carried out repairing trenches and roads. When the trenches were manned there was a system of defence in depth on a two company basis with only a thin presence in the front line where the men were in small teams armed with Lewis guns to minimize casualties.

*   *   *

The original Pal volunteers were now a minority in the Battalions and tended to be concentrated in the non-combat sections such as the transport section, signallers, the bandsmen, cooks and other specialist units.

When the two Bradford battalions were broken up in February, 1918, the 18th West Yorks compiled a complete muster roll giving the number and function of each soldier. The roll reveals the scale of change and how the battalion had become a slimmer more sophisticated technical unit with many more specialisms than in 1915. The total roll of other ranks was a slimmed down 733 compared with 995 in December, 1915. Of the original 995 other ranks who went to Egypt, only 280 were still with the Battalion in February, 1918, and many of them had been wounded at Serre or Gavrelle before returning to the Battalion later in 1917. The number of officers had grown to forty-two, but only seven were original Pals: Major Albert W. Robinson (second in command), Captain Leslie Bakes (31st Division, Salvage) , Captain Morris Clough, Captain Arthur Cockerham (Transport), Captain Walter Peace, Lieutenant John L. Wood (31st Division Signals) and Lieutenant Benjamin Hammond (Quartermaster).[1] Appendix A gives full details of the muster roll.

Despite the wretched daily grind in the trenches, casualty figures in the Pals were to be much lower over the next nine months than they had been over the previous ten months. There was certainly fear and tedium, illness and depression, but casualty figures reflected the change of tactics. In the First Pals, over a period of nine months after they came out of the line at Gavrelle, thirteen officers and men were killed (twelve by artillery, three by gunshot, one by suicide), whilst one hundred and twelve were wounded (two gunshot, twenty-four by gas, eighty-six by artillery). In the Second Pals, the figures were ten officers and men killed and thirty-eight wounded. In addition there were three self-inflicted wounds by men in both battalions who had reached the end of their tether. But even though there were fewer casualties from enemy action, the long slog of daily living conditions in the trenches wore men down. Many years later, Herbert Bradley of the Second Pals described the effect and pondered on his own pain and discomfort in old age.

> *Oh, sludge and sludge, and sumps, well you couldn't drain water away. That was the trouble you know. It was the conditions men had to live in. It's a wonder half of the lads wan't dead with rheumatics or summat like that. I wondered if this was part on it now, it can be you know, in a way, but...up to t'knees in mud.*   Private Herbert Bradley 18/95[7]

When the Pals came out of the line after the attack at Gavrelle, they were joined by a new chaplain, the Reverend John Calderbank. The previous Padre, the Reverend John G. Thornton had been with the Pals since their Skipton days. Padre Thornton was mentioned in dispatches for his efforts

Reverend John Calderbank.

to help the wounded, but following his marriage in April he was transferred to the 18th Casualty Clearing Station 10 May, 1917. He saw the surviving Pals again when he gave the address at the laying up of the Pals' Colours in Bradford Cathedral in November, 1920.[8]

John Calderbank, a graduate of Selwyn College Cambridge in 1913, came from Barrow in Furness. After ordination at Carlisle he became a Curate at Penrith Parish Church. In July 1915, at the age of twenty-eight, he enlisted in the R.A.M.C. and was commissioned as a Chaplain in December 1915, serving with the 21st Middlesex in the Lens area.[9] His diary contains a detailed record of his time with the Bradford Battalions in 1917 and 1918. He gave a vivid description of his arrival at 93 Brigade HQ beyond St. Catherines to await the Bradford Battalions coming out of the line from the support trenches at Gavrelle on Saturday 12 May, 1917.

> *The dust raised by the continuous stream of traffic was simply appalling, one seemed to breath nothing but dust. I soon came to what was a short time ago No Man's Land, and the scene was such that words almost fail to give an adequate picture. The old German front line had been simply obliterated by shell holes which were simply touching each other over a vast area. A tank had evidently come to grief and was resting on its side. An aeroplane was in close company a sharer in misfortune. The roads had been repaired by logs of wood. The plain was now full of encampments and troops, and judging by the noise of the guns they seemed to be innumerable. I finally reached the old railway cutting where 93 Brigade had its HQ. The scene was beyond description, shelters, dug-outs, some blown to pieces, some in use and devastation at every step.*

Overhead there were innumerable aeroplanes like a cloud of locusts.

On the way back (to 31st Division HQ at St. Catherines) I discovered that no one is allowed on a lorry without a pass. It seemed an endless journey and one was almost dying of thirst due to the intense heat and dust. I was absolutely wet through with sweat and felt like dropping from sheer exhaustion. In the house where I was billeted the windows had been blown out and a blanket was hung over the windows in the room I occupied to keep out the wind and cold at nights. REVEREND JOHN CALDERBANK, CF[10]

The determined new Chaplain soon had a run in with the brusque and earthy Colonel Croydon of the First Pals. It was an episode which says much about both men.

When the 16th came out of the line after I arrived, I interviewed the C.O. to see about fixing up services for the men. Thornton, my predecessor, had informed me that he had not been able to arrange any services owing to the action of the C.O. When I approached the C.O. he told me that there were not going to be any services. I would have to wait until we got back into rest billets. I told him I had held services much nearer the line. This caused him to explode, and as he had been an old Regimental Sergeant Major the language was very florid. He went home on leave the next day.

In a few days we went into the line again and when we came out again I fixed up with Major McGavin Greig (Brigade Major in temporary command of 16WY) for a parade service with the band. When the C.O. returned after our next tour in the line I again approached him about services. I was met with, "I have told you that you are not going to have any services here, you will have to wait". By this time I had got the old boy fairly well summed up, so I looked him straight in they eye and said, "while you were away on leave we had a service and the men enjoyed it. I don't see why we cannot have another". He looked at me as if he could kill me, and I retaliated by looking him straight in they eye in return. After a pause, he said, "Go and tell the Adjutant what you want. Fix it up with him".
REVEREND JOHN CALDERBANK, CF[11]

What the Chaplain didn't know was that the night before the original confrontation on 14 May Colonel Croydon suffered a second dose of concussion within ten days of being badly concussed during the Gavrelle attack on 3 May. Enemy artillery clearly had their old lines registered and scored a direct hit on Battalion HQ. Two men were killed and nineteen wounded in the incident during the night of 13 May. The Colonel was allowing his men to rest and the War Diary indicates a rest day with no parades other than a foot and a rifle inspection.[12]

The day after his concession on services, the Colonel did make a significant gesture. He gave the Padre his second charger, Polly, an excellent mount with a splendid turn of speed. Within days the Padre and the C.O. were riding together to visit the wounded in hospital, and Croydon had thawed out sufficiently to astonish the Officers' Mess with his singing :

After tea played songs on the harmonium while the C.O. sang.[13]

Walter Hare tells another story about besting the fearsome Colonel Croydon:

"I'm the brigadier... give it to me!"

> *I was a runner and just after the Gavrelle attack I was sent with a message from Colonel Croydon to Brigade Headquarters. I was travelling light for speed and safety when I saw an officer coming towards me with red tabs. It was Brigadier Ingles. I tried to dodge out of his way to avoid him but he saw me and shouted,*
>
> *"Soldier ! What are you doing ?"*
>
> *"I'm taking a message to Brigade HQ, Sir". I replied.*
>
> *"Well, give it to me. I'm the Brigadier", he said.*
>
> *"Shouldn't do that, Sir. My orders are take it to Brigade HQ. If anything happens to you they won't get it".*
>
> *"I suppose you're right", he said. "Now get about your business but don't let me see you improperly dressed again. Carry your rifle next time".*
>
> *Well, I got back to Battalion HQ and all hell had broken loose. Colonel Croydon sent for me and said the Brigadier was furious and I'd caused trouble for the Battalion. I was improperly dressed and all runners must wear full kit with rifles in future. He shouted me down and swore when I tried to say how difficult that was. Anyway, next day I was told to take him on a tour of the captured German trenches which were now our front line. There was an easy way and a hard way, and I took him the hard way. There was a bit where a German light railway had crossed a trench and there was a gap they had a sniper on. I told the Colonel to stay where he was and I dived over the old line. I then explained he would have to crawl under because the sniper always got the second man. Well, he swore but he had no choice but to crawl through the mud. I brought him back the same way. He grunted a sort of thanks when we got back and I said, "Sir, you see how difficult it is. Do runners really have to wear full kit?" He stomped off to clean up and said,"You can wear what you bloody well like !"*
>
> *He was a good soldier, though, and we all respected him.*

"Shouldn't do that sir!'

37468 PRIVATE WALTER HARE, 16 WY[14]

Walter, a Methodist lay preacher, always had a way with words, and was never afraid of authority. In the Summer of 1917, he was lucky enough to receive a leave pass. He was convinced his journey would be interrupted and that he would be sent back to the front. After a tedious journey through France, a rough Channel crossing and a train to London, his heart sang at the familiar Yorkshire names on the Great Northern departure board at Kings Cross. But at Peterborough his heart sank,

"You can wear what you bloody-well like!'

> *"All service Personnel must leave the train at once" was the announcement. I thought, Oh, heck. They must be sending us back for a Summer offensive. I'm never going to get to see my family and Emily'* [Walter's girlfriend]. *There were military police everywhere shouting at us, telling us to get into line. When everybody was sorted out the Station Master appeared in his top hat and told us that the Prime Minister wanted to see us – Mr. Lloyd George. Well he came down the line chatting to everybody and when he got to me he asked where I'd come from. "France,*

Sir", I said. "Whereabouts ?" he asked. "Sorry, Sir, can't tell you that. Official Secret". Well he really enjoyed that and laughed, and eventually we got on the train again. I was so tired I fell asleep on the train and didn't wake up until we'd gone past Selby to York. I walked all the way back to Cawood, and my mother nearly dropped when she saw me. I was filthy and covered in fleas. She told me to get a bath and get changed, but didn't. I went straight off to see Emily. 37468 PRIVATE WALTER HARE, 16 WY[15]

Walter didn't see Emily again for nearly eighteen months, and when he did they got married. Walter and his brother had just been released from a German Prisoner of War Camp.

Over the course of the nine months the pattern was usually six days in the front line followed by six days of mixed rest and labouring working parties followed by six days in reserve. There were tragedies and accidents. On 27 May as the First Pals were cleaning up and preparing to move out, eleven men were wounded as a result of a bomb being accidentally thrown into an incinerator as the Battalion was clearing up at Maroeuil. On 23 June a direct hit was made on the Second Pals Orderly tent near Gavrelle killing three clerks, all of whom were original Pals, and wounding Colonel Carter. Padre Calderbank met Colonel Carter the next day.

I met Colonel Carter who informed me that they had been shelled in their camp the previous evening. Three of the orderly room staff had been literally blown to pieces, and he himself had had a miraculous escape. He had been sleeping in a tent next to the other men, and although his tent was literally riddles with holes, and his British Warm which had been laid across his chest had been badly gashed, and his tunic full of holes, he had only received a small flesh wound. I arranged to hold a funeral service for the men who had been killed on my way back from the trenches.

The Chaplain visited the Front Line on the same day and went on to give a vivid description of the conditions the men had to endure.

We went across country between the support and front lines keeping close to a bank until we reached the ruins of Gavrelle. It was not a pleasant journey as we were under observation from the German lines, and two or three German observation balloons were in close proximity. There was a lot of shelling going on just on our left, and it was a case of ducking, then bobbing up again to see where the shells had fallen, and then off again. There was no actual trench, and it was a case of working along ditches, and using shell holes to secure as much cover as possible. We reached the front line, got into the trench and went round to see the Companies, and then made our way back along Widow Trench. A lot of shrapnel was coming over on our right, and on one occasion just as we threw ourselves into the bottom of the trench, a perfect hail of shrapnel swished over the top of the trench.

REV. JOHN CALDERBANK, CHAPLAIN 93 BRIGADE [16]

The Colonel was probably underplaying his wound because he was on sick leave until 3 August and Major Albert Robinson took charge of the Battalion in that time.

On 21 July there was an even more devastating event. The First Pals were lined up ready to march to the front at Arleux outside their billets at Neueville St. Vaast when one isolated H.E. shell landed on the front of D Company killing Lieutenants Buchanan and Robb (who had only arrived the previous day and had never even been in the trenches) and five men. Forty men were wounded in the incident. Again, one suspects this was no lucky hit. The Germans still had a powerful air presence and it is likely an observer noticed the movement at the camp and signalled the information to his artillery. In his diary, Padre Calderbank expressed his sadness and described how he borrowed a lantern from a military policeman and conducted the funeral service at 11.00 p.m. accompanied by the bandsmen and Captain Ashforth.

The next day, one Corporal Ingram was reported missing believed captured as he went to the latrine at an isolated forward post at Acheville. Again at Acheville, one of many First Pals patrols took a bad hit when Sergeant Nelson was killed, two men were missing and one man wounded during a six man patrol in No Man's Land, 29 July. On the same night a shell fell on C Company HQ killing Second Lieutenant Paus and wounding Second Lieutenant Carney and three other ranks. Oscar Paus had been with the 16th West Yorks for only two months but had a local connection. He was a thirty-seven year old textile buyer in Bradford and the son of a Norwegian shipping merchant. He was commissioned in March, 1917 having joined the Royal Fusiliers as a private. He had been wounded on the Somme and was an old boy of Bradford Grammar School.[17]

On the same trench tour in the First Pals, twenty-one year old Captain Frank Hoffmann, commander of D Company and an original officer from 1914, was sent to hospital with a severe infection. It may be his condition was exacerbated by the events of 21 July. Like Oscar Paus, he was an old boy of Bradford Grammar School. He never returned to the Battalion he had joined three years before. His medical record describes him as being, 'In poor general condition. Suffering from debility. Has dyspnoea and palpitation on exertion. Tachycardia 110 per minute.'[18] Frank's twenty-two year old brother Harry had been struck off the battalion strength in August, 1916 after suffering severe shell shock at Serre. A year later Harry's medical record still showed major long term problems: 'Variability of his heart, pulse 136, some of which acceleration is probably due to excitement. Complains of exhaustion after any severe form of exercise and complains of nightmares.'[19]

In August the Germans started to use more gas shells. Nineteen men were gassed in the First Pals, 2 August, when the Battalion was in support in Canada Trench at Vimy. As a result of this incident, all gas respirators were examined and both Bradford battalions had to pass through the gas chamber when they came out of the line. Later that month, George Morgan, by now a sergeant but still only nineteen, had a run in with Brigadier Ingles over the gas incident on one of the few occasions when the Brigadier was in the front line.

The only other time I saw him I got into bother. We used to have gas helmets called P.H. helmets and they were horrible things. They were dipped in some sort of chemical and had eye pieces and a nose piece, you know. It looked like the Klu Klux Klan. You used to have to wear them here [pointing] when you were in the trenches, ready to put on if any gas came over. And the Brigadier came down with his retinue of hangers on and he says to me,"Why haven't you got your gas helmet at the alert?" I said, "I don't need to put it at the alert. I can get it on just the same without". He says, "Oh, can you. We'll see", and he got his watch out and shouts, "Gas!"

I put me hands in me pockets and I remember they were in like a kind of an envelope, light plastic envelope (but it weren't plastic then) and I got it out of me pocket and tab ends came out of me pocket and bits of baton and match – bits of nails and all that you put in your pocket. I got it out of my pocket and I got it on. Just got it on in time. I think I'd have been court-martialled or shot at dawn I think if I hadn't have done.

16/1205 SERGEANT GEORGE MORGAN[20]

George himself was wounded shortly after this incident.

The trenches in the Arleux sector were in a dreadful condition.

In some places one sinks almost to the knees, also in places the mud is so sticky that one has to be careful not to leave gumboots behind in the mud. It was a miserable wet day raining all the time. The poor fellows seem to get very little rest for they have to work on the trenches during the day and then go out on working and carrying parties at night. Sometimes they get in absolutely wet through, and there is no question the small tot of rum warms them up and helps them to get off to sleep in the small shelters dug in the side of the trench. REV. JOHN CALDERBANK, CHAPLAIN 93 BRIGADE[21]

Walter Hare, as a Methodist Lay Preacher and teetotaller, was thought an appropriate person to bring up the rum ration. He remembered being very unpopular when he dived for cover one night at Vimy and the rum jar smashed and ended up all over his tunic. The men were more than miffed to miss their rum. As a runner, Walter had to travel up and down the trenches, and with a rum soaked tunic his presence was noted. 'Here comes our bloody rum ration', was one of the more polite greetings.[22]

At the end of August, the Germans launched a trench raid at Mericourt which had been manned by the Second Pals for seven day. Colonel Carter made sure the West Yorks weren't caught napping as they had been at Neuve Chapelle the previous year. His suspicions were first aroused when no less than ten enemy aircraft flew low over the Brfitish lines earlier in the day. The Colonel then noticed a different pattern to the German artillery barrage and acting on hunch assumed a raid was going to take place. He analysed the map and calculated exactly where a raiding party would come given the maximum cover they would need. The Colonel's hunch was right and two raiding parties totalling at least fifty Germans were met and driven off by massive Lewis gun fire. There was an added bonus in that a wounded German was captured and brought in. This was some achievement given that the Pals were so spread out with only 120 men holding a 1,200 yard section of front line and only had eighty men in reserve.[23] One of those reserves was Private Jack Morris (18/911) who made it home, but only as a casualty after he went forward to help deal with the raid. Jack gave a vivid description of the horrors of being wounded and what trench warfare meant on an individual basis.

I went up at night and I got into't line at ten minutes to twelve. Captain Peace, he were a gentleman if ever there were one, he says, "Jack, take your team out. There's been a noise coming over since twelve o'clock. You get up there". I'd fired two magazines, if you see 'em, you pot ' em, drop 'em and run. He had a gun had Jerry and you never heard it. Well you felt it drop at side of you. Well at twenty past twelve I was on a stretcher and Captain Peace come and he says "You lucky blighter" and threw a twenty packet of Gold Flake where I was. Anyway they put me in t'Ambulance, Frank Burn and RSM Scott, lifted us and a German. Well the German died and they dropped him out at a barrage balloon place. Well they sent me down to t'base and first thing I saw were a chap stropping a razor. Next thing I saw were a barrow full of arms and legs going to 't incinerator. Well they took me in and operated. It were a couple of days when I came round. Anyway a night orderly came on duty one night and he says "By blooming heck, What you doing?" I says "What you mean?" He says "You're going raving mad. Aye, you've won war by yourself". Anyway I see one of them Queen Alexandra's Nurses coming up t'ward. I'd been at point o' death more than once, you know, and she knelt down at side of me and she said "Don't do that again, Tommy. That's the only way we get to know what's going on. You don't tell lies when you're coming out of that stuff. All you tell me were the truth" So anyway, from there down to Rouen. Doctor comes round and that were first time I seen a leg cut off. You know you've seen ham in a shop haven't you, well your leg's just like that. All fat, you know what I mean?

18/911 PRIVATE JACK MORRIS[24]

The Summer turned to autumn and then winter. The round of trench life continued. On 17 October Lieutenant John Stanley who had won the D.S.O. at Gavrelle was wounded. A steady trickle of casualties occurred in both Battalions. In mid December the Pals came out of the line and Colonel Croydon got his wish – a full Ceremonial Drill in front of Major-General Wanless O'Gowan. The General congratulated Colonel Croydon on the Battalion's demonstration.[25]

The winter of 1917/18 was particularly harsh with temperatures consistently well below freezing and heavy snow covered the trench lines. The cheerful optimism of the autumn of 1914 was a dim and distant memory for the remaining original Pals. The Battalion War Diaries record a number of self inflicted wounds in this period as desperate men at the end of their tether were driven to self mutilation in an attempt to get away from an existence they could no longer tolerate. In his duties as a runner, Private Walter Hare recalled coming round a traverse to an empty section of the line between the outposts in the Arleux Sector. There he found one of the Battalion military policemen exposing a foot over the parapet in the hope of achieving a 'Blighty' wound. 'I told him we all felt just as bad as he did, but what he was doing was wrong After a bit he calmed down and went back We never spoke about it again.'[26]

But Christmas was coming and all hoped that the New Year would see an end to the War.

*   *   *

Christmas Day, 1917 saw the 16th West Yorks busy on working parties carrying ammunition up to the line, making dug outs in the Lievin line and wiring in front of Baby Trench. It was also a particularly busy day for the Reverend John Calderbank, Chaplain the to 93 Brigade. In his diary he records his hectic round in the Arleux sector to the north of Vimy Ridge.

> *25/12/17 8.30 a.m. Holy Communion at Brigade H.Q. Stayed for breakfast. 10.00 a.m. Holy Communion for L.T.M.B. and M.G.C. & and 'B' and 'C' Coys of 18 West Yorks in some old German gun pits. 11.30 a.m. H.C. in the new dug out at Tunnel Dump. Stayed for lunch. 1.30 p.m. H.C. for 'A'Coy 18 West Yorks & 'D'Coy 16 West Yorks at Sugar Post. 3.00 p.m. H.C. 'D'Coy 18 West Yorks and 'C' Coy 16 West Yorks at Willerval North. 5.00 p.m. H. C. for 'A' and 'B' Coys 16 West York.s and HQ. Just as we were about to start this service the S.O.S. alarm sounded. It turned out it was a section on our right that was affected, so after about twenty minutes we proceeded with the service. The dug outs in which the services were held were packed to overflowing and in some cases the men were packed so tightly that one could hardly move. The altar was generally an old box or a makeshift with a frontal I carried about with me, together with a small crucifix and two small candlesticks. The only light was from the two candlesticks, and a few candles in bottles round the dug-out. This was a day which will never be forgotten.*

REV. JOHN CALDERBANK, CHAPLAIN 93 BRIGADE[27]

In West Hartlepool, the Metcalfe family was enjoying a well earned rest after a hectic period in their confectionary and pastry shop. Despite the shortages and rationing, they had done their best to provide cakes and all manner of Christmas goodies for their customers. No doubt they raised a toast to their eldest son Lawrence who was serving as a second lieutenant with the 16 West Yorks. They were not to know that for them too, Christmas Day, 1917, would be a day never to be forgotten.

On 25 January, 1918, the Hartlepool *Northern Daily Mail* announced that twenty-two year old Second Lieutenant Lawrence Metcalfe of the l6th West Yorks had been killed in action. There were two entries in the column, one from Lieutenant Metcalfe's parents and younger brothers and sisters, and another from his uncle, aunt and cousins. [28] Family grief was compounded by a fact concealed in the announcement. Young Lawrence Metcalfe had shot himself in the head at 6.30 p.m. on Christmas Day, 1917 in his dug out at C Company H.Q. at Willerval North to the east of the village of Arleux-en-Gohelle.

Lawrence Metcalfe was a nineteen year old and a stockbroker's clerk when he became a Kitchener volunteer in September, 1914. After serving with the Hussars, he was transferred to the 3rd and later the 2nd Royal

31st Division signallers after the Armistice.

Irish Regiment where he was promoted to corporal four days after the opening of the Somme offensive. He was commissioned in April, 1917 and joined D Company of the 16th West Yorks on 23 May filling one of the gaps left after the attack at Gavrelle. On the night of 19 August 1917, he was wounded by machine gun fire when visiting advanced posts in the Arleux sector. He recovered sufficiently to return to the battalion 22 September, where he joined C Company. According to Dr. Charles Roche, the Battalion Medical Officer:

> *The wound received on 19/8/17 was very slight and could not have affected his general health or state of mind. Since his return to the Battalion he has never reported sick.*
>
> CAPTAIN CHARLES ROCHE M.C., R.A.M.C., ATT 16WY[29]

The M.O.'s comment on the state of Metcalfe's mind is debatable. The Commander of C Company, Captain Louis L. de Souza, gave a different view to the Court-of-Inquest.

> *I noticed he was very highly strung and very excitable. Very little drink seemed to influence him. He had had no alcohol this tour in the line to my knowledge except the rum ration until the 25th instant. His nerves were in a very bad state and were badly affected by shell fire. When under fire he always tried to get drink He could never sleep much in the line. I never heard that he had any troubles in his private affairs.*
>
> CAPTAIN LOUIS L. DE SOUZA 16WY[30]

On the 23 December, Regimental Sergeant Major Cussins had complained to the Adjutant, Captain Greenwood,

Out of eighty men in C Company, nineteen had at Stand Down that morning been without an issue of rum, and that the Orderly Sergeant had complained that the Officer issuing rum, Second Lieutenant Metcalfe, appeared to be the worse for liquor and unfit to issue rum.[31]

Sufficient rum for nineteen men is an enormous dose, and Captain Greenwood decided the evidence was too conflicting to proceed with a charge. Nevertheless, Greenwood gave Metcalfe a severe warning and reported the matter to Lieutenant Colonel Croydon. The C.O. decided to take no further action. Metcalfe was in an environment where he had lost his grip and could no longer control his fear or emotions. What happened in the darkness of a dug out on a Christmas Day evening is a vivid illustration of what could happen when a soldier's mind passes breaking point. Captain de Souza gave evidence as to what happened.

About 2.00 p.m. on the 25 December, 1917, I warned him [Metcalfe] and another Officer to take charge of a carrying party to parade at 4.30 p.m. and take Stokes shells up to the Stokes gun positions near the Front Line. Between 2.00 p.m. and 4.00 p.m. he [Metcalfe] was sitting in Company H. Q. dug-out and he had had two whiskeys and water. He had had three whiskeys and water at midday dinner between 1.00 p.m. and 2.00 p.m. Tea was brought in about 4.00 p.m., and he said "Tea's up" and got up from his seat in front of the fire to take his place at the table. He appeared slightly unsteady on his feet, and as he sat down he almost upset a cup of tea. Immediately after sitting down he rested his head on his hand, with his elbow on the table, and seemed very drowsy. He sipped his tea but didn't eat anything. As it was nearly time for parade, I tried several times to rouse him, and warned him to get ready, but he did not rouse himself and only muttered "Rollocks" or some such word. After several attempts I threatened to inform the Adjutant that he was incapable of taking the part. This made him angry and he told me "Go and tell him ".

CAPTAIN LOUIS L. DE SOUZA 16 WY[32]

One wonders why Captain de Souza permitted Metcalfe to have two further whiskeys after warning him for duty at 2.00 p.m., and having seen three previous whiskeys consumed by him at lunchtime. De Souza was aware of the rum incident only two days before. One can only question whether de Souza was slack, or was finding a pretext to allow a weak officer to compromise himself in a situation where he could be more easily got rid of through his being incapable of fulfilling his duties. By an odd irony the Stokes gun positions, which should have been Metcalfe's destination, were located in trenches named Brandy, Beer, Benedictine, Tee and Total.

The other officer... had already gone out to put on his equipment. Seeing [Metcalfe] did not make an effort to go I detailed Second Lieutenant Ward to go in his place... [Metcalfe] called out 'Ward won't go', and told him to sit down. He then went into the bedroom which is connected with the outer Mess by a passage about five yards long and there is a door at each end. No one went in with him. Whilst he was in there the other officer who was going came in to report that the party was ready to move off and [Metcalfe] called out "Wait for me. I'm coming". After about three minutes he returned to the Mess with his overcoat on and was trying to do up his belt which would not meet over his overcoat. He called for a man to help him to fasten it, and his servant, 37497 Private Percy Walker, came to help him but could not manage it, and he had to take off his overcoat. Whilst his servant was helping him he leant up against the table apparently in a dazed condition. Seeing his state I warned Ward to take the party. While Ward was getting ready, Metcalfe went out into the trench. About half a minute later Ward followed him. About five minutes later Metcalfe returned and threw down his hat and stick and went into the bedroom. As he passed he asked me if I was writing to the Adjutant and I said 'Yes', and he replied "But you sent Ward to relieve me". He went on into the bedroom mumbling something which I could not hear. Shortly afterwards I wrote out and sent a note to the Adjutant reporting that Metcalfe was incapable of taking the party, being under the influence of drink, and that I awaited instructions. Metcalfe remained in the bedroom about an hour. When he returned and sat beside me in front of the fire with a book to read, he asked again if I had sent the note to the Adjutant. I answered "Yes". After a few minutes I was rung up by the Adjutant. I went to the phone in the Signallers' dug-out and received instructions that [Metcalfe] was to be put under close arrest and that an officer was being sent down to be with him. [Metcalfe] heard this communication through the receiver in the Mess and on my return he said "Thanks". I told him to consider himself under arrest. I said I was sorry but had no other course open to me. He agreed but stated that as it was Christmas I ought to have sent out Ward and said nothing about it. He seemed in a very excited condition and kept repeating words to the effect that it was Christmas and I should have let him off. I told him I was very sorry but that after what had occurred on the 23rd I felt it my duty to report it. I then reminded him that an officer was coming down to look after him. He said nothing but went on reading at the table. After a short pause he said "He need not come down" and got up and walked into the bedroom, as he got into the passage, just as he was closing the door of the Mess he mumbled something about a revolver. I had a suspicion of what he meant and called out "Don't be idiotic". I got up and called for Private Walker and went round the table to follow [Metcalfe]. I heard a shot fired and called out "Don't be a damned fool". I opened the door and heard another shot. I hurried into the bedroom with Private Walker following me and found Metcalfe lying huddled in a heap half under the bed. There was a bullet wound in his head I bent down and felt his arm and saw he was dead at once.

CAPTAIN LOUIS L. DE SOUZA 16 WY[33]

A Court of Inquest was assembled the following day consisting solely of officers from the 16th West Yorks. Their finding was that,

Death was caused through a revolver wound to the head, which was self-inflicted whilst the deceased was temporarily of unsound mind, which was

caused through drink and worry at being reported as unfit for duty in the trenches.[34]

An anguished and more profound verdict came from James Metcalfe, the officer's father. In a letter to the War Office after requesting that 'self-inflicted' be removed from the death certificate because it disqualified payment from Lawrence's life insurance policy, James wrote,

Whatever made our Dear Son do such a rash act it was through the War for he was a keen soldier and was in three years and nearly four months.[35]

The Reverend Calderbank ended his diary for Christmas Day on a bleak note. 'Just after dinner word came in that one of the Officers, Metcalfe, had shot himself.'[36] The War Office refused to alter the death certificate. 'Killed in Action' was used only in the Hartlepool *Northern Daily Mail.* Chaplain Calderbank conducted the funeral service and Lawrence Metcalfe was buried in Roclincourt Military Cemetery, Grave 2, Row F, Plot 2. His grieving parents later moved from their home in Musgrave Street to a more prosperous home in Wansbeck Gardens. The new house was named as an act of rememberance for their lost son, 'Lauriedene'.[37]

The 16th West Yorks came out of the line on 3 January, 1918 when they were relived by the Hull Commercials. They were given a ride by light railway to the billets at Ecoivres well away from the line and had a period of rest. They had their official Christmas Dinner 4 January and had the luxury of a hot bath in wine vats 12 January. There was a tour in the Front line when they relieved the Leeds Pals at Arleux 19 January until 27 January. Rumours were rife that the battalion was about to be broken up,

PoW camp in Germany.

particularly when news filtered through that the Second Pals were to be disbanded. There was one more tour at Arleux between 5 and 11 February. The First Pals saw off a German raid on their trenches 8 February killing a number of Germans. Private Clifford Creek (38812) from Leeds and Corporal William Forster (20/93) were the last casualties. On 11 February they came out of the line for the last time and went to billets the town of Maroleuil. The disbandment was formally announced by Colonel Croydon.[38]

For the 18th West Yorks there was a period of rest in the New Year followed by one more tour of the front line trenches and reserve lines at Arleux. They came out of the line for the last time 27 January and moved to Bray Camp for training. On 31 January orders came to disband the Battalion. Colonel Carter addressed his Battalion 1 February and informed them of what was to happen.[39] A major reorganisation in the British Army was begun in January, 1918. The cause was a shortage of men – although the Prime Minister, David Lloyd George was also accused of deliberately holding back troops because he was unwilling to allow Haig to conduct another expensive offensive. It was thought better to give the impression of the same number of Divisions in France rather than to bring the existing battalions up to strength and reduce the number of divisions. In future brigades were to consist of three rather than four battalions. The new 93 Brigade was to consist of the 15/17th West Yorks, the 13th Yorks and Lancs, and the 18th Durham Light Infantry.

It marked the end of the Bradford Pals.

NOTES

1. Battalion War Diary
2. John Terraine,Haig, *The Educated Soldier*.
3. CCorrespondence, WFA magazine, July, 1991, and response by John Terraine.
4. Ibid.
5. Analysis of Battalion War Diaries and Medal Rolls at Public Record Office.
6. WO95/2342 31st Division War Diary
7. Herbert Bradley, taped conversation with Steve Kerry, op.cit.
8. *Bradford Weekly Telegraph*, 24th November, 1920.
9. Crockfords, and additional information including Mr. Calderbank's diary supplied to the author by his family. In 1920, John Calderbank became a Curate at Bradford Cathedral and was later Vicar of Barnoldswick and Calverley.
10. Reverend John Calderbank, diary, kindly loaned by his daughters.
11. Ibid.
12. Battalion War Diary
13. Calderbank, opus cit.
14. Walter Hare, taped conversation with the author, December, 1992.
15. Ibid.
16. Calderbank diary. Op.Cit.
17. PRO339 Paus
18. PRO339 Hoffmann
19. PRO339 Hoffmann
20. Morgan. Tape interview with Malcolm Brown. Op.cit.
21. Calderbank. Op.cit.
22. Hare. Op.cit.
23. Battalion War Diary.
24. Jack Morris, taped interview with Steve Kerry. Op.cit.
25. Battalion War Diary.
26. Walter Hare, op.cit.

27. Reverend John Calderbank, diary. 25/12/1917.

28. *Northern Daily Mail*, Hartlepool, 'Killed in Action' Column, 25 January, 1918.

29. WO 339/83990, PRO, Statement by Captain Charles Roche, M.C., (R.A.M.C.) to Court-of-Inquest, 26th December 1917.

30. WO 339/83990. Witness evidence by Captain Louis Lovell de Souza to Court-of-Inquest, 26th December 1917.

31. WO 339/83990, de Souza, ibid.

32. Ibid

33. Ibid

34. Members of the Court of Inquest were Captain Philip Henry Battishill, M.C., (President), Captain Charles Roche M.C. (R.A.M.C.), who also gave evidence, Lieutenant Alec Bethune Peter Wood and Lieutenant Frank de Bell Price.

35. WO339/83990. Letter from James Metcalfe to the War Office.

36. Calderbank, ibid.

37. Commonwealth War Graves Commission entry for Laurence Metcalfe records the parents' new address.

38. Battalion War Diary.

39. Battalion War Diary.

Prisoner of war camp at the Armistice.

Some Bradford Pals pose in a PoW camp.

Chapter Seventeen

AFTERWARDS

The men of the Bradford Pals were scattered amongst other battalions. The 18th West Yorks transfers were completed by 15th February and the 16th West Yorks by 28th February, 1918.

Destination	Officers	Men
16th West Yorks		
15th West Yorks	4	192
3rd Entrenching Battalion (Labour Corps)	12	583

23 officers went to XIII Corps reinforcement base and were scattered throughout the Corps.

18th West Yorks		
1st West Yorks	5	90
2nd West Yorks	2	45
1/5 West Yorks	5	90
1/6 West Yorks	2	90
1/7 West Yorks	2	90
9th West Yorks	5	90
10th West Yorks	5	90
15th West Yorks	5	90
21st West Yorks	2	45
XIII Reinforcement Camp	8	42

The Transport Section left for attachment to the 1st Brigade of Guards whilst the Band transferred to the 8th West Yorks.

A number of subsequent transfers came over the coming months, especially in the group sent to the 3rd Entrenching Battalion.

Colonel Carter ended up in Vladivostok advising the White Russian forces, but died of double pneumonia shortly before the birth of his daughter in 1919. He was thirty-three. His wife later married Air Marshal Sir John Slessor.

Colonel Croydon lived to the age of sixty-six in Carshalton. He too was a victim of War office financial nitpicking. He was not awarded travel expenses when he came to collect his Military Cross in 1917 because he arrived too early – and his wife was not allowed a pension when he died because she was twenty-five years younger than he was and he married her after the war.

Major Albert Robinson became commanding officer of the 3rd Cheshires and survived the war. He left teaching and went into farming in Suffolk.

The group going to the Leeds Pals included R.S.M. Cussins and Walter Hare (who was captured in the German Spring offensive). Sadly Captain Murgatroyd D.C.M., the other hero of Serre was killed, as was Captain Morris Clough.

Captain Walter Peace received a bar to the Military Cross he had won at Serre in September 1918 when serving with the Leeds Pals, again leading his men by example even though he himself was wounded. Corporal Harold Cowgill (18/1514) must have been seventeen when he joined the Second Pals. He was awarded the Distinguished Conduct Medal in July 1918 for rushing and capturing a German machine gun when serving with the Leeds Pals, but sadly died from his wounds at the age of twenty. Douglas Hunter (16/228) serving with the Trench Mortar Battery was more fortunate, he too was awarded the Distinguished Conduct Medal but survived to returned to work in the mill in Batley.

Lieutenant Stanley D.S.O. survived the war, but died at the early age of forty-one, largely as a result of his wounds. Dr. Roche died in 1921 of tuberculosis picked up in the trenches. Harry Dalley also died young in 1937. Dr. McTavish returned to Canada and lived to the age of eighty-two in Alberta practising medicine, talking an interest in Veteran Affairs, and serving as a District Medical Officer in the Second World War. R.S.M. Scott, like RSM Cussins, came back to the Bradford City Police Force. John McGrath survived the fire at Valley Parade and lived well into his nineties pedalling his exercise bicycle.

Walter Hare came home from prisoner of war camp, married his Emily, managed the local Co-op grocery stores, preached in the Methodist Chapel and followed Yorkshire cricket. He also wrote poetry and became a TV star in his final years. He just missed his century – achieving ninety-nine happy years just before his death in 1997. The author misses him enormously.

Brigadier Ingles lived to a ripe old age of eighty-three in Devon, as did General Wanless O'Gowan in Surrey. General Hunter-Weston continued as a Tory M.P. and lived until 1941 when, at the age of seventy-seven, he fell to his death from an observation tower where he used to watch the shipping in the Clyde at Hunterston. He had to negotiate a high wall to achieve the feat. His study remains untouched with all his personal effects.

There were services and parades when the survivors came home to Bradford in 1919. The Bradford War Memorial was unveiled 1 July, 1922, the sixth anniversary of the Palls' disaster at Serre. The Roll of Honour carries no fewer than 37,000 names, massive testament to the sacrifice and contribution made by the city in the Great War. Arthur Wild's family insisted on his name being included.

In 1928, the Bradford Pals Comradeship Association was formed with a base at Claremont, just up the road from the War Memorial near the Alhambra Theatre, and close to Windsor Baths where the First Pals held their farewell entertainment in January, 1915. The family of nineteen year old Norman Waddilove, who died at Serre, owned Claremont.

Annual Dinners and visits to France took place over many years, but their numbers inevitably dwindled. The surviving Pals became television stars in 1976 when Yorkshire Television made a programme 'Reunion' marking their return for the 60th Anniversary of the Battle of the Somme.

The colours now hang in Bradford Cathedral and there is a Memorial window there. There are no memorials in France, only the names at Thiepval and Arras and the countless headstones. But there is still a presence there. As George Morgan said,

> *To me they're holy places. It was consecrated ground where we walked when we got to the Somme.*

We can never know the suffering of the survivors, or how they coped with the grief. It is impossible to tell the stories of so many men.

Let us give the last words to George Morgan and Walter Hare.

> *It was the biggest incident in my life. I've lived sixty years afterwards, and I've never, never got over it. It's always been there in my mind. It was the biggest thing that ever happened to me. We'd all got to know each other very well and we were all very good comrades, in fact I don't think there's ever been better comradeship ever...and then all at once when this day, this terrible day of July 1st, we were wiped out.*

SERGEANT GEORGE MORGAN, 16WY[1]

> *And did we waste our time in days gone by,*
> *As there we stood*
> *Knee deep in mud.*
> *And was it just a waste of human life*
> *To try to find a way*
> *Of turning evil into good.*
> *Oh no, we still must try to find the goal*
> *Which is the hope of every soul*
> *That wars must cease,*
> *Then we shall know that love, not hate*
> *Can rule the day*
> *And we can say*
> *Goodbye to this fair earth, our time has passed,*
> *And we can rest in perfect peace at last.*

PRIVATE WALTER HARE, 16WY[2]

NOTES

1. George Morgan, taped interview with Malcolm Brown. Op Cit.
2. Walter Hare. Poem written in 1991 on a journey to the Somme with the author.

Bradford Pals march past the Town Hall again. Armistice Day, 11 November, 1920.
Sergeant Harold Saville MM, behind the tall figure of Fred Conquest.

Pals in Manningham Park, 1981.